Get the eBook FREE!

(PDF, ePub, Kindle, and liveBook all included)

We believe that once you buy a book from us, you should be able to read it in any format we have available. To get electronic versions of this book at no additional cost to you, purchase and then register this book at the Manning website.

Go to https://www.manning.com/freebook and follow the instructions to complete your pBook registration.

That's it!
Thanks from Manning!

Lead Developer Career Guide

SHELLEY BENHOFF

FOREWORD BY STEVE BUCHANAN

MANNING
SHELTER ISLAND

For online information and ordering of this and other Manning books, please visit www.manning.com. The publisher offers discounts on this book when ordered in quantity.

For more information, please contact

> Special Sales Department
> Manning Publications Co.
> 20 Baldwin Road
> PO Box 761
> Shelter Island, NY 11964
> Email: orders@manning.com

Manning Publications Co.
20 Baldwin Road
PO Box 761
Shelter Island, NY 11964

Development editor:	Rebecca Johnson
Technical editor:	Stephen Mizell
Review editor:	Dunja Nikitović
Production editor:	Kathy Rossland
Copy editor:	Julie McNamee
Proofreader:	Melody Dolab
Typesetter:	Tamara Švelić Sabljić
Cover designer:	Marija Tudor

ISBN 9781633438071
Printed in the United States of America

*This book is dedicated to my parents who bought me my first computer,
the Tandy 1000, and recognized my aptitude for technology.
I also dedicate this book to my husband, Jason,
and my sisters, Jennifer and Tricia,
who have supported me through all the ups and downs
I've experienced over the years.*

brief contents

contents

foreword

My name is Steve Buchanan, and I'm honored to write this foreword. With more than 20 years of experience in the tech industry, I've worked as a generalist, led internal and consulting teams, and gained extensive knowledge in various facets of technology, including development. Recently, I've been advising startups and leading a research team at Microsoft, collaborating cross-functionally with executives, engineers, designers, and customer teams to evaluate end-to-end experiences across multicloud environments, with a focus on improving Azure.

I've known Shelley Benhoff for several years, meeting her as a fellow author of Pluralsight courses in the tech space. She is an established expert with more than 20 years of experience in the tech industry, much of it spent in development and leading development teams. Her most recent role is as a Senior Developer Experience Manager at Docker. I've always respected Shelley and followed her remarkable accomplishments throughout her career.

When I heard she was writing the *Lead Developer Career Guide*, I was ecstatic. I knew she would bring a wealth of real-world knowledge to the topic. When she asked me to write a use case for the book, I didn't hesitate to contribute. And when she asked me to write the foreword, I was even more excited because it gave me the opportunity to read the book early and recognize how invaluable it is for developers.

Shelley is a leader, whether she is leading teams in her day-to-day job, supporting the community, or creating content to help others develop their skills. Manning could not have chosen a better author to write this book.

In the world of development, especially as a junior developer, there is often little guidance on how to advance your career and start leading teams. Navigating the transition from a junior role to a leadership position can be daunting without a clear road map. Many developers who have successfully made this leap did so without direct guidance, relying on their own experiences and learning through trial and error. This lack of structured support means that valuable lessons are often learned the hard way, with mistakes serving as the primary teacher.

Recognizing this gap, the *Lead Developer Career Guide* steps in as a crucial resource. This book is designed to be a comprehensive, step-by-step guide for developers who are ready to move from junior or individual contributor roles to positions of leadership. The guidance it offers is not just theory but grounded in real-world experience. The author, along with other carefully selected contributors, shares practical advice and insights gained from years of navigating the tech industry. The collective wisdom in this book provides readers with a solid foundation on which to build their leadership skills.

What sets this book apart is its focus on actionable advice and real-world use cases. Each chapter is filled with practical examples that illustrate the challenges and rewards of moving into a leadership role. The author, as a seasoned professional, offers a unique perspective on various aspects of the transition, from developing essential soft skills to mastering the technical competencies required for effective leadership. This diverse array of insights ensures that readers can relate to and learn from multiple experiences, making the journey to becoming a lead developer more accessible and achievable.

As a reader, this book takes you, the junior developer, on a journey to understanding what it means to be a lead developer. It covers the career trajectory for the role and the necessary skills, both soft and technical: how to write technical documents, work with project teams, and optimize development processes. You'll also explore the world of consulting, working with clients, increasing your emotional intelligence, stepping into leadership roles, and even becoming a mentor.

The book is enriched with real-world use cases from experts in the tech field, and it includes numerous charts, graphs, diagrams, and other graphics to provide a visual breakdown of complex concepts and processes. By the end, you'll have a comprehensive understanding of what it truly takes to become a lead developer.

For the foreseeable future, this book will be my go-to recommendation for junior developers who aspire to level up into a lead developer role. It stands out as an essential resource, providing the structured guidance that so many developers need but often lack. Whether you're just starting to think about advancing your career or are already on the path to leadership, this book offers invaluable insights and practical advice to help you achieve your goals.

I hope you enjoy this book as much as I have, from start to finish. It offers a wealth of knowledge that is not only valuable for a full read-through but also serves as a lasting reference. You can return to it anytime you need specific advice on the many aspects of a career as a lead developer. Whether you're dealing with technical challenges, team dynamics, or personal growth, the guidance in this book will be a reliable companion throughout your career.

This book is designed to grow with you, offering insights and guidance at every stage of your journey into leadership. Its practical examples and real-world use cases make it easy to apply the lessons learned to your own experiences. As you progress in your career, you'll find that this book continues to provide relevant and actionable advice, helping you navigate the complexities of leadership in the tech industry.

— STEVE BUCHANAN
PRINCIPAL PROGRAM MANAGER, MICROSOFT

preface

Throughout my 25-year journey as a developer, my focus wasn't always on leadership. Starting out as a junior developer, I found immense satisfaction in the technical intricacies of the job, thriving in research and training. It wasn't until my boss, recognizing my potential, broached the subject of leadership that I began to contemplate its possibilities.

Initially, I hesitated, uncertain of what leadership entailed or whether I possessed the necessary skills. However, driven by my aspirations, I embraced the challenge. With time, I progressed from senior developer to team lead, eventually attaining the role of lead developer.

Reflecting on my journey, I recognize that perhaps a bit more preparation beforehand would have eased some of the early struggles. I encountered my fair share of challenges, particularly in navigating conflicts within my team, which proved to be stressful. Yet, each obstacle was a learning opportunity, shaping me into a more resilient leader.

The inspiration for this book struck me when I stumbled upon Alyssa Miller's *Cybersecurity Career Guide*. Realizing the lack of resources specifically tailored for lead developers, I felt compelled to fill the gap. My own experiences as a novice lead developer fueled my determination to create a comprehensive guide for those embarking on a similar path.

Being a successful lead developer demands a delicate balance of technical prowess and interpersonal finesse. Within these pages, I not only delve into enhancing technical skills but also provide practical examples to cultivate crucial soft skills, such as effective communication. Additionally, I've curated a selection of supplementary resources to facilitate a deeper exploration of the topics discussed.

It's my sincere hope that this book serves as a beacon for aspiring lead developers, guiding them away from the pitfalls I encountered and toward a smoother, more fulfilling journey in leadership.

acknowledgments

I want to thank my husband, Jason Benhoff, for supporting me to reach my goals. Writing a book is hard work, and it takes time away from quality time with my family. This was my first book, and I didn't know what to expect. I often felt discouraged because everything took longer than I intended, but you were there for me, and you listened to my concerns, which helped me push through to the finish line.

I also want to thank the contributors to the case studies throughout the book: Ryan Lewis, Deborah Kurata, Dan Wahlin, Chloe Condon, Maureen Josephine, Scott Hanselman, Jamie Maguire, Edidiong Askipo, and Gabriela Martinez-Sanchez. Thank you for your time and for sharing your real-world experiences to create engaging case studies to tie into the topics presented. I appreciate every one of you, and I'm lucky to know you.

Next, I'd like to acknowledge my editor at Manning, Rebecca Johnson. Thank you for your guidance and patience when life got in the way of my progress. Your dedication to the quality of this book has truly enhanced the experience for all who delve into its pages. Thank you to everyone at Manning who worked with me on the production and promotion of the book. It was truly a team effort, and I enjoyed working with the team at Manning throughout the development of this book.

I also want to extend my heartfelt gratitude to the reviewers who generously dedicated their time to reading my manuscript at different points in its journey, offering invaluable feedback along the way: Alex Rios, Ari-Pekka Lappi, Avinash Kumar, Avishek Roy Chowdhury, Balraj Singh, Bill LeBorgne, Dinesh Kumar, Foster Haines, Giacomo Gamba, Greg MacLean, Greg White, Ian De La Cruz, Javid Asgarov, Johannes Lochmann, John Kasiewicz, Leonardo José Gomes da Silva, Marc Taylor, Mario (Plamenov) Pavlov, Matt Deimel, Matthias Bartsch, Mike Baran, Neil Croll, Nolan To, Philippe Vialatte, Raul Murciano, Steve Goodman, Stuart A. Schmukler, Tam Nguyen, Tim O'Leary, and Zeynep Nur Aktaş.

Special thanks to Stephen Mizell, technical editor, for your detailed reviews. Your knowledge regarding the lead developer role was crucial to crafting the storytelling aspects of this book and aided me in writing relatable scenarios in which lead developers may find themselves. The quality of your reviews was always excellent, and I appreciate the time you spent making sure my book was of the highest quality. Stephen is a leader in the API industry and has helped companies such as Autodesk, SmartBear, Apiary, and Optic build great API products. He's the author of *API by Design* and *The Language-Oriented Approach to API Development* and is a co-author of the API standard RESTful JSON.

And finally, thank you to Steve Buchanan for your contributions, including a case study and the book's foreword. Your enthusiasm for mentoring lead developers exemplifies mentoring excellence that we should all strive to uphold. I learned a lot from you, and I appreciate the thought that went into your case study and foreword. I feel very honored that you spent so much time on this, and your efforts are much appreciated.

about this book

Being a lead developer was one of the hardest roles I've taken on in my career. Moving from a senior developer into leadership has a very steep learning curve. Most lead developers lack the soft skills or training to achieve true leadership, and they need guidance to set themselves up for success. In this book, you'll learn how to lead teams, work with project managers, present solutions to clients, and use critical thinking during emergencies. You'll also learn how to mentor teams and provide accurate estimates to help project managers keep projects on track and within the budget. When you're finished reading this book, you'll understand how to combine your technical skills with the leadership skills necessary to become a successful lead developer.

Who should read this book

If you're a junior developer, this guide will help you plan your career path to becoming a technical lead. If you're a senior developer, you'll master the leadership abilities that will turn your technical knowledge into an asset for your whole team. If you're a team leader, hand this book to your best developer to help them mature into the role of lead.

How this book is organized: A road map

The book has 12 chapters:

- Chapter 1 defines the role of lead developer, including the daily tasks and what team members expect in a successful lead developer.
- Chapter 2 discusses the lead developer career trajectory starting with junior developer and moving through different career paths into technical leadership.
- Chapter 3 lists lead developer skills you should learn, including different leadership styles and how to choose the right one for your personality.
- Chapter 4 provides tactics and tools you can use to learn any developer skill, apply these skills on the job, and overcome learning blockers.

- Chapter 5 details the importance of technical documentation and how to write documentation that is easily accessible to your team.
- Chapter 6 discusses the optimization of development processes and how to maintain a streamlined development process to follow best practices in the Software Development Lifecycle (SDLC).
- Chapter 7 reviews how to work with project teams and communicate effectively to avoid miscommunication and improve project management processes.
- Chapter 8 describes how to form relationships with your clients and stakeholders while catering to their needs and resolving conflicts with difficult clients.
- Chapter 9 defines what it means to be a mentor and how you can help your team members achieve career and personal growth.
- Chapter 10 provides examples of hurdles that lead developers face when taking the lead for the first time and how to overcome them to improve confidence and lead a successful team.
- Chapter 11 defines emotional intelligence and its importance to the role of lead developer.
- Chapter 12 discusses how to decide when you're ready to take the leap into a lead developer role and set yourself up for success.

liveBook discussion forum

Purchase of *Lead Developer Career Guide* includes free access to liveBook, Manning's online reading platform. Using liveBook's exclusive discussion features, you can attach comments to the book globally or to specific sections or paragraphs. It's a snap to make notes for yourself, ask and answer technical questions, and receive help from the author and other users. To access the forum, go to https://livebook.manning.com/book/lead-developer-career-guide/discussion. You can also learn more about Manning's forums and the rules of conduct at https://livebook.manning.com/discussion.

Manning's commitment to our readers is to provide a venue where a meaningful dialogue between individual readers and between readers and the author can take place. It's not a commitment to any specific amount of participation on the part of the author, whose contribution to the forum remains voluntary (and unpaid). We suggest you try asking the author some challenging questions lest her interest stray! The forum and the archives of previous discussions will be accessible from the publisher's website as long as the book is in print.

Other online resources

If you want to deep dive into the soft skills presented in this book, you can watch Shelley's online courses on Pluralsight: https://pluralsight.com/authors/shelley-benhoff. She also has courses on LinkedIn Learning: www.linkedin.com/learning/instructors/shelley-benhoff.

about the author

SHELLEY BENHOFF has 25+ years of experience in IT as a lead developer, trainer, Docker Community Leader, and Sitecore MVP. She has a passion for tiaras, technology, gaming, and general nerdery. She loves to learn new things as well as mentor and teach others. She teaches leadership, communication, Docker, and Sitecore development on Pluralsight and LinkedIn Learning. Shelley aims to provide her students with an immersive learning experience based on real-world scenarios. She has studied soft skills and technical skills to become a well-rounded leader. Many of her online courses include entertaining animated scenarios using real experiences from her career to walk students through common workplace events to help visualize learning objectives.

about the cover illustration

The figure on the cover of *Lead Developer Career Guide*, titled "Saint Lazare Vénérienne," or "A Female Prisoner at Saint-Lazare Prison Paris," is taken from a book by Louis Curmer published in 1841. Each illustration is finely drawn and colored by hand.

In those days, it was easy to identify where people lived and what their trade or station in life was just by their dress. Manning celebrates the inventiveness and initiative of the computer business with book covers based on the rich diversity of regional culture centuries ago, brought back to life by pictures from collections such as this one.

What is a lead developer?

This chapter covers

- Lead developer definition
- Senior developer versus lead developer comparison
- Lead developer responsibilities
- Lead developer expectations beyond daily tasks

So you want upward mobility in your career as a developer? The lead developer role may be for you. If you've researched the lead developer role or are a newly appointed lead developer, then you've probably encountered resources that focus on the technical expertise you must achieve before being hired for this role. However, the title "lead developer" includes the word "lead," and you must have a combination of both technical and leadership skills.

A lead developer, also known as a technical lead, is a senior-level software developer who takes on additional responsibilities within a development team. The lead developer is often responsible for guiding and mentoring other team members, making technical decisions, and coordinating the development team's work. They represent the development team and work with project managers to prioritize development tasks. The lead developer may also play a key role in the planning and execution of software projects and may be involved in the management of the team and the development process. In my experience, the role of a lead developer varies in different types of organizations and cultures, and there is no one-size-fits-all approach.

Lead developers are often expected to handle communication and support the development needs of project teams. To be a successful lead developer, you must have a high level of critical thinking and people skills. It's vital to make quick and effective decisions and communicate those decisions among the team. There may be times when team members disagree with your decisions, and you must be able to handle conflict and difficult conversations.

Many senior developers are promoted to lead developer positions based solely on their technical skills. The focus on soft skills is lacking for technical positions; however, when a developer is in a leadership position, they need support in mastering the soft skills necessary for success in working on teams and interfacing with clients and stakeholders. I've witnessed this far too often, and it happened to me too. I felt like I was thrown into a pool without knowing how to swim, and while it was difficult at first, I was able to learn on the job, and I eventually learned how to be a great leader. To start, you need to understand the demand for lead developers and who can be successful in this role.

1.1   Who can be a lead developer

Lead developers can be from anywhere in the world, have many different backgrounds, and represent all genders. Today, there is a need for more diversity in developer roles. According to the United States Bureau of Labor Statistics (BLS), only 21.5% of software developers in the United States are women. White developers equal 55.0% of the industry, Asians are 36.4%, followed by Black, Hispanic, or Latino at 5.7% (see figure 1.1). It's estimated that 8% of all developers are LGBTQIA+. Companies that champion diverse development teams can create innovation, as they can create products and services for a wider audience. Being a champion for diversity is something you need to consider as a lead developer when you're hiring new developers.

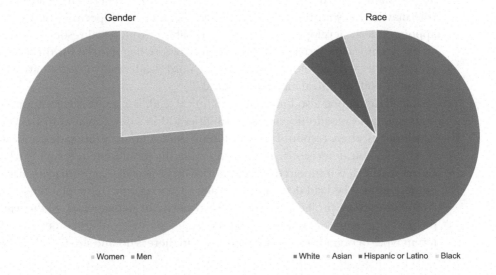

Gender   Race

■ Women ■ Men   ■ White ■ Asian ■ Hispanic or Latino ■ Black

Figure 1.1   Developer Demographics – USA (Source: www.bls.gov/cps/cpsaat11.htm)

According to the Stack Overflow Developer survey, the global gender disparity is even greater. More than 73,000 developers from 180 countries took this global survey, and it suggests that almost 93% of developers are men, 4.8% are women, and 1.39% are non-binary, genderqueer, or gender nonconforming. Regarding race at the global level, 39.38% of all developers are white, 37.25% are European, 9.7% are Indian, 9.48% are Asian, and 5.71% are Hispanic or Latino. The top industries for lead developers are Fortune 500 and technology followed by finance, manufacturing, and retail (see figure 1.2): 65% of developers work in the public sector, 32% are in the private sector, 2% are in education, and 1% are in government.

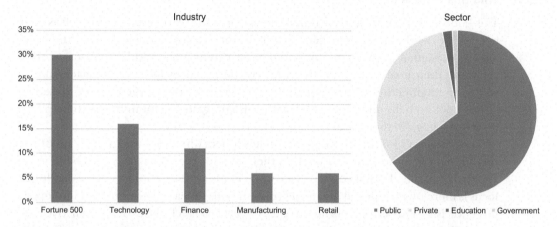

Figure 1.2 Developer Demographics – Worldwide (Source: https://survey.stackoverflow.co/2022/ #demographics-gender-prof)

Most jobs I've had have included a global team of both employees and contractors. In the United States, many tech companies outsource a portion of their software development staff, so I've had the pleasure of working with people from various backgrounds. However, most of the full-time employees I've worked with were not people of color. When I hired a team for the first time, I hired three white women and one white man. This was my unconscious bias, and I should have done a better job of seeking talent from different demographics. I could have required a wider talent pool from the recruiter, including an equally diverse demographic. Don't make the same mistake that I did! Many organizations that I'm involved with support diversity, equity, and inclusion, including Black Girls Code, Girls Who Code, Women Who Code, and Latinas Who Code, to name a few. Being involved in these communities has taught me valuable lessons and connected me with some of the most talented developers I've had the pleasure of knowing.

Another important demographic to note is education level. Many people think a computer science degree is necessary to be a developer and even more so for a lead developer. While this was true at one point, it's no longer the case. Patrick Collison, CEO of Stripe, and Sahil Lavingia, founder of Gumroad, don't have college degrees, and they went on to excel in leadership and form successful tech companies. Only some people can adhere to the strict approach to education offered by universities. Some people want to learn on the job, and that's fine! Many people also don't find coding until later in life, and they studied something vastly different in college.

Many of the industry experts that are featured throughout this book come from different backgrounds, including gender, race, and educational level. They are diverse, representing many groups in tech from around the world to show that you can be successful as a lead developer no matter your background.

1.1.1 Who this book is for

This book is for aspiring and current junior, senior, and lead developers as well as engineering or development managers. People in these roles can benefit from the information presented in this book to outline their career plans and have a clear path to achieving their goals using current industry best practices in technical leadership. If you're an engineering or development manager, you can use the content presented in this book to help others achieve their goals and gain insight into how to help lead developers grow in their careers.

This book isn't for nondevelopers and developers who don't work on a team. If you don't have a team to lead and mentor, then most of the concepts in this book won't apply to your role. Even if you interface with clients and stakeholders occasionally, the focus is more on technical skills and less on soft skills or leadership. For nondevelopers, this book isn't a fit, as it covers how to gain expert-level technical skills as well as leadership skills for development teams. Lead developers must balance technical and leadership skills, and we'll cover both throughout this book.

If you're a junior developer, this book will help you learn how to study and hone your technical skills effectively. There are also many soft skills discussed in this book that you'll benefit from in your current position, such as communicating with your co-workers and using active listening to ensure that you're not only understanding what you're building but also why you're building it. This goes a long way to help you create excellent software and websites with the end user in mind.

For senior developers, this book will help you prepare to move into a leadership role. You're already a technical expert; now you must learn how to discuss your technical approach for a project with project teams and get their buy-in. Learning soft skills will help you sell your idea and build a collaborative communication culture within your team. You also need to be an excellent mentor and support your team. These expectations may require you to step outside your comfort zone, which I encourage you to do. Some people don't want to do this, and that's ok! However, I can tell you from experience that going outside your comfort zone can lead you to opportunities that you never thought possible.

If you're an engineering manager with or without development skills, you'll want to share this book with junior, senior, and lead developers on your team to help them grow in their careers. If your career includes development roles, then you may want to stay current with your skills so that you can communicate with your lead developers about their technical approaches. Even if your career didn't include development roles and you have little to no development experience, as an engineering manager, you do have technical skills. You may not be able to sit down and code, but you're able to understand technical concepts, and this book will help you understand and empathize with your lead developers and their struggles.

1.1.2 Reviewing top industries for lead developers

As a lead developer, it's important to be aware of the industries that offer the most opportunities for employment. The most popular industries for lead developers include the following:

- Retail
- Technology
- Healthcare
- Banking/fintech
- Manufacturing
- Business services
- Government

I've worked in most of these sectors, and historically, government jobs (at least in the United States) are the most stable and come with good benefits. The downside is that you'll often not work on cutting-edge technology; instead, you'll work with legacy code and systems. This can have its benefits, as you'll learn a bit of programming history. However, these jobs often go to developers who specialize in legacy systems. These systems aren't going away any time soon, and COBOL programmers are still in high demand.

I've also done a lot of work in the healthcare industry and business services industry. In healthcare, I learned a lot about security due to privacy laws dealing with patient information. And working in business services gave me the experience of working with external clients and customers. Each industry comes with its benefits, and I suggest you work for companies that provide you with opportunities to work on projects that interest you.

Each industry focuses on many different types of products and services. For example, in the fintech industry, you would focus on consumer products and business solutions for handling payments or investments. Big technology companies focus on innovative consumer products such as apps, streaming services, video games, and business-facing or business-to-business (B2B) solutions. Manufacturing and retail industry companies create the items that we use every day, including cars and clothing, which they sell on e-commerce websites. Table 1.1 lists the top industries and companies for lead developers and the pros and cons for each industry.

Table 1.1   Top industries and companies for lead developers

Industry	Top Companies	Pros	Cons
Retail	Walmart, Amazon, Kroger, and Costco	Specialize in e-commerce, employee discounts	Prone to frequent lay-offs based on sales, long hours during the holidays
Technology	Facebook/Meta, Apple, Amazon, Netflix, and Google	Learn from the best talent in the industry, excellent perks, high salaries, vesting options	Very high competition and expectations, stringent performance review process, long hours
Healthcare	CVS, UnitedHealth, Johnson & Johnson	Gain experience with high-level security systems and data privacy	Many codes to keep track of pertaining to health data
Fintech	American Express, PayPal, Mastercard, Fiserv, and Visa	Highly profitable, more job security, work on creative app solutions	Responsible for preserving sensitive data, constant hacking attempts
Manufacturing	Tesla, Samsung, Toyota, and Lockheed Martin	Variable project opportunities, learn different technologies and systems	Fewer remote jobs, not always on the cutting edge of technology

Whatever industry you're interested in, most companies need developers. You may work on different types of products and services, such as building apps and websites or consulting for an agency; however, the role of the lead developer remains the same. The expectations and struggles for this role are applicable across all industries and sectors.

1.1.3   *Being a successful lead developer*

A successful lead developer will learn technical skills throughout their career by working in roles such as junior developer, senior developer, or developer advocate/ developer relations. In these positions, you'll develop your technical skills as you build systems based on business or functional requirements and write technical requirements for tasks assigned to you. You'll also understand the deployment process, as you're responsible for deploying your code for testing before it goes into production.

Lead developers are expected to have the technical expertise to build systems and lead the development team. You may work with a lead architect responsible for providing the technical requirements and approach. Lead developers focus mainly on development tasks; however, these roles are often combined into one, which is the focus of this book. It's best to know too much instead of too little to prepare you for anything.

When you move into a lead developer position, you'll combine your technical skills with leadership skills (see figure 1.3). Facilitating communication is a key skill that you'll need to master to ensure that the development team is productive and produces high-quality work. Decision-making is another leadership skill that takes some time to learn, especially making quick decisions in an emergency by gathering feedback from your team. You need empathy and self-awareness to build trust and cultivate relationships. When you build trust, your team will work together well, and you'll see productivity increase. These relationships are important to not only your success but also your team's success.

Technical Skills	Leadership Skills
✓ Learn programming languages ✓ Write technical specifications ✓ Develop features, components, and systems ✓ Deploy code	✓ Facilitate communication ✓ Make final decisions ✓ Gather feedback ✓ Emotional intelligence ✓ Self-awareness

Figure 1.3 Technical skills vs. leadership skills

The success of a lead developer is based on the success of your team. This includes ensuring that your team works within the projected timeline and that you take on minimal technical debt. To accomplish this, you must prioritize the most important tasks and help unblock your team so they can complete their tasks on time and ensure high-quality work. An important metric to compare is the tasks to be completed in each iteration or release versus what was completed. The quality of your team's work will be reflected in the open/close rates of tickets, problems, or bugs. When code is deployed to production, it should be the final version with no critical errors, which will reflect an attention to detail by the team.

You don't have to have both technical expertise and leadership skills to apply for your first lead developer job. If you're lucky, you'll be able to get promoted to a lead developer position at your current job. However, since you're reading this book, you're already ahead of the curve, and you'll understand more about what lies ahead when you're finished. Many senior developers are thrown into lead developer positions and expected to "learn on the job." This only works if they are given the support they need to navigate their new leadership position. Some companies offer access to learning platforms such as Pluralsight; however, you need mentoring as well. I suggest having a group of mentors from different backgrounds including gender, race, education level, and experience. When you have a diverse group of mentors, you'll be inspired by their different points of view to find your own leadership style.

1.2 Lead developer tasks

Understanding the tasks and responsibilities of a lead developer is an important step in your career journey. Whether you're building products or offering services, you'll have leadership responsibilities within project teams and potentially also at the organizational level. These can seem like daunting tasks, but with the proper preparation and support, you'll be able to take them head-on. While roles and responsibilities can vary across cultures, the most common scenarios are presented throughout this section.

When you're a senior developer, your focus is mainly on your own work. Senior developers may also mentor junior developers to assist them in learning new skills and to collaborate with them on their work. The spotlight is on their technical skills and consistently improving their technical expertise. This role requires a high level of experience and knowledge that is incredibly valuable to development teams. Problem-solving skills help senior developers use their critical thinking to troubleshoot errors, fix bugs, and help remove blockers for other team members. This is a department-facing role with little to no direct communication with clients and stakeholders, such as project managers, development managers, marketers, and so on.

In contrast, lead developers are responsible for working with project managers, clients, and stakeholders. As a lead developer, you'll represent the entire development team, gather their feedback, form your technical approach, and present it to the project team. The focus is more on business and communication skills, as you're the face of the development team, and you act as the go-between to communicate client or stakeholder requirements to the developers. This role also requires some project management skills because the lead developer works closely with the project manager to calculate project estimates and keep the development team on track. Figure 1.4 shows a comparison of senior versus lead developer skills.

	Senior developer	Lead developer
Development tasks	✓	✓
Mentor junior developers	✓	✓
Troubleshooting errors and bugs	✓	✓
Build technical architecture	✓	✓
Documentation	✓	✓
Communicate project specs to the dev team		✓
Calculate project estimates		✓
Develop coding standards		✓
Present the technical approach to project stakeholders		✓

Figure 1.4   Senior vs. lead developer

An important lead developer task is assisting in the project proposal phase when starting a new project. At the beginning of any project, the lead developer is tasked with forming a technical approach and creating project estimates. This process begins with gathering feedback from all project stakeholders, including business and technical requirements. This feedback supports the overall technical approach, which will enable you to create the project estimates with the help of your team since they will be the ones doing the work. After you present your technical approach, your estimates will need to be refined. Project estimates change frequently, and it's essential for the lead developer to constantly gather feedback from the team. Figure 1.5 shows a lead developer's process to start a project and gather estimates.

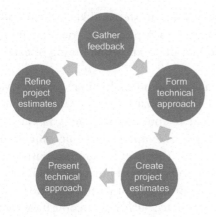

Figure 1.5 Starting a new project

The following list contains the main responsibilities of a lead developer:

- Leading the development team
- Working with project teams
- Communicating with clients and stakeholders
- Setting development standards
- Building technical architecture

When you're working through these tasks, keep in mind that this will take practice. No one is comfortable with everything at first. You'll learn as you go, and you'll improve your skills. Communication is the key skill that every lead developer needs to be successful. When you're in a leadership position, your main job will be facilitating communication within your team. Lead developers play an important role in ensuring that the development team is given the support they need. This also goes a long way to retaining talent when your team is constantly learning, growing, and improving.

1.2.1 Leading the development team

Leading by example, building trust, and mentoring the development team make up the first step on your path to leadership success. Lead developers are responsible for supporting the development team to ensure their success both as a team and individually. This is ultimately how your success as a lead developer will be measured, not by your success alone but rather by your team.

When you're in a leadership position, you can make or break an employee's day. Leading by example means setting a positive tone for your team and coaching them through difficult times, especially in emergencies. For example, what do you do when a website goes down? Hopefully, you have an emergency plan in place that you can follow. If not, you should make one before emergencies happen. You must stay calm, formulate a plan of attack, and assign tasks to resolve the problem quickly. You should also tell everyone on the project team what the plan is step by step and keep them updated as each step is completed. If the resolution requires a deployment, you'll need to get the Quality Assurance (QA) team involved and let them know the timing of each step so they can prepare to start testing.

Building trust in your team will help you understand each other's points of view and improve your team's morale. If your team doesn't trust you, they won't come to you when they have a problem. If they can't come to you, they may not go to anyone, and their needs will never be met. When this happens, employees can become disengaged from their work and potentially quit their jobs. Turnover is more expensive than you think, and it can take a developer up to a year to be fully acclimated to their job.

A study from LinkedIn (https://mng.bz/NB6x) states that the turnover rate in the tech industry is 13.2%. Furthermore, in recent years, 50% more people have voluntarily quit their jobs. According to a study by the Work Institute (https://mng.bz/Dpgg), the cost of employee turnover is approximately 33.3% of their annual salary. It's estimated that it can take up to two months to hire a new software developer and another six months to bring them up to speed. If there is no knowledge transfer, the costs are even higher, which is why lead developers must ensure that they provide proper onboarding documentation (covered in depth later in this book). You want to avoid the loss of knowledge by retaining top talent and building trust in your team.

A good way to build trust is to back up your employees. When someone has an idea, and you think it's a good idea, then you need to back them up. Defending your team's ideas will make them feel listened to and appreciated, which will help you form a bond with them. If the idea isn't exactly what you had in mind, you should keep an open mind and consider options that build upon the original idea. You can say, "That's a good start, but what do you think about (xyz)?" Asking questions is how you'll draw out the talent within your team.

The first time I led a team, we implemented a project tracking system that was suggested to us by a director. The system didn't work well for our types of projects, and my team suggested that we switch to Atlassian Jira. I wasn't keen to go against the director's suggestion, but I knew that we would have a problem if we didn't switch. When I had a one-on-one with the director, I explained our problems with the system he suggested and how Atlassian Jira would solve these problems for us. It was an uncomfortable conversation for me as a first-time leader, but in the end, I explained our position, backed up my team, and we came to an agreement. When we implemented Atlassian Jira, I kept my team involved. I listened to them, and we selected the best processes that worked for the team. This went a long way in building trust and comradery on my team.

One of the most important behaviors you can exhibit is open communication. Clear, honest communication builds a foundation of trust and sets expectations for how your team interacts. If you make a promise, ensure you can deliver on it to show your team that you follow through on commitments. Being receptive to feedback shows that you value your team members' opinions and ideas. You must also act honestly, objectively, and in the best interest of the community. Misusing information or treating people unfairly can erode trust and destroy morale. Handling information and requests respectfully and treating people with respect and fairness can help create a positive and productive team dynamic. By exhibiting these behaviors, you can build a culture of trust within your team, leading to greater collaboration, productivity, and success.

It's also important to ensure that your team isn't stretched too thin and working too many hours because that results in burnout and lower productivity. You should promote work–life balance and encourage your team members to take breaks when needed. Additionally, it's essential to foster a culture of open communication and collaboration, allowing team members to share their workload and work together to achieve goals. Providing support and recognizing their hard work and achievements can also help boost morale and reduce stress levels. By taking a proactive approach to addressing burnout, you can help your team members feel valued, supported, and motivated, which can ultimately lead to higher productivity and better outcomes. It's of utmost importance to get feedback from your team on project estimates and coordinate timelines with the project manager.

1.2.2 Working with project teams

Lead developers are a crucial part of the project team. They work closely with project managers, QA, clients, and stakeholders to provide their technical expertise and assist in project planning. Their skills directly contribute to the success of the project as they provide estimates and facilitate communication between the clients, stakeholders, and development team.

Working well with project managers is an essential skill for a lead developer. You should understand the project management framework and where you can assist. For new projects, you'll provide estimates of the development work that needs to be done and the overall approach. As the work progresses, you'll work closely with the project manager to organize tasks, priorities, bugs, and technical debt. The lead developer is the liaison between the project manager and the development team, and you must rely on their feedback to come up with estimates and to weigh in on priorities.

For example, if a developer on your team has been working on a product or feature and the priorities change, they should be given the time to get to a good stopping point, document where they left off, and then check it into a repository. The lead developer should ensure that their work is properly documented so that they or someone else can pick it back up in the future. This happens a lot because priorities change all the time. If that weren't the case, we wouldn't need project managers!

Another important task for a lead developer is working with QA to ensure that the quality of the development work matches the requirements, the code is ready for testing, and everything works as intended. This entails assisting with QA's testing strategy, ensuring that the technical requirements are well documented, and answering questions when necessary. The QA process is critical to a project's success, and as a lead developer, you'll be expected to work with them to figure out common problems so that you can adjust your development approach to avoid these problems in the future.

Working directly with clients and stakeholders is probably one of the hardest skills for a lead developer to master. I had a very hard time at first being the face of the development team, which can be a daunting experience, especially if you're an introvert by nature. The development team attends meetings, including project kickoffs, sprint planning, and retrospectives, to name a few. This is a good learning experience for any developer even before they become a lead developer. Lead developers may work with both internal and external stakeholders and vendors for services that they are using for the project. When a lead developer works directly with project stakeholders, the development team will get the technical information from them and not the project manager. This goes a long way to avoid miscommunication and ensure that everyone is on the same page, which will help to minimize technical debt and improve productivity.

1.2.3 *Communicating with clients and stakeholders*

So how do you communicate with clients and stakeholders? Everyone is different, so you should start by assessing their level of comfort, understanding their point of view, and building relationships. Remember, clients and stakeholders are people with lives outside of work. You should always get to know the people you work with as human beings, consider their emotions, and attend to their needs.

You can assess a client's level of comfort by observing how they interact with the rest of the project team. If the project is going poorly, are their arms crossed? Is there a frown on their face? Or are they open to suggestions and collaborating to resolve the problems? If they aren't collaborative, this suggests that they don't trust that the project team has their best interests in mind. An example of this is when the client only asks "when" and "how much," as this doesn't assist in finding a solution. You can always tell the status of a working relationship when things go wrong. How do people react? Teams that work well in the face of adversity and show the client or stakeholder a unified front will ease their concerns and make them more comfortable with the status of the project. Table 1.2 lists body language references that you can use to understand different reactions.

Table 1.2   Body language references

Title	Link
The Dictionary of Body Language: A Field Guide to Human Behavior	https://mng.bz/lrxR
Your Body Language Speaks for You in Meetings	https://mng.bz/BgMl
How to Get Better at Reading People from Different Cultures	https://mng.bz/dZ21

Another key aspect of providing professional support for your clients and stakeholders is understanding their points of view. You shouldn't design their systems until you have business requirements and you've spoken to the team to ensure that you're all in agreement. Without solid business requirements, you may introduce scope creep. Thinking about not only how but why your team is building certain products or features will help the development team be more accurate when they begin working on new tasks. Developers need to test their work before it's deployed, and they need real-world examples to work with. You may also get feedback from the developers for improvements to run by the rest of the team. When you suggest improvements to clients and stakeholders and you understand their needs, you'll provide them with added value, and they will think highly of the work that the team is doing.

Getting to know your clients as people helps to diffuse tension and build important relationships. Meetings should start with a quick "How is everyone doing?"; don't shy away from asking people about their life outside of work. This goes for both offshore and domestic teams—they should be treated the same. If you have a meeting on a Friday, you can ask, "What is everyone doing this weekend?" Or ask the opposite on a Monday! You'll often find things that you have in common with them, and you can work them into the conversation from time to time. You may follow the same sports teams, watch the same movies, or read the same books. Even if you come from different backgrounds, you can often find something that you have in common with anyone. You can also inject some mild humor from time to time to lighten the mood.

Everyone struggles with communicating with clients and stakeholders, especially if you're providing a service to a client and not working on an internal project. Providing services such as consulting or working on business-to-business (B2B) solutions is a bit harder because the company is relying on you to ensure that the clients and stakeholders are happy so that their business is retained. I've worked for consulting agencies on projects that included building enterprise websites for Fortune 500 companies, and some of these projects had multimillion-dollar budgets. The level of responsibility was high for me as the lead developer on those types of projects, and it was a struggle to find my voice at first.

When you're working on an internal project to build a product or support your organization's infrastructure, communication is a bit different. Although no less important, it's often easier, as you already have common ground working for the same company. You may also work with third-party vendors, which is a different relationship because they are business partners who work for your organization. You should offer everyone that you work with the same level of professionalism and consideration of their needs. I've worked on internal products where the project team was mostly internal with a few external vendors. The atmosphere during meetings was much more casual with more chit-chat, but we were still focused on the project and committed to building the best products possible.

This was just a quick summary of this topic. Later in this book, I devote a full chapter to help you oversee clients and stakeholders with real-world examples.

1.2.4 *Setting development standards*

An especially important part of your job as a lead developer will be setting and maintaining development standards. You want to ensure that the development team is using the same coding style to bring symmetry to your codebase; the goal is to not be able to tell who the developer is just by looking at the code. One of the main reasons that organizations have standards is so that any developer can easily find the code they are looking for to fix a bug or improve a feature. This helps improve productivity, as developers don't always have to reverse engineer code to find what they need.

Development standards should be as granular as possible, including items such as where to place the curly brace after an `if` statement, adding comments before every function, and especially naming conventions. It's helpful to have a clear pattern in your file and directory names, modules, functions, and features.

Whether you're working on products or services, you must ensure that the development team adheres to the development standards. These standards must be well-documented and reviewed with every team member when they are being onboarded to the project. During the onboarding process, the lead developer should review the development standards with everyone on the team to ensure full adoption. During code review, standards should be enforced. You can also find common errors during code reviews that you can discuss with the entire team to ensure that everyone understands the development standards.

When you set development standards for a project, you may or may not have standards at the organizational level to rely on. If development standards exist, your priority is to learn and maintain them. Organizations may have custom libraries that should be included in all projects or a specific approach they take to technical architecture. These standards should change over time when the tech stacks your organization uses are upgraded or when new technologies come out that you want to adopt. Lead developers can also influence the development standards at the organizational level, and you should never shy away from presenting new ideas for improvements.

Maintaining development standards is essential, as technology is changing all the time. Lead developers need to keep their skills current and alert the project team and potentially the organization about updates that need to be made. Subscribing to newsletters for the technologies that you're using is a great way to keep up with the latest news and updates. Being active in the tech community and networking with people on social media is another way to remain up to date. Almost every technology has a community on Slack or Discord that is run either by a company or by community members.

I work with many different technologies, including Docker, which has an excellent community Slack and newsletters. Their Slack provides you with access to Docker Captains, Docker Community Leaders, and Docker employees who are always available to answer your questions. I'm also in similar groups for .NET and Sitecore, where we share current standards and updates. This helps me stay up to date with frequently changing standards and practices.

You can also rely on your development team to suggest improvements to the development standards. Every developer should have a say in the development approach. When people from different backgrounds come together to share ideas, this drives innovation. Including them in the standards process is a great way to motivate the team to keep their skills current by engaging in continuous learning.

1.2.5 *Building technical architecture*

Lead developers are expected to understand how to build technical architecture from scratch using current industry standards and practices. You'll need to work with project teams to ensure that the approach you're implementing fits within the budget but also provides a stable system. I've often worked with teams where I was the main decision-maker, but I leaned on other lead developers to ensure that I was making the right decisions if I was struggling. It's important to ask for help when you need it.

Being able to build out and document the technical architecture of a project from scratch isn't a skill that is easy to come by. You may be able to build a simple application using a tutorial, but when it comes to consumer products and enterprise solutions, you'll need to understand much more advanced concepts, which takes time and experience. When we start as junior developers, our main task is to fix bugs or add features to already-existing projects. The best way to learn how to build systems from scratch is to shadow and observe what the lead developer is doing. Ask them questions, get copies of the documentation they're using, and work on prototypes or personal projects. Working on personal projects is a great way to learn new skills, and it should be fun. You can get ideas for projects and guidance from boot camps, online courses, and architecture pattern books. Case studies are also a good resource, and you can find them by searching for the specific technology you're using. You can build yourself a portfolio website, app, or software that is related to your industry. If you become part of a community of developers, you should share your code with them for support.

In my experience, I've learned a lot from other developers within the organization. I would ask them for advice about the project I was working on even if they weren't working on that project. It's a good practice to get an outside opinion from someone who is impartial because they can often see things that you can't. I was often asked to help on projects that I didn't work on, and we would discuss what worked well with our projects and what didn't. This helped me learn more about the organizational approach to their products and keep my skills up to date.

One of your tasks as a lead developer may be to help plan out the budget for the technical architecture. This includes items such as server costs, software, web hosting, databases, and security protocols. The lead developer must get as granular as possible with these costs up front to avoid a price hike during the project. Furthermore, whenever you upgrade a project, you should reassess these costs and try to find solutions that will minimize the expense for your organization. To estimate server costs, you can use tools such as the Amazon Web Services (AWS) or Microsoft Azure cost calculators. Most cloud providers have tools to help you with estimates, including software and hosting. The budget for the technical architecture must include everything needed for every instance, including development, testing, staging, and production.

The lead developer is also responsible for creating an illustration of the technical architecture, usually in the form of a flowchart or diagram. Doing this will help you envision everything that you need to estimate for the budget. The illustration also shows how systems interact with each other as well as the users. The overall purpose of a technical diagram (see figure 1.6) is to plan how to build your project from the ground up, including every stage of the software development lifecycle.

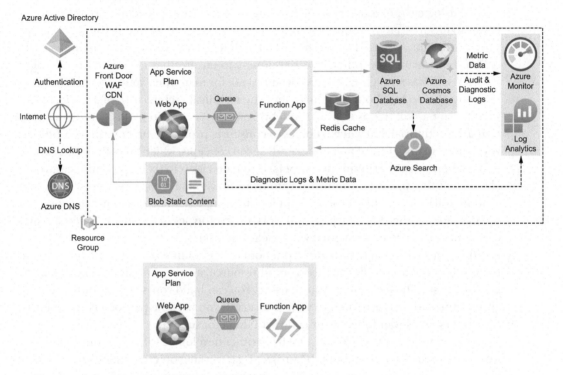

Figure 1.6   Example technical architecture diagram

When you're creating technical architecture diagrams for projects, you should try to be as consistent as possible. Check to see if your organization already has standards for creating technical architecture diagrams that you can follow. Make sure that the usage of shapes, lines, colors, and legends follows the same pattern to avoid miscommunication. These diagrams are crucial to the project's success, as they provide a clear map to show the team how everything will be built from start to finish and how it all supports the budget. Throughout this book, we'll discuss creating and presenting technical architecture diagrams to clients and stakeholders.

1.3   *Lead developer expectations*

Now that we've discussed lead developer tasks, we need to discuss the expectations for that role. It's important to understand the difference between responsibilities and expectations. Responsibilities are the tasks and duties that you're accountable for in your role, while expectations are the standards that others have for you. It's essential to take ownership of your responsibilities and ensure that you fulfill them to the best of your abilities. At the same time, you should also be aware of the expectations others have of you, such as being a good communicator, mentor, and leader. Balancing your responsibilities and expectations can be challenging, but it's crucial for your success and your team's success. Remember to always approach your role with a positive attitude and a willingness to learn and grow.

The lead developer role comes with many responsibilities, and you'll be held to a higher standard than junior or senior developers. A successful lead developer must be highly communicative and show true leadership skills. This is a completely different skill set than development work, and you'll need to find a balance between your technical skills and leadership skills. When you're working with project teams, they expect to be able to rely on you heavily to support everyone on the team, not just the development team. When you're working with the development team, you're expected to deliver requirements from the project team to the developers who are implementing the features or fixing bugs.

The following list contains the main leadership expectations of a lead developer:

- Providing team support
- Forming working relationships
- Being a leader

When you're working with nondevelopers such as marketing, QA, product designers, and executives, they will expect you to speak their language. If you use too many technical terms, they may get frustrated if they don't understand. Cultivating a language style that is technical but doesn't go too far into the weeds of specific development tasks will take time and a lot of observation of how the nondevelopers on the team speak to one another. Remember, they do have technical skills, and you can always coach them a bit to support them and help them learn more about the technologies you're using in a project.

1.3.1 *Providing team support*

One of your main expectations as a lead developer is to provide support to your team. This entails being communicative and answering questions as quickly as possible. This is a hard task because you're the technical expert, and as such, you'll most likely be inundated with questions from the team. You also have your own work to do, so you can't stop everything you're doing every time someone pings you with a question. You must ensure that your needs and your team's needs are met.

The hardest part about being communicative is when you're concentrating on doing your development work. If you stop when you're in the middle of something, you'll lose productivity because it's hard to get started again, especially if you're working on a very complex feature or task. My rule for myself and the lead developers I've hired is to try to answer questions within one hour. This will give you some time to wrap up what you're doing or at least get to a good stopping point so that you don't lose productivity. We live in a world where people are very busy and tend to want immediate answers. You must set some boundaries so that you can accomplish your tasks, but a compromise must be made to ensure the success of the team. You need to find your balance.

A good way to reduce the number of questions you get daily is to anticipate the team's needs. When you're asked questions in a meeting, for example, you should explain the answer to its full and logical conclusion and not leave anything out. Often, people will ask a question in a meeting and then ask for further clarification after they have had time to think about it. Put yourself in their shoes and anticipate the information they need to complete their tasks. If someone asks the same question repeatedly, don't get frustrated. They ask the same question because they may not understand the answer or there is no documentation. Taking the time to answer their questions and asking them to reiterate their understanding will help to mitigate this problem while increasing productivity.

Documenting FAQs in a central document repository and sharing it with the entire team is also a great way to ensure that everyone knows where to look for the information they need, which will also help you balance your work. You should maintain separate FAQs for nondevelopers and developers on the project team. For developer FAQs, adding documentation directly to the code repository is a popular approach. The entire team should have access to add FAQs on their own, and the lead developer should work with them to ensure that the answers are correct and there are no duplicates.

Creating a glossary of terms also helps nondevelopers understand the language that is being used. The terms should include everything that is included in the architecture diagram and should be linked to the diagram. This is a great reference for everyone on the team, including developers. The glossary should also include terms such as acronyms written in full with an explanation of what it is and what it does. Some acronyms are organization-specific, so if anyone googles that term, they may find other results with the same or similar acronym, causing even more confusion.

When you're writing project documentation that includes a glossary, you should format it for readability and maximum retention. Most people organize a glossary in alphabetical order, but you can also group terms by industry or organizational terminology. I like to include a background knowledge section for industry-standard terms that already have their documentation. The background knowledge section should have links to existing documentation for industry terms and concepts to support different roles and varying degrees of expertise on the team.

When you go the extra mile to anticipate the needs of your team and provide them with the support they need to be successful, you're also supporting your success, as you can be more productive. Writing documentation and glossaries for an entire team isn't an easy task, as there are many different roles and experience levels within the team. A successful lead developer needs to understand how the people on the team think, what information they need to know, and how to help them learn.

1.3.2   Forming working relationships

Lead developers must form working relationships so that there is cohesion and the team works well together. This entails respecting the expertise of your team members, appreciating them, and having open communication. Developing trust and comradery among your team members can lead to a more productive and enjoyable work environment. When you take the time to get to know your colleagues, you can understand their strengths and weaknesses, communication styles, and work preferences. This can help you delegate tasks better and foster a sense of collaboration, which can ultimately lead to more successful outcomes. When you have good working relationships, you'll be better able to support the needs of your team.

Respecting the expertise of your co-workers seems like a no-brainer, but you must be self-aware to be sure that you're being respectful. You should respect everyone you work with, including developers, project managers, clients, and so on. We are all prone to unconscious bias, as it's built into our culture, and you must raise your level of self-awareness to ensure that you're being respectful. *Unconscious bias* is a social stereotype someone automatically forms about a person or group of people. It's often unintentional and outside of their conscious awareness, so it can take time for people to realize that they're creating unconscious biases toward others. You and your team need to know how to properly identify unconscious bias and immediately stop it.

The following list contains the most common examples of unconscious bias:

- *Ageism*—Holding the idea that older people slow down and therefore aren't as competent or capable at work
- *Beauty bias*—Unfairly judging people based on their appearance
- *Conformity bias*—Applying basic peer pressure in which a person is pressured to agree with the opinion of the entire group, even if they have stated that they disagree
- *Affinity bias*—Being drawn to people who are like us
- *Confirmation bias*—Actively seeking to confirm ideas or success that we've had in the past that has little to no bearing on the current situation
- *Attribution bias*—Making assumptions about others based on their actions to understand why they're acting that way
- *Gender bias*—Favoring one gender over another
- *Ableism*—Being prejudiced against individuals with disabilities or those who are perceived as having disabilities
- *Cultural bias*—Tending to judge or evaluate people, events, or behaviors based on the standards and values of our own culture or group, without considering the cultural norms and values of other groups
- *Racism*—Upholding a system of prejudice, discrimination, and power based on the belief that certain races are superior or inferior to others

Being self-aware is your first step in combatting unconscious bias and being more respectful to your co-workers. Lead developers should ensure that they have a diverse team so that there is an even amount of representation. You need the expertise of people from different backgrounds to create products and services that are usable by your target audience. A lead developer needs to be open to learning from anyone. You can learn a lot from both nondevelopers and developers and rely on their expertise when you keep an open mind.

Good working relationships are formed by appreciating your co-workers. Tell the project team during a meeting how successful someone was in building a feature or fixing a bug. Say "thank you" when someone answers your questions or helps you find the answers that you need. Take your team out to lunch occasionally. Or if you're remote, schedule a fun activity that you can do together online, such as a virtual happy hour, playing video games, or playing *Dungeons and Dragons*. I've participated in a virtual happy hour where everyone could order drinks of their choice and the company paid for them. The only problem was waiting until the happy hour to have their drink!

Open and consistent communication is a key component of every good working relationship. This can lead to having difficult conversations; however, moving through those conversations becomes easier when you already have a relationship with that person or group of people. When you're working with internal co-workers, don't lie, and don't sugarcoat things. When there's a problem, let the team know, and be honest and direct. It's so much worse when you try to cover things to protect yourself or your team. If you aren't honest or consistent with your messaging, your team will lose trust in you. They may also follow your lead and avoid conflict or be dishonest themselves, which will only lead to more conflict. When you're consistent in your honesty, people will come to expect it, and they will respect you for it.

1.3.3   *Being a leader*

A leader is a person who is in a position of authority or influence and who is able to guide and direct others. Leaders may be responsible for making decisions, setting goals, and developing strategies for achieving those goals. They may also be responsible for inspiring and motivating others and for building and maintaining relationships within a team or organization. Leadership styles and approaches can vary widely and may depend on the specific goals and needs of an organization, as well as the personalities and abilities of individual leaders.

Finding your leadership style is important, so throughout this book, we'll review current best practices. As a lead developer, you can't "set it and forget it"; in other words, you need to check back in on things from time to time. You'll be expected to make decisions, ensure accountability, and lead change. You want to inspire your team and lead by example while at the same time understanding that you can't please everyone.

Making decisions takes a high level of critical thinking. A lead developer must consider risk, form a plan, and execute that plan. You need to keep a level head during this process to avoid making baseless decisions or going off course. Part of decision-making is ensuring that the action plan is carried out as you described. Therefore, you should check in throughout the project because people may deviate from the plan. When you have an action plan, you must work together with your team to gather consistent feedback to ensure that everything is going as planned. When things aren't going as planned, sharing information among the team can help you get back on track. Communicating the action plan shouldn't include just telling your team what the plan is, but rather sharing information so that you can make informed decisions.

As a lead developer, everyone on your team looks to you, and you must lead by example. Establishing accountability for yourself is one of the first steps in becoming a true leader. You need to hold yourself accountable for deadlines and follow-through. If you promise to do something, then do it. If for some reason, you can't, then let the person know when they can expect what you promised. You should also apologize when you drop the ball on a project or offend someone unintentionally. Some people avoid apologizing because they don't want to admit that they're wrong and sometimes fear losing their job over it. This should never be the case, and you need to show your team that apologizing when you're wrong is a part of the team's culture.

Leading by example is an important concept for all leaders to master. When you show your values through your behavior, then others will notice and follow your lead. At my first job as a lead developer, I was constantly promising that tasks would be done by a certain deadline, and then I was so overloaded with work that I couldn't live up to that promise. Of course, you want to be enthusiastic about your work, but you must ensure that you're able to do the work in the amount of time given. I eventually learned how to push back on things that weren't a priority so that my schedule was more realistic. In doing that, I found that my team felt comfortable coming to me when they felt overloaded so that we could work out a plan together.

We live in a world of change, and people often don't like change because it can cause them anxiety. Anxiety is one of the most common mental health disorders, and it affects almost everyone at some level. Being a positive leader of change for your project team and organization will ensure your success as a lead developer and provide a safe and trusting workplace to mitigate anxiety among your team. Whether the change is suggested by you or another person on your team, you're expected to carry it out. You need to set an example by following the purpose and vision of the project while proposing necessary changes. Another component of this is to empower your team to be change leaders as well. They should feel comfortable sharing ideas, proposing new features, and streamlining processes. This will help raise their confidence level and give them the support they need to develop their careers.

Inspiring the best in your team will help you draw out their talent. People are at their most productive when their leaders make them feel supported and take an interest in their careers. However, being inspirational doesn't mean that you'll always agree with everyone. You don't have to be a people pleaser to be inspirational. Being a people pleaser is dangerous and can cause unintentional conflict if you tell one person one thing and another person another thing. They may feel lied to or even betrayed, and then you'll need to sort that out. It's better to handle difficult conversations up front and tell everyone why a decision must be made. If someone is unhappy, you should take them aside and listen to their concerns. Even if they aren't happy with the decision, when you listen to co-workers, they will feel respected and appreciated, which will inspire them to treat others the same way.

Being a leader applies to other roles in development besides lead developer. Everyone at every level of their career should learn leadership skills to help prepare them for the next phase of their career. In the next chapter, we'll talk about your career trajectory from junior to lead developer and beyond.

1.4   Case study

I've been a developer since 1998, and my career has spanned many different industries and job titles. I'm currently the co-owner at HoffsTech, LLC, where I write and produce technical content, including online courses for Pluralsight and Linkedin Learning, with my husband, Jason Benhoff. I'm also a senior developer experience manager at Docker. My technical skills include web development using .NET/C#/MVC, Sitecore CMS, Azure DevOps, Docker, and Kubernetes. I'm a four-time Sitecore MVP and Docker Community Leader. I speak at conferences worldwide, and I'm very passionate about mentoring future technology leaders. In the following case study, I'll discuss my career leading up to and including being a lead developer to help you gain insight into the role and what it means to be a lead developer.

1.4.1   What was your first experience as a lead developer?

I first became a lead developer after leaving a job where I was a manager, so my career trajectory was a bit different. Before I was a manager, I was a web developer and trainer. My responsibilities included creating courseware for developers to learn a specific platform. I had very complementary technical skills, and I was highly organized, so I got promoted to management. However, I had no management experience. I also had no project management experience, and I didn't realize I would manage both the team and the projects. I tried to ask management for training in these skills, but I never received it. So I made use of the knowledge of people on my team and other managers within the organization. I can't say I was successful in that job (I wasn't really set up for success), but I did learn a lot.

When I left that company, I wanted to get back to my developer roots, and I was offered a lead developer role at an agency specializing in web development. This was the classic lead developer role where I had a project team, and I represented the development team to project stakeholders. Even with my management experience, I felt a bit like a fish out of water, because unlike my previous job, I was now speaking with external clients. This came with an extra level of stress for me because I wanted to ensure that the clients were happy with our team's work.

At first, I struggled in all aspects of being a lead developer. I have somewhat of an introverted personality (at least until I get to know people), so my main struggle was speaking up and asserting my opinion. I also tried to please everyone, which is a topic we'll get into in a later chapter. My technical abilities were fine, but I struggled in meetings, and I avoided conflict at all costs, which I learned only leads to more conflict.

Over the years, I found my way by engaging with multiple mentors and reading leadership publications such as the *Harvard Business Review*. I also learned to lean on my team for advice and not be afraid to tell someone that I didn't know the answer to their question. I failed a lot, but I always learned valuable lessons from failures, which helped me in the long run.

1.4.2 What did you enjoy the most as a lead developer?

My greatest joy as a lead developer is watching my mentees succeed. Being a support system for the team comes with a high level of responsibility, and when one person is successful, we are all successful. One of my greatest success stories was when I worked with a very talented developer who had a hard time trying new things. But he also wanted to be a lead developer, so I coached him in the areas he was struggling with, including being confident in his technical approach and presenting his approach to the project team. He wasn't comfortable with presentations at first, and I told him that I get nervous every single time I present. Sometimes, it's so bad that I have a hand towel on my desk because my hands get sweaty. He found that very relatable and told me that he was inspired by my willingness to go outside my comfort zone. I told him that his career would take a major turn when he was able to break through that self-imposed barrier. He is an engineering manager now at a big company, and I'm so proud of him!

1.4.3 How did your experience as a lead developer set you up for success in your current job?

As mentioned earlier, I'm currently the co-owner at HoffsTech, LLC, and we produce technical content. I also create content as part of my job as a senior developer experience manager at Docker. This is very different from being a lead developer because I'm working with technical writers, editors, and producers instead of developers and clients. My experience as a lead developer has set me up for success in my current roles, as I oversee hiring and overall team management at HoffsTech. At Docker, I work with teams to create content to fit our audience and support our business goals. I support the developer community and mentor everyone who works with me, whether they are an employee of the company or a freelancer. I add mentoring opportunities to any job description that I post because I want potential candidates to know that they will be supported, which often attracts top talent. I understand how to manage the day-to-day tasks of my team and ensure that our processes are reviewed and updated constantly.

Being a lead developer taught me not only how to lead but also what true leadership means. I learned how to stay on my toes and figure out how to handle constant changes while remaining (relatively) calm. I understand how to resolve conflict in my team without blaming anyone. The main thing I realized that has helped me the most is that people work with me, not for me. That change in my mindset helped me be a better mentor and leader because my job isn't to tell people what to do; my job is to draw out their talent by working together to figure out what to do.

Summary

- Lead developers are responsible for leading and mentoring development teams as well as communicating with project teams.

- Lead developers can come from any background, including any gender, race, and education level.

- The day-to-day tasks of a lead developer include leading the development team, working with project teams, communicating with clients and stakeholders, setting development standards, and building technical architecture.

- The expectations of a lead developer are to provide team support, form working relationships, and be a leader.

- Lead developers must possess technical expertise and be capable of writing technical specifications, developing features, troubleshooting errors, and deploying code.

- Lead developers must learn leadership skills, including facilitating communication, decision-making, gathering feedback, emotional intelligence, and self-awareness.

- The career path for a lead developer normally begins with junior developer, then senior developer, and developer advocate/developer relations.

- The success of a lead developer is reflected in the success of the development team and can be measured in the amount and quality of work completed in an iteration or release.

Lead developer career trajectory

This chapter covers

- Roles leading to lead developer
- Management and technical roles beyond lead developer
- Crafting effective résumés and cover letters
- Succeeding in technical reviews
- Differentiating with strong writing, presentation, and interview skills
- In-demand technical skills review

Everyone must start somewhere, and no one gets a job as a lead developer with no experience. The most common path is junior developer > senior developer > lead developer > management. However, this isn't the only path, and in this chapter, we'll explore various options for your lead developer career trajectory.

Once you have a clear career path in mind, you must write a winning résumé to get in the door for interviews. Not only does a strong résumé help you stand out in a competitive job market, but it also helps you secure more lucrative job offers and better career opportunities. By highlighting your strengths and accomplishments, you can communicate your value proposition to potential employers and convince them that you're the right person for the job. Investing time and effort in creating a winning résumé can pay off in numerous ways, both in terms of your career advancement and your personal growth.

Technical interviews are the hardest part about landing any developer position. As a lead developer, you're expected to be a technical expert, and you will be tested. Being prepared by asking the right questions beforehand will help you achieve success in these sweat-inducing interviews. To start planning your career trajectory, you need to understand the software developer roles available to you and how these roles support your efforts in becoming a lead developer.

2.1 Reviewing software developer roles

When you're looking for jobs, it can be difficult to stick to one role, especially after being laid off and needing to get another job quickly. It's even harder for people who are on a work visa that is sponsored by their employer because they have the extra hurdle of not only looking for the right role but also finding a company that offers sponsorships for foreign visas.

When I first started, I couldn't find any junior developer positions that were open to people with zero years of experience. I'm very adamant that the junior developer role shouldn't require any experience, but sadly, this is still a problem today. Instead of becoming a junior developer, I started out working help desk jobs. Many people champion this route because help desk representatives are exposed to various technologies and processes. Help desk work also helps you learn critical thinking skills by troubleshooting errors.

Throughout my career, I've deviated from the developer path several times, but I ultimately landed lead developer positions. I've had roles as a help desk representative, web developer, courseware designer, manager, and lead developer, and now I'm a business owner! No career path is set in stone. You just make it up as you go.

2.1.1 Starting as a junior developer

A junior developer is a person who possesses basic programming skills that they learned in higher education, by attending a boot camp, or by practicing on their own. They generally have less than a year to three years of experience, but I wish employers would revise that to allow people with no years of experience. This means that you need to have development experience before getting a job as a junior developer, which, in my opinion, is gatekeeping.

The following list contains the main requirements for junior developer jobs:

- Less than a year to three years of experience
- Passion for technology
- Basic programming skills
- Detail-oriented
- Willingness and ability to learn new skills

- Ability to work on teams
- Flexibility

Companies are looking for someone with general programming and development knowledge. They may not have the specific skills for the tech stack that the company is using, but they should be able to learn quickly. They need to be able to learn on the job and apply their knowledge to the task at hand. We're often placed in positions throughout our careers as developers where we're asked to work with a technology unfamiliar to us. Learning how to break concepts down and find the documentation you need are key skills you'll learn as a junior developer.

Because junior developers are new to the industry and to learning organizational processes, they often spend most of their time researching best practices, asking questions, and taking advice from senior and lead developers. One of the hardest parts of being a junior developer is feeling like you know nothing and are a burden to your team. Junior developers are a critical part of any organization. Without training and mentoring junior developers, we would never have any senior or lead developers!

The following list contains the main responsibilities of a junior developer:

- Continuously improving programming skills
- Assisting the development team
- Attending team meetings
- Troubleshooting errors and fixing bugs

Junior developers focus on learning and applying their knowledge to assist the development team in software design and coding. They will learn a lot in this role, and their skills will improve over the years as they gain experience. Critical thinking is a skill anyone should master in this role, as junior developers work on bug fixes and errors. Tracking down the source of an error isn't always easy and sometimes seems impossible. Learning how to troubleshoot effectively will help junior developers achieve success when they move into a senior developer position.

2.1.2 *Becoming a senior developer*

A senior developer must have technical expertise as well as mentoring skills. As junior developers gain experience, they should help their peers learn new skills by guiding them to the proper resources. Mentoring your team is a skill that you'll need to learn to become a senior developer.

The following list contains the main requirements for senior developer jobs:

- More than three years of experience
- Experience working with complex projects
- Successfully implementing high-quality features
- Navigating all phases of the Software Development Lifecycle (SDLC)
- Self-managing tasks and projects

These requirements are variable based on the organization. Some companies also offer a mid-level developer role to help you move your career forward, and this role is basically an extension of the junior developer role. The major difference is your level of experience and expertise, but your responsibilities are the same. I was a junior developer for five years before I was promoted to mid-level developer. I went straight to management from there, making me think that I should have either been promoted from junior to senior developer or received another promotion after becoming a mid-level developer. But I never asked to become a senior developer, and promotions are rarely given automatically. This is a topic we'll dive into in a later chapter.

As a senior developer, you're expected to mentor others, communicate your opinions on technical planning, and be independent. You also need to be comfortable speaking up in development team meetings. Senior developers must understand higher-level technical concepts and be able to apply them to build new features. Junior developers are often assigned bugs to help them acclimate to the programming languages used for specific projects. As you progress in your role as a senior developer, there are several key soft skills that you should focus on before becoming a lead developer (see figure 2.1).

Figure 2.1   Soft skills

When I'm hiring senior developers, I'm looking for people who are willing and able to assist the team and support their success. They must be highly skilled in the tech stack the company is already using and have experience with the preferred programming language within the organization. This doesn't mean that they must be an expert in every programming language the company uses, and in my experience, that is often hard to find. Instead of looking for someone who possesses 100% of the skills listed in the job description, companies look at their ability to learn new skills quickly. Table 2.1 lists junior developer versus senior developer responsibilities.

Table 2.1 Junior developer vs. senior developer responsibilities

	Junior developer	Senior developer
Continuously improve programming skills	✓	✓
Assist the development team	✓	✓
Attend team meetings	✓	✓
Troubleshoot errors and fix bugs	✓	✓
Develop basic features		✓
Mentor junior developers		✓

As you grow in the senior developer role, observing the lead developers who work with you and learning from them is important. Watch how they create architectural diagrams, and offer to help them write documentation. You can also find opportunities to show initiative by taking on responsibilities, including presenting technical information and identifying areas of improvement. Reflecting on what went wrong with a project and lessons learned is a great way to improve your leadership skills. Showing that you have these soft skills will set you on your way to becoming a lead developer.

2.1.3 *Moving to lead developer or lead architect*

There are a few different variants for the lead developer position. *Lead architects* are like lead developers, but they are mainly responsible for detailing the technical architecture and how to build it. They may also draw diagrams to illustrate how each component in the technical architecture is connected to each other. They are the people who plan what to do and how to do it. In contrast, a lead developer has the skills of a lead architect, but they also execute the plan and write code. They are responsible for maintaining coding best practices and standards, which require the highest level of technical knowledge. Lead developers must have full expertise in every aspect of a project at the technical level, whereas lead architects don't have to be experts to plan projects. Table 2.2 lists lead developer versus lead architect skills.

Table 2.2 Lead developer vs. lead architect skills

	Lead developer	Lead architect
Create technical architecture diagrams	✓	✓
Explain how the technical architecture will be built	✓	✓
Illustrate component/module/feature relationships	✓	✓
Estimate technical tasks	✓	
Develop infrastructure and features	✓	
Mentor the development team	✓	

Some companies split these roles into two different positions, but in my experience, it's a combined role. This may vary across different industries and organization sizes. I've found that the roles are often combined because generally a lead developer is expected to possess all the skills of a lead architect as well. Hiring managers are looking for lead developers who can build systems from the ground up and conduct code reviews, which require programming expertise. You may also be required to build the initial infrastructure for a project and write instructions for your team members to configure their local development environments.

As a lead developer, you need to understand the business side of things and the technical side. Part of project planning includes meetings with clients and stakeholders to list their business requirements. Understanding what they expect to see as a result is a skill that you must master. You'll also work with the project manager to help them plan the budget and hopefully avoid increasing project costs during the development phase.

Lead developers are expected to translate business requirements into technical requirements, which is why they need to understand the product domain. You can't plan accurate technical requirements or estimates if you don't fully understand what the client or stakeholder needs. If your estimates are off, you need to work with your project team, including the stakeholders, to ensure that you are all on the same page. You need to think about the result and why the stakeholders need this result. What are their business drivers? Are they increasing brand awareness, supporting their end users, or driving sales? Usually, it's a combination of things. If you're working at an agency or company delivering products and services to customers, you need to consider what the project you're working on means to the company. This situation's main goal is customer retention because you want people to be loyal to your company or brand.

The following list contains the business skills required for lead developer jobs:

- Assisting in project planning
- Working with budgets
- Understanding business requirements
- Understanding business goals and desired outcomes

A lead developer is also expected to possess important soft skills. When your team members ask questions or need help, you'll be the person they look to for answers. If you don't know the answer, you need to help your team find the answers they need from internal co-workers or external clients, stakeholders, and vendors. You can also ask the senior developers on your team for their input and give them the opportunity to shine. It's also important to document the answers to avoid repeat questions. Lead developers need to lead by example and provide their team with the skills they need to grow in their career. This is done by recognizing learning opportunities and facilitating communication between teams, which will help the team members understand how to self-manage.

Lead developers must be comfortable communicating with clients and stakeholders and presenting information to them. This may involve informal conversations or formal presentations. Becoming familiar with creating effective slides will help make your presentations engaging for the audience. Public speaking isn't always easy for everyone, especially if you're an introvert. Employers are looking for lead developers who can communicate effectively with people both internally and externally. A lead developer is the face of the development team, and they are required to have excellent communication skills.

The following list contains the soft skills required for lead developer jobs:

- Mentoring other team members
- Presenting information to project teams
- Facilitating communication between teams
- Communicating directly with clients and stakeholders
- Leading with empathy and emotional intelligence
- Providing feedback
- Resolving conflict

The combination of technical, business, and soft skills is what companies look for in a successful candidate for a lead developer position. You need to show that you have a proven track record of success in planning and implementing technical architecture, assisting with project planning, understanding the business side of things, and being able to lead teams. Learning business skills and soft skills to complement your technical expertise will help you be successful if you want to go into management and leadership.

2.1.4 Considering management and beyond

If you enjoy the business side of being a lead developer, you may want to consider a career in management and executive leadership. Many opportunities are available to you as an engineering manager, technical director, or even CTO. You won't write code as a part of your daily tasks, but your experience as a developer will greatly aid your success as a manager. If you don't want to lose your programming skills, you can work on personal projects or study skills with the development team. The best managers I've had asked questions about programming and were open to learning from anyone. Learning is a two-way street, and managers can learn from any team member.

If you want to continue coding daily, then management may not be a fit for you, and that's fine! Even if you enjoy business skills, that doesn't mean you must push yourself into a management position. We often focus on an upwardly mobile career trajectory, but keep in mind that once you become a senior or lead developer, you can stay in that role for the remainder of your career. Management and leadership require different skill sets, especially when you're managing people.

As a manager, one of the hardest skills to master is hiring. You want to find the best talent for your team, which requires the ability to read people and assess their skills. During the interview process, you want to uncover specifics about what the interviewee's contribution was on a project instead of focusing on the significance of the project itself. They need to be a fit for your organization and your types of projects. You must hire developers at all levels whose skills complement one another. If you hire the wrong people or don't support the success of the right people, you'll manage turnover for your team. A survey by Forbes (https://mng.bz/ZVRN) showed that recruiting a new person costs approximately 33% of their first-year salary. This can be very costly if you have a high turnover. Managers must be able to have difficult conversations and resolve conflicts. Lacking these skills will result in high turnover, which is costly because you lose talent.

Managers handle the budget for the entire team, which includes project costs and salaries. It's the managers' responsibility to ensure that projects are delivered within the proposed budget and that the result is high quality. This involves a lot of spreadsheets and meetings with upper management. You must be prepared to state your case when project costs increase and work with the management team to make decisions to get the project back on track. This complex system requires proactive thinking to avoid budget problems in the future.

Solid business processes help keep your budget on track and increase your team's productivity. Processes should be updated regularly to keep up with industry changes. Holding on to outdated processes will set your team back, even if those processes have always worked. Managers must be up to date with best practices in development and implement new systems and technologies to ensure high productivity. Figure 2.2 shows an example of a software development career trajectory.

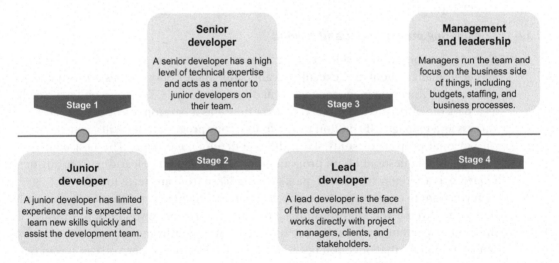

Figure 2.2   Software development career trajectory

This career trajectory is the standard, but it's not the only path you can take as a software developer. Many different paths can set you up for success as a lead developer or manager. Everyone is different, so you should carve out the right career path for you.

2.1.5 *Considering your career options*

Many people think you must get a degree in computer science to be a developer. This isn't the case anymore, as boot camps and certification programs have become more popular. I know many developers who studied nontechnical topics in college, including history, philosophy, and psychology. You don't have to stick with the same career your entire life. You can switch it up and do different things that will enable you to bring a unique perspective to working on a development team. If everyone on a team has the same background, they won't be set up for success because innovation will be stalled if everyone has a similar mindset. Innovation comes from diverse teams with different perspectives who come together to create products and solutions that apply to many different types of people and businesses.

Starting a software development career as an intern can provide many benefits. *Internships* can be hard to find, but they offer an opportunity to gain valuable experience and practical skills. Internships provide exposure to real-world projects and challenges, which can help you build critical thinking and problem-solving skills by working with experienced developers. I started my career as an intern for Black & Decker, which I found through my college. Some boot camps may also offer job support, and you can also find internships by building your professional network.

I'm a proponent of beginning a career in tech by doing help desk or tech support work. This will get your foot in the door and allow you to network with tech professionals who can help you find a development position. You'll also learn critical thinking skills as you help troubleshoot errors and find solutions for users. If you work with users who aren't technically proficient, you can be a teacher and help them learn new skills so that they don't have to call or chat with the help desk in the future. When you work any type of customer service job, you gain valuable skills that are transferrable to any role, as you always seek solutions for the customer.

Data science is another field that lends itself to a development career. In this role, you extract meaning from and interpret data. This requires skills in statistics, machine learning, and software development. A data scientist uses tools to collect, clean, and organize data to find patterns and build models. This role collects data on product or app usage to quantify a product's health for continuous improvement. You're expected to be detail-oriented to ensure the accuracy and uniformity of the data you extract for analysis. Data science is a growing area at the moment with artificial intelligence (AI), and many jobs will require some knowledge of prompt engineering.

A career in AI and machine learning (ML) is highly conducive to a development career due to the interdisciplinary nature of these fields, which blend advanced algorithms, data analysis, and software engineering. AI/ML professionals are adept at creating intelligent systems that can learn from and adapt to new data, skills that are directly applicable to developing robust, scalable software solutions. The iterative process of training models and optimizing algorithms also aligns closely with the agile methodologies commonly used in software development. This background ensures that AI/ML experts are proficient in coding, problem-solving, and system design, all of which are essential for a successful development career. Additionally, as AI/ML technologies continue to integrate into various industries, there is a growing demand for developers who can innovate and implement these advanced capabilities, making this career path both versatile and future-proof.

Another role that lends itself well to a development career is *technical training*. Even if you're not pursuing a career in training, it's helpful to have experience teaching at least one course or workshop and interacting with students. When students have questions, it's a good practice to ask them how they might solve the problem instead of answering yourself. This type of dialogue helps them retain knowledge when they are led to the answer, which will teach them critical thinking skills. I have experience in both writing and delivering training, and I became a lead developer afterward. Writing technical training requires you to learn instructional design where you understand the learner, their goals, and learning objectives for the course. A key skill in instructional design is understanding how people learn and the different teaching methods they can use. Some people like to get training up front before they begin a task, and others prefer learning on the job. There are different formats for learning, including written, video, and audio. You can learn from blogs, books, online video training, or audiobooks. Technical training involves a lot of research, and you must be on your toes to troubleshoot and fix any problems that your students encounter during a class.

Technical writing is another role that can lead to a development career, which is different from technical training. Technical training focuses on teaching people skills by providing them with instructions on how to build something. Technical writing is documenting the technical aspects of a product. Both roles require a lot of research; however, the output format is different. Instead of writing a how-to guide from start to finish, technical documentation is organized by feature or product. This aims to allow developers to find answers to specific questions, not to build something from scratch.

I've worked with many *quality assurance (QA)* professionals who transitioned into a development career. This is a good career path because you'll learn how to thoroughly test your code from the user's perspective. Many developers (including me) tend to ensure that the technical requirements have been met and only test for those. However, sometimes you'll find that the technical requirements may not support the business requirements. You can uncover these problems by looking at the overall user experience to ensure that all requirements are met. QA professionals also provide regression testing, an excellent skill for developers to avoid breaking code that was once working.

Being a *technical marketer* or *content creator* is a great way to learn development skills and move into a development position. You'll work closely with software developers and product managers to understand complex technical concepts and communicate technical information to nontechnical audiences. This role also provides an opportunity to develop marketing and communication skills, such as creating compelling technical content, developing marketing strategies, and building relationships with customers and clients.

Technical marketers also work closely with sales, and you could become a sales engineer. *Sales engineers* use their technical expertise to help customers solve complex problems and make informed purchasing decisions. This requires a deep understanding of software development processes and the ability to communicate technical information to nontechnical stakeholders. In this role, you'll work closely with product managers, software developers, and customer support teams, which can provide exposure to different aspects of the software development lifecycle. I've worked with many sales engineers who transitioned into developer roles, and they are often excellent at zeroing in on the problem to provide ideas for improvement to ensure customer satisfaction.

Finally, there is the *developer advocate* or *developer relations* role. You can do this before or after becoming a lead developer as a lateral move. This role requires a lot of public speaking, so you must be comfortable speaking in front of a large group of people. Developer advocates also create content to promote learning for a specific technology. This often involves filming live videos, screen sharing, webinars, and live streams. They are the face of the development community, which gives them influence, and they are role models. Developer advocacy is great for people who enjoy development work, teaching, and connecting directly with an audience to help them learn new skills.

Whatever career path you choose, don't feel like you must stick to one path; we all have room to grow, and sometimes that takes our careers in different directions. In my career, I've been a help desk associate, web developer, courseware developer, technical trainer, lead developer, author, speaker, developer relations manager, and business owner. I certainly didn't take the traditional path even though I have a degree in computer science. There are many different roles that involve technical skills that will help you eventually land a job as a lead developer. It's up to you to make it happen.

2.2 Moving through a software development career

Development positions are highly competitive, and getting your foot in the door is hard. When you're applying for jobs through public job boards or recruiters, it's even more difficult to get an interview. My number one tip for any professional in any career is to start networking early. The sooner you don't have to apply for jobs anonymously, the better off you will be. With a large professional network, you'll find jobs more easily, as people can suggest jobs to you and help you get an interview.

As a lead developer, it's important to continuously expand your professional network to stay up to date on industry developments, seek out new opportunities, and grow your career. Some ways to do this include actively participating in online developer communities and forums, attending industry events and conferences, contributing to open source projects, and joining local meetups and networking groups. You can also contact other professionals in your field through LinkedIn, email, or other online channels to ask for advice, request introductions, or simply connect and exchange ideas. Building relationships with others in your field can also be a great way to learn new skills, get feedback on your work, and find new collaborators. I spend a lot of time building my brand on LinkedIn by posting relevant articles about the technology I'm working with. This has helped connect me with hiring managers who are looking for someone with my skill set. Even if you find a job through your professional network, you still need to impress the hiring manager and show that you're a match for the position by successfully navigating the interview process.

2.2.1 Writing a résumé

Your résumé is the main tool that will get you an interview. You should tailor your résumé for different types of positions to highlight your experience that matches the job description. I don't generally tailor a résumé for each job that I apply for. Instead, I keep copies of résumés for different job types. For example, I have different résumés for lead developer and developer advocate roles. While both positions have related skill sets, you must highlight the most applicable skills to the role (see an example résumé in figure 2.3). A good résumé should include the following:

- *Your name and contact information*—Phone number and email (optionally, you can include your address, LinkedIn Profile, and portfolio website URL)
- *Career objective*—A simple objective that lists the position title you're applying for
- *Career summary*—A bulleted list of high-level highlights from your career
- *Technical skills summary*—A bulleted list of programming languages, methodologies, and tools
- *Professional experience*—A table of your employment history over the past five to seven years, including company names, locations, dates, and a bulleted list of your job tasks and accomplishments
- *Additional experience*—A shortened list of your job experience for the past seven+ years
- *Education and certifications*—Everything you've accomplished, even if it's not related to the job description

You should keep your résumé relatively short, which is why most people suggest only listing the past seven years of experience under the Professional Experience heading. An Additional Experience section is a place for you to summarize other positions you've held throughout your career that apply to the career objective. Hiring managers see a lot of résumés, and this format has landed me a lot of interviews over the years, even when I was applying for junior developer positions. Many companies use automated systems that look for frequency of keywords; therefore, having more pages isn't seen as a downside. Keeping your experience succinct and including keywords that are relevant to the position you're applying for can help these automated tools pull your résumé from a long list of others.

Shelley K. Benhoff

Address
Phone Number
Email
LinkedIn Profile

OBJECTIVE
Lead Developer

CAREER SUMMARY

- More than 20 years of professional programming and development experience in both backend and frontend programming languages.
- A Sitecore Certified Developer, Sitecore MVP, and Official Sitecore Trainer with 11 years of Sitecore implementation experience.
- A published author and professional trainer well-versed in the most current technologies.
- An excellent problem-solver, able to quickly grasp complex systems and identify opportunities for improvements and resolution of critical issues.
- An effective leader, skilled in supporting team members in aligning with the project and organizational goals.

TECHNICAL SKILLS SUMMARY

- Advanced Web Applications Programming/Design: ASP.NET 1.0-Current, C#, Web Forms, MVC5, HTML5, CSS3, VB.NET, AJAX, JSON, RESTful APIs, JQuery, JavaScript, Angular, Bootstrap, VBScript, XML, XSLT, ActiveX, Java, DHTML, DOM, IIS, Azure, SQL, SSMS, GitHub, Subversion, TFS, NuGet, Sitecore 6.5 – Current
- Oculus Rift VHD, Unity 2D, Gamemaker Studio 2, and RPG Maker MV video game development.

PROFESSIONAL EXPERIENCE

5/2015 - Present   **HoffsTech, LLC**, City, State
Senior Consultant and Professional Trainer

- Provided Sitecore consulting services to multiple clients. Services included Sitecore upgrades, new implementations, maintenance, and training.
- Managed Sitecore Enterprise multi-site solutions including setting up server farms and working with Rackspace load balancers.
- Published various online training courses on Pluralsight:
  - Tactics and Tools for Troubleshooting Docker
  - Moving From Technical Professional to Management
- Published books on Amazon Kindle: Technical Interview Study Guide For ASP.NET Web Developers and The Fundamentals of Web Development: Using HTML5, CSS3, and JavaScript
- Created an online self-paced training course teaching beginners How to Build a Simple Microsoft Azure .NET Website.

Shelley K. Benhoff

Address
Phone Number
Email
LinkedIn Profile

Additional Experience
Software Development Team Lead, *Company, Location*

- Worked full time from a home office managing a project to convert the existing CDC Ventures application in Microsoft Access to a web application using ASP.NET 3.5.

Systems Analyst, *Company, Location*

- Created and maintained two database applications using VBA with Microsoft Access.

EDUCATION AND TRAINING

Bachelor of Science, Computer Information Systems, *College, Year*
Sitecore Certified Professional Developer and Official Sitecore
Sitecore MVP
Docker Community Leader

Figure 2.3   Example lead developer résumé

Examples of common résumé errors

The following list contains examples of common errors that you should avoid to ensure that your résumé ends up in the yes pile:

- Errors in spelling, grammar, and punctuation
- Missing contact information
- No Technical Skills section
- Not well organized
- Not tailoring a résumé for the job requirements

Using AI tools to write a résumé can significantly enhance the quality and effectiveness of these crucial job application documents. AI tools such as ChatGPT can analyze job descriptions and highlight key skills and experiences required for the position. By comparing this analysis with your résumé, AI can suggest specific keywords and phrases to include, ensuring your résumé aligns with what employers are seeking. I like to use Grammarly to review my résumé for grammatical errors, stylistic improvements, and overall readability. These tools can suggest more effective word choices and help eliminate unnecessary jargon or repetitive language. By using these AI capabilities, you can create a polished, targeted, and professional résumé that stands out to employers and increases your chances of landing interviews.

2.2.2 Creating a cover letter

The development industry is extremely competitive, and getting a recruiter or hiring manager to review your résumé can be difficult. Recruiters and hiring managers are inundated with job applications when they post a new job. They hardly ever read every word of a résumé, and having a cover letter (whether required or optional) can help get you an interview by summarizing your qualifications and piquing their interest in a few short sentences.

If you're a recent college graduate, congratulations, you're now competing against hundreds of thousands of developers just like you. If you didn't go to college, congratulations, you're now competing against hundreds of thousands of developers just like you. Either way, you're going to have a lot of competition. So how do you get potential employers to read your résumé? As someone who has been both the interviewee and interviewer, I know it all starts with the cover letter. A well-written cover letter goes a long way toward getting an employer to read your résumé. You should have the following items in a cover letter:

- The position title and company
- Where you found the job posting
- Highlights from your résumé that match the job description
- Your availability for both an interview and a potential start date
- Your contact information

You should always keep a general cover letter template for yourself and tailor it to each position you apply for. If you send a generic cover letter to every employer, then it will look like you're spamming employers from job boards. To simplify the process, I suggest creating a Microsoft Excel spreadsheet listing each position, résumé highlights, and so on, and then using a Microsoft Word mail merge to automate your cover letter easily. Keeping a spreadsheet of your job applications will also help you avoid applying for the same job multiple times, which will land your résumé in the no pile. Figure 2.4 shows an example cover letter.

Shelley K. Benhoff
Address
Phone Number
Email
LinkedIn Profile

Dear Hiring Manager,

I am extremely interested in the Lead Developer position with *Company Name* that was posted on your website. My resume is attached for your review.

I hope that you will find my attributes beneficial to your company. I am constantly striving to extend myself to learn and grow. You will find me to be hardworking, dedicated, and independent. My career achievements have included over 20 years of experience in the tech industry as an ASP.NET C# Web Developer. For the past 10 years, I have focused on Sitecore CMS Development and I have worked on multiple Sitecore implementations. I also worked for Sitecore where I developed and delivered technical developer training to Official Sitecore Trainers and Sitecore Partners globally. I worked very closely with the Sitecore Product Teams to determine best practices and coding standards that are currently used by Sitecore Developers worldwide.

I look forward to hearing from you and hope that we can arrange an interview at that time. Please feel free to contact me by phone or email. I can be reached at *Phone Number* or *Email Address*.

Thank you for your consideration.

Sincerely,

Shelley Benhoff

Figure 2.4 Example lead developer cover letter

A well-written cover letter can be a great tool to use to get an interview, and if you're applying for a job on a company's website, they often require one. Understanding how to write a cover letter will set you up for success and move you through the interview process and on to the next step.

2.2.3 *Achieving success in technical interviews*

Technical interviews are an important part of the interview process for developers, and they are crucial for the lead developer role. You're expected to be a technical expert, which often requires a coding test followed by an interview where you discuss the coding test and best practices in the industry. You must show your skill level and stay calm during this phase of the interview process.

When given a coding test, ensure you understand what they are asking you to do. Ask for clarification if you don't understand something about the coding test. You must go into it with a full understanding of the expected result. It's human nature to want to proceed without asking questions to appear self-sufficient, but that is detrimental to your interview success. As a hiring manager myself, I like when people speak up because I'm not looking to hire "yes" people. I want to hire people to bring their opinions to the table to help the team learn and grow. The following list includes resources to help you practice skills for taking a coding test:

- LeetCode (https://leetcode.com/)
- HackerRank (www.hackerrank.com)
- Project Euler (https://projecteuler.net/)
- Interview Cake (www.interviewcake.com)
- Cracking the Coding Interview (www.crackingthecodinginterview.com)

As you go through the coding test, make sure that you pay attention to the details and follow each specific instruction to the letter. Developers must be detail-oriented to ensure that all requirements are completed so that clients are happy with the result. Hiring managers want to see a high level of consistency and well-thought-out code when they're hiring a lead developer. This will show that you not only possess technical expertise, but you're also a person who can look at every aspect of a task to drive high-quality results.

After you pass the coding test, you'll move on to the interview where you'll most likely be asked to answer questions about your approach to the coding test. A good thing to do is walk them through your logic in solving the coding test and give well-rounded answers. Don't just tell them how you did something; tell them why. Go into detail, and don't give short answers. What best practices have you learned, and where did you learn them? Try not to second-guess yourself. Be confident in your approach! If you got an interview, then the hiring manager liked your approach; otherwise, you wouldn't have moved on in the interview process.

You should also discuss other approaches you could have used to complete the coding test. This will show that you have an open mind and can see opportunities to go a different route. Companies tend to have set coding standards within the organization, which may vary from company to company in terms of architecture and style. Adapting to different coding standards is a good skill for any lead developer.

During the technical interview, if you're asked a question and you don't know the answer, talk about how you would go about finding the information that you need to get the answer. No one should be expected to know everything off the top of their head. The best interviews I've participated in allowed people to use a laptop to look up answers if they were unsure. As developers, most of our day is spent doing research anyway, and I want to see that skill in practice when I'm hiring a lead developer.

Technical interviews can be very stressful, but you must remain calm. If you have spent time preparing for the interview, this will greatly increase your chances of success. You can outline your answers ahead of time based on questions you've been asked in previous technical interviews. You should always be prepared to walk through your coding test in detail to explain the logic in your approach. Being prepared for a technical interview will help you remain calm, cool, and collected so that you're successful.

2.2.4 *Interviewing for development leadership positions*

If you're interested in the business side of things, you can begin to think about the next steps in your career progression. Leadership interviews differ from technical interviews, as they focus on business goals, budgeting, and staffing requirements. You may be asked some technical questions, but they will be more abstract at a higher level instead of walking through your approach to individual lines of code in a coding test. You should be prepared to talk about how you'll lead teams and your general leadership approach.

A good way to cultivate your leadership style is to work closely with project managers and team managers across the organization. Observe how they handle leading meetings, organizing projects, and maintaining budgets. Work with them to create solutions that will enable them to automate processes to increase productivity and decrease costs. Showing that you can decrease costs is a key skill that hiring managers look for in a development manager.

There are generally multiple interviews included in an interview process for leadership positions. You may have to meet with executives and people you wouldn't normally work with as a lead developer. When you meet with executives, prepare a slide deck. Part of being a manager and leader is organizing engaging presentations. Even if you're not asked to prepare a presentation, prepare one anyway! This will show that you'll go above and beyond to achieve success and that you're comfortable with public speaking. Your slides should walk through your résumé and discuss current industry trends and how you would ensure that your projects follow best practices. In addition, list any applicable successes you achieved as a lead developer, and focus on the success of your team, not yourself. Leaders support teams and must be team players; you shouldn't be focused on yourself, as this can show a tendency to take credit for the work of others. Hiring managers are looking for leaders who give credit where credit is due.

If you've spent your entire career as a developer, you must be prepared to shift gears when you apply for a leadership position. Leadership requires a different skill set, so it's important for you to keep a record of your success as a lead developer. This will make it easy to keep your résumé updated in the future. Make sure that you focus on the skills required to manage development teams instead of being the technical expert on the team. You need to be forward-thinking and use data to predict future staffing needs and mitigate costs. You'll learn these skills as a lead developer when you work closely with project managers on task estimates and statuses to reduce costs for the organization. This will help set you up for success as you advance in your career and apply for leadership positions.

If you're lucky, a position in leadership may open up at your current job that you can apply for. But before a position becomes open, you should begin to step up in your current job and show that you have leadership skills. When you're a lead developer, you'll show your leadership skills by supporting your team's success. You can do this by taking responsibility for mistakes that were made, as the key decision-making is up to you. Mistakes happen, and no one is infallible. Being a responsible person will show that you're leadership material.

Being proactive instead of reactive is another great skill for a leader. For example, you must schedule maintenance periods to avoid system failures. Your team should be empowered to think ahead and predict future problems, especially when large changes are made, such as upgrading to a new version of the programming language you're using. Taking a proactive approach will reduce emergencies and costs due to time lost fixing critical errors that could have been prevented. If you find that the company is experiencing consistent emergencies across multiple projects, you should voice your opinion and offer solutions to avoid future emergencies. You can schedule automated nightly maintenance tasks and send out a status report once the maintenance is complete. Over time, keep track of the reduction in emergencies, and communicate your team's success to the leadership team.

2.3   *The job market for lead developers*

Developers are in high demand, and plenty of jobs are available—but there is also a lot of competition. Because you're reading this book, you're already ahead of the competition by taking an interest in your career plan! It also helps to know what your peers are doing to get jobs so that you can prepare for interviews accordingly. Being competitive includes observing the actions of others to inspire your own approach to maintaining your development career.

2.3.1   *Assessing the competition*

As a lead developer, you should assess your competition in the job market to position yourself better to attract top talent and stay competitive in the industry. The following list includes some ways that you can assess your competition in the job market:

- *Research job postings.* You can review the job postings for lead developers and note the required qualifications, job responsibilities, and compensation packages. This will give you a better understanding of the skills and experience that are in demand in the current job market.
- *Analyze job descriptions.* You should pay attention to the specific technologies and programming languages that companies seek in their job descriptions. This will help you identify the most important technical skills to develop and highlight in your own job postings.
- *Track market trends.* Joining online communities and forums where developers discuss their experiences and job opportunities will give you a better understanding of the current market trends and the demand for certain skills. Look for emerging technologies and programming languages that may become more popular soon.
- *Monitor your competitors' online presence.* Look at your competitors' websites and social media accounts for information about their team structure, the types of projects they're working on, and any recent hires or promotions. This can give you insight into their hiring strategies and help you stay current on industry news.
- *Attend industry events.* Attending industry events and conferences gives you the opportunity to network with other developers and stay current on the latest technologies.

Another way to assess your competition is by speaking to mentors. Everyone needs a group of mentors to help them navigate their careers. Having mentors who have hired people in the past or who are current hiring managers helps a great deal, as they can help you assess your competition. They can guide you, suggest skills to learn, and tell you what areas you excel in. It's even better if you have multiple mentors who can do this for you because mentors should only guide you to career solutions that are right for you. We're all different, and we should take inspiration from multiple people to forge our own path. Asking your mentors what drives them to read a résumé, put it in the yes pile, and hire developers will enable you to be competitive during the interview process and get the job that you want.

2.3.2 Standing above the crowd

How do you stand out to get job interviews when hiring managers receive piles of résumés for every job they post? Customizing your résumé for each job application is a great way to pique the hiring managers' interest. You should list your skills that match the job requirements listed in the job description. This will demonstrate your ability to apply your skills in real-world situations and draw attention to your relevant skills. Showcase your relevant skills in an engaging way by using action verbs to describe your accomplishments and quantify any applicable results. For example, I like to use verbs such as *achieved*, *built*, *optimized*, and *automated*. Hiring managers prefer to see a concise list of what you've achieved in your career, so you should focus on actions.

Contributing to open source projects is another good way to stand out from your competitors. When you join tech communities, there are often channels where people post links to the community projects they're working on. You can work with a team of developers in a GitHub repository where you can report bugs, write code, and submit pull requests. Most of the time, you don't have to request to join community projects, as the repositories are public, so anyone can join at any time. However, it's good to get to know other people who are working on the project and discuss the most important features that need to be implemented and errors that need to be addressed. This will show hiring managers that you can work with a team and that you understand code repositories and how they relate to the SDLC. Being active in programming communities is a great sign that you're a team player and provide value by giving back to the community. Contributions to open source projects aren't often listed on the résumés that I've seen, so having this experience will help you stand out and land you an interview.

I suggest that any developer should start a blog. This is another way to show that you give back to the community by posting helpful tips for your peers. The best blogs are the ones that explain a problem that the author encountered and how they fixed it. If you're struggling with a specific error, chances are that someone else is too, and your blog post could be the resource they need to resolve the error quickly. You can also blog about your work contributing to open source projects and get others interested in joining the team. Plus, you can use your blog to help you find an answer that you need if you can't think of it off the top of your head. Most developers that I know often use their own blogs to help them if they're struggling, and I do this too! (You can find my blog at https://hoffstech.com/blog/.) Your blog can act as a notebook if you need to revisit an error or process you previously documented.

You can build up your GitHub profile by contributing to open source projects and writing blog posts. Having an active GitHub account is a great way to show everything you've learned and are currently working on. When you write blog posts that contain walkthroughs of code, you should create a GitHub repository even if it's not a full project. Did you know that hiring managers can search GitHub to find interview candidates? GitHub settings allow you to add a job profile and check a box if you're available for hire. This is a little-known fact, and it's a great way for you to get noticed by hiring managers and receive invitations to apply for jobs that you wouldn't have known about otherwise. GitHub also has a feature for you to create your portfolio website and add it to your profile. You can even host your portfolio website on GitHub and include the link in your résumé. Many developers miss these features, as they aren't really promoted or intuitive.

2.3.3 Reviewing in-demand technical skills

It's often confusing for developers to figure out what programming skills, platforms, and technologies they should focus on. The number of skills that you can learn is overwhelming, and you can't be an expert in everything. It's good to specialize in related skills that complement each other, such as JavaScript, as well as frameworks and libraries, including Angular and React. Keep in mind that these trends change frequently, and just because a skill becomes less in demand doesn't mean that you should switch to another skill. You want to remain somewhat consistent throughout your career and build your skills according to your interests and what jobs are available. Figure 2.5 shows the top desired programming skills for 2024 according to Stack Overflow.

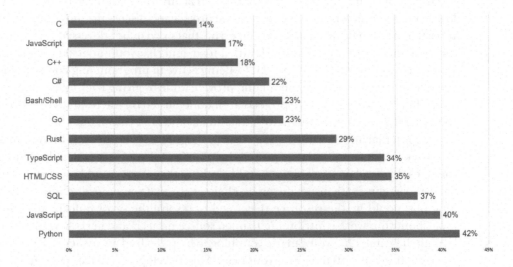

Figure 2.5   Top desired programming skills for 2024 according to Stack Overflow (https://mng.bz/ RNmR)

The landscape in the tech industry for developers is constantly changing, and there are many different types of jobs and roles that you can specialize in. Full-stack developers are the most sought after, as they have well-rounded expertise. As a lead developer, you'll be required to manage all aspects of the development process and work with different developers. If you're creating web applications, you'll work with both frontend and backend developers, so you need to understand their day-to-day tasks. A full-stack developer may not be an expert in everything, but that role will set you up for success as a lead developer if you're responsible for managing full teams.

Lead developers must understand the continuous integration/continuous delivery (CI/CD) process, and it's important to learn DevOps skills to manage releases. You should be able to configure all environments, including a local development environment, QA, staging, and production. This requires expertise in the full SDLC and organization skills to work on multiple releases simultaneously. Understanding cloud architecture is necessary to manage deployments to minimize downtime for your users. This includes skills such as using Amazon Web Services (AWS) and Microsoft Azure to integrate your development workflow and configure pipelines for CI/CD. Learning Docker and Kubernetes will help you streamline your deployment processes and automate much of the heavy lifting. The SDLC process varies between different companies and industries depending on the approach and methodology. Lead developers should understand all aspects of the SDLC.

Application developers are in high demand, as they focus on building applications for multiple operating systems (OSs), including Linux, Mac, Windows, iOS, and Android. You're required to have in-depth knowledge of managing code for each OS. You can specialize in building apps specifically for mobile devices, which is also a very in-demand role for developers. However, most applications exist both on the web and as mobile apps, so many companies look for lead developers who can manage both. Figure 2.6 shows the top five in-demand development jobs for 2023.

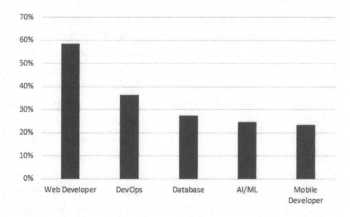

Figure 2.6   Top five in-demand development jobs for 2023 according to CodinGame (https://mng.bz/ 2gKo)

A well-rounded skill set will help you succeed as a lead developer, as you're expected to manage the entire SDLC. You'll work with people from different roles, and when they need help, you should be able to point them in the right direction. Keeping your skills current is a great way to stay ahead of the curve and provide the organization with a proactive approach to future upgrades. Understanding current trends will help your team succeed as they continue to learn and grow in their careers. We'll discuss how to keep your technical skills current in a later chapter.

2.4   Case study

Dan Wahlin is a principal/director at Microsoft helping developers use services across the entire Microsoft Cloud (Azure, Microsoft 365, Power Platform, and GitHub). In addition to his work at Microsoft, Dan creates training courses for Pluralsight, speaks at conferences and meetups around the world, and offers webinars on a variety of technical topics. Prior to joining Microsoft, Dan was CEO of a consulting, architecture, and training company called Wahlin Consulting for 20 years, helping enterprises build great software. Follow Dan on Twitter at https://twitter.com/danwahlin or subscribe to his *Code with Dan* newsletter at https://blog.codewithdan.com. In this case study, Dan offers his experience and advice about the career trajectory for lead developers.

2.4.1   *What advice do you have for developers who are setting a career plan?*

It's important to think through and visualize what achievements you want to reach in your career. As Stephen R. Covey said, "Begin with the end in mind." You should read his book, *The 7 Habits of Highly Effective People*, if you haven't already; it's an excellent career resource. He's saying that you should make time to visualize what it would feel like to reach your goals. For example, athletes visualize themselves performing well in a game, and salespeople visualize themselves giving a successful pitch and winning the sale. Visualization applies to many other scenarios, including your career success. Visualize yourself in the role you want, and think through what it would take to get to that level. Your inner voice may kick in and say, "You can't do that, who are you kidding?" That's normal, and it happens to everyone, no matter who they are. Keep at it, and develop a belief that you can achieve what you're visualizing. Planning and documenting the specific steps you need to take to achieve your career goals is a great start to begin your career plan.

This next one is extremely important! Build your plan into your daily routine. Want to manage a team someday? Research what highly successful managers do, and start practicing what you learn in meetings, in interactions with colleagues and customers, and in other situations. You don't have to be a manager to start applying the skills that a manager needs. Want to be a CEO? Learn what successful CEOs do, practice the skills you'll need to get that type of job, learn about what paths different CEOs took to get there, and apply what you learn to your current job and overall life. Don't wait for the "perfect time." The perfect time is now.

Be consistent and persistent. Have a plan to actively work toward your goals. Roadblocks will certainly be thrown at you along the way. Your muscles get stronger by applying consistent stress to them. You get stronger in life by viewing roadblocks or walls as opportunities that help you learn, improve, and move to the next level. You can stay at the bottom of the wall, or you can put in the effort to climb it.

Let me share a quick story about myself and my career journey. I can honestly say that way back in my early 20s, I visualized myself doing things in my career such as these, as well as other things:

- Managing a team
- Writing a book
- Releasing a training course
- Giving corporate training around the world
- Speaking at conferences
- Publishing articles for magazines
- Running a company

While I experienced plenty of fear, doubt, and anxiety along the way, I knew I could achieve these goals and believed in myself. It took a lot of planning, consistent practice, persistence, and hard work, but I was able to reach all of my key goals. I want to emphasize that it wasn't because I was smarter than others or better than them. On the contrary, I view myself as pretty "normal." But I was willing to visualize my goals and had the belief that I could achieve them. I'll admit that I wasn't as good at documenting the steps, but in hindsight, I realize how important the planning process is. Having said that, no amount of visualization or planning will help you achieve your career goals without consistent and active effort. Plan to roll up your sleeves, dig in, and get dirty. Action speaks louder than words, so you must be willing to consistently work smart and work hard.

2.4.2 How can developers stay on top of the competition in today's job market?

Become a lifelong learner. I've had to learn many different concepts and technologies over my career. The secret to success in today's job market is being willing to step outside your comfort zone, learn something new, practice it, and increase your skills by actively using it.

Be willing to admit that you don't know it all if pressed. "Imposter syndrome" is completely normal, and everyone feels it from time to time. Push through it, and be open to asking for help when you need it. Nobody knows it all. If you feel like someone does know it all, they're just a good actor. Don't act like a "know-it-all" in the interview.

It's OK to be wrong, and it's OK to fail. Embrace that, and take advantage of it in interviews. View failures as learning opportunities that you can use in future scenarios to help you stand above the crowd. Apply failures and lessons learned to scenarios you work with every day. Share how you failed, what you learned, and the approach you now take with others (in interviews, with your team, with your career community, etc.).

Actively contribute to your community. If you're a developer, contribute your own projects to open source, submit pull requests as you find problems in projects you use, and write about how you personally learn, lessons learned, and so on in your blog, in social media (if you use that), and other areas. If you don't have enough time to contribute to your community or work on personal projects, try asking your current employer if you can write blog articles for them detailing technical problems you've faced and how you fixed them.

Be willing to put yourself out there. If you enjoy sharing your knowledge, you can create videos, submit to speak at conferences, and offer to give "lunch and learns" at work. A little-known fact about me is that when I began submitting to speak at conferences, I received nothing but rejections. It literally took a few years before I got my first "yes," and that changed everything. Although I'd argue it's much easier to speak at conferences nowadays (there are a lot more of them), don't take a rejection personally. Reach back out to the conference if possible and ask what you could do differently. Let them know that you'd really like to speak and that you're willing to volunteer the first time around. Get creative!

2.4.3   *How can developers stand out during the interview process?*

Smile and be friendly. Is that stupid to mention? I don't think so. It's amazing how far a smile and a friendly and cooperative attitude will get you in life. I'm not saying that you should be fake, but I'm saying that it's easy to see when someone is truly excited to be there for the interview. If you feel the interview isn't going well, do your best to continue having a positive attitude and demeanor. You may be doing way better than previous interviewees without knowing it. Some interviews are designed to test people's resilience and ability to deal with stress, so keep that in mind.

Be prepared, and practice, practice, practice. Learn as much as you can about the interview process, and have friends interview you and give feedback. Practice how you'll respond when you don't know something. Practice what questions you'll ask the interviewers when that opportunity presents itself. Interviews are a two-way street, and you should ask questions to see if the employer is a fit for you. Learn how to deal with stress appropriately. Be sure to have an answer to the often-dreaded question, "Where do you see yourself in five years?" The more you practice, the more you can be yourself, which will instantly put you above the people who are nervous and struggling during the interview.

Another little-known fact about me is that I didn't have the years of experience required for my first technology job interview. I got the job, though, so what was the secret? I was extremely interested in the job, and my enthusiasm showed through to the point that the interviewers were excited to give me a chance. They interviewed many people but remembered me the most, I was told.

I had a project ready to show that related to the job I was interviewing for. Although I didn't have an extensive background using the skills they wanted, I was able to demonstrate that I had all the skills needed by showing them a "real" project I built. The fact that I was prepared and had something ready in advance impressed them.

Be willing to say "I don't know" when you're not sure about something, and practice how you'll respond (as mentioned earlier). But—and this is very important—follow up any "I don't know" statement with what you would do to figure it out, and walk the interviewer through your problem-solving skills if they'll let you.

Have project work, articles/blog posts, videos you've created, and so on that are directly related to the job ready to go for the interviewers. Be proactive and prepared rather than showing up with nothing aside from the ability to answer questions. If you really want the job and don't currently have a project to show, put in the time to create the project. Some interviews require you to build a project and then turn it in later. I'd only do that if you're very interested in the job. (I'm not a big fan of that interviewing approach, by the way; they should instead give preference to the proactive interviewees that have something ready to show in advance.) If you do have that type of interview, though, and are very interested in the job, use that project as an opportunity to show off your skills and stand out.

Summary

- The most common career trajectory for developers begins with the junior developer role, then progresses to senior developer, and then lead developer.
- There are many positions related to development that will help you achieve success as a developer, such as help desk, data science, AI/ML, QA, technical training, technical writing, and developer advocacy.
- You must show that you have leadership and business skills to get promoted into management.
- Your résumé should list your career objective, career summary, and technical skills summary at the top to highlight your career achievements in a condensed format to make it easier for hiring managers to read.
- Development positions have a high level of competition, and you can stand out by possessing certifications, working on open source projects, starting a blog, and creating a GitHub portfolio.
- Achieving success in technical interviews can be accomplished by being detail-oriented, addressing every task required in the coding test, and being able to walk through your approach to the coding test during the interview process.
- Lead developers should focus on staying current with in-demand skills in programming and DevOps.

Learning lead developer skills

3

This chapter covers

- Updating skills with study resources
- Practicing leadership soft skills
- Prioritizing and scheduling learning
- Understanding leadership styles
- Matching leadership style to personality
- Improving presentation skills and engagement

To be a successful lead developer, you'll need to learn many key skills. Learning everything you need to know takes a lot of time, so it's important to know what skills to learn and prioritize them accordingly. Lead developers are expected to strike a good balance between technical and soft skills, which is very hard to do.

As developers, we must keep our technical skills current if we want to be competitive in the job market. This is especially true for lead developers, as you're expected to lead the technical aspects of a project. You must stay up to date with the latest technologies and trends. We're often using many different technologies in a single project, and it can be difficult to keep ourselves up to date. This is especially true when brand-new programming languages are developed. Throughout my career, I've probably worked with more than 15 different languages and frameworks. I'm constantly reading technical blogs, white papers, and announcements from technology companies to stay current with industry best practices. It helps me to study architectural patterns for every programming language before I begin working with them. That way, I have a reference for when I start a new project using that language.

Soft skills are often difficult to learn because you can't always put yourself in specific situations so that you can practice soft skills, such as conflict resolution. Plus, there's no one-size-fits-all approach to each situation that will occur on your watch. You must learn how to navigate situations and communicate effectively to support the team's success.

It may take time for you to find your leadership style as you learn and apply soft skills that are new to you. Leadership can be scary, especially when you're responsible for key decisions that affect the budget of a multimillion-dollar project. You must learn to embrace failure and not fear it because failure is a learning experience. The real failure is never trying in the first place. If you fear failure, you may opt for no decision instead of the right decision. Making no decision is a decision in and of itself, and it can be very detrimental to the morale of your team. Some companies also defer decisions until the last minute as a best practice to allow time to consider all possible approaches and outcomes.

Public speaking is a skill that many people avoid at all costs. To be a good lead developer, you should continually work on improving your presentation skills. Learning best practices in slide design, cadence, and tone can make all the difference in keeping your audience engaged throughout your presentation. However, unlike most soft skills, you can practice presentations beforehand to ensure success when you're presenting.

Being a lifelong learner is the key to being successful in your entire career, not just as a lead developer. I don't believe anyone ever reaches an ultimate understanding of 100% of any topic. There are always new things to learn, especially when you observe things from other people's points of view.

3.1   *Prioritizing learning new skills*

Learning technical skills isn't new to you as a developer because you're constantly having to learn new skills to complete your day-to-day tasks. It's often hard to find the time to set aside for studying, but it must be done. When your skills are outdated, you may miss key upgrades that must be executed to avoid a security problem or bug. Lead developers aren't always given a heads-up when new technologies need to be implemented. Often, it's the lead developers who suggest the adoption of new technologies for the entire organization.

Learning and applying soft skills is equally important to keep your tech skills up to date. Leadership skills change over time as culture shifts and new processes are adopted. In recent years, emotional intelligence has become a key skill that all leaders must have, but it wasn't that way back in the industrial era when they used the command-and-control style of leadership. We are in the participation era, and people want meaning and purpose in their work. Lead developers must keep up with these changes so that they can lead using current best practices.

3.1.1   *Learning current technical skills*

There are many ways that you can keep your technical skills current. When you don't prioritize learning, you'll waste a lot of time muddling through difficult tasks. If you encounter an error that you don't recognize, the first thing you do is search for that error. You may find quick answers, but then you're faced with new errors, and you're nowhere close to figuring out the solution. At this point, you should look at the documentation for the technology that you're working with or find blogs that explain the error and the solution step-by-step.

An effective way to keep your technical skills current is to subscribe to get email notifications from any technology that you're currently using or may use in the future. There have been major shifts in the industry, and companies often change their tooling and deployment processes to keep up with current best practices. Companies send out announcements and helpful blog posts when they have released an update to their technology. You should read the release notes to learn what has changed and think about how these changes will affect the projects your team is working on.

Tech communities also provide announcements for upcoming releases, known problems, and hotfixes. If you join tech communities that are run by a tech company, they usually also provide support so you can ask employees questions directly. Plus, joining tech communities is a great way to expand your professional network and work on community projects. This community interaction can also lead to awards as you give back to the community and help others learn new skills. You should never interact with a community to earn a reward; it should simply be the byproduct of your efforts. The point of joining a community is to provide as much support as you get.

Popular tech communities

The following list includes popular tech communities where people work together to learn new skills and collaborate on projects:

- 100 Days of Code (www.100daysofcode.com)
- 100 Devs (https://leonnoel.com/100devs/)
- Black Tech Twitter (https://mng.bz/1aGQ)
- Dev.to (https://dev.to/)
- GitHub Community (https://github.com/community/)
- GitLab Community (https://about.gitlab.com/community/)
- Hashnode (https://hashnode.com)
- Hacker News (https://news.ycombinator.com)
- Women Who Code (www.womenwhocode.com)

I also like to follow tech influencers and developer advocates on social media because they often provide product updates as well as tips and tricks. To find qualified tech influencers, start by searching for keywords related to your industry on social media platforms such as X/Twitter, LinkedIn, and YouTube. Attend industry events and conferences to meet tech influencers in person, and search for online communities and forums related to your industry to see who is actively contributing valuable insights and information. Focus on individuals who have a track record of producing high-quality content and engaging with their audience, and be wary of those who seem more focused on self-promotion than on providing valuable information and insights. You should interact with them and start conversations with their followers who comment on their posts. This is a different type of community than joining developer Slack or Discord communities, and your experience will vary across different platforms. Social media is full of opinionated people, and developers have curious minds and shouldn't shy away from a public academic debate.

Keeping your technical skills current will enable you as a lead developer to provide ideas for continuous improvement of the projects you're working on. You can also pass your knowledge along to the development team and get their opinions on upgrading your current systems or adopting new technology. Making sure that your projects are using up-to-date technology will keep your systems running smoothly and help them avoid security problems. You'll support the growth of your team, and this will result in successful projects.

3.1.2 Reviewing necessary soft skills

While everyone who works in a professional setting must have some soft skills, lead developers are required to possess leadership soft skills to be successful. Being a great leader takes time, and learning the necessary soft skills up front will help ease you into a leadership position. When you're a lead developer, the development team looks to you for guidance not only in their daily tasks but also in their overall careers.

You must be prepared to communicate effectively by understanding the needs of your team members. Looking inward will raise your self-awareness, and this will make you emotionally intelligent. You'll be able to manage your own emotions in a positive way, which will help you communicate effectively and resolve conflict. It's important to be able to put yourself in someone else's shoes and see their point of view. This helps you to gain the trust of your team, as you're open to thinking about things from different perspectives. Being an empathetic leader also helps you to manage conflict and resolve it effectively by considering everyone's opinions. As a lead developer, you must keep an open mind and be able to have difficult conversations. It helps to be prepared and to understand what soft skills to focus on, why they are important, and how to learn them (see table 3.1).

Table 3.1   Soft skills for lead developers to learn

Soft skill	Why it's important	How to learn
Communication	Lead developers are expected to be the go-between for development and nondevelopment teams.	*The Art of Communicating* by Thich Nhat Hanh *Crucial Conversations: Tools for Talking When Stakes Are High* by Kerry Patterson, Joseph Grenny, Ron McMillan, and Al Switzler
Mentoring	Developers need guidance to help them learn current skills and support their career success.	*The Mentor's Guide: Facilitating Effective Learning Relationships* by Lois J. Zachary *Becoming an Effective Mentoring Leader: Proven Strategies for Building Excellence in Your Organization* by William J. Rothwell and Peter Chee
Emotional intelligence	Being self-aware and managing your behavior in positive ways will help you communicate effectively and overcome challenges.	*The Emotionally Intelligent Manager: How to Develop and Use the Four Key Emotional Skills of Leadership* by David R. Caruso and Peter Salovey *The Ride of a Lifetime* by Bob Iger, CEO of Disney
Empathy	Seeing things from others' points of view will help you form quality working relationships.	*Applied Empathy: The New Language of Leadership* by Michael Ventura *Empathy Works: The Key to Competitive Advantage in the New Era of Work* by Sophie Wade
Conflict resolution	Effectively resolving conflict will support a positive working environment to help you attract and retain top talent.	*Difficult Conversations: How to Discuss What Matters Most* by Douglas Stone, Bruce Patton, and Sheila Heen *The Anatomy of Peace: Resolving the Heart of Conflict* by the Arbinger Institute
Providing feedback	Learning to provide both positive and negative feedback will help your team improve and grow in their careers.	*Radical Candor: Be a Kick-Ass Boss without Losing Your Humanity* by Kim Scott *Thanks for the Feedback: The Science and Art of Receiving Feedback Well* by Douglas Stone and Sheila Heen

One of the first steps in developing your leadership skills is to take a step back and reflect on your strengths and weaknesses: What are your natural talents and areas of expertise? What areas do you need to improve? Reflecting on these questions can help you identify where you need to focus your efforts. I like to perform my own retrospective at the end of each year, looking back on what went well and what did not, to come up with a plan of action for the following year.

Another important step in developing your leadership skills is to seek feedback from others. This can include colleagues, managers, and even team members. Ask for their honest feedback on your leadership style and be open to constructive criticism. This feedback can help you identify areas for improvement and give you a better understanding of how others perceive you as a leader. Reading books, articles, and blog posts on leadership can be a great way to learn from others and gain new perspectives. You can also attend workshops or training sessions, or even take a course on leadership. The key is to stay curious and open to learning new things.

Leadership isn't just about giving orders or making decisions; it's also about leading by example. Take on additional responsibilities, be a role model for your team, and set the standard for excellence. Be a good listener, be responsive, and be open to feedback. One of the best ways to learn leadership skills is to surround yourself with good mentors. Look for individuals who have experience and are skilled in leadership. Learn from their experiences, and ask for guidance and advice. Mentors can provide valuable feedback and can help you see the bigger picture. When you take the time and effort to learn these soft skills, you may find it hard to apply them right away. When you're facing new responsibilities, it's important to jump right in to figure out solutions and not approach things tentatively. Applying soft skills is very different from applying technical skills because there is no predefined script for what you should say in every single situation that you encounter. You'll have to learn as you go.

3.1.3　Practicing soft skills on the job

Part of learning soft skills is putting them into practice in the workplace. When you're leading teams, you must embrace failure. A friend of mine, Hetal Dave, Sitecore MVP, once told me, "You should fail. Without failure, you'll never know what success looks like." You'll fail at times, and that's ok. You learn far more from failure than you do from success. Understanding what not to do and why is a powerful skill to have.

One of the hardest skills to master is conflict resolution. The first time you resolve conflict on your team, it will probably feel uncomfortable. You must try your best to listen to all sides of the conflict and keep an open mind. You may go into a mediation session with a predetermined solution, but you should allow everyone to be heard and ensure you are a good listener. This is especially difficult when leadership is involved, and you want to impress them with your handling of the situation. You must remember that it's not about you and your success. Your goal should be the success of the team.

Conflict isn't always reported, so a good way to learn how to resolve conflict is learning how to recognize unspoken conflict. Try paying attention to nonverbal cues, such as body language, tone of voice, and changes in behavior that indicate underlying tension. If team members aren't listening to each other, they may go off on their own and take their own approach despite what was agreed upon. In addition, notice when people have their arms crossed or appear indifferent when a team member is speaking. Once unspoken conflict is recognized, it's essential to address it in a constructive manner. You should encourage open communication and listen to team members' concerns to find a mutually beneficial resolution. By recognizing and addressing unspoken conflict, teams can work more effectively together and achieve their goals. It took me a long time to get used to resolving conflict. You shouldn't expect to master this skill right away because it takes practice. For more information on this topic, you can read my e-book, *Conflict Management Playbook* (available on Amazon).

Applying emotional intelligence and empathy is something you can do in your personal life as well as in the workplace. When you're always self-aware and can apologize if you've done something wrong, people will feel listened to. You should ask questions to find out how people view events or tasks they're working on. One of the responsibilities of a lead developer is to reduce technical debt; however, this shouldn't come at the expense of your team. You must observe how much they are working and ensure that they aren't getting burnt out. Understanding that people have lives outside of work will help you gain their trust, and they will be more honest with you.

You can practice emotional intelligence and empathy by actively listening to team members' concerns, acknowledging their feelings, and responding with compassion and understanding. This could involve scheduling regular one-on-one meetings with team members to discuss their concerns, provide constructive feedback, and recognize their accomplishments. You should take the time to understand the challenges and pressures that team members may be facing outside of work and provide support and flexibility as needed. You can start the conversation by telling your team about your life and your own struggles. Some people may not be comfortable sharing personal information, so it's up to you to provide an example for them to follow. Lead developers should build strong relationships with their team members and build trust.

Trust goes a long way to establishing honesty in your team. When people are honest with you and you don't have to read between the lines to determine how they feel, this is a great step in establishing proper communication. Communicating openly among your team makes it easier to provide frequent feedback, whether it's positive or negative. If there is a sense of trust between you and your team members, they will be empowered to share their opinions, and this will help you drive innovation on your projects.

3.1.4 *Setting aside time for learning*

It's easy to say, "You should set aside one hour for learning every day." But will you be able to stick to that? I know I can't! You can block off time in your calendar, but priorities are constantly changing, and you may find that you're not able to study every single day. I also suggest that you don't spend too much of your personal time studying, as that is your time to relax. If you study in your personal time, you should read books and spend some time away from the monitor and keyboard. This is important for both your physical and mental health.

So how do you stick to a learning schedule? I like to plan learning objectives for the week to support timeboxing my learning schedule. We are often overly positive when planning our goals for the week, so you should aim to achieve 70% or more of your goals. Outrageous goals are called "moonshot goals," and while they are useful to inspire you to do your best, keep in mind that you shouldn't make yourself feel bad if you don't achieve 100% of your goals.

Example weekly learning objectives

The following list contains example learning objectives for a developer's learning schedule:

- Create a GitHub repository.
- Create a simple website from scratch, including a heading, paragraph text, and dropdown box.
- Add CSS to a simple website, and style all page elements.
- Commit the completed website to the GitHub repository.

If you have time blocked off in your calendar for learning, you should try your hardest to stick to it. If you're in a meeting that is going over, ask yourself if it's necessary for you to speak up and end the meeting. Everyone has a busy schedule, and they may also want the meeting to end on time so that they can move on with their day. This is where you can use emotional intelligence and observe the body language of the meeting attendees to assess if they have checked out of the meeting already. When people are clearly multitasking or have already packed up to leave, these are signs that they want the meeting to end. If you're not able to get through the entire agenda during the meeting, suggest that the team schedule a follow-up or handle the missed topics asynchronously. They will thank you for speaking up, especially if they are already late for their next meeting.

When your calendar is blocked off, you're not required to provide instant answers when people send you messages. Turn off notifications, and close your email, Slack, Microsoft Teams, and all social media apps. Multitasking is the killer of productivity. When you concentrate on one thing for even 15 to 30 minutes, you'll do more in that time than you would if you allowed distractions and your task ended up taking three times longer. Table 3.2 shows an example of a calendar that incorporates a learning schedule.

Table 3.2   Example learning schedule

Learning schedule	Monday	Tuesday	Wednesday	Thursday	Friday
9:00 AM	Daily Standup	Daily Standup	Daily Standup	Daily Standup	Daily Standup
10:00 AM	Project Meeting			Project Meeting	Heads Down on Tasks
11:00 AM	1-on-1 With Manager	Project Meeting	Heads Down on Tasks	Backlog Grooming	
12:00 PM					
1:00 PM	Heads Down on Tasks	Study Time		Study Time	Sprint Planning
2:00 PM		Heads Down on Tasks		Heads Down on Tasks	
3:00 PM					
4:00 PM	Study Time		Study Time	Sprint Retrospective	Study Time
5:00 PM					

You must learn to set boundaries for your study schedule. You're allowed to tell people no when they ask you to do things right away that aren't emergencies. In these cases, the person requesting something from you may not be aware of your existing workload. You can put it back on them and say that you would be happy to work on their task, but you already have a full workload. Then, ask them what you can cut from your workload to make the time you need for them. You can also delegate the task to someone else on the team who is equally capable.

Making time to study new skills is very hard when you're new to the lead developer role. If you can't find large blocks of time, you can study for 15 to 30 minutes at a time. If you're always finding time to learn, you're doing what is necessary to be a successful lead developer.

3.2 Finding your leadership style

Many leadership styles have been identified and studied over the years. These styles are often updated, and it's difficult to find a list containing every leadership style and variant because there are so many. Leadership styles vary across industries and cultures. What works for one person may not work for another, which is why every leader must find their perfect fit.

The best leaders test out multiple leadership styles for various situations and personality types. Your approach to leadership shouldn't be defined by one leadership style; rather, it should include many different leadership styles to support both your needs and the needs of your team. Understanding your own personality traits and how they apply to different leadership styles will help you figure out what styles are best for you. You should also observe the personality types of the people on your team. This will help you support them and their needs so they can perform at a high level and produce quality work.

3.2.1 Reviewing popular leadership styles

As I've studied leadership over the years, I've come across up to 30 different leadership styles in various industries. For the purposes of this book, I'll narrow it down to the top 10 most popular leadership styles for tech companies. Every leader should master several leadership styles that match their personality type and business needs. As you read through this list, think about how you already interact with your co-workers and how they respond to the leadership styles that are used in your workplace. The following list includes the top 10 most popular leadership styles:

- *Autocratic*—This style involves a leader making decisions on their own, without input from team members.
- *Democratic*—This style involves leaders seeking input and feedback from team members before making decisions.
- *Transformational*—This style involves leaders inspiring and motivating team members to be their best selves and to work toward a shared vision.

- *Transactional*—This style involves leaders setting clear goals and expectations for team members, as well as providing rewards or consequences based on performance.
- *Servant*—This style involves leaders focusing on their team members' needs and using their own skills and resources to help them grow and develop.
- *Visionary*—This style involves leaders setting a clear and compelling vision for the future, as well as inspiring team members to work toward that vision.
- *Coaching*—This style involves leaders providing guidance and support to help team members develop their skills and reach their goals.
- *Laissez-faire*—This style involves leaders taking a hands-off approach and allowing team members to make their own decisions.
- *Affiliative*—This style involves leaders focusing on building strong relationships and creating a harmonious team environment.
- *Commanding*—This style involves leaders taking charge and issuing orders, often in high-pressure situations or emergencies.

Learning to combine these leadership styles and use them in different situations is difficult because there is no one correct answer in your approach to each situation. You'll learn as you go, but it does help to understand the strengths and weaknesses of each leadership style by discussing the pros and cons of each (see table 3.3).

Table 3.3   Pros and cons of popular leadership styles

Leadership style	Pros	Cons
Autocratic	Quick and efficient decision-making	May lead to low morale and a lack of creativity and innovation
Democratic	Can lead to higher job satisfaction and commitment to the team	May make decision-making slower
Transformational	Can inspire and motivate team members	May not be effective in situations where quick decision-making is necessary
Transactional	Can be effective in achieving specific goals and improving performance	May not foster a long-term commitment to the team or company
Servant	Can lead to a strong team culture and high levels of job satisfaction	May not be effective in situations where quick decision-making is necessary
Visionary	Can inspire team members and lead to long-term success	May not be effective in times of crisis or when quick decision-making is necessary
Coaching	Can help team members develop their skills and reach their goals	May not be effective in situations where quick decision-making is necessary
Laissez-faire	Can foster creativity and innovation	May not be effective in achieving specific goals or in times of crisis
Affiliative	Can create a harmonious team environment	May not be effective in achieving specific goals or in times of crisis
Commanding	Can be effective in emergencies or when quick decision-making is necessary	May lead to low morale and a lack of innovation

While the autocratic leadership style is listed, I don't recommend any lead developer make decisions without the input of their team members regularly. However, sometimes you may need to make quick decisions, and you won't have time to rely on your team. In this case, it's good to have autocratic leadership skills so that you can make effective decisions.

The same can also be said about the commanding leadership style: you don't want to implement the old school "command and control" leadership style by telling people what to do 100% of the time. However, this is a good skill to have in emergencies when people are scrambling and you need to regain order quickly and formulate a plan. As a lead developer, you should expect emergencies to happen. Even if you're at the top of your game, system errors and failures happen, and you need to be prepared to handle them.

Lead developers are in a support role, so you'll focus mainly on supportive leadership styles, including transactional and servant leadership. You must ensure the productivity of your team and support them by answering questions and removing blockers so that they can complete their tasks. Part of supporting your team includes mentoring, which is included in the coaching and transformational leadership styles.

As a lead developer, you may not need higher-level leadership styles in your current job, but it's good to practice these if you want to move into managerial roles in the future. A visionary leader is usually attributed to a company's CEO, as they are responsible for communicating the company's vision and direction. However, you can do this at the team level, which is something you would do as an engineering manager or director. The following list includes popular leadership books to help you learn more about different leadership styles:

- *Drive: The Surprising Truth about What Motivates Us* by Daniel H. Pink
- *Good to Great: Why Some Companies Make the Leap and Others Don't* by Jim Collins
- *Leadership and Self-Deception: Getting Out of the Box* by the Arbinger Institute
- *Start with Why: How Great Leaders Inspire Everyone to Take Action* by Simon Sinek
- *The 7 Habits of Highly Effective People* by Stephen R. Covey
- *The Five Levels of Leadership: Proven Steps to Maximize Your Potential* by John C. Maxwell
- *The Power of Servant-Leadership* by Robert K. Greenleaf

There are many learning resources to help you in your journey to becoming a successful lead developer. The books listed here are excellent sources and should be a staple in any leader's library. You may also want to listen to popular leadership podcasts such as *Leadership and Business* by *The Harvard Business Review* and *The Leadership Lab* by The Center for Creative Leadership. Understanding the main leadership styles will help you navigate your responsibilities as a lead developer. You should give every single one a go and observe the results to assess what works for you and what doesn't. Not all leadership styles are a fit for everyone, and you'll need to consider your own personality type when forming your own personalized leadership style.

3.2.2 *Assessing your personality type*

Most people believe that you must be an extrovert to be an effective leader, but that is simply not true. I have introverted tendencies and have known many introverts who were effective lead developers. Many developers are introverted, so they think that leadership isn't for them. Research has shown that introverts can bring unique strengths to leadership positions, such as the ability to listen carefully, think deeply, and communicate clearly. It's important to remember that leadership isn't only about your personality type but rather about your abilities and skills. Both introverts and extroverts can be successful leaders, provided they can effectively communicate, inspire, and motivate their team.

Several personality assessment tools are commonly used in the industry for leadership development and selection. Some of the most well-known and widely used include the following:

- *Emotional Intelligence Quotient (EQ) assessment*—Measures an individual's emotional intelligence, which includes their ability to recognize and understand their own emotions and the emotions of others
- *DISC assessment*—Measures four dimensions of personality, including dominance, influence, steadiness, and compliance
- *Five-Factor Model (FFM)*—Measures five broad dimensions of personality, including openness, conscientiousness, extraversion, agreeableness, and neuroticism
- *Leadership Styles Inventory (LSI)*—Measures an individual's leadership style and helps them understand their strengths and areas for development
- *Myers-Briggs Type Indicator (MBTI)*—Helps individuals understand their personality preferences and how they perceive and make decisions

The results of a personality assessment can be a helpful tool for understanding your own leadership style and how you might be perceived by others. By understanding your personality traits, you can gain insight into your strengths as a leader and areas where you may need to work on developing your skills. For example, if you score high in conscientiousness, you may be organized, reliable, and detail-oriented, which could be beneficial for your leadership style. If you score high in extraversion, you may be confident, energetic, and skilled at motivating others. To determine your leadership style using the results of a personality assessment, try the following steps:

- Review the results of your personality assessment, and identify your dominant personality traits.
- Reflect on how these traits might influence your leadership style. For example, if you score high in agreeableness, you may be inclined to build consensus and foster positive relationships with team members.
- Consider how your personality traits might bring both strengths and challenges in your role as a leader.

- Identify any areas where you would like to develop your leadership skills, and consider what specific actions you can take to do so.
- Seek feedback from others, such as team members or colleagues, about your leadership style and how it's perceived by others.

Use this information to adapt and refine your leadership style as needed. It's not accurate to say that certain personality types make better leaders than others. Leadership may be influenced by your personality type, but it's your abilities and skills that will make you a good leader. As mentioned earlier, both introverts and extroverts can be successful leaders, and each personality type has its own unique strengths and weaknesses.

Some research has suggested that certain personality traits may be more conducive to leadership. For example, individuals who are confident, decisive, and able to adapt to changing circumstances may be more likely to succeed as leaders. These personality traits aren't necessarily tied to any specific personality type but rather can be found in individuals of all types. A *personality trait* is a specific characteristic or aspect of a person's behavior, thoughts, and feelings that describes how they tend to behave or respond to certain situations, whereas a *personality type* is a broader categorization that groups individuals based on a combination of several traits, often in a systematic way, as in the case of the MBTI assessment. In simpler terms, a personality trait is a building block, and a personality type is a collection of those building blocks put together to form a bigger picture. A successful leader doesn't have to be a specific personality type, but they do need to have personality traits that complement leadership skills.

Ultimately, the most effective leaders are those who can understand and work with their own strengths and limitations, and who can adapt their leadership style to the different personalities of the people on their team and the situation at hand. Leadership is always in flux, and your style will change and adapt with experience.

3.2.3   *Observing personalities on your team*

Understanding team members' personalities can help you communicate and interact with them more effectively. For example, if you know a team member is introverted, you might approach them differently from an extroverted team member. If an introvert doesn't want to speak up in a meeting, then you can ask for their opinion. They may not feel comfortable speaking up unless spoken to first. Observing team members' personalities can help you identify and address any potential conflicts or misunderstandings within the team. By understanding how team members approach problem-solving and decision-making, you can facilitate more productive and harmonious interactions.

Understanding team members' personalities can also help you tailor your leadership style to better suit the needs and preferences of the team. If you know that a team member is highly motivated by recognition and praise, you might praise them more frequently. You can also identify potential growth and development areas. By understanding what drives and motivates your team, you can help create a supportive environment that encourages personal and professional growth.

One popular method is using personality tests such as the MBTI. We discussed this test earlier, as it's also useful to assess your personality type to determine your leadership style. The MBTI categorizes individuals into 16 personality types based on four dichotomies: Introversion/Extraversion, Sensing/Intuition, Thinking/Feeling, and Judging/Perceiving. By understanding these types, lead developers can gain insights into how their team members prefer to work, communicate, and make decisions. This knowledge can help in assigning tasks that align with each member's strengths, improving team dynamics, and fostering a more collaborative and productive work environment.

However, relying solely on the MBTI has its limitations. Critics argue that the MBTI lacks scientific validity and reliability. The binary nature of its categories can oversimplify complex human behaviors and lead to pigeonholing. Therefore, it's beneficial for lead developers to consider alternative personality assessments. One such alternative is the Big Five personality traits model, which measures individuals in five dimensions: Openness, Conscientiousness, Extraversion, Agreeableness, and Neuroticism. This model is widely accepted in the psychological community for its empirical support and capability to provide a more nuanced understanding of personality.

Another alternative is the DISC assessment, which focuses on four primary behavioral traits: Dominance, Influence, Steadiness, and Conscientiousness. The DISC assessment is particularly useful in workplace settings, as it highlights how individuals are likely to behave in team interactions, respond to challenges, and approach their work. Understanding these traits can help lead developers tailor their leadership strategies to suit different team members, enhance communication, and manage conflicts effectively.

There are many ways that a lead developer can observe the personalities of their team members. You should pay attention to how team members communicate and interact with one another. Do they tend to be more introverted or extroverted? Do they prefer to work independently or as part of a team? You need to adjust your communication style to suit the preferences of different team members. For example, an introverted team member might prefer written communication or one-on-one conversations, while an extroverted team member might thrive in group discussions.

You should take notice of how team members approach problem-solving and decision-making. Do they tend to be more analytical or intuitive? Do they prefer to consider all the options before they make a decision, or do they prefer to act quickly? An analytical team member might appreciate access to data and research materials, while an intuitive team member might benefit from more hands-on learning opportunities. By providing tailored support and resources, a leader can help team members feel more supported and valued.

Consider how team members respond to feedback and criticism. Do they tend to be more open and receptive to feedback, or do they become defensive? Supporting team members who are receptive to feedback and those who aren't can be a challenge for any leader. For team members who handle criticism poorly, it can be helpful to provide it in a private setting, rather than in front of the whole team to reduce feelings of embarrassment or shame and create a more open and supportive environment for feedback. I've handled giving negative feedback in a private setting many times for my own employees, and I've witnessed employers who handled it publicly. Public shame kills morale, and it doesn't help the person feel supported. If a team member is struggling to accept and respond to feedback, consider offering additional support and resources to help them improve. This might include coaching, mentorship, or access to training and development opportunities.

Take the time to notice how team members handle their workload. Do they tend to become overwhelmed, or do they remain calm and composed under pressure? Different team members may have different preferences when it comes to how they work best. Some may prefer a more structured environment, while others may thrive in a more flexible setting. By offering flexibility and allowing team members to work in ways that suit their personalities, you can help create a more positive and productive work environment.

Pay attention to team members' values and motivations. What is important to them, and what drives them to succeed? Different team members may have different goals and areas for growth and development. By providing opportunities for learning and personal development, and by offering support and guidance as needed, a leader can help team members reach their full potential. By observing these and other aspects of team members' personalities, you can gain valuable insights into how best to support and manage your team.

3.3   *Improving your presentation skills*

Public speaking can be a daunting task, but it doesn't have to be. Whether you're presenting to a group of co-workers, clients, or students, it's natural to feel anxious about speaking in front of others. However, with proper preparation and the right mindset, you can calm your nerves and deliver a confident and effective presentation. In this section, we'll explore some strategies for overcoming nervousness before a presentation, including practicing and visualizing your success, getting feedback, arriving early and setting up equipment, and relaxing with breathing exercises and positive self-talk. While it may take time to master the art of being calm before, during, and after a presentation, with practice, you can become an excellent public speaker. Some desired outcomes from professional presentations can include the following:

- A clear and concise message that is easily understood by the audience
- A single takeaway or a few key points that the audience can remember and apply
- Increased understanding or knowledge of the topic at hand
- Inspiration or motivation for the audience to take action
- Changed minds or perspectives on a particular problem or topic

- Increased interest in or engagement with the subject matter
- Building credibility and establishing oneself as an expert in the field

Whether the outcome should be a single takeaway, a few key points, or changed minds really depends on the purpose of the presentation and the audience. Ideally, a good professional presentation should aim to achieve a combination of these outcomes. Being able to present information is a requirement for conducting demos and walk-throughs or training. When you're mentoring developers, you must be able to discuss technical architecture in detail. These discussions should be short and to the point, so you must organize the information so that it's easily consumable. If you give a bad presentation, you may lose the trust of your team or, even worse, of clients and stake-holders. When you can't communicate effectively, this can lead to miscommunication and time wasted working on the wrong things. The following list includes examples of effective presentations that have helped me in my career:

- ".NET Overview & Roadmap" by Scott Hanselman and Scott Hunter (https://mng.bz/PNZ8)
- "The Art of Computers" by Scott Hanselman (https://mng.bz/JNZz)
- "Everything You Thought You Already Knew about Orchestration" by Laura Frank Tacho (https://mng.bz/w5xB)
- "Forward thinking: What's next for AI" by IBM (https://mng.bz/q0ON)

Effective communication is crucial for lead developers to convey technical informa-tion to their team and stakeholders. You need to be prepared and remain confident throughout your presentation, which isn't easy at first. As time goes on, you'll get bet-ter with practice—trust me. Learning how to engage with and manage an audience is a very important skill that lead developers need in order to convey the appropriate message to both developers and nondevelopers.

3.3.1 Calming your nerves

The best advice anyone ever gave me about public speaking is that you should be ner-vous. You feel nervous because you want to do a good job and convey your message in its entirety. If you aren't nervous, kudos to you! Most of the public speakers in my network get nervous before speaking at an event or giving a presentation. You're not alone!

You should always practice your presentation beforehand. The more comfortable you are with your material, the less nervous you'll be. This also helps you keep the pace and ensure proper timing so your presentation isn't over or under the allotted time. As you practice, visualize yourself giving a successful presentation. Imagine yourself feel-ing confident and in control. This will go a long way to ensure your success because if you think you'll succeed, then you're in a mindset to support your own success. If you think you'll fail, you're setting yourself up for failure. Instead, focus on your audience. Remember that they want you to succeed and are rooting for you.

When you practice your presentation, you can also record yourself and play it back to assess your performance. You may notice that some parts of your presentation are confusing or that you need to rearrange certain sections. Practicing and recording your presentation allows you to identify and fix these problems before you give the actual presentation. Seeing yourself give the presentation can help you feel more confident and prepared when it's time to give the actual presentation. It also allows you to get feedback from others. Showing your practice presentation to a friend or colleague can give you valuable feedback on your delivery, content, and overall effectiveness, which can help you feel more confident.

Arriving early and setting up your equipment beforehand will help you feel more in control and prepared. Doing this will also mitigate any technical problems that may arise in the conference room or videoconference. If you're doing an in-person presentation in a conference room, make sure that someone who knows the equipment is there to help you in case you need assistance. If you're doing a videoconference and you're not the host, ask the host to join 15 minutes early to help you get set up to ensure everything is working properly before the meeting starts.

On the day of your presentation, try to participate in relaxing activities such as breathing exercises and meditation. Taking a few moments to sit quietly and think of nothing at all is a proven method that will reduce stress and tension. If you're tense at the beginning of your presentation, it will be hard for you to give a good performance throughout. Try taking deep breaths. Inhale slowly and exhale slowly to help calm your nerves. Use positive self-talk. Tell yourself that you're prepared and that you can do this. Try to relax your body. Tense and release different muscle groups to help release tension.

Being calm before, during, and after your presentation will take time for you to master, so don't be worried if it doesn't happen immediately. I used to get so anxious before a presentation that my hands would shake, and it was hard to operate the mouse and keyboard. Practicing by yourself or with friends is different from giving a presentation to a room full of people that you may not know very well. But the more you do it, the more you'll improve to become an excellent public speaker.

3.3.2   *Creating effective slides*

As a lead developer, it's important to communicate technical information effectively to your team and other stakeholders. One powerful tool for achieving this is the use of visual aids, such as slides. When done well, slides can help you clarify your points, illustrate complex concepts, and engage your audience. However, creating effective slides requires careful planning and attention to detail.

To create effective slides, it's important to keep them simple and focused. Begin with an agenda, and end with a summary and next steps. Avoid cluttering your slides with too much text or too many graphs and charts. When there is too much text, the viewers may not listen to you and just read the slides. Instead, choose a few key points, and use clear, concise language to convey them. Use headings, subheadings, and bullet points to organize your content and make it easy to follow. If your company has a style guide for presentations, you should study it and ensure that you follow any guidance provided.

Another important factor to consider is the use of fonts and images. Choose a font that is easy to read from a distance, and use a large enough font size to avoid straining your audience's eyes. When it comes to images, be sure to select ones that are relevant to your content and of high quality. Poorly designed or low-resolution images can distract from your message and make your presentation appear unprofessional.

In addition to these general tips, there are a few considerations specific to development teams that you should keep in mind when creating your slides. For example, you may want to include code examples or debugging output to illustrate specific points. In these cases, it's important to use a font and layout that make the code easy to read and understand.

Finally, use color and layout effectively to highlight important points and create a visually appealing presentation. Choose a limited color palette and use it consistently throughout your presentation, such as the color palette for the company brand. Use headings and subheadings to organize your content and make it easy for your audience to follow along. For an example of an effective slide, see figure 3.1.

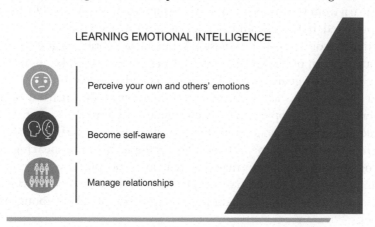

Figure 3.1 **Example of an effective slide**

While you may be comfortable speaking to other developers, communicating technical information to nondevelopers can be more challenging. Before diving into the technical details, it's important to provide some context and establish a common understanding. Begin by explaining the problem you're trying to solve or the goal you're trying to achieve. Use clear, concise language, and avoid using jargon or technical terms that may be unfamiliar to your audience.

Use analogies and examples, as they can be a powerful tool for explaining complex concepts to a nontechnical audience. For example, you might use an analogy to explain how a particular software component works by comparing it to something in the real world, such as a car engine or smart home device. Similarly, you can use examples to illustrate how a particular technology or process works in practice.

By following these tips, you can create effective slides that will help you communicate your message effectively and professionally to your development team. Remember, the purpose of your slides is to support and supplement your presentation, not to distract from it. With careful planning and attention to detail, you can create slides that will help you effectively communicate your message and engage your audience.

3.3.3   Giving a great performance

A passive audience isn't a good audience. You must keep your audience engaged by asking questions, soliciting feedback, and encouraging discussion. Use a variety of delivery techniques, such as storytelling or anecdotes, to keep your audience interested. At the beginning of your presentation, you should ask the audience leading questions so that you can tailor your material for them. If you're working on a project team or consulting gig, it's best to ask the team about your audience beforehand, but you should also ask at the beginning of your talk to mitigate any misinformation you may have been given about your audience previously. For example, ask everyone what they hope to learn from your presentation. Hopefully, their answers will be in line with what you've prepared, but you should be ready to improvise on the fly.

Improvisation is a difficult skill to master. While most people suggest that you join a class or group to learn public speaking skills, I suggest that you take an improv class. These classes are mostly geared toward performers and comedians, but you need to think of your presentations as performances. Whenever you're in front of an audience, it's a performance. People expect to engage with what you're saying, and if they aren't engaged, then you'll need to quickly change gears to improve your performance, which is where improv skills come in handy. For example, if you're speaking about an advanced programming topic, you may find that some people in your audience are beginners. In this case, you should try to explain things in full without leaving out key information so that the beginners can understand what you're talking about, even if it's at a lower level.

Confidence is key to giving a great performance. Remember that you're the expert on the topic you're presenting, and your audience is looking to you for guidance and information. Believe in yourself and your abilities, and your confidence will shine through in your delivery. Don't let imposter syndrome get to you. You were selected to present because of your expertise. (We'll discuss imposter syndrome in detail later in this book.)

It's also helpful to seek support and feedback from colleagues and mentors. They can provide valuable insights and encouragement as you work to build your confidence as a public speaker. Finally, remember that it's okay to make mistakes or not know all the answers. No one expects you to be perfect, and acknowledging that you don't have all the answers can make you more relatable to your audience. If someone asks you a question that you don't know the answer to, tell them that you'll research the topic and get back to them after your presentation is over. I find it useful to create a "parking lot" that includes the outstanding topics. Then, when I find the answer, I let everyone know, not just the person who asked, because someone else may be wondering the same thing.

Thinking of your presentations as performances will help keep your audience engaged and interested in what you're talking about. You don't have to be a professional actor to learn the art of performance or improvisation. But learning a bit about these skills will help your confidence level improve as you gain experience.

3.4 Case study

Maureen Josephine is a software engineer and a Google Developer Expert in Flutter and Dart. She was the first female Flutter Google Developer Expert in sub-Saharan Africa and the first Flutter Google Developer Expert in Kenya. She is a technical speaker, technical writer, and the lead Community Organizer for Flutter Kisumu. She is a recipient of the McKinsey & Company Next Generation Women Leader Award 2020. She enjoys exploring and learning new things. Besides coding, she is passionate about fashion and design, and she gets her inspiration from nature, African culture, and technology. In this case study, she provides insight into her experiences learning lead developer skills.

3.4.1 What soft skills have you learned that helped you most in your career?

Communication skills have helped me a lot because no one can know what you want or need other than you. You must effectively communicate your needs to others and not be afraid to ask questions. Good communication goes two ways—you also need to be able to receive feedback from others. If you receive good feedback, that's great! No feedback isn't good because without feedback, how will you improve? And negative feedback can be difficult to take, but you can't take it personally. Put yourself in their shoes, and think about the negative feedback with an open mind so that you can assess the need for your own professional development.

You should ask people what they need if you notice them struggling. Some people shy away from asking tough questions because they are afraid of looking like they don't know something. I studied CS at university, and I felt afraid to ask questions at my first internship. You learn a lot of theory at the university, but then you get out into the real world that requires more practical work, and you realize that you don't know that much. I got stuck trying to complete tasks based on the reading assigned to me by my mentor because I didn't ask questions. I almost quit because of this! Finally, I discovered the need to communicate with people and be proactive about learning new skills and asking questions.

3.4.2 How do you prepare for giving a presentation?

The most important thing is to be confident. People are attending your presentation to listen to you and learn something new. It helps to do your research so that the information you're presenting is accurate. One time, I gave a talk on AI, Flutter, and machine learning. I had to read a lot about machine learning, and I learned a lot. But it was good that I did that because I was able to share my insights so that the audience learned something from my presentation.

As you're preparing for a presentation, you shouldn't procrastinate on creating your slides. Make them about two weeks before your talk. I regret procrastinating on my slides for some of my previous presentations because I didn't have enough time to think about the slide design and make good slides. It's also nerve-wracking to be making slides a few days or even hours before your presentation.

Right before your presentation, you can calm your nerves by massaging your jaw and cheeks for a few minutes. This helps to relax your jaw and reduce anxiety. You can also write down or tell yourself positive affirmations such as "you can do it" or "you look great." Looking good will also boost your confidence because you don't have to worry about what people think of your appearance.

Don't be afraid to engage with your audience. You should start your presentation by asking the audience if they know about the topic. This is a good way to get to know the audience before you start talking. When I did my first talk in Hamburg, Germany, it was the first time I gave a tech talk physically in Europe coming from an African background, and I felt nervous because I didn't know what to expect from the audience. When I asked them what they knew about my topic, I got some really good feedback that I incorporated into my presentation.

3.4.3   Why is it important to observe personalities on your team?

When you're working in a global community, you must realize that people are very different based on their culture. You may think you're making jokes, but in some cultures, what you're saying is offensive. You should observe your environment and how things work, considering the energy that the team gives off. When you or someone else on your team is giving feedback, you can assess if a person takes that feedback well or not. You can't treat everyone equally as to how they react to things. People are different, and you'll have to approach giving feedback differently for different types of personalities. Putting yourself in their shoes helps to gain insight into where they are coming from. The last thing you want to do is accidentally create enemies.

3.4.4   What advice do you have for lead developers with a busy schedule to help them prioritize learning new skills?

When you're busy, it seems like every day something new comes up. It's important for you to maintain discipline. You should learn to use a schedule that suits you. Some people learn better and are more alert in the morning, while others prefer the evening. Don't set a schedule based on someone else's schedule. Their life is probably much different from yours, and their schedule may not work for you. Your schedule can be as little as 30 minutes per day, but the important thing is to be consistent.

Also, think about what is next after you learn the new skill. What is the end goal or main objective? What is driving your motivation toward learning that skill? When you're learning new skills, you need to also practice your new skills. You need practical skills and textbook knowledge to implement what you've learned. You can make your own project to practice and share your learning with others. When you learn something new, you can create videos, blogs, articles, or even tweets. I see a lot of people sharing knowledge on Twitter, and I think that's really cool! I've written many articles and answered questions on Stack Overflow, and then later I've forgotten the information on that topic and googled it only to find my own work. That goes to show that you can help not only the community but also your future self by sharing the information that you've learned.

If I'm researching something for a problem at work, I will take time from my workday to learn that specific topic. Sometimes, you need a small bit of information to make something work, and if you have a deadline, you need to find the solution for your specific problem quickly. But afterward, you can take the time for a more in-depth overview of how it works overall. This will help you balance your learning between your work hours and personal time.

Summary

- Lead developers must have a balance of both technical and soft skills.
- Being a lifelong learner and prioritizing learning versus your daily tasks is essential for success as a lead developer.
- There are 10 popular leadership styles for tech companies: autocratic, democratic, transformational, transactional, servant, visionary, coaching, laissez-faire, affiliative, and commanding.
- Lead developers should prioritize supportive leadership styles such as transactional, servant, coaching, and transformational.
- Lead developers should also be prepared to use higher-level leadership styles, such as visionary and commanding, in the future or in emergency situations.
- It's normal to feel nervous before giving a presentation, but practicing beforehand can help reduce nerves and ensure a successful performance.
- Visual aids, such as slides, can help clarify points and engage an audience, but it's important to keep them simple and focused with clear language and high-quality images.
- To communicate technical information effectively to a nontechnical audience, it's important to provide context, use analogies and examples, and avoid jargon. It can also be helpful to seek support and feedback from colleagues and mentors.

Learning any
developer skill

4

This chapter covers

- Finding your learning style and content types
- How health affects memory retention
- Overcoming learning obstacles
- How community projects boost skill growth
- Creating projects for experience and portfolio
- Setting realistic skill-learning goals

Learning new technical skills is a crucial part of being a developer, but it can also be a challenging and overwhelming process. Whether you're just starting out or you're a seasoned pro, there's always something new to learn and ways to improve your skills.

One of the biggest problems that developers face when learning new skills is feeling overwhelmed by the amount of information available. With so many resources and tutorials at our fingertips, knowing where to start and what information is most relevant can be difficult. When developers find the necessary information, they may lack the time needed for practice or application. It's one thing to read about a new concept or technology, but it's another thing to put it into practice. Developers often struggle to find the time or opportunity to apply what they're learning in real-world scenarios.

Developers also face the problem of imposter syndrome. It's easy to feel like you're the only one who doesn't understand a new concept or technology, especially when you're surrounded by more experienced developers. Plus, working with experienced developers can be intimidating, and you want to impress them with your skill level. This happens to everyone, even me (especially me)! Just remember—you're not alone. We'll come back to this topic later in this chapter when discussing physical and mental health.

Another problem that developers face is a lack of patience and perseverance. Learning new technical skills takes time and effort, and it's easy to get discouraged when progress is slow. Developers' goals during one-on-one meetings with their manager are often too aspirational, so they aren't set up for success. It's great to have goals, but they can also make you feel like a failure when you don't achieve them. This often prevents you from progressing or even causes you to ditch your learning goals entirely.

Many developers face these problems, but you can overcome them. Even if we set attainable goals, life happens, and priorities shift. Remember that learning is a lifelong journey, and the most important thing is to enjoy the ride.

4.1 Improving your learning methods

It's important to consider your own learning style and ways to reflect on the format that makes you comfortable and helps you retain the information better. Assessing your preferred content types is important in effectively learning new technical and soft skills and improving your learning methods. The most popular content types include textbooks, blog posts, online courses, instructional videos, and audiobooks. With so many options available, it can be overwhelming to know where to start and which types of content will be the most effective for you. When you encounter learning blockers, it can be difficult to overcome them if you don't know where to go to find the information that you need. Many developers (me included) will often try to break through learning blockers by just continuing to work without a break until the solution presents itself. However, there are healthier ways to deal with learning blockers without over-working yourself.

You can retain information at a high level while you're learning new skills by using tactics such as mnemonic devices. A *mnemonic device* is a tool or technique that helps you remember something. It's a simple and fun way to make learning new information more efficient and effective. Mnemonic devices can take many forms, such as a catchy phrase, rhyme, or acronym, making recalling complex information or a list of items easier. They're like little memory helpers that can make it a lot easier to remember important facts, figures, and dates. We'll discuss these devices further in section 4.1.2.

Lead developers must balance their time between their work responsibilities and keeping their skills current. This can be difficult without guidance and setting attainable goals. As discussed in the previous chapter, you must make the time to learn new skills. It's a good idea to block off your calendar to ensure that you have the time necessary to learn new skills on a regular basis. When it comes to learning new skills, it's ultimately up to you to balance your time and keep your mind sharp to learn quickly and retain what you've learned.

4.1.1   *Understanding how you learn*

Sifting through the endless resources available to learn new technical and soft skills can take a lot of time and patience. Many options are available, making it difficult to know where to start and, more importantly, how to choose the types of content you'll learn from most effectively.

To determine your preferred content types, you should experiment with different formats and evaluate which ones work best for you. Some common formats include the following:

- Video tutorials
- Written tutorials and documentation
- Interactive coding exercises
- Code samples
- Podcasts
- Audiobooks

By trying out a variety of formats, you can gain insight into which content types are most effective for you and use that knowledge to guide your future learning. Many people find it interesting that I prefer written tutorials, even though I create video-based online courses. My preference comes from beginning my development career before video tutorials were available. Now that they are available, I like combining a video with written instructions. One way that you can assess if video tutorials are for you is by watching a tutorial on a topic that interests you. After watching the video, try reading an article or documentation about the same topic. Take note of how you process and retain the information from each format. Are you able to absorb more from the video tutorial? Or does reading the documentation make it easier for you to understand the material?

Another effective method is to practice what you've learned. Try working through some interactive coding exercises that apply the concepts you've learned. This will allow you to apply what you've learned hands-on and see if you can successfully implement the concepts on your own. For example, you can find something small to automate, such as a simple timekeeping application. As you learn a new language, database, or framework, rewrite your application using the new technology. As you work through the exercises, take note of how you feel and how well you're able to understand the material. Are you feeling more confident in your abilities? Or are you having a hard time following the instructions? Code samples can also be a great way to assess yourself. Read through code samples in a language or technology you're trying to learn to see how well you understand the code. Take note of any areas where you're struggling, and plan to study those concepts more thoroughly.

It's also important to consider your own learning style. Individuals are different in the way they process information. Some people are visual learners who prefer to see information presented in diagrams, illustrations, or pictures. Some are auditory learners, who prefer to hear information in lectures, podcasts, or audiobooks. Lastly, some people are kinesthetic learners, who prefer to use their hands to touch and manipulate objects while they learn. Reflect on the format that makes you comfortable and helps you retain the information better.

By trying out different content types, practicing what you've learned, and reflecting on your own learning style, you'll be able to better understand which types of content will be the most effective for you in the future.

4.1.2 Boosting your memory

Boosting your memory while learning new skills can help you retain information more effectively and become a more efficient and effective developer. This will help you reduce the time you spend studying as you work smarter, not harder. You'll be better equipped to use critical thinking, keep in mind similar skills you've learned in the past, or overcome common errors you've encountered before.

Practicing *active recall* is the process of retrieving information from your memory without the aid of prompts or cues. Instead of passively reading through documentation or tutorials, try to actively recall what you've learned by testing yourself or teaching the material to someone else. This helps strengthen the connections in your brain and makes it more likely that you'll remember the information later. As you gain experience, you may see the same errors occurring frequently. When this happens, you'll be able to quickly fix those errors, especially if you've seen them before and it took you and your team a long time to fix them. Trust me, you'll remember how to resolve errors like this off the top of your head when you've been through the stress of trying to figure them out in the past.

As mentioned earlier, mnemonic devices are memory aids that can help you remember information more easily. For example, you could use an acronym to remember a list of programming terms or create a mental image to help you remember a specific syntax. Mnemonic devices can be especially helpful when you're trying to remember something that's difficult to visualize, such as a complex algorithm or data structure. Developers can use several different types of mnemonic devices to retain information about programming skills. Table 4.1 lists some mnemonic devices that I use to remember information.

Table 4.1   Mnemonic devices with examples for developers

Mnemonic device	Definition	Example
Acronym	Word made up of the first letters of a phrase or name	SOLID: Single Responsibility, Open-Closed, Liskov Substitution, Interface Segregation, and Dependency Inversion
Acrostics	A sentence or phrase in which the first letter of each word represents a letter in another word or phrase	CRUD (Create, Read, Update, Delete) application = "Careful Reading Uncovers Deeper Meaning"

Table 4.1   Mnemonic devices with examples for developers *(continued)*

Mnemonic device	Definition	Example
Chunking	The process of breaking down information into smaller, more manageable chunks	Break down long code strings into smaller groups, like a specific function or a group of related variables.
Imagery	The use of visual images to help remember information	An image of a tree to represent the hierarchical structure of a program, with the trunk representing the main function and the branches representing subfunctions
Rhymes	Correspondence of sound between words or the endings of words	"Agile projects go round and round, with planning, doing, checking, and adjusting to being found" = key stages in agile project management.

Large amounts of information can be overwhelming and difficult to retain. Instead of taking everything in at once, break complex concepts down into smaller, more manageable chunks. Try focusing on one aspect of a new skill or technique at a time and gradually building on what you've learned. If the concept includes building a new mobile application, the main components could include developing the backend functionality and components. You can create a task list or a to-do list for each component, with smaller, more specific tasks that need to be accomplished to complete that component.

4.1.3   *Taking care of your physical and mental health*

Research has shown that sleep, stress level, and mental health play an important role in consolidating new information in our memory. Ensure you're getting a good amount of restful sleep and managing your stress level, as both can affect your physical health, making it harder to learn and retain information. Your mental health is equally as important to keep yourself balanced and alert. You should exercise regularly, watch your nutrition, and not overwork yourself. Being healthy will enhance your ability to learn and retain new information.

Taking care of your physical and mental health is important for overcoming imposter syndrome as well. Ensure you're getting enough sleep, eating healthily, and taking breaks when needed. Exercise can also be a great way to relieve stress and improve your mood. Additionally, consider talking to a therapist or counselor if you're struggling with imposter syndrome or other mental health problems. I still get imposter syndrome, and something that helps me is reframing my negative thoughts into positive ones. Instead of thinking, "I don't know what I'm doing," try thinking, "I'm still learning, and that's okay." Instead of focusing on your mistakes, focus on what you've learned from them. Remember that everyone makes mistakes, and they're an opportunity to grow and improve.

As developers, we often find ourselves in a fast-paced and ever-changing environment. While this can be exciting and stimulating, it can also be stressful. Stress can take a toll on our physical and mental health, and it's important that we take the time to manage it effectively. It's easy to get caught up in the hustle and bustle of our work, but it's crucial that we make self-care a priority. This can include things such as exercise, meditation, and hobbies. Make sure you have time for yourself and your loved ones. Don't hesitate to contact colleagues, friends, or a professional if you're feeling overwhelmed. Remember that it's okay to take a step back, take a deep breath, and regroup. You're not expected to know everything, and it's important that you ask for help. Your well-being matters, and taking care of yourself will ultimately help you be more productive, effective, and fulfilled.

Another vital skill is setting boundaries and being able to say no to people. Lead developers are often approached numerous times daily to answer questions or engage in project conversations. If you have a full workload and someone comes to you with a request, it's a good practice to tell them that you want to help them, but you can't help them right now. When people make requests like this, they are often not expecting immediate action anyway. Project managers exist to help you manage your workload, and you should always refer to them if you're feeling overwhelmed.

> **NOTE** I was never good at saying no to people early in my career. I couldn't set boundaries, and I was a people pleaser. I once had a boss who requested that I take a train from London to Belgium at 8 P.M. to meet with a client the next morning, and I agreed to it. Not only was it dangerous for a young woman to arrive in an unfamiliar country late at night by herself, but I didn't get to sleep at all that night because I had to prepare for the meeting. I had every right to decline my boss's request.

When you don't set proper boundaries, the stress of overworking yourself will take a toll on your physical and mental health. After getting very sick and being hospitalized for a week because I had been traveling internationally twice a month for too long, I still went right back to work and continued to overwork myself. It took four more years before I realized I wasn't getting better, and a mental breakdown finally forced me to take time off. It changed my life, and now I put my health first. You can't help other people until you help yourself.

4.1.4 Teaching while you learn

Finding opportunities to teach others while you learn new programming skills can be a great way to solidify your understanding of the material and give back to the community. Let's say you're working on a new project, and you're setting up a local development environment. You continue to get the same networking errors, and you try to implement fixes from Stack Overflow, but nothing is working. Or you are pair programming with a junior developer, and neither of you can figure out how to fix an error and what is causing it. When you do figure out the solution, you should create content to help others who are facing the same errors. You can write a blog post, make a tutorial video, or give a talk detailing both the problem and the solution.

One way to find opportunities to teach is to look for meetups or user groups online or in your area that focus on the programming languages or technologies you're interested in learning. These groups often need speakers to give presentations or lead workshops on specific topics, and as a member, you can volunteer to lead a session or give a talk about the errors you've experienced and how you fixed them. These are my favorite types of presentations because they are engaging and can gain an emotional response from the audience if they have also experienced the same errors.

You can also create your own opportunities by offering to teach a class or workshop online or at a local college, university, or community center. This can be a great way to give back to your community and share your knowledge with others. If you can't find a user group, you can always create one! Don't be afraid to create your own community, as being the creator of a community will teach you leadership skills. You have to organize your group, schedule events, and moderate discussions, which are all great skills to have as a lead developer.

Another way to find opportunities is to look for mentorship programs or apprenticeships. Many companies and organizations have mentorship programs for developers looking to learn new skills and gain experience. As a mentor, you'll be responsible for guiding a more junior developer through the process of learning a new technology or skill set. The wonderful thing about being a mentor is that you have the opportunity to learn from your mentees as well. I've learned so much from my mentees over the years, as they are studying the latest and greatest technologies that I hadn't studied yet. This will help them reinforce their confidence when they're able to teach new skills to an experienced lead developer.

Additionally, you can also use the power of social media and other online platforms. Creating a blog, a YouTube channel, a podcast, or a Twitch channel about your own learning experience can help you attract followers and students who want to learn from your experience and methods. Remember, you don't always have to share technical skills that you've learned; you can also share leadership skills. Telling stories about situations you found yourself in, how you handled them, and how you would handle them now is a great way to connect with your audience and get feedback on your leadership skills.

Teaching while learning new skills can be a mutually beneficial experience. It allows you to deepen your understanding of the material while giving back to the community. There are many ways to find opportunities to teach, including volunteering to speak at meetups or user groups, participating in mentorship programs or apprenticeships, creating online content, or teaching a class or workshop at a local institution. As you prepare your teaching materials, you may also uncover other teachable moments that you didn't think of before. All of this will go a long way toward ensuring that you're consistently improving your skills and that you're set up for success in your career as a lead developer.

4.2 *Applying your skills*

Working on personal projects, helping with community projects, and creating prototypes are valuable skills for any lead developer to have in their career. Prototypes are early versions of a product or feature that are used to test and validate design concepts. They can take many forms, from rough sketches on paper to highly detailed mockups built with software. Creating a prototype is a great way to explore different design options and get feedback on your ideas. Along with mockups mentioned earlier, there are many other tools and techniques you can use to build prototypes, including wireframing and even coding.

When it comes to learning new skills, working on community projects can be extremely helpful, as they allow developers to experiment with new technologies and techniques in a supportive environment and get a sense of how something will work before committing to a full implementation. Additionally, working on a personal or community project can help develop problem-solving skills, as developers learn to identify and work through challenges that arise. Prototypes allow you to test and validate your ideas quickly and cheaply, and they also help you communicate your vision to stakeholders and team members. When you're starting a new project, a prototype can be a great way to explore different design options and identify potential problems early on. This can save a lot of time and resources in the long run, as changes are much more difficult and expensive to make once a project is well underway. A good example of a simple prototype that you can build for any programming language or framework is a Create, Read, Update, and Delete (CRUD) application, as described in figure 4.1.

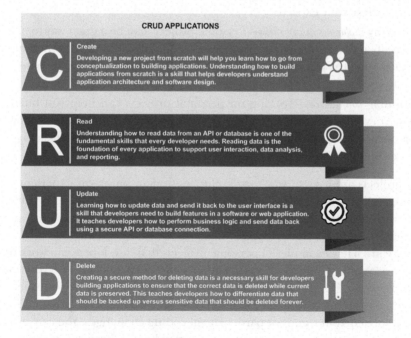

Figure 4.1 Example CRUD prototype

Prototypes can help with the development process and demonstrate a project's value to stakeholders. By providing a tangible example of what the final product will look like, it can be much easier to secure funding, gather feedback, and build buy-in from key decision-makers.

Prototypes can also be a great tool for team collaboration and communication. They can help developers clearly communicate their ideas to the rest of the team and gather feedback and input from other team members. This can lead to a more efficient and effective development process, as everyone is on the same page and working toward the same goal. You should take the time to learn and practice creating prototypes—it will pay off in the long run.

4.2.1 *Developing personal projects*

Working on personal projects can be incredibly beneficial for a career in development. Not only do they allow you to gain hands-on experience with various technologies and tools, but they also demonstrate your passion and commitment to your craft. Personal projects allow you to experiment with new technologies and tools that you may not have the opportunity to work with in your day-to-day job. This can help you stay current with the latest industry trends and improve your skills. The following list includes some of the benefits of working on a personal project:

- *Building a portfolio*—Personal projects can be used to create a portfolio that showcases your abilities and skills to potential employers. Having a portfolio of real-world projects can be a great way to stand out from other candidates and demonstrate your expertise.
- *Improving problem-solving skills*—Personal projects can be a great way to challenge yourself and improve your problem-solving skills. Building something from scratch requires you to think critically, identify and fix bugs, and come up with creative solutions to problems.
- *Increasing confidence*—Working on personal projects can help you build confidence in your abilities as a developer. Completing a project, no matter how small, is a great feeling and can give you the motivation you need to tackle bigger and more complex projects.

Personal projects are a great way for developers to gain hands-on experience, build a portfolio, and showcase their skills to potential employers. But it can be difficult to come up with ideas for personal projects. Table 4.2 lists a few examples of personal projects that developers can work on.

These are just a few examples of personal projects that developers can work on. The possibilities are endless, and the key is to choose a project that aligns with your interests and skills. However, it's also a good idea to work on projects that are outside of your comfort zone to broaden your skill set. To come up with ideas for personal projects, you can explore current trends or participate in coding challenges. You can also create something that solves a problem you or someone you know is having. For example, one of the featured contributors for this book, Jamie Maguire, works on his own personal projects using the Twitter API. He was interested in creating a robust tool to manage his account, so he learned how to work with the tools provided by Twitter.

Table 4.2 Examples of personal projects for developers

Project	Benefits
Build a website or web application	Gain experience with frontend technologies such as HTML, CSS, and JavaScript, and web frameworks such as React or AngularJS.
Create a mobile app	Gain experience with mobile development technologies such as Swift for iOS and Kotlin for Android. Developers can also use cross-platform development tools such as React Native or Flutter to build apps that run on both iOS and Android.
Create a game	Learn game development technologies such as Unity or Unreal Engine as well as game development frameworks such as Pygame or Godot to create 2D games.
Create a personal assistant	Learn natural language processing and machine learning technologies using platforms such as Dialogflow or Rasa to create an AI-powered personal assistant that can help with tasks such as scheduling, reminders, and more.
Create a chatbot	Gain experience with natural language processing and machine learning technologies using platforms such as Dialogflow or Botkit to create a chatbot that can interact with users in natural language.

By working on a personal project, developers can gain valuable experience, improve their skills, and build a portfolio of work that can help them advance their careers. So take some time to explore new technologies and tools, and start working on a personal project today!

4.2.2 *Working on community projects*

Working on community projects can be incredibly beneficial for developers for a number of reasons. For one, it allows you to collaborate with other like-minded individuals, which can lead to the creation of innovative and high-quality projects. Additionally, participating in community projects can help you build a strong network of professional contacts, which can prove invaluable in your career.

But how do you get started? The first step is to find a project that aligns with your interests and skills. There are many different types of open source projects, from software development to documentation and translation. Browse through popular open source platforms such as GitHub, SourceForge, and GitLab to find projects that catch your eye. You can also become a contributor to many libraries and frameworks, such as React. You can address any problems that you find and suggest new features.

Before you reach out to contribute to a project, it's a good idea to read through the documentation to get a sense of the project's goals and how it's organized. This will help you understand how you can contribute and what skills are needed. Once you've found a project that you're interested in, reach out to the project's maintainers or community members. Introduce yourself, and explain why you're interested in the project. Be sure to mention any relevant experience or skills you have that could be helpful to the project.

When you first get started, it's best to start with small, manageable tasks. This will help you familiarize yourself with the project's codebase and workflow and give you a chance to build a relationship with the other members of the community. Open source projects are built on collaboration, so it's important to communicate effectively with other members of the community. Be sure to ask questions when you need help and provide updates on your progress.

One of the most popular tech communities for developers is GitHub, a platform that allows developers to share, collaborate on, and review code. It's widely used by developers of all skill levels and offers a variety of projects to work on, including those related to open source software, machine learning, and data science. GitHub also provides developers with a range of tools to help them collaborate more effectively, including code reviews, issue tracking, and project management.

Another popular community for developers is Stack Overflow, a platform where developers can ask and answer questions related to programming. Stack Overflow is a great resource for developers looking for help with specific programming problems, and it also provides a wealth of information on best practices and common pitfalls. Additionally, Stack Overflow has a reputation system that rewards users who contribute high-quality answers and questions, which can help to build your reputation as a developer.

A third popular community for developers is the Linux community, which is dedicated to the development and promotion of the Linux operating system. Linux is an open source operating system that is widely used in servers, desktops, and mobile devices. The Linux community is made up of a diverse group of developers, system administrators, and users who work together to create and maintain the operating system, and they are always looking for contributors.

Remember, getting involved in open source projects isn't just about writing code, it's about building a community. By contributing to a project, you're helping to improve the project, and you're also building a network of like-minded developers who can help you grow both personally and professionally. So don't hesitate to take the first step and reach out to get involved today!

4.2.3   *Creating prototypes*

As a developer, one of the most important skills you can have is the ability to quickly learn new technologies and programming languages. One of the best ways to do this is by creating prototypes that can be adapted to a variety of different situations. One of the main benefits of creating prototypes is that they allow you to build a solid foundation of knowledge in a particular area. For example, if you're learning a new programming language, you can start by creating a simple project that demonstrates the basic syntax and structure of the language, such as a CRUD application. As you become more proficient, you can then adapt the project to include more advanced features and functionality. This process helps you gradually build your skills and become more confident in your ability to work with new technology.

Something that helped me learn a new language was recreating code that was written in one language in another language. I learned C# this way because when C# was becoming popular, I was a VB.NET programmer. I used tools including a VB-to-C# code converter to help me learn the differences between the two languages. I also read blogs and textbooks to further hone my skills to become proficient in C#.

Another benefit of creating prototypes is that they can serve as a reference point for future projects. For example, if you're working on a project that requires the use of a specific library or framework, you can refer to a previous project where you used the same technology. This can save you a lot of time and effort, as you'll already be familiar with the basics of how the technology works. Additionally, you can also reuse the code that you created for the previous project, which can help to speed up development time and reduce the risk of errors.

Creating reusable projects can also be a great way to demonstrate your skills to potential employers or clients. If you're a lead developer looking for a new job, you can create a portfolio of reusable projects that demonstrate your abilities in different programming languages or technologies. This can be a powerful tool for landing new jobs and building a successful career.

One example of a prototype is creating a library or framework for a specific language or technology. For example, a developer who is interested in learning Python can create a library for handling CSV files that can be used in multiple projects. This not only helps you improve your Python skills, but it also saves time for future projects that require CSV file handling.

Another example is creating a boilerplate or starter project for a specific use case. If you're interested in learning React, you can create a starter project that includes a basic file structure, a few commonly used libraries, and some example code. This can save a lot of time for developers who are just getting started with React and want to quickly set up a new project.

Creating prototypes also helps to improve code quality and maintainability. By writing code that can be reused across multiple projects, developers can ensure that the code is well-structured, easy to understand, and easy to maintain. Additionally, prototypes can be shared with other developers, which can lead to collaboration and feedback that can improve the overall quality of the code. You can also make your prototype an open source project to get community feedback and contributions. That way, you're giving back to the community and allowing others to learn new skills.

Prototypes are a great way for developers to learn new skills and improve development time. They allow developers to apply their knowledge to real-world problems, provide a sense of accomplishment and satisfaction, and improve code quality and maintainability. So next time you're looking to improve your skills and save time, consider creating a prototype.

4.3   *Overcoming learning blockers*

Lead developers often face a variety of challenges when it comes to learning new skills and technologies. You may encounter learning blockers, which are a common and natural part of the learning process. They occur when our brain needs a break from information overload or when we hit a snag in our understanding. This doesn't mean that we're not capable or intelligent, but rather, our brain needs time to process and make connections. Taking a step back, trying a different approach, or seeking help can often break through these blocks and help us continue our learning journey with renewed energy and understanding.

4.3.1   *Taking breaks*

As developers, we often find ourselves in the middle of a difficult problem or stuck trying to learn a new concept. It can be frustrating and demotivating, and it's easy to get caught up in the feeling that we should just push through and work harder. Taking a break is one of the best things you can do when you encounter a learning blocker.

Taking a break can help you see the problem from a different perspective. When you've been staring at the same piece of code or trying to understand the same concept for hours, it can be hard to see the bigger picture. Stepping away from the problem for a bit can help you come back to it with fresh eyes and a renewed perspective. I tend to have my best ideas while I'm taking a shower or bath because that's when I am most relaxed.

Just like your body needs rest to function properly, your brain needs a break too. When you're feeling mentally exhausted, it can be hard to focus and absorb new information. Giving your brain some time to rest and recharge can help you return to the problem feeling refreshed and ready to tackle it again.

Taking a break can also help you avoid burnout. When we're feeling blocked and frustrated, it's easy to fall into the trap of working longer and harder in an effort to make progress. You may find yourself working on the same thing over and over but never getting anywhere. This approach can lead to burnout, which can make it even harder to make progress in the long run. By taking a break and giving yourself permission to step away from the problem, you're allowing yourself the time and space you need to come back to it with renewed energy and focus.

So when should you take a break? The answer will vary depending on the individual and their specific needs, but a good rule of thumb is to take a break every hour or so. This will give your brain a chance to rest and recharge and help you stay focused and productive when you return to your studies. During your breaks, it's important to engage in activities that are different from studying. This could be something as simple as taking a walk outside, stretching your muscles, or chatting with a friend. Doing something that is enjoyable and diverting your focus from your studies helps you come back with renewed energy.

Another important thing to consider is the time of day. If you're a morning person, you may find that you're most productive in the early hours of the day and need more frequent breaks. On the other hand, if you're a night owl, you may be able to push through for longer periods of time before needing a break.

Ultimately, the key to successful studying is finding a balance between hard work and rest. By taking regular breaks, you can ensure that you're getting the most out of your study sessions and avoid feeling overwhelmed or burnt out. So the next time you're hitting the books, make sure to take a break every now and then. Your mind and body will thank you!

4.3.2 Setting attainable goals

As a developer, you're constantly learning new skills and technologies to stay ahead in the field. But with so many options out there, it can be overwhelming to decide what to focus on next. That's why setting attainable learning goals is so important. When setting your goals, it's important to be realistic about what you can accomplish in a set amount of time. If you're just starting out, for example, it's unlikely that you'll be able to master a complex framework like React in a week. Instead, start with something smaller, like learning the basics of JavaScript or a particular library.

Another important aspect of setting goals is making sure they align with your overall career aspirations. If you're working toward a specific job or role, make sure your goals align with the skills required for that position. For example, if you're interested in becoming a full-stack developer, make sure you're learning both frontend and backend technologies.

You should also make sure to set both short-term and long-term goals. Short-term goals can be things like learning a specific language or library, while long-term goals might be more general, like becoming an expert in a particular field or earning a specific certification. Having a mix of both will help you stay motivated while also giving you a sense of direction in the long term.

When you set learning goals for yourself, you're able to stay on track and make sure that you're focusing on the skills that are most important to you. This can help you achieve your career aspirations, whether you're looking to move into a new role, advance in your current position, or simply stay up-to-date with the latest technologies. Having attainable learning goals also helps keep you motivated and engaged. When you're working toward a specific goal, you're more likely to stay focused and make steady progress. This can help you avoid feeling overwhelmed or burned out, which is all too common in the fast-paced world of development.

Another benefit of setting learning goals is that it allows you to measure your progress. You can track your progress and see how far you've come by setting specific and measurable goals. This can be incredibly motivating and help you remain focused as you work toward your goals. A good way to stay on track is to break down your goals into smaller, more manageable tasks. For example, instead of setting a goal to "learn React," you might break it down into smaller tasks like "learn the basics of React," "build a simple app using React," "learn advanced features of React," and so on. This will make the goal more manageable and help you track your progress more easily.

A moonshot goal is a highly ambitious and transformative target that aims to make a significant positive effect. Having a moonshot goal is a great way to inspire creativity and innovation, push boundaries, and drive progress. By setting a moonshot goal, you're setting your sights high and challenging yourself to aim for something truly meaningful and effective. Having a moonshot goal can also provide a sense of purpose, motivation, and direction in your personal or professional life. Just keep in mind that these are the end goals, and you should focus on achieving success with attainable goals that will lead you to your moonshot goals. Table 4.3 lists examples of moonshot goals versus attainable goals.

Table 4.3   Examples of moonshot goals vs. attainable goals

Project	Moonshot goal	Attainable goals
Build an app.	Build the next big social media app.	■ Learn the basics of React. ■ Build a "Hello, world!" app. ■ Learn advanced React skills. ■ Develop user interactions.
Create artificial general intelligence (AGI).	Create the next ChatGPT.	■ Learn the basics of AI. ■ Build a simple AI algorithm capable of performing a specific task. ■ Improve the accuracy and efficiency of the algorithm. ■ Study cognitive psychology to create human intelligence models.

Setting attainable learning goals is essential for any developer looking to improve their skills and advance their career. It helps you stay on track, stay motivated, and measure your progress. Make sure your goals align with your career aspirations, break them down into smaller tasks, and seek out resources and support. With a solid plan in place, you'll be well on your way to achieving your goals and becoming a better developer.

4.3.3   Seeking help

As a lead developer, it's natural to want to be self-sufficient and able to handle any challenge that comes your way. But let's face it, no one has all the answers, and even the most seasoned developers encounter learning blockers from time to time. In these moments, seeking help can be the key to overcoming those obstacles and moving forward with your learning journey.

Let's talk about why seeking help is so important. It can save you a lot of time and frustration. When you're stuck on a problem or don't know how to proceed, it can be easy to get bogged down and waste hours or even days trying to figure things out on your own. By seeking help, you can get a fresh perspective and some guidance that can help you make progress much more quickly. Seeking help allows you to learn from the experience of others and can expose you to new ways of thinking and working that you might not have discovered on your own.

So how do you go about seeking help? One of the best ways is to reach out to more experienced colleagues or mentors. They can provide valuable insights and guidance that can help you overcome the obstacle you're facing. You should approach experienced colleagues or mentors with respect and a clear understanding of their needs. Before asking for help, take the time to research and try to solve the problem on your own. This will show that you're motivated and capable of tackling the problem at hand. When asking for help, you should be specific about the problem you're facing and provide any relevant background information. It also helps when you're open to feedback and willing to take constructive criticism. Remember to be gracious and thank the colleague or mentor for their time and assistance.

Additionally, you can also look for help within the developer community. There are a variety of online forums and communities where developers come together to share knowledge and help each other out. The following list includes developer communities you can use to ask for help:

- *Stack Overflow*—A popular Q&A platform for programmers to ask and answer technical questions.
- *GitHub*—On this platform, developers can host and share their code, as well as collaborate on open source projects. Many developers use GitHub's Issues feature to ask for help with specific problems.
- *Reddit*—The /r/LearnProgramming and /r/Programming subreddits are both popular communities where developers can ask for help and share their knowledge with others.
- *Quora*—This Q&A website allows developers to ask and answer questions on a wide range of programming-related topics.
- *Dedicated communities*—Many programming languages and frameworks have dedicated communities where developers can ask for help and share their knowledge with others. Examples include the Docker community, the React community, and the Angular community.
- *Meetup*—Many cities have meetup groups for developers where they can meet, network, and ask for help from others in their field.

When you reach out for help, it's important to be specific about what you're looking for. Be clear about what you're trying to accomplish and what you need help with. This will make it easier for the person you're asking to give you the guidance you need. It's also a good idea to be open to feedback and to be willing to try different approaches. Remember, seeking help isn't a sign of weakness; it's a sign of strength. It shows that you're willing to learn and grow and that you're not afraid to ask for help when you need it.

Seeking help is an essential part of the learning process for lead developers. It can save you time, expose you to new ways of thinking, and help you overcome obstacles that might otherwise hold you back. By reaching out to more experienced colleagues or mentors, or by finding help within the developer community, you can get the guidance you need to keep moving forward with your learning journey. So the next time you're faced with a learning blocker, don't be afraid to ask for help. It could be the key to unlocking your full potential.

4.4   Case study

Scott Hanselman has been a developer for 30 years and has been blogging at hanselman .com for 20 years. He works in open source on .NET and the Azure Cloud for Microsoft out of his home office in Portland, Oregon. Scott has been podcasting for more than 15 years, and he has produced 800 episodes of the Hanselminutes podcast and 700 episodes of the Azure Friday podcast. He's written a number of technical books and spoken in person to more than 1 million developers worldwide! He's also on TikTok, which was very likely a huge mistake. In this case study, Scott shares his thoughts on learning any developer skill.

4.4.1   How can a developer find community projects, and how can they get involved?

One of the things that I struggle with when I'm coaching people is the unspoken vibe when you meet someone who you know is going places. Like if you're at Chipotle and you've seen someone a few times and you notice them. There's just something about them, and you think to yourself that they have the potential to do more. We think these things, but we never say them. But now that I'm an old man with big Dad energy, I do say these things! I'll talk to them and say something encouraging and watch them light up.

There are so many developers who are going places, and they are so desperate to get there, and it shows. They do things like send me random emails saying, "Let me pick your brain," or they spam my LinkedIn inbox. It doesn't come from a bad place; they are clear self-starters who want to achieve success, but they are going about it in the wrong way. Starting with negative interactions doesn't make me want to help you. On the other hand, there are these other people that you just have a feeling about, and you want to help them and offer them mentorship. So how do we prepare people for these moments? A lot of it is just plain luck.

When you're reaching out to someone to get involved in the community and find community projects, make sure you're prepared first. Have you searched for community projects on your own? Have you looked for relevant social media accounts or interacted with anyone else in the community? You need to do these things first to be prepared for when the opportunity becomes available. Luck is opportunity plus being prepared. I could point you to a project that you can contribute to, but you must show up and do the work.

There are soft skills involved in finding community projects and interacting with other developers. You must warm up to people and not try to fast-forward the process of getting to know someone. Offer your help first before asking for help. With community projects, a lot of the tasks can be grunt work, but it's still something that you'll learn from. Having a positive attitude and making helpful comments will establish you as someone who is a good community contributor. Think about the humans behind the project. What do they need? What problems are they trying to solve? How can you help them? Offer to do the dirty work. That's how you build trust.

4.4.2 How can a developer find the help they need to overcome learning blockers?

I think that it's common for developers to get overwhelmed with all the things that we must learn in tech. This happens to people who are new in their careers and people like me who've been doing this for many years. What do you do when you're completely overwhelmed? There's a concept called rubber ducking where you get a rubber duck and explain the problem to them. Say you're trying to reverse sort a linked list. You just explain it to the duck, and in the process of getting it out of your mouth, back into your ears, and into your brain, you can solve the problem. Explaining it to even a nontechnical partner, spouse, or roommate is also something you can do.

You should wake up and be mentally present and intentional. I'm a big believer in deliberate practice. If you're searching for an error and staring at the screen looking for the answers you need and not finding them, it's time to talk to somebody. If you can't find somebody, then talk to a rubber duck. Put it on top of your monitor, and when you have a problem, explain it to the duck. You can also go for a walk and talk to yourself. That's also rubber duck debugging. You don't need an actual duck.

Overcoming learning blockers is a waking-up process. If you don't understand the answers you're getting from Google or Stack Overflow, you need to take a step back. If you're trying to copy and paste code you found on Stack Overflow for unit testing, and you don't know what async means, but you're trying to do async programming, then you need to step back and learn about async programming first. I'm a big fan of going one level below your comfort zone. You don't have to go all the way down to assembly, but it does help if you understand the overall concepts that you're implementing in your code.

4.4.3 What would you tell a developer who feels inadequate because they aren't working on as many community projects as other developers in their network?

I'm inadequate compared to Rihanna and Beyoncé. I can give you a list of all the people I'm inadequate when compared to. The only person you should be comparing yourself to is yourself. You don't know what's going on in other people's lives. Do you have kids? Then you won't have as much time to work on community projects as some college kid who lives with their parents. You have different life experiences and responsibilities. We need to stop apologizing for what we're not doing and start thinking about what we're doing and what we can be doing and only comparing ourselves to our past selves.

You should also think about how you value your time. I like to play video games, so in my off hours, I'm playing *God of War*. But what are my colleagues doing for those extra 3 to 4 hours a day? Some of them spend that time coding, and that can make me feel bad. But coding helps them relax and unwind, so their experience is different. I'm not going to apologize for playing video games; it's what helps me relax. We're all on our own journey and shouldn't apologize for what we're not doing.

4.4.4 *How do you like to learn new skills?*

I like to learn in public, but that is a privilege because I'm less likely to have mean people comment on my work. I think if you're learning in public, you need to be able to ignore those comments and delete those unwanted DMs and just move on. My favorite way to learn in public is through trusted mentoring groups. One-on-one mentoring can be threatening, but if you can find a group of three to four, you can keep each other accountable. Codenewbie (www.codenewbie.org) is a great community, and they are very welcoming. You can create a mini study group where everyone is on the same level so you can collaborate with people who are similar to you without feeling like you're at the bottom of the food chain. Everyone is equal in their skills and accountability, and everyone has the opportunity to be both the mentor and the mentee.

Summary

- Assessing your preferred content types is important in order to determine which formats are most effective for you.
- Experimenting with different content formats, practicing what you've learned, and reflecting on your own learning style can help you gain insight into which types of content will be the most effective for you in the future.
- Boosting your memory while learning new skills can help you retain information more effectively and become a more efficient and effective developer. This can include practicing active recall, testing yourself, teaching the material to someone else, and using mnemonic devices.
- Creating prototypes can save time and resources by allowing you to test and validate ideas early on and communicate your vision to stakeholders and team members.
- Prototypes can be used to learn new skills and demonstrate the value of a project to stakeholders to improve collaboration and communication within a team.
- Personal projects can be beneficial for a career in development by providing hands-on experience with new technologies, building a portfolio, finding networking opportunities, improving problem-solving skills, and increasing confidence.
- Overcoming learning blockers can be achieved by taking regular breaks, setting clear and attainable goals, and seeking help and guidance from more experienced colleagues or mentors.

- Taking breaks can help overcome learning blockers by providing a fresh perspective, recharging the brain, and avoiding burnout.
- Setting attainable goals provides you with direction and focus, gives you a sense of accomplishment when met, and helps you navigate the learning process effectively.

Writing technical documentation

Lead developers must learn how to write and manage technical documentation because it helps to clearly communicate the design and functionality of a software system to both internal and external stakeholders. This includes other developers on the team, as well as project managers, QA engineers, and other nontechnical team members.

Technical documentation also helps to ensure that a software application is easy to maintain and update over time. Clear documentation can make it easier for new developers to understand the codebase and quickly become productive. It also can help to prevent errors and confusion by providing a clear and accurate reference for how the system is supposed to work. Additionally, technical documentation can be used as a training tool for new team members, and it can also be used to create user manuals and other forms of end-user documentation.

Technical documentation is important for communication, maintainability, and clarity. It helps others to understand the system, prevents errors and confusion, and can be used during the onboarding process for new team members. When you invest time in creating and maintaining technical documentation, you'll improve the developer workflow. You'll also provide project teams with a centralized location to reference when they have questions. When there is turnover on your team, you won't lose important knowledge, as it's already documented. With clear and concise technical documentation, your life as a lead developer is made easier with proper organization and communication.

5.1 Setting the team up for success

When there is proper technical documentation, developers clearly understand the codebase and how it should be maintained. As a result, the codebase is more consistent, easier to read, and more maintainable. Additionally, developers can quickly find the information they need, which can help to reduce the amount of time spent on resolving problems or debugging code. Furthermore, proper technical documentation also helps to ensure that decisions aren't lost over time, which can improve the codebase's long-term maintainability. Table 5.1 lists the effects of proper technical documentation versus development without documentation.

Table 5.1 Effects of proper technical documentation on the development workflow

With proper technical documentation	Without proper technical documentation
Developers clearly understand how the code works and how to use it.	Developers are left to figure things out independently, which can lead to confusion and mistakes.
Developers can easily find the information they need to complete their tasks.	Developers may need to spend a lot of time searching for information and experimenting to understand how things work.
Developers can quickly identify/fix bugs and make changes to the code.	Developers may have a harder time identifying/fixing bugs and making changes to the code.
Developers can easily collaborate with other team members.	Developers may have difficulty working with other team members because they aren't on the same page.
Developers can easily onboard new team members.	Developers may have difficulty onboarding new team members because they lack the information they need to get started.

When there's little to no documentation, developers may have difficulty understanding the codebase and how it should be maintained. This can lead to a lack of consistency in the codebase, making it difficult to read and keep updated. Additionally, developers may have a hard time finding the information they need, which can lead to delays or mistakes. Without proper documentation, decisions may be lost over time, which can lead to a higher level of technical debt and increased maintenance costs.

5.1.1 Documenting everything

As a lead developer, one of the most important things you can do to set your team up for success is to document everything having to do with developer processes. This includes documentation on coding standards, development workflow, and deployment processes. There are several collaboration tools that you can use to manage your documentation including Confluence, Microsoft Word, Google Docs, and GitHub Wiki pages.

Developing and maintaining coding standards is an essential aspect of any software development project. It ensures that the codebase is consistent, easy to read, and maintainable. Coding standards serve as a guide for developers to follow when writing code, and they also provide a consistent reference for code review and maintenance. Some companies have coding standards at the organizational level, which must be reviewed and updated frequently. Establishing and documenting coding standards can also help to prevent common coding mistakes and improve the overall quality of the codebase.

It's important to ensure that the coding standards are easily accessible to all team members as a part of your technical documentation. This can be accomplished by making the document available on a company intranet or shared drive or by including the standards in the team's code review process. You should also keep the coding standards up to date. As new technologies and best practices emerge, you should review the standards and make any necessary updates. Additionally, the team should be encouraged to provide feedback on the standards, and any problems or concerns should be addressed in a timely manner.

Documenting the development workflow is an essential part of ensuring that your team is working efficiently and effectively. By creating clear and detailed documentation of the development process, you can help streamline the workflow and improve communication among team members. To start, it's important to gather input from the team on their current workflow and identify any areas that may be causing delays or confusion. Once you have a clear understanding of the existing workflow, you can begin to document it in a step-by-step format, including information on how to handle bugs and problems that arise, how to review and merge code, and how to test and deploy code. An example of a development workflow may include the following steps:

- *Planning*—Team members gather to discuss new features or updates for the project and create a plan for implementation.
- *Development*—Team members work on implementing the new features or updates, following established coding standards and best practices.
- *Code review*—Team members review each other's code and provide feedback, ensuring that the code is of high quality and adheres to the established coding standards.

- *Testing*—Team members test the new features or updates to ensure that they are functioning correctly and fix any bugs that are found.
- *Deployment*—Team members deploy new features or updates to a staging environment for further testing and validation before being released to production.
- *Maintenance*—Team members continue to monitor and maintain the codebase, addressing any problems that arise and implementing any necessary updates.

Development workflows can vary depending on the specific project or organization, and you need to find what works best for you. Documenting the workflow is important, as it helps to ensure that everyone is aware of the different steps and that the team is aligned in the same direction. Gitflow is a popular software development methodology that provides a development workflow for managing the Git version control system. The main branch contains the production-ready code, while the development branch is where all the new features are developed. You should document the process for naming features and hotfix branches, pushing code to QA, and merging code into the main branch once the feature is complete. You can also document how to handle merge errors, cherry-picking code changes to commit, and deployment procedures.

Documenting the deployment process is an important step in ensuring that your team can quickly and efficiently deploy new features and updates to production. By creating clear and detailed documentation of the deployment process, you can help reduce the risk of errors and improve communication among team members. To start, you should gather information on the existing deployment process, including the steps involved, the tools and technologies used, and any best practices that have been established. Once you have a clear understanding of the existing process, you should document it in a step-by-step format, including information on how to handle any problems that may arise during deployment. It's also a good idea to include diagrams or flowcharts to help visualize the process. Effective documentation of the deployment process is key to ensuring that your team can deploy new features and updates quickly and efficiently. Figure 5.1 shows an example of documenting the deployment process.

Documentation not only helps new team members understand how things are done within your organization but also serves as a valuable reference for experienced developers when they encounter a problem and need to troubleshoot it. By providing clear and detailed documentation, you can help your team work more efficiently and effectively, which in turn will help the organization. Your team will be set up for success because there are transparent standards for everyone to follow. In addition, proper documentation can also help to reduce the risk of errors and improve communication within the team. When everyone is on the same page and understands the processes that are in place, it's easier to identify and correct any problems that appear.

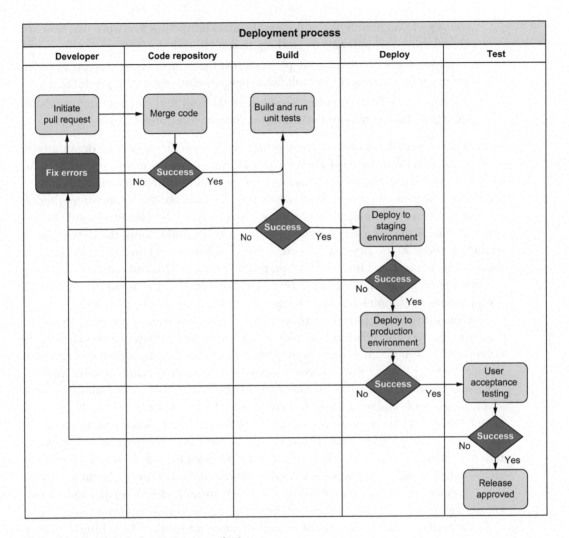

Figure 5.1   Example deployment process chart

5.1.2   *Managing technical debt*

Technical debt is a term used to describe the cost of maintaining and updating code that has been developed in a hurry or without proper attention to quality. It's important to understand that technical debt isn't always a bad thing, as it allows teams to quickly deliver features and updates to meet deadlines or respond to changing business needs. However, when not managed properly, technical debt can quickly accumulate and become a significant burden on a project. Think of technical debt as a loan, like a mortgage or a credit card debt. It allows you to achieve your goals faster, but it also means you'll have to pay interest in the form of added complexity, increased maintenance costs, and longer development cycles. Just like financial debt, technical debt can be manageable if it's monitored and paid off over time. On average, developers waste 33% of their time managing technical debt. By writing proper documentation, including coding standards and the deployment process, you'll manage technical debt, which reduces time spent researching "unknowns," re-implementing work that doesn't meet standards, or introducing new errors.

As a lead developer, it's important to be aware of technical debt and to take steps to manage it effectively. When you take the time to document your code and systems, you're effectively creating a road map for your team to follow. You're also creating a record of what has been done and how it has been done. This can be incredibly valuable when it comes time to make updates or changes, as you'll have a clear understanding of what needs to be done and how to do it. This can help to reduce confusion and errors and can also make it easier for new team members to get up to speed quickly.

One way to effectively manage technical debt is to maintain a historical record of decisions made in the technical documentation. By keeping track of why certain decisions were made and what tradeoffs were considered, you and your team will have a better understanding of the codebase and be able to make more informed decisions in the future.

For example, if a certain design pattern was chosen because it was the best fit for a specific use case, documenting that decision can help the team understand the reasoning behind it and make similar decisions in the future. The same is true when a specific technology is chosen that offers better performance; documenting that decision tells the team why the choice was made and informs similar future decisions.

Including this historical record in the technical documentation also helps to ensure that the decisions aren't lost over time as team members come and go. This means that anyone new to the project will have access to the context and understanding of the decisions made in the past, which will help them make better decisions going forward. Retaining this information and documenting it will help you reduce technical debt when turnover results in lost expertise from your team. Although there should be a knowledge transfer before a person leaves the team, that doesn't always happen, so it's best to document everything. Preserving a historical record allows lead developers and the team to make more informed decisions, understand the codebase better, and ensure that the decisions aren't lost over time. It's not only beneficial for the present but also for the future of the project.

5.1.3 Onboarding new developers

As a lead developer, one of the most important responsibilities you have is ensuring that new developers are able to quickly and easily onboard to your team. One of the best ways to do this is by writing clear and comprehensive documentation. Proper technical documentation can help new developers understand the overall architecture of the project, as well as the specific details of how different components and systems work together. This can save a significant amount of time and reduce bugs, as new developers won't have to spend as much time trying to figure out how everything works on their own.

In addition, clear and well-organized technical documentation can also make it easier for new developers to identify and fix any bugs that they come across. This can be especially useful if the documentation includes detailed information about how different parts of the code are supposed to work, as well as any known problems or edge cases. Writing proper technical documentation is a simple but powerful tool that can help you as a lead developer reduce the time it takes to onboard new developers and make the process smoother and more efficient for everyone involved. The following list includes topics that should be included in developer onboarding documentation:

- *Code of conduct*—A list of the team's expectations for behavior and communication, including guidelines for working with others and resolving conflicts
- *Coding standards*—Detailed information on the team's coding standards, including naming conventions, formatting, commenting, and best practices
- *Development workflow*—A step-by-step guide to the team's development workflow, including information on how to handle bugs and problems, how to review and merge code, and how to test and deploy code
- *Deployment process*—A step-by-step guide to the team's deployment process, including information on how to handle any problems that may arise during deployment
- *Tools and technologies*—A list of the tools and technologies used by the team, including any required software or libraries
- *Communication channels*—Information on the team's communication channels, including email, chat, and videoconferencing tools, and how to use them effectively
- *Resources and documentation*—A list of useful resources and documentation for the team, including any internal wikis, documentation, or tutorials
- Onboarding checklist—A list of tasks that new developers should complete as part of their onboarding, including training, code reviews, and other requirements
- *Technical debt management*—Information on the team's approach to managing technical debt and how new developers can help to minimize it
- *Mentorship program*—Information on the team's mentorship program, including how new developers can find a mentor and what is expected of new developers

It's important to note that the specific items on this list may vary depending on the organization or project, but these are some of the most common items that should be included in developer onboarding documentation. The most important thing is that the documentation should be complete, clear, and easy to understand, and it should be reviewed regularly to make sure that it stays up to date.

I've worked at many companies that lacked technical documentation, and I took it upon myself to write documentation so that future developers wouldn't struggle with onboarding as I did. Many organizations don't document the process for setting up your local development environment, and this causes confusion and frustration. One time, it took me two whole weeks to reverse engineer a development environment configuration because there was no documentation, and the previous developers who worked on the project had all left the company. When I went through the process over the two-week period, I wrote down step by step what I had to do to configure my environment and the errors I encountered along the way. When I hired new developers for my team, it took them one day to set up their local development environments versus two weeks.

Don't be afraid to invest time in this task, and remember that keeping your documentation updated is a key aspect of reducing the time it takes to onboard new developers as the project and team evolve over time. It's a good practice to have new developers edit the documentation as they go through the onboarding process so that it's always up to date. This has the added benefit of giving them experience in maintaining documentation so that they can contribute regularly. Lead developers don't bear the full responsibility of maintaining documentation—it's a team effort. With proper documentation in place, you'll be able to onboard new developers more efficiently and ensure that your entire team is working together effectively.

5.2 Structuring documentation

Structuring technical documentation is extremely important for ensuring that the information is easy to understand and navigate for developers and other users. Well-structured documentation makes it easy for developers to find the information they need quickly and get up to speed with a new project or technology. This can save a lot of time and frustration and help ensure that projects are completed on time and to a high standard.

When documentation isn't structured, it can be difficult to find the information you need, which can lead to confusion and mistakes. This can be especially problematic when working on a large or complex project, where there may be a lot of different documentation to navigate. Poorly structured documentation can also make it difficult for new developers to get immersed in a project, which can slow down the development process and lead to delays.

5.2.1 Chunking the content

When it comes to technical documentation, it's important to keep in mind that your audience is made up of busy developers who want to quickly find the information they need. One of the best ways to make this happen is by breaking up your documentation into easily consumable chunks. *Chunking,* as it's often called, is a technique for organizing information into small, manageable pieces so that it's easy for readers to find what they need and understand it quickly. Figure 5.2 shows an example of chunking used in developer documentation in Confluence.

Following are tips for structuring your documentation using chunking:

- *Headings and subheadings*—Use headings and subheadings to break up your document into sections. This makes it easy for readers to scan and find the information they're looking for.
- *Bullet points*—Use bullet points and numbered lists to organize information into bite-sized chunks. This makes it easy for readers to quickly absorb the information and understand the main points.
- *Images and diagrams*—Use images and diagrams to supplement your text. This helps to break up the text and make the document more visually appealing, which can make it easier for readers to understand.
- *Examples and case studies*—Use examples and case studies to illustrate key concepts. This helps to make the information more concrete and easier to understand.
- *Simple language*—Keep your language simple and easy to understand. Avoid using jargon or technical terms that your readers may not be familiar with.

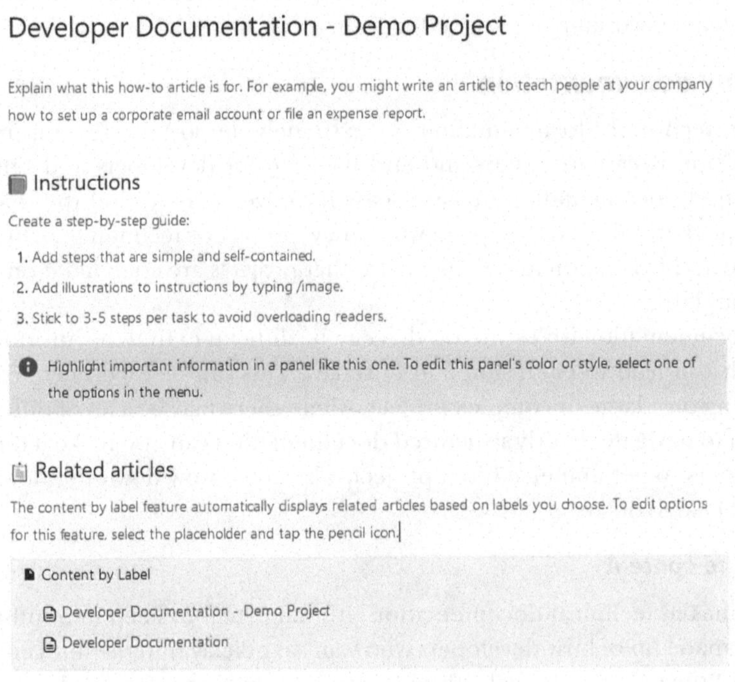

Developer Documentation - Demo Project

Explain what this how-to article is for. For example, you might write an article to teach people at your company how to set up a corporate email account or file an expense report.

Instructions

Create a step-by-step guide:

1. Add steps that are simple and self-contained.
2. Add illustrations to instructions by typing /image.
3. Stick to 3-5 steps per task to avoid overloading readers.

> ℹ️ Highlight important information in a panel like this one. To edit this panel's color or style, select one of the options in the menu.

Related articles

The content by label feature automatically displays related articles based on labels you choose. To edit options for this feature, select the placeholder and tap the pencil icon.

📄 Content by Label

   📄 Developer Documentation - Demo Project

   📄 Developer Documentation

Figure 5.2   Example developer documentation in Confluence

By following these tips, you can ensure that your technical documentation is structured to help your readers find the information they need and understand it quickly. Remember, the goal of technical documentation is to help developers be more productive and effective, so make easy-to-use documentation a priority.

5.2.2 Using visual aids

Visual aids have a positive effect on technical documentation in several ways. They can make complex information more easily understandable by breaking it down into smaller, more manageable chunks. Visual aids can also make technical documentation more engaging and interesting to read, which can keep the reader's attention. They can be used to convey the overall structure and flow of a system or program, making it easier for the reader to navigate and understand the codebase. Using visuals helps to break up text and make the documentation more visually appealing. The use of visual aids can greatly enhance the effectiveness of technical documentation and make it easier for developers to understand and work with the codebase (see table 5.2).

Table 5.2 Examples of visual aids

Visual Aid	Purpose
Flowcharts	Flowcharts are a great way to visualize the flow of control in a program or system. They can be used to show the different paths a user can take through the system or explain the logic of a particular function or module.
Diagrams	Diagrams can be used to show the overall architecture of a system or to illustrate the relationships between different components. They can also be used to show the flow of data or control between different parts of the system.
Screenshots	Screenshots are a great way to show what a user interface looks like and how it works. They can also be used to show the output of a program or the results of a particular test.
Code snippets	Code snippets are an essential part of technical documentation. They should be used to illustrate specific examples of how to use a particular function or class.

When I'm writing technical documentation, I rely heavily on screenshots and code snippets. As you list the steps to walk a developer through a task, such as setting up their development environment or connecting to a test server, it helps to see a visual representation of what the developer sees on their screen. It also helps if you draw their attention to specific areas of the screen using callouts such as boxes and highlighting. This can be difficult to keep updated, as developer tools are constantly changing, so you should keep that in mind as you update your documentation. We'll discuss this in detail later in this chapter.

5.2.3 Including an introduction and summary

When it comes to technical documentation, the introduction is crucial. It should provide an overview of the purpose of the document, as well as any background information that may be useful. The introduction should also include a list of any assumptions or prerequisites the reader should be aware of before diving into the document. The following is an example of an introduction to developer documentation:

> *Welcome to the developer documentation for setting up a local development environment. This document will provide a step-by-step guide for setting up a local environment on your computer for development purposes. This guide assumes that you have a*

basic understanding of computer systems and software development. Additionally, it's important to note that the instructions provided in this document are for a Windows operating system.

After the introduction, you should include a summary of the document's contents. This summary should give the reader a high-level understanding of what the document covers and what they can expect to learn from it. This can be a great way to help the reader decide if the document is relevant to their needs and can also help them navigate the document more easily. The following is an example of a summary for developer documentation:

> *This document provides step-by-step instructions on how to configure a development environment on a local machine, including the installation of required software, tools, and libraries, as well as the configuration of relevant settings. It includes an overview of the development environment, explaining its purpose and how it differs from production environments. It then provides a list of prerequisites needed for the installation, such as the operating system and hardware requirements. The document covers the installation of software dependencies and tools, including compilers, code editors, and package managers. It explains how to set up environment variables and configure the necessary paths. Finally, this document provides a troubleshooting reference that includes common errors.*

In addition, it's essential to include a conclusion summary at the end of the document containing the key takeaways. The conclusion should summarize the main points of the document and provide any additional context or background information that may be useful. It's also good practice to provide a section for further reading that can include resources, relevant documents, or external links to help the reader gain a more-in-depth understanding of the subject matter. There are different types of conclusions depending on the subject matter of the documentation. If the document covers deep technical detail or has iterated through several topics, a more complete conclusion is needed. I like to work with the development and project team to gather the necessary information for the conclusion. The following list includes examples of a conclusion for a document that contains deep technical detail:

- Install a local web server, such as Apache or Nginx.
- Install and configure a database management system, such as MySQL or PostgreSQL.
- Install a programming language runtime, such as PHP or Python.
- Install a version control system, such as Git.
- Clone the project repository to your local machine.
- Set up a virtual host or local domain for the project.
- Configure environment variables and settings specific to your local development environment.
- Run any necessary setup or installation scripts, such as database migrations.
- Test the project to ensure that it runs correctly in your local environment.

- Related Documents and Resources:
    - Contact list
    - Project stakeholders
    - API documentation

If you're writing technical documentation that is a reference instead of a how-to guide, you can write a more general conclusion or wrap-up where applicable. An example of this is application programming interface (API) documentation that provides detailed information on the endpoints, parameters, and responses of the API, enabling developers to integrate it into their applications. This type of documentation isn't a walkthrough of specific steps, so it's not appropriate to have a conclusion with bullet points. Instead, you should summarize the key takeaways in a paragraph. The following is an example of a conclusion for reference documentation:

> *This API reference document has provided a reference of the API's capabilities. We understand that developers may have additional questions or require further assistance during the integration process, and we encourage you to reach out to our support team for help. Additionally, we're continuously updating and improving our API to provide the best possible experience for our users, so we recommend regularly checking our documentation for updates.*

By using introductions and summaries, as well as clear and concise writing, diagrams, code examples, and conclusion sections, developers can ensure that their documentation is easy to understand and navigate. With these best practices in mind, lead developers can make sure their documents are well structured to maximize their effectiveness.

5.3 Creating the content

As a lead developer, you have a lot on your plate. With so much to do, it can be easy to feel overwhelmed when it comes time to create technical documentation. You may ask yourself where you should even begin. It helps to delegate content creation to your team and not take on everything yourself. Creating technical documentation can be a daunting task, but it doesn't have to be overwhelming. It's important to remind yourself that creating technical documentation is a necessary and important task because it not only helps the team to understand the project better but also serves as a reference point for future projects. Having complete documentation will help your team be more productive by providing them with a place to find the answers to their questions. That way, it frees up more of your time to focus on your leadership duties. By investing time and effort in creating technical documentation, you're helping to ensure the success of your project and your team.

5.3.1 Starting with an outline

One of the most important steps in creating technical documentation is writing an outline. An outline is a road map for the documentation that helps to organize the information and ensure that it's presented in a logical and easy-to-follow manner. Before writing an outline, it's important to understand the purpose of the documentation. Who is the audience? What is the goal of the documentation? What information needs to be included? Understanding the purpose of the documentation will help to ensure that the outline is focused and relevant.

Once the purpose of the documentation is understood, the next step is to break the documentation down into sections. This can be done by identifying the main topics that need to be covered. For example, if the documentation is a user manual for a software application, the following sections might be included: "Introduction," "Getting started," "Using the application," "Troubleshooting," and "References."

After the sections have been identified, it's important to create subheadings for each section. These subheadings will help to organize the information within each section and make it easier for developers to find the information they need. Under the "Getting Started" section, the subheadings might include "Installing the application," "Creating an account," and "Navigating the user interface."

You also can use bullet points and numbered lists as an effective way to present information in a clear and easy-to-follow manner. These can be used to organize information within each section and subheading. If you have an "Installing the application" subheading, the numbered list of instructions might look like this:

1 Download the installation file.
2 Run the installation wizard.
3 Activate the application.

Once the outline is complete, it's important to review and revise it. The outline should be clear and easy to follow, and it should include all the information that is necessary for the documentation. It's also a good idea to ask for feedback from other developers to ensure that the outline is clear and easy to understand. An outline for a developer guide of an application could look like this:

- Introduction
  - Description of the application
  - Audience and purpose of the guide
- Summary
  - High-level overview
  - Key takeaways
- Getting started
  - Setting up the development environment
  - Cloning the repository
  - Installing dependencies
- Application architecture
  - High-level overview of the application structure
  - Detailed description of each component

- Building and deploying the application
  - Building for different environments
  - Deployment options
  - Best practices
- Troubleshooting and maintenance
  - Common problems and solutions
  - Upgrading the application
  - Maintenance tasks
- Conclusion
  - Main points of the document
  - Additional context or background information
- Appendices
  - References and external resources
  - Glossary of terms

Writing an outline for technical documentation can be a time-consuming task, but it's well worth the effort. A well-written outline will help ensure that the documentation is clear, concise, and easy to understand, which will save developers time and frustration and aid them in completing projects on time and to a high standard.

5.3.2 *Writing specific instructions*

Writing specific instructions for technical documentation can be a challenging task, but it's essential for ensuring that developers have the information they need to work efficiently and effectively. Specific instructions should be clear and concise, with no room for confusion. Use active voice, and be specific about what action should be taken and what the expected outcome should be.

Writing step-by-step instructions is an effective way to ensure that developers know exactly what to do and when to do it. Each step should be clearly numbered, and the instructions should be presented in a logical order. When giving instructions, be as specific as possible. Instead of saying "configure the settings," say "configure the settings in the config.txt file." It's also a good idea to include screenshots or diagrams to help illustrate the instructions. The following list includes an example of step-by-step instructions for a developer to pull a Docker image:

1 Open a command line interface (CLI) on your local machine.
2 Make sure you have Docker installed by running the command `docker -version`. If the command runs successfully and you can see the version of Docker, that means you have installed Docker.
3 Search for the image on the Docker Hub registry by running the command `docker search <image_name>`, where "image_name" is the name of the image you want to pull.

4 Once you've found the image you want to use, pull it down to your local machine by running the command `docker pull <image_name>`.

5 Verify that the image has been pulled successfully by running the command `docker images` and checking that the image is listed.

In the previous example, notice that I have the code for the developer to execute in a different font to clearly define the executable instructions versus the documentation text. This makes it easy for a developer to copy and paste the code into the CLI of their choice, which saves time and reduces misspellings due to human error. You want to make sure that you write in full sentences, and be as descriptive as possible.

Along with the specific instructions, it's a good idea to include tips and best practices to help developers work more efficiently and effectively. You could include tips on how to troubleshoot common problems or best practices for working with certain tools or technologies. Examples and use cases are effective ways to illustrate how the instructions and best practices should be used. These can clarify the instructions and make it easier for developers to understand how the instructions apply to their specific situations.

Before publishing the documentation, it's important to test the instructions to ensure that they are accurate and complete. Have other developers who aren't familiar with the content follow the instructions and provide feedback to ensure that the instructions are accurate, clear, and easy to follow. That way, you know that the documentation that is available to the entire team is targeted to the right audience and will help set them up for success.

5.3.3 *Getting right to the point*

When it comes to technical documentation, it's important to get right to the point. Not only is this approach more efficient, but it also helps to ensure that the instructions are clear and easy to follow. One of the biggest problems with poor technical documentation is that it can be overly wordy. This can make it difficult for readers to understand what is being asked of them and can even lead to confusion and frustration. Consider the instructions in table 5.3 for setting up a new software development environment.

As you can see, the clear and concise version is much easier to understand and follow. It eliminates any unnecessary information and gets straight to the point. In contrast, the overly wordy version includes too much information. You must strike a balance between providing specific instructions and keeping them short enough that the content is easily consumable. I hate to break it to you, but most developers will skim your documentation looking for the key instructions that they need to get the job done. When you include too much information, this will slow the reader down and cause confusion.

When writing technical documentation, lead developers need to be clear and concise. By getting right to the point and eliminating any unnecessary information, you can make the instructions easy to understand and follow. This will ultimately save time and lead to a more efficient and effective development process.

Table 5.3 Overly wordy documentation vs. clear and concise documentation

Overly wordy documentation	Clear and concise documentation
To properly set up your new development environment, you'll need to first install the necessary software components. This includes the latest version of the programming language that you'll be using, as well as any associated libraries and frameworks. Once these components have been installed, you'll then need to configure your environment to properly connect to any necessary external dependencies. This may include setting up access to a remote database or configuring your environment to use a specific version control system. Finally, you'll need to run any necessary tests to ensure that your environment is properly set up and configured.	To set up your new development environment, install the programming language, libraries, and frameworks. Then, connect to the remote database. Finally, run tests to ensure everything is working properly.

5.3.4 Using a style guide

When it comes to technical documentation, having a consistent and clear writing style is crucial for ensuring that your readers can easily understand and use the information you provide. One of the most effective ways to achieve this consistency is by using a *style guide*, which is a set of guidelines for writing and formatting documents. It typically includes rules for grammar, punctuation, and word usage, as well as recommendations for document structure and layout. By adhering to a style guide, writers can ensure that their documents are clear, consistent, and easy to read. Two of the most widely used style guides for technical documentation are those provided by Google (https://developers.google.com/style) and Microsoft (https://learn.microsoft.com/en-us/style-guide/welcome). Both guides are designed to help writers create clear and consistent documentation, but they do have some key differences.

The Google developer documentation style guide is focused on helping writers create clear and concise documentation that is easy to understand. It includes rules for grammar, punctuation, and word usage, as well as recommendations for document structure and layout. The guide includes guidelines for writing for different audiences and for different types of documents.

The Microsoft Writing Style Guide is designed to help writers create documentation that is both clear and professional. It includes rules for grammar, punctuation, and word usage, as well as recommendations for document structure and layout. The guide also includes guidelines for writing for different audiences and for different types of documents, and it also puts emphasis on the importance of accessibility and inclusivity in language usage.

Both guides are comprehensive and provide a wealth of information for writers. However, the Google guide is more focused on clarity and concision, while the Microsoft guide puts more emphasis on professionalism and accessibility. If your organization focuses on Microsoft technologies and programming languages such as .NET, you'll want to use the Microsoft style guide; otherwise, use the Google style guide.

Using a style guide for technical documentation is essential for ensuring that your documents are clear, consistent, and easy to understand. Whichever style guide you choose, it will help you create high-quality, user-friendly documentation that your readers will appreciate.

5.4   *Implementing a documentation maintenance cycle*

As a lead developer, you understand the importance of keeping your codebase up to date and maintainable. The same principle applies to technical documentation. A documentation maintenance cycle is a regular process of reviewing, updating, and improving technical documentation. This ensures that the documentation remains accurate, user-friendly, and easy to understand.

Keep in mind that technical documentation isn't a one-time task. As the codebase evolves, so too should the documentation. Keeping documentation up-to-date is crucial for maintaining the efficiency and productivity of your team. When documentation is outdated, developers may spend more time trying to understand the codebase and troubleshoot problems, which can lead to delays and mistakes. The documentation review process should include testing the documentation, soliciting feedback, and publishing regular updates.

It's essential to keep technical documentation up to date to ensure that developers have access to accurate and relevant information. Outdated documentation can lead to confusion, errors, and inefficiencies, as users may rely on inaccurate information. Additionally, technology solutions are continually evolving and improving, so keeping documentation up-to-date ensures that users have access to the latest features and functionalities. Regularly updating technical documentation also demonstrates a commitment to quality, which can improve user satisfaction and promote customer loyalty.

5.4.1   *Testing the documentation*

As a lead developer, you know how important it is to ensure that your code is thoroughly tested and working correctly before it's released to users. But did you know that it's just as important to test your technical documentation? Testing technical documentation helps ensure that it's accurate, easy to understand, and user-friendly. This is especially crucial for developers, as clear and accurate documentation can save a significant amount of time and effort when it comes to understanding and implementing new features or troubleshooting problems. So how can you go about testing your technical documentation?

Make sure to test the documentation in the same environment where it will be used. This will help you identify any problems or inaccuracies that may arise when the documentation is being used in a real-world scenario. If problems are found, it's important to update the documentation to address these problems before it's published to the whole team. This will avoid miscommunication and confusion due to inaccurate instructions.

You should also ask anyone who tests your documentation to list any errors they encountered that were environmental, but for which the instructions in the documentation were correct. These types of errors should be included at the end of the document in a section for "Known Issues" or "FAQs." I've worked for many companies that attempted to provide every full-time developer with the same exact local development environment, but contractors had different environments because their equipment wasn't provided by the company. If this is the case in your organization, you should have at least one contractor test your documentation so that any error they may encounter is covered.

There are several automation tools available that can help you test your documentation, such as Doxygen. These tools can automatically check for syntax errors, broken links, and other problems that may arise. They can save a lot of time if you use them before you even have anyone else test your document. You should also use a spelling and grammar tool such as Grammarly to ensure that your documentation is written properly. This is especially important when you work with people who don't speak English as a first language. I like to avoid using contractions, and I keep in mind that the English language is hard to learn. Wherever possible, have nonnative English speakers test your documentation to ensure that it's accessible to them.

Testing technical documentation is just as important as testing the code itself. By following these best practices, you can help ensure that your documentation is accurate, user-friendly, and easy to understand, which will save time and effort for developers and end users alike. Remember that clear and accurate documentation is essential for successful development and user experience. So always take the time to test and improve your technical documentation.

5.4.2 Getting feedback

When it comes to technical documentation, feedback can be especially valuable. It can help you identify inaccuracies, areas that are unclear, or even areas where the documentation could be improved in terms of usability. By incorporating this feedback, you can help ensure that your documentation is accurate, user-friendly, and easy to understand. But how do you go about getting this feedback?

When asking for feedback, make sure you're asking the right questions. For example, you might ask "Is this documentation clear and easy to understand?" or "Did you find everything you were looking for in the documentation?" Some people need a prompt so that they know what type of feedback you're looking for and how best they can help. You can add these prompts using collaboration tools for your documentation such as Confluence, Microsoft Word, Google Docs, or GitHub.

You should also aim to get feedback from different stakeholders, as they can provide different perspectives on your documentation. This may include feedback from other developers, QA testers, project managers, or end users that can help you identify different problems. Each person has a different perspective based on their role, so you may get varied opinions. Keep in mind that feedback, even if it may not be directly applicable, may be beneficial. If feedback from an end user isn't applicable to the technical documentation, it could still be useful for improving the user experience. In these cases, it's important to keep an open mind and consider the feedback in the context of the overall user experience. For example, if an end user suggests a feature that isn't currently in the documentation, it could be an indication that the feature is missing from the codebase as well.

Getting feedback on your technical documentation is an important part of the development process. By asking the right questions and being open to feedback, you can help ensure that your documentation is accurate, user-friendly, and easy to understand. Remember that feedback is an ongoing process, and you should be prepared to iterate and improve as needed. Keep in mind that feedback can be beneficial even if it may not be directly applicable—it could be an indication of areas that need improvement in other aspects of the project.

5.4.3   *Setting a documentation maintenance window*

Even the best documentation can become outdated or inaccurate if it's not properly maintained. That's where a documentation maintenance window comes in. A *documentation maintenance window* is a dedicated time during which the team can focus on updating, reviewing, and improving the project's documentation. This can include tasks such as fixing typos, updating code samples, and ensuring that the documentation is still accurate and relevant.

To form a successful documentation maintenance plan, you should schedule regular maintenance windows. Depending on the size and complexity of your project, it may make sense to schedule maintenance windows on a weekly or monthly basis. This will help ensure that the documentation stays up to date and that small problems are addressed before they become big problems. Most of the documentation that I've written was updated at least quarterly or after a large update. It helps to put a reminder in your team's calendar so that you don't forget these important updates.

During the maintenance window, assign specific tasks to team members to ensure that all areas of the documentation are covered. One team member could focus on code samples, while another could focus on user documentation. As a lead developer, you should learn how to delegate responsibilities to others so that you're not overworked. This has the added benefit of empowering your team to take on new tasks and learn new skills to help them level up their careers.

You can also use documentation tools such as Docusaurus, Read the Docs, or MkDocs to manage the documentation process. These tools make it easy to collaborate on documentation, track changes, and ensure that the documentation is always up to date. If those tools aren't available to you, there are also good collaboration features in Microsoft Word and Google Docs, which are commonly used in organizations.

It's a good idea to measure and track progress by keeping a record of the tasks that were completed during each maintenance window. This will help the team see what has been accomplished and identify areas where additional work is needed. I like to use a changelog or release notes to list all changes that have been made to technical documentation. You can even incorporate these changes into the release notes for a deployment.

Having a documentation maintenance window is an essential part of any software development project. By scheduling regular maintenance windows, assigning specific tasks to team members, and using documentation tools, you can ensure that your project's documentation stays accurate, relevant, and up-to-date. By following these tips, you can create a successful documentation maintenance plan that will help your team work more efficiently and effectively.

5.5 Case study

Edidiong Asikpo is a senior developer advocate based in Lagos, Nigeria. She is passionate about sharing her knowledge of DevOps through technical articles, videos, and social media. Edidiong has given more than 100 talks at tech events worldwide and continues to play a significant role in building developer communities in Africa. She is a Certified Kubernetes Application Developer and an open source contributor. When she's not doing anything tech-related, she travels across the world, takes beautiful pictures, and analyzes movies. In this case study, Edidiong shares her experience with technical documentation and provides advice for writing and maintaining documentation.

5.5.1 How has writing proper documentation helped you set your team up for success?

When I worked as a developer advocate at Hashnode, we didn't have product documentation. This led our users to be unaware of certain features or how to implement the ones they were aware of. To solve this, users often contacted us via Discord to ask questions and share their concerns. But as a small team, we could answer only so many questions while trying to complete our normal day-to-day tasks. So we decided to create documentation to address this problem!

Creating this documentation didn't just set up our team for success, but it also gave our users and community members a one-stop place to find every piece of information they needed about Hashnode. They no longer had to wait for minutes or hours to get a response, and we (the team) no longer had to spend hours of our day responding to questions via Discord or retyping responses we had already shared with someone else the previous week. The documentation also eliminated confusion within the team—if you were unsure about the right answer to give a user about a question, you could head over to the documentation to read about it before reverting to the user.

Another example of how writing proper documentation helped me set up my team for success was when I worked as a software engineer in the Developer Relations team at Interswitch. For context, Interswitch is the biggest fintech company in Africa, so there were over 300 people in the company. One of the negative effects of having so many people in a company is that sometimes two teams could be working on the same thing without knowing this. For us, it was APIs. Several teams would build APIs that did the same thing or almost the same thing. This significantly affected our documentation and the developer experience of external developers integrating with our APIs.

We needed to fix this, and we knew having better documentation was the first step to take. So we set up meetings with all engineering managers, compiled all those APIs, merged the ones that were similar, and ensured every team took responsibility for updating their documentation when a change was made to the API. In addition to this, we also added a brief description of each API so that developers could quickly find the right API, as well as code snippets of how to implement these APIs with several programming languages. In summary, this updated documentation and structure of updating made our APIs more discoverable and easier to keep up to date and increased the sales we made as a company.

5.5.2 Have you received feedback from other developers about your documentation? Did they suggest any improvements, and what were the suggestions?

Yes, I have. During the process of updating the Interswitch API documentation, we would reach out to external and internal developers and ask them for feedback on what we could do or improve. One of the feedback items they shared was regarding the outdatedness of the documentation in relation to the APIs. So we thought through some possible solutions and decided to use a tool called Swagger, which allowed us to automatically publish an update to the documentation when the codebase of the API was updated through the deployment pipeline. This completely removed the forgetfulness of humans to update the documentation when the API was changed, and it ensured that the API was always up-to-date.

Another feedback they shared was how the API documentation wasn't properly organized based on the different types of APIs. To solve this, we adopted a tool called Readme to make it easier to collaborate with all engineering teams and add as many code snippets as possible to ensure every developer had a good developer experience while using our documentation and APIs. Making the documentation open source also allowed external developers to contribute to the documentation as well.

5.5.3 What if someone has never written technical documentation before? What is your advice to help them get started?

Five things: Take a course. Read more. Follow a style guide. Understand the goal of the documentation. Always proofread before publishing:

1 I always recommend taking a course first because it enables you to discover several things to do when writing technical documentation. I highly recommend the technical writing course by Google. It was written by some of the best technical writers and developers in the industry. The great thing about this course is that it's free. So you don't have to spend anything to learn how to write better technical documentation.

2 Reading is essential because it will help you enrich your vocabulary, keep you abreast of current trends, help you discover what's going on in the writing world, and also keep the spirit of writing alive. This quote by Lisa See, "Read a thousand

books, and your words will flow like a river," says it all. The more you read other technical documentation or articles, the better you'll be able to express yourself or structure your documentation in a better way.

3 Technical writing isn't like any other form of writing. There are specific rules and formatting to think about. Following a style guide will help define things like when to use sentence case versus title case and writing introductions and summaries. Both Google and Microsoft have style guides that are industry standard and good to start with.

4 Before you begin writing, think through what you're going to write. What is the purpose of the documentation? Is it explaining a process or answering a specific question? If it's the latter, you want to make sure the documentation only answers the question without any extra information that would be distracting. An example would be someone searching for information about how to center a `div` in HTML. You just want to give them the code they need, instead of beating around the bush.

5 My final piece of advice is that when you finish writing the documentation, don't publish it right away. Take an hour or so and do other things, and then come back and read it again. That helps you notice things that maybe you could have crafted better, aren't necessary, or that you need to add. You should read your documentation thinking about the reader's mindset and what they need to accomplish. Doing all these things and taking into account the readers' perspective will help you write outstanding technical documentation.

5.5.4 Have you used any AI tools for writing technical documentation, and what was the result?

Almost everyone is talking about AI and its effect these days. Companies have incorporated AI into their tools, developers use AI to improve their development workflow, and technical writers use it to create articles and documents. Here are some AI tools I use for writing:

- *Grammarly*—It's excellent for many things. It helps you correct grammatical errors, suggests ways to update the tone of your message to reach your target audience, and checks if the content is plagiarized (assuming someone else wrote a document for you and you want to confirm it's brand new before payment). Grammarly is that tool!

- *ChatGPT*—I've used this much more often, especially to shorten messages or make them more understandable. It also helps generate code snippets, suggest content topics, and explain concepts I don't understand like I'm five, which gives me the context I need to write a documentation in a better way.

- *Inkeep*—To improve the developer experience on our documentation, we've added Inkeep's new documentation search and AI assistance to our documentation site. This enables our users to quickly search for relevant documentation and get AI-powered aid to common questions.

- *WriterAI*—I haven't used it personally yet, but a colleague of mine did try it and sent me a document to review, and it was pretty impressive.

Summary

- Proper technical documentation leads to a clear understanding of the codebase, consistency, readability, maintainability, efficient problem resolution, and improved long-term maintainability.

- Lack of documentation can lead to a lack of understanding of the codebase, lack of consistency, difficulty reading and updating the code, delays and mistakes in problem resolution, loss of decisions over time, and increased technical debt and maintenance costs.

- Documentation not only helps new team members understand how things are done within your organization but also serves as a valuable reference for experienced developers when they encounter a problem or need to troubleshoot a problem.

- Clear and well-organized technical documentation can make it easier for new developers to identify and fix bugs by providing detailed information about the code, how it's working, and known problems, which can help reduce onboarding time and make the process smoother and more efficient for everyone involved.

- Technical documentation should be structured to make it easy for developers to quickly find the information they need by using proper headings, an introduction and summary, visual aids, code samples, and case studies.

- Writing an outline is an important step in creating technical documentation, as it's a road map that helps organize the information and present it in a logical and easy-to-follow manner.

- Testing and revising technical documentation are just as important as testing the code. These involve getting feedback from users, testing the documentation in the same environment that it will be used, asking for any known problems, and incorporating the feedback during a documentation maintenance window.

Optimizing the
development process

6

This chapter covers

- Workflow and project management with and without proper optimization
- Pain points in development processes
- Suggesting improvements using best communication practices
- Being open to constructive feedback
- Automation opportunities and the best tools
- Optimizing processes to reduce technical debt

The development process refers to the series of steps and tasks involved in creating a new product or feature, from ideation to delivery. This process includes everything from conceptualizing an idea to testing, refining, and ultimately launching the final product. The development process can vary depending on the nature of the product or service being created, the team working on it, and the resources available. It's a complex and iterative process that involves several steps. The first step is market research, where the product team identifies a need in the market and gathers information about customer preferences and behavior. This information is used to inform the design of the product. The design phase involves creating a blueprint for the product, including its features, functionality, and user interface. Once the design is complete, prototyping begins. This involves creating a rough product model to test its feasibility and get user feedback. Developers work with the project team as product development progresses to develop, test, and debug the application. Quality assurance is an important step because this is where the product is tested thoroughly to ensure it meets the necessary standards. Finally, the product is deployed or launched to the market. Deployments may involve an initial release followed by updates as customer feedback informs the product's development. Throughout the entire process, feedback is collected and incorporated to improve the product and ensure it meets the needs of its users. The development process is critical to the success of a product or service, as it ensures that the final product meets the needs and expectations of its users while being feasible to produce and maintain. Figure 6.1 illustrates the six stages of the development process.

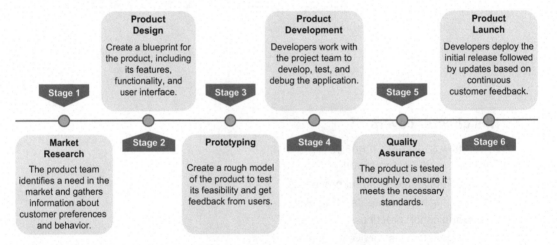

Figure 6.1   The six stages of the development process

The importance of a well-defined development process can't be overstated. A well-structured development process ensures that all stakeholders are aligned, project goals and timelines are clear, and tasks are completed efficiently and effectively. An optimized development process also helps teams avoid common roadblocks and pitfalls, such as scope creep, delays, and miscommunication. There are several key benefits to optimizing the development process, including the following:

- *Improved efficiency*—Optimizing the development process helps teams work more efficiently and reduces the time it takes to complete tasks and deliver high-quality products.

- *Increased collaboration*—A well-optimized development process fosters better collaboration among team members and helps ensure everyone works together effectively.
- *Enhanced quality*—Optimizing the development process helps teams focus on delivering high-quality products and reducing the number of bugs and errors.
- *Improved project management*—A well-optimized development process makes it easier for teams to manage projects, track progress, and make course corrections when necessary.

Optimizing the development process is essential for delivering high-quality products and ensuring that teams work efficiently and effectively. A well-defined and optimized development process helps teams align on project goals, avoid common roadblocks, and focus on delivering the best possible product to customers.

6.1 Identifying opportunities for process improvement

Lead developers play a critical role in ensuring that the development process runs smoothly and efficiently. By identifying opportunities to improve the process, they can help their teams work more effectively, deliver better results, and ultimately improve the quality of the products they produce. An optimized development process can mean the difference between delivering projects on time and within budget versus missing deadlines, producing low-quality products, and running over budget.

For example, consider two organizations: one with an optimized development process and another with a process that hasn't been optimized. In an organization with an optimized process, project deadlines are more likely to be met because the team has a clear road map and a streamlined process for success. This means that they can deliver high-quality products on time and within budget, leading to greater customer satisfaction and a stronger reputation. On the other hand, an organization with an inefficient development process may miss project deadlines, leading to decreased customer satisfaction and lost revenue. Product quality may also suffer due to rushed development, limited testing, and a lack of attention to detail. This can lead to losing trust in the organization and reduced customer loyalty.

Team morale is another important factor to consider. In an optimized development process, the team feels confident and supported, leading to higher morale and greater productivity. However, in an organization with an inefficient process, team members may feel frustrated, overwhelmed, and unsupported.

Optimizing the development process provides greater flexibility for organizations to respond to changes in the market. Organizations can quickly adapt to new trends and customer demands by streamlining the development process. This allows them to stay ahead of the competition and remain industry leaders. In contrast, an inefficient process may limit an organization's ability to respond to changes in the market, putting them at a disadvantage.

I've worked for many different types of organizations with various levels of development process optimization. One of the worst jobs I ever had involved a management team that expected project managers and developers to act as QA and perform all the testing tasks. I can't stress this enough: QA professionals have specific skills, and they are an integral part of the team. Proper testing practices aren't followed or documented without them, and chaos ensues. When I worked for organizations that included proper QA, project teams could preemptively find and fix problems before they went to production. This made our clients and customers happy with the quality of our work. We retained a lot more business and were able to hire top talent due to our excellent reputation.

By taking the time to evaluate and improve the process continuously, lead developers can help their teams work smarter, not harder. This leads to greater job satisfaction, improved morale, and a stronger sense of teamwork among the development team. A well-optimized development process is a win-win for everyone involved, so it's worth taking the time to identify and act on opportunities for improvement.

6.1.1   Recognizing pain points

The development process can be challenging and demanding. Producing high-quality products that meet users' needs requires a great deal of effort, attention to detail, and dedication. However, despite our best efforts, pain points often arise during the process that can negatively affect our ability to achieve these goals. *Pain points* are areas of difficulty, frustration, or dissatisfaction that arise during a process.

One of the most common pain points that developers experience is the lack of clear direction or communication. When project goals aren't clearly defined or there is a lack of communication between team members, it can lead to confusion, missed deadlines, and increased costs. To address this problem, it's important to establish clear lines of communication, set achievable project goals, and hold regular meetings to keep everyone on the same page.

Another pain point that many developers experience is a lack of proper tools and human resources. When teams don't have access to the development tools needed to do their jobs effectively, it can cause team members to become frustrated and burned out. A lack of development tools can result in inefficient processes that produce poor-quality products that don't meet users' needs. To resolve this problem, it's essential to research and invest in the right tools and resources continually and to provide ongoing training and support to help developers stay up-to-date with the latest technologies and best practices. It's also important to ensure that the developers on your team aren't overworked. You can achieve this by working with project managers to manage their tasks regularly. Table 6.1 contains valuable information on how to recognize and address common pain points.

Table 6.1 How to recognize and address common pain points

Pain point	Symptom	Result	Solution
Lack of clear direction or communication	Decreased productivity and efficiency	Confusion and mis-communication among team members	Establish clear lines of communication, set achievable project goals, and hold regular meetings.
Lack of proper tools	Poor quality products	Subpar products that don't meet the needs of users	Continually research and invest in the right tools.
Lack of proper human resources	Demotivated and disengaged team members	Frustration and burnout among team members	Provide ongoing training and support, and work with project management to ensure developers aren't overworked.
Decreased customer satisfaction	Reduction in future business opportunities	Negative effect on the reputation of the organization	Produce high-quality products by addressing all pain points.

I've frequently encountered one pain point throughout my career: lack of clear direction or communication. Communication skills are imperative for any leader, and as a lead developer, you must ensure that everyone is on the same page to improve productivity and motivate your team. Miscommunication often occurs when you think you don't have the time to have important conversations or you assume that everyone is on task. You can't avoid having important or even difficult conversations with anyone you work with. It's up to you and the project manager to establish clear lines of communication both within the development team and with the project teams.

When pain points in the development process aren't addressed, the consequences can be significant and long-lasting. It's important to recognize and address these pain points in the development process because they can significantly affect our ability to produce high-quality products and services. Lead developers can also prioritize pain points by evaluating their effect on the development process and the product. By focusing on pain points that will have the greatest effect, you can make the most significant improvements with your available resources. In addition, you can use data and analytics to identify pain points and track the effectiveness of the solutions they implement. By improving communication, investing in the right tools and resources, and reducing technical debt, we can ensure that our development process is as efficient, productive, and enjoyable as possible.

6.1.2 *Providing ideas for improvement*

As a lead developer, you're in a unique position to drive your team's success. Not only are you responsible for delivering high-quality code, but you can suggest ways to improve the development process. The following list includes steps you can take to provide valuable ideas that will have a real effect:

- *Stay up-to-date.* Technology is constantly evolving, and staying on top of the latest trends and developments in your field is important. Attend conferences, read articles, and follow industry leaders on social media. Use this knowledge to identify new tools, techniques, and processes that could benefit your team.

- *Embrace change.* Change can be scary, but it's also essential for growth. Encourage your team to embrace new ideas and be open to trying new things. This can be as simple as experimenting with a new tool or as complex as changing the entire development process. Lead by example to show your team that you're willing to take risks and try new things.

- *Collaborate with other teams.* Collaborating with other teams within your organization can help you get a wider perspective on the development process. This can be especially valuable if your team is facing a specific challenge that another team has already overcome. Work with other leads to find common solutions and share best practices.

- *Focus on continuous improvement.* The development process is never perfect, and there's always room for improvement. Encourage your team to evaluate the process continuously and make changes as needed. Regular retrospectives and continuous improvement workshops can be great ways to gather feedback and identify areas for improvement.

It's essential to communicate your ideas for improving the development process clearly, be concise, and inspire your team. When presenting your ideas, make sure to highlight the benefits to the team and the organization. Explain how the changes will improve the development process and lead to better outcomes. You can also use visual aids to help explain your ideas, such as flowcharts, diagrams, and graphs. This can help make your ideas more engaging and easier to understand.

Encourage open and honest feedback from your team. This can help you refine your ideas and ensure that they are well received. Show your team how passionate you are about the ideas you're presenting. Your enthusiasm will be contagious and will help get your team on board. Always make sure that your ideas are clearly communicated and that everyone understands what is expected of them. Be sure to follow up with regular updates to make sure everyone knows what's going on.

Effective communication is key to making meaningful changes, so take the time to make your ideas as clear and effectual as possible. Leading by example and providing valuable ideas for improvement are excellent ways to motivate your team and inspire them. By embracing change, collaborating with other teams, and focusing on continual improvement, you can help your team deliver better results and achieve their full potential.

6.1.3   *Using AI coding tools*

In recent years, the landscape of software development has been significantly transformed by the advent of AI-powered coding tools. Among the most notable of these is GitHub Copilot, an AI code assistant developed by OpenAI in collaboration with

GitHub. Powered by the GPT-4 architecture, Copilot is designed to assist developers by suggesting code snippets, autocompleting lines of code, and even generating entire functions based on contextual cues within the development environment. However, Copilot isn't alone in this space; several other tools have emerged, each with unique capabilities to enhance developer productivity. Table 6.2 lists the most popular AI coding tools available.

Table 6.2 Most popular AI coding tools

Name	Description
GitHub Copilot	As one of the pioneers in AI coding assistance, Copilot integrates seamlessly with Visual Studio Code (VS Code) and other popular editors. It uses machine learning models trained on vast amounts of open source code to provide intelligent code suggestions and completions. Copilot excels in enhancing productivity by reducing the amount of boilerplate code developers need to write and helping with syntax and language nuances.
Tabnine	Tabnine supports a wide range of programming languages and integrates with multiple IDEs. Tabnine's strength lies in its ability to learn from the specific codebase it's applied to, providing more contextually relevant suggestions as it adapts to the project's style and patterns.
Kite	Kite offers intelligent code completions and documentation lookups within the developer's editor. It emphasizes speed and privacy by running its AI models locally on the developer's machine. Kite supports popular languages such as Python, JavaScript, and Go, making it a versatile choice for many developers.
IntelliCode	Microsoft's IntelliCode integrates with Visual Studio and VS Code, providing AI-assisted recommendations based on best practices and patterns observed in high-quality codebases. IntelliCode enhances code reviews and encourages the adoption of standard coding conventions.

The introduction of AI coding tools has been a game-changer for many developers, significantly boosting productivity in several ways. AI tools can generate repetitive code structures, allowing developers to focus on more complex and creative aspects of their projects. By providing suggestions that adhere to best practices, AI tools help maintain a higher standard of code quality and consistency across teams. AI-powered autocompletion and instant code suggestions accelerate the coding process, enabling developers to write code faster and with fewer interruptions. For junior developers or those learning a new language, AI tools act as mentors, offering guidance and code examples that facilitate quicker learning and understanding.

Despite their benefits, AI coding tools aren't without their challenges and potential problems. As a lead developer, you may need to provide arguments against AI coding tools if upper management is focused on using these tools to save money. Developers might become overly dependent on AI suggestions, potentially undermining their ability to write code independently or think critically about their implementations. AI models trained on public code repositories might inadvertently suggest insecure or outdated coding practices, posing security risks if not carefully reviewed. AI tools can sometimes produce incorrect or suboptimal code suggestions, especially in complex or unique scenarios where the training data doesn't adequately cover edge cases.

While AI tools offer substantial support, human intervention remains crucial in several scenarios. AI-generated code should always be reviewed by experienced developers to ensure correctness, security, and adherence to project-specific requirements. Human creativity and expertise are irreplaceable for intricate algorithms, novel problem-solving approaches, and innovative software design. Developers must consider the broader context and potential implications of their code, something that AI tools aren't yet equipped to understand fully. AI tools aren't a replacement for human expertise and oversight. Striking the right balance between using AI assistance and applying human judgment is key to maximizing the benefits of these tools while mitigating their potential drawbacks. As the technology evolves, it will be fascinating to see how these tools continue to shape the future of software development.

6.1.4   *Managing the development process*

Managing the development process is critical to any organization's success, as it ensures that work is completed efficiently and effectively. In development, process management refers to the systematic approach of designing, executing, controlling, and monitoring development processes. It involves defining the steps involved in a process, ensuring that they are followed consistently, and improving the process over time.

If you have a well-defined development process in place, work can be completed more efficiently and with fewer errors. Properly defining and communicating the development process encourages collaboration and communication among team members. As each step in the process is defined and monitored, work is completed to a high standard and meets the users' needs. When lead developers continuously review and improve the development process, organizations can find new and more efficient working methods. Applying process management to a development process involves the following steps:

1 *Define the development process.* Defining the development process should include all the steps involved in taking a project from start to finish, including requirements gathering, design, coding, testing, and deployment. To help you define the development process, gather feedback from the development team, other managers, QA, and project teams. Everyone involved in the development process has equally valid expertise that you should rely on.

2 *Document the process.* Once the development process has been defined, it's important to document the process so that it can be easily referenced and followed. We'll discuss this topic in detail later in this chapter.

3 *Communicate the process.* To communicate the development process to the team, hold a meeting to introduce the process and ensure everyone understands it. You can make a formal presentation or walk the team through the documentation that you've created.

4 *Assign roles and responsibilities.* Assign clear roles and responsibilities to each team member so that everyone knows what their part in the process is. Lead developers shouldn't be solely responsible for managing processes. You need to use the entire team's expertise to form effective processes.

5 *Establish deadlines.* Establish clear deadlines for each step in the process so that everyone knows when work needs to be completed. Maintain a calendar and set reminders for anyone contributing to forming, documenting, and maintaining the development process.

6 *Encourage collaboration.* Encourage team members to collaborate and communicate regularly to ensure that everyone is on the same page. Lead developers should empower their team to seek out the people who possess the information they need by introducing them to other teams and providing a contact list for all stakeholders involved in the development process. That way, they can take it upon themselves to reach out when they need help.

7 *Use tools to manage the process.* Consider using tools such as project management software or version control systems such as GitHub to help manage the process and keep everyone on track. Some popular project management systems include Jira, Trello, Asana, and Microsoft Project.

8 *Regularly review and update the process.* Review the development process regularly, and make changes as needed to ensure that it continues to be effective and efficient. We'll discuss this topic further later in this chapter.

Process management is a critical aspect of successful development. By following these steps, you can apply process management to your development process and ensure that work is completed efficiently and effectively. Having a clear and well-defined process in place can help your team work together more efficiently and deliver high-quality results.

6.2 Receiving feedback

As a lead developer, receiving feedback from the project team during the development process is essential. This feedback on the development process can help to ensure that the final product meets the needs and expectations of all parties involved, leading to better outcomes for everyone. Stakeholders' feedback helps facilitate open and honest communication between teams while maintaining the development process. Feedback allows lead developers to understand the needs and expectations of stakeholders, and it allows stakeholders to understand the constraints and limitations of the development process. This improved communication can lead to better collaboration and a more efficient development process.

Feedback from stakeholders can help lead developers make informed decisions about the development process. For example, stakeholders may provide insight into the needs of the end users, which can inform design and functionality decisions. This information can help lead developers make better decisions that result in a product that meets the needs of all parties involved. By receiving feedback from stakeholders, lead developers can then adjust their approach to make the development process more efficient and productive.

6.2.1 *Interviewing stakeholders*

As a lead developer, it's important to understand the perspectives and needs of all stakeholders involved in the development process. This means reaching out to not only developers but also nondevelopers who are affected by the software being created. Developers are key players in the development process, but they don't always completely understand the goals, constraints, and challenges that stakeholders face. On the other hand, nondevelopers may not have the skills necessary to write code, but they have a deep understanding of the technology, business requirements, customer needs, and how the software fits into the larger organization.

By gathering insights from both developers and nondevelopers, you can create a more comprehensive view of the development process and identify opportunities to improve it. This could mean optimizing workflows, reducing the time it takes to launch new features, or creating better collaboration between teams. The following list includes example questions to ask developers and nondevelopers when looking to improve the development process:

- Developers:
  - What are the biggest challenges you face when developing software?
  - What tools or processes would make your job easier?
  - How do you collaborate with other teams in the organization?
  - How do you stay informed about the latest technologies and trends in software development?
- Nondevelopers:
  - What are the most important considerations when developing software for your team or department?
  - How do you measure the success of software projects?
  - How do you prioritize competing demands for resources and time?
  - What are the biggest pain points in the current development process?

By asking these questions and listening to the answers, you can gain valuable insights to help you improve the development process. With a more comprehensive view of the needs and perspectives of all stakeholders, you can create better software that meets the needs of the business and delivers value to customers.

6.2.2 *Being open to constructive criticism*

Constructive criticism is a type of feedback that focuses on improving an individual's or team's performance. It's an essential tool for personal and professional growth, and it's especially crucial in the software development industry. As a lead developer, you play a critical role in managing the development process and ensuring that your team delivers high-quality products. In this role, you must be open to constructive criticism, as it can provide valuable insights into areas that need improvement.

When receiving constructive criticism, it's important to approach it with an open mind and not take it personally. The goal of this feedback is to help you and your team grow and improve, and it's not meant to be an attack on your abilities. Instead, it's an opportunity to learn and make positive changes. One of the benefits of constructive criticism is that it can help you identify weaknesses and areas for improvement that you may not have otherwise noticed. By accepting and incorporating feedback, you can make changes that can increase productivity, improve problem-solving skills, and create better results.

When you're open to constructive criticism, you set a positive example for your team. When team members see that their leader is willing to listen to feedback and make changes, they are more likely to be open to it themselves. This can create a culture of continuous improvement, where everyone is encouraged to grow and learn. An example of constructive criticism I once received from a manager was "Your presentation was well-organized and clear, but I think you could improve by incorporating more visuals to help illustrate your points." Constructive criticism highlights specific areas for improvement while also offering suggestions for how to make those improvements. The feedback is offered in a respectful and constructive manner, with the ultimate goal of helping the person improve their presentation skills.

I used to take it personally when I received constructive criticism, and I viewed it as an attack on my skills and abilities. I would continue to struggle, and I was afraid to ask questions, so my work would often take much longer than expected. After a co-worker recognized this and suggested that I keep an open mind and not take things so personally, I began to incorporate improvements that were addressed in the feedback. I learned from others, including co-workers and people in the tech community from all levels and areas of expertise. They encouraged me to improve in certain areas, including studying the latest programming languages and tools we used to evolve the development process continually. I'm thankful that this happened because it's what led me to become a lead developer and, eventually, a manager.

Being open to constructive criticism is essential to your personal and professional growth, as well as to the success of your team. Don't be afraid to listen to feedback, embrace it, and use it to make positive changes. Remember, constructive criticism is a gift, and it's up to you to use that criticism to improve and grow.

6.2.3 *Keeping an open mind*

As a lead developer, you play a vital role in the software development process. It's crucial to keep an open mind when receiving feedback from both developers and non-developers, regardless of their skill level. This openness to feedback is important for personal and professional growth and can lead to better team results.

Receiving developer feedback can provide valuable insights into the development process and help you identify areas for improvement. Junior developers may have fresh perspectives and new ideas that can lead to innovative solutions. By being open to their feedback, you can foster a culture of growth and encourage the development of new skills.

Nondevelopers, such as project managers, clients, or stakeholders, can provide valuable feedback and suggestions that can improve the development process. By being open to their feedback, you can ensure that the process meets all stakeholders' needs and is understood by everyone involved.

Lead developers play a crucial role in the software development process, but it's important to remember that no one has all the answers. This is where checking your ego comes into play. As a lead developer, it's essential to have confidence in your abilities, but it's equally important to have the humility to acknowledge that you don't know everything and to be open to new ideas and perspectives.

One of the benefits of keeping your ego in check is that it opens the door to collaboration and teamwork. When you're willing to listen to others and learn from their experiences, you can work together to find the best solutions. This can lead to more innovative ideas, better problem-solving, and improved results for your team. Moreover, being open to feedback and new ideas can help you grow as a leader. By embracing new perspectives and approaches, you can broaden your skill set and become a more well-rounded leader. This leads to improved decision-making and better results for your team.

As a lead developer, you must keep an open mind and not think you have all the answers. By embracing feedback and new ideas, you can collaborate with others, grow as a leader, and ensure the success of your team. Remember, the best leaders are those who are open to learning and growth and who lead by example.

6.3   *Reviewing the software development lifecycle*

The development process refers to the overall process of creating a software product from idea to launch and beyond, including all the activities involved in the software's design, development, testing, and maintenance. On the other hand, the software development lifecycle (SDLC) is a more specific and structured approach to the development process. It outlines the steps or phases a software development team should follow to ensure the product meets quality standards, business objectives, and user requirements. The SDLC provides a road map for the development process, outlining the activities that need to be performed at each stage of the process.

The SDLC is a series of steps that a software development team takes to design, build, and maintain a software product. It outlines the process of creating a software product from idea to launch and beyond. The SDLC is a crucial aspect of software development and helps ensure that the product meets quality standards, business objectives, and user requirements.

Lead developers play a crucial role in the SDLC, as they oversee the entire process and ensure it runs smoothly. They must continually review the SDLC to identify areas for improvement and to ensure that it remains relevant to the changing needs of the software development industry. Figure 6.2 shows the six stages of the SDLC.

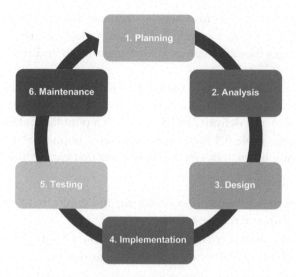

Figure 6.2
Software
development
lifecycle

There are several benefits to continuously reviewing and improving the SDLC. First, it helps to keep the process efficient and streamlined, reducing the risk of bottlenecks and delays. This can lead to faster project completion times, lower costs, and better customer satisfaction. Second, the process also helps to ensure that the development team is using the most up-to-date methods and techniques, which can improve the quality of the product. Third, reviewing and improving can keep the software development process relevant to the changing needs of the business and its customers, ensuring that the end product meets their evolving needs.

When the SDLC is never reviewed or updated, it can lead to several problems. The process may become outdated and inefficient, leading to delays and increased costs. The product may also be of lower quality and not meet the changing needs of the business and its customers. In addition, the software development team may be using outdated methods and techniques, limiting their ability to innovate and create new and exciting products.

The SDLC is a crucial development aspect and must be continuously reviewed and improved by lead developers. This helps to ensure that the process is efficient, effective, and relevant to the changing needs of the software development industry. By continually reviewing the SDLC, lead developers can help ensure that their development team produces high-quality products that meet the needs of the business and its customers.

6.3.1 Identifying opportunities for automation

As a lead developer, you play a critical role in ensuring the smooth functioning of the SDLC within an organization. One way to streamline the SDLC is by identifying opportunities for automation. Automating repetitive and manual tasks can save time, reduce errors, and improve overall efficiency.

The first step is to examine the current processes within your SDLC closely. Make a list of repetitive, manual, and time-consuming tasks. Examples include generating documentation, creating backups, and performing code reviews. These tasks are ideal candidates for automation. Ask your team to help you identify tasks that take time and resources. Discuss the challenges they face daily, and work together to find automation solutions.

There are many third-party tools available in the market that can help you automate tasks within the SDLC. For example, Jenkins is a popular open source tool that can be used for continuous integration and delivery, and Selenium is a popular tool for automating web application testing. Table 6.3 lists some of the most popular SDLC automation tools, and the following list includes examples of tasks that can be automated within the SDLC:

- *Code testing and deployment*—Automating code testing and deployment can help you reduce errors and improve release speed.
- *Continuous integration and delivery (CI/CD)*—Automating the CI/CD process can help you quickly and efficiently deliver new features to customers.
- *Reporting*—Automating report generation can save you time and reduce errors.
- *Backup and recovery*—Automating backup and recovery can help you quickly restore systems after a failure.

Table 6.3   SDLC automation tools

Tool	Purpose
Git	Version control and collaboration
Jenkins, Azure DevOps, GitLab CI/CD, GitHub Actions	Continuous integration and delivery
Selenium	Automated testing
Jira	Project management and bug tracking
Puppet, Chef, Ansible	Configuration management
Docker	Containerization
Gradle, Maven	Build automation
Microsoft Power BI, Tableau	Reporting automation
Microsoft Azure Backup, Veeam Backup & Replication	Automated backups and replication

By using automation tools, you can improve productivity and streamline your SDLC. These tools are constantly changing, so you must keep up with the latest updates and products by attending industry events, joining user groups, and being active in tech communities. When you integrate automation tools into your SDLC, you'll support your team's success and help them work smarter, not harder.

6.3.2   *Removing bottlenecks*

Software development is a complex process that involves many moving parts, and it's essential to keep everything flowing smoothly to ensure the success of a project. Unfortunately, bottlenecks can arise at any stage of the SDLC and can significantly affect the speed and quality of delivery. A *bottleneck* is anything that slows down or obstructs the progress of a project. In software development, bottlenecks can occur due to a lack of resources, conflicting priorities, and process inefficiencies. Whatever the cause, bottlenecks can significantly affect the delivery timeline, project budget, and overall product quality.

If a team lacks the necessary resources to complete a task, it can quickly become a bottleneck. In this situation, you can work with the project manager to allocate more resources to the project, such as hiring additional team members or outsourcing specific tasks. If this isn't possible, then the project plan must be revised so that the development team isn't overworked, which can cause burnout.

When different stakeholders have conflicting priorities, it can lead to a backlog of work and delay the delivery of the final product. To fix this bottleneck, it's essential to align the priorities of all stakeholders and ensure that everyone is working toward the same goals. Having conversations with the stakeholders, especially the project manager, will help you manage the backlog and get back on track.

Process inefficiencies are a major cause of bottlenecks and can arise from various sources, including outdated methodologies, manual processes, and poor communication. It's important to adopt modern methodologies, automate manual processes, and improve communication channels to fix process inefficiencies. However, sometimes, the lead developer can become a bottleneck in the development process, slowing down the entire team and affecting the final product's quality. That is why lead developers need to delegate tasks and remove themselves as a bottleneck in the SDLC.

First and foremost, delegation helps to distribute the workload more evenly, allowing the team to work more efficiently and effectively. Understanding your team's skills and abilities can help you delegate tasks effectively. This will help you identify which tasks each team member is most suited to and which tasks require your attention. You should also trust your team to get the job done, which will improve their confidence. Taking on too much responsibility can lead to burnout and negatively affect the team's morale. By delegating tasks, you can focus on the most critical aspects of the project, while others can tackle the smaller but still essential tasks.

Additionally, delegation helps develop other team members' skills and expertise. When lead developers delegate tasks, they allow team members to grow, learn new skills, and take on more responsibility. This not only helps the team work more efficiently but also builds a more capable team overall. However, delegation isn't just about shifting tasks from one person to another. It's also about creating a culture of trust and collaboration, where everyone is encouraged to contribute their ideas and expertise. When lead developers create an environment where everyone feels valued and their contributions are recognized and appreciated, this builds a more engaged and motivated team and reduces the likelihood of bottlenecks in the development process.

Removing bottlenecks is essential for the success of any software development project. Whether it's a lack of resources, conflicting priorities, process inefficiencies, or lack of delegation, it's important to identify and resolve bottlenecks quickly to ensure the smooth delivery of the final product. When you continually update your processes to remove bottlenecks by working with stakeholders and the development team, your projects will run more smoothly, and you'll achieve better results.

6.3.3 *Using a preventative versus reactionary approach*

Software development involves making a constant stream of decisions that affect the quality and maintainability of your codebase. Lead developers must take it upon themselves to take the correct approach to optimize the SDLC. Two common approaches are preventative and reactionary:

- *Preventative approach*—Preventative approaches to software development focus on avoiding problems before they occur. This can involve taking the time to design a solution that is scalable, maintainable, and adherent to best practices. Preventative approaches aim to reduce the risk of introducing technical debt and ensure that the codebase remains healthy over time.
- *Reactionary approach*—Reactionary approaches to software development focus on fixing problems as they arise. This can involve patching bugs, addressing security vulnerabilities, or refactoring code to make it more maintainable. Reactionary approaches aim to address problems quickly and efficiently but can lead to a codebase that is more complex and harder to maintain over time.

Using a preventative approach helps lead developers reduce technical debt. By taking the time to consider the long-term effect of their solutions, lead developers can make decisions that reduce the risk of introducing technical debt. This can involve considering scalability, maintainability, and best practices when designing a solution.

For example, lead developers can implement code review practices to catch problems early in the development process and prevent technical debt from accumulating. They can also encourage their team members to follow best practices and write clear, well-documented code. Lead developers can use tools to automate code analysis, such as code linters and automated testing frameworks, to help catch problems early and make code review more efficient.

> ### Preventative approach in action
>
> One of the problems I've seen throughout my career is a lack of proper maintenance, which causes systems to go down periodically. I once worked for an organization that favored a reactionary approach because they thought it saved time, as running maintenance tasks took too long. However, their clients often had the impression that they didn't build stable systems because they were always going down. When I took over as the lead developer on their flagship project, I took a preventative approach. I automated maintenance processes to run overnight, and I set email alerts so that I didn't have to check in on the processes manually. My changes improved productivity because we had far fewer emergencies to take care of. The clients were impressed with their systems' stability, and the organization adopted my preventative approach.

Using a preventative approach to software development is an effective way for lead developers to reduce technical debt and optimize the SDLC. By implementing best practices throughout the SDLC, lead developers can help ensure that their codebase remains healthy and efficient over time. Using a preventative approach will help ensure high client or stakeholder satisfaction as you provide high-quality systems.

6.4 Maintaining the development process

As a lead developer, it's essential to maintain the development process to ensure that your projects run smoothly and meet their goals. A well-structured development process not only saves time and effort but also helps maintain the project's quality and ensures that everyone involved is updated and aware.

Having a solid development process helps keep track of progress. Lead developers can easily monitor what has been accomplished, what is currently being worked on, and what still needs to be done. This enables them to make informed decisions about allocating resources and avoiding potential roadblocks.

Another crucial aspect of maintaining the development process is communication. A well-defined process promotes clear communication between team members, stakeholders, QA, and management. This helps ensure that everyone knows their responsibilities and that work is divided effectively. This reduces the risk of misunderstandings and conflicts and helps to keep projects moving forward.

Having a robust development process that includes the QA process can help lead developers identify and resolve problems more efficiently. By using a clear and organized approach, lead developers can quickly spot any problems that may arise and take corrective action before they become larger and more time-consuming. This allows the project to remain on track and avoid delays that can significantly affect the timeline and budget.

Maintaining the development process provides the project a sense of stability and reliability. This can help to build trust with stakeholders and increase their confidence in the team's ability to deliver quality work. Additionally, having a structured process in place can make it easier for new team members to join and become productive more quickly.

Maintaining the development process provides a road map for the project, promotes clear communication, helps identify and resolve problems, and provides stability and reliability. As a lead developer, you play a crucial role in ensuring that the development process remains robust and effective. Ensure that the development process is consistently updated and maintained, and it will pay off in the long run.

6.4.1 Documenting the development process

Lead developers play a critical role in software development and are responsible for ensuring a project's success. One of your key responsibilities as a lead developer is documenting the development process, which can greatly benefit the entire team and the project. Documentation serves as a reference for future development and maintenance, helps to ensure consistency in coding practices, and facilitates knowledge transfer between team members. You can use documentation to track the development process from concept to product launch.

To create effective documentation, you should start by creating a documentation plan that outlines the steps in the development process, including research, writing technical requirements, and implementation. Documentation of the development process should also include a list of the stakeholders involved, such as IT support, DevOps, and QA. This plan should be reviewed and updated regularly to reflect any changes in the development process.

As we discussed in the previous chapter on technical documentation, lead developers can use a variety of formats to document the development process, including written documentation, diagrams, and code comments. By using a combination of formats, lead developers can ensure that the documentation is easy to understand and accessible to all team members. Table 6.4 includes the stages of a product development process.

Table 6.4   **Stages of a product development process**

Phase	Definition	Stakeholders
Concept	This is the initial stage of the development process, where you brainstorm and come up with ideas for the project. To document this stage, you can create a concept document that outlines the project goals, objectives, and expected outcomes. This document can serve as a reference for future development and maintenance.	■ Marketing ■ Project management ■ Lead developer
Research	In this stage, you work with stakeholders to research and gather information about the project to determine feasibility and identify potential challenges. To document this stage, you can create a research report that includes information about your findings and any recommendations for the project.	■ Marketing ■ Lead developer ■ Legal ■ Project management
Analysis	In this stage, you analyze the research and determine the best approach for the project. To document this stage, you can create an analysis report that outlines your approach and the steps you plan to take in the development stage.	■ Marketing ■ Project management ■ Lead developer ■ UX/UI
Development	In this stage, you begin the actual development of the project. To document this stage, you can create detailed development documentation that includes information about each step of the development process, including code snippets and diagrams.	■ Development ■ DevOps ■ QA
Launch	In this stage, you launch the project and make it available to the public. To document this stage, you can create a launch report that includes information about the launch process and any challenges that arose during the launch.	■ Development ■ DevOps ■ QA ■ Marketing ■ Project management ■ UX/UI

By documenting the development process from concept to implementation, lead developers can ensure a smooth and efficient workflow that benefits the entire team and the project. By using a variety of formats and involving team members in the documentation process, lead developers can create a documentation plan that works for their team and helps ensure the success of their project.

6.4.2 *Documenting the quality assurance process*

As a lead developer, it's important to remember that the QA team is an asset when it comes to suggesting improvements for the development process. The QA team brings a unique perspective and expertise to the table, and by including them in the conversation, you'll have a better understanding of how changes will affect the overall quality of the product. Using their expertise can help you identify potential problems before they arise and ensure that improvements are implemented to benefit the entire team. By working together, you and the QA team can create a stronger, more efficient development process that delivers high-quality results. It's important to understand the significance of documenting the stages of the QA process, which not only provides a clear and comprehensive understanding of the process for your team but also helps to ensure consistency and accountability across different projects.

Combining unit testing with integration testing and manual testing is a highly effective approach for QA in software development projects. Each type of testing is described here:

- *Unit testing*—Unit testing provides automated checks that can quickly and efficiently identify problems at the code level, ensuring that algorithms and integrations are working properly.
- *Integration testing*—Integration testing focuses on testing the interactions between different parts of a system rather than testing each part in isolation to identify any inconsistencies or problems that may arise when the modules are integrated together.
- *Manual testing*—Offers a more human perspective that can catch problems that may have been overlooked in the unit testing and integration testing processes, specifically whether or not the user experience matches the requirements.

By combining these approaches, you can gain a comprehensive understanding of the quality of your software and ensure that all relevant scenarios have been tested. Furthermore, by using the strengths of these methods, you can save time and resources and ultimately produce a higher-quality product. Combining unit testing, integration testing, and manual testing is a smart investment in the success of your software development projects.

The QA process typically involves four key stages: planning, test design, execution, and reporting. Each stage plays an important role in ensuring the overall quality of the software and should be documented clearly and concisely. Figure 6.3 shows an example

QA process for an e-commerce website, and the following list includes each stage of the QA process and its definition:

- *Planning*—The planning stage involves determining the scope and objectives of the QA process. This stage is crucial for setting the foundation for the rest of the process and involves tasks such as defining the acceptance criteria, identifying potential risks, and determining the resources needed.
- *Test design*—Once the planning stage is complete, the next step is to design the tests. This involves creating a list of test cases, identifying the criteria for each case, and determining the test environment. This stage is important for ensuring that all relevant tests are covered and that the results will be accurate and reliable.
- *Execution*—The execution stage is where the tests are run. This stage is where the design and planning stages come together and where the test results are obtained. It's important to ensure that the tests are run according to the design and that the results are recorded and analyzed.
- *Reporting*—The final stage is reporting, where the test results are documented and communicated to the relevant stakeholders. This stage is important for ensuring that the results are understood and for making recommendations for any improvements that need to be made.

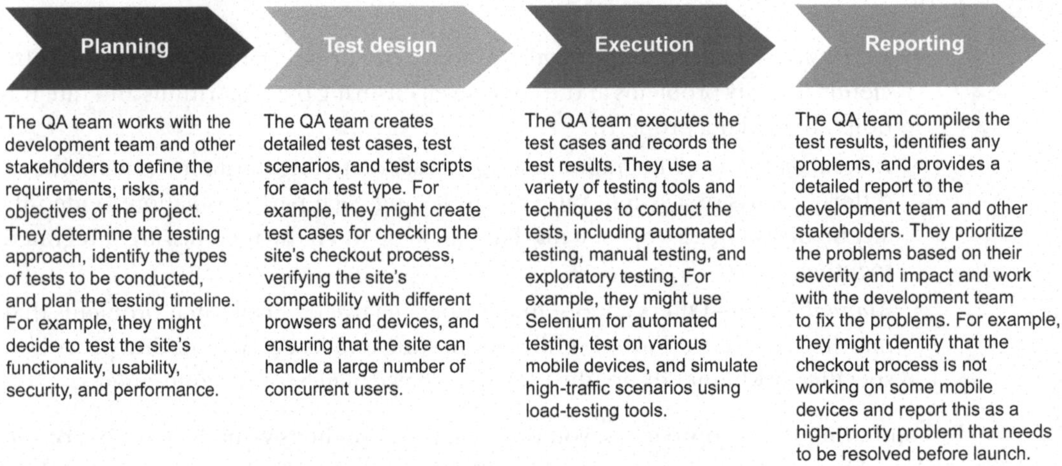

Planning	Test design	Execution	Reporting
The QA team works with the development team and other stakeholders to define the requirements, risks, and objectives of the project. They determine the testing approach, identify the types of tests to be conducted, and plan the testing timeline. For example, they might decide to test the site's functionality, usability, security, and performance.	The QA team creates detailed test cases, test scenarios, and test scripts for each test type. For example, they might create test cases for checking the site's checkout process, verifying the site's compatibility with different browsers and devices, and ensuring that the site can handle a large number of concurrent users.	The QA team executes the test cases and records the test results. They use a variety of testing tools and techniques to conduct the tests, including automated testing, manual testing, and exploratory testing. For example, they might use Selenium for automated testing, test on various mobile devices, and simulate high-traffic scenarios using load-testing tools.	The QA team compiles the test results, identifies any problems, and provides a detailed report to the development team and other stakeholders. They prioritize the problems based on their severity and impact and work with the development team to fix the problems. For example, they might identify that the checkout process is not working on some mobile devices and report this as a high-priority problem that needs to be resolved before launch.

Figure 6.3   Example QA process for an e-commerce website

Documenting the stages of the QA process is an important part of the development process for lead developers. It provides a clear and comprehensive understanding of the team's process and helps ensure consistency and accountability across different projects. By following best practices in technical documentation, you can create clear and concise documentation that will benefit your team and your projects.

6.4.3 Setting a development process maintenance schedule

Lead developers oversee the entire development process, from concept to launch, and ensure that their team has the tools and resources they need to deliver high-quality software on time and within budget. One of the most important tasks in this role is setting a maintenance schedule for documenting and continually improving the development process. To set a maintenance schedule for documenting and improving the development process, follow these steps:

- *Schedule regular reviews.* Schedule regular reviews of the development process, such as monthly or quarterly, to ensure that it remains up-to-date and relevant.
- *Involve all team members.* Encourage all team members to provide input and suggestions for improving the development process. This will help ensure that everyone is invested in it and that changes are made that benefit the entire team.
- *Document changes.* Document any changes to the development process and the reasoning behind the changes to ensure that the process remains transparent and accountable. Preserve the history of the document by using a document management system such as OneDrive or Dropbox.
- *Continuously improve.* Continuously review and update the development process to ensure that it remains efficient, effective, and relevant.

In my experience, new teams or organizations should set a frequent maintenance schedule for the development process because they are still forming their teams and finding out what works for them. In this case, I suggest reviewing the process both during and after deployments. I've worked on many web development projects for enterprise clients, and we tried as best we could to fix any problems in the development process before launch. This isn't always an option, as staging environments often can't replicate the production environment 100%. However, revising your documentation of the development process before you launch a product or website will help you avoid errors on launch day.

Setting a maintenance schedule for documenting and continually improving the development process is essential to ensuring the success of your projects. Lead developers must regularly reflect on the development process and identify areas for improvement. By asking yourself, your team, and stakeholders the preceding questions, you can ensure that the development process is efficient and that you continue delivering high-quality software on time and within budget.

6.5 Case study

Ryan H. Lewis is a staff software engineer at Reddit specializing in high-performance cloud-based web applications. He hosts *Building Reddit*, an engineering podcast focused on how Reddit builds software. More than 20 years ago, he started building websites to promote his bands and record label. After traveling around the world playing music, he settled down in the Pacific Northwest and started his professional software career.

Since then, he has led teams at T-Mobile, Expedia, and several startups. He has taught online with Pluralsight and O'Reilly and in person at Seattle Central College and the University of Washington. He is the author of *The Cloud Developer Workbook*. In this case study, Ryan shares his thoughts on the development process and his experience with process improvement.

6.5.1   What pain points have you encountered in the development process, and how did you address them?

When I think about pain points, I lump them into two categories: things that slow velocity and things that lower morale. As a lead developer, you often work on things that unblock your team but aren't that fun to work on, such as the deployment pipeline and CI/CD. I was on a team where we had a deployment pipeline that broke often. This pipeline was essential because it deployed our code, but it wasn't robust, and we didn't have a lot of automated tests for it. We needed to add a testing framework into the pipeline to catch bugs and improve the pipeline configuration. No one else had experience with it, so that was something that I worked on to keep from slowing down the team. I modified the pipeline to run the automated tests and added a few additional tests. It helped make the pipeline more resilient and lowered the number of bugs making it into production. Overall, it solved a major pain point. If you take on tasks that no one else wants to do, it can also set a positive tone and improve morale. Just make sure you're pitching in and being helpful.

Another problem I've encountered is being asked to develop software or new features without sufficient product requirements. I've worked in teams with inexperienced product managers that wanted us to start building features with vague descriptions. A practical approach was to push back during the planning phase and develop a standard for necessary requirements. In the same vein, lead developers should also be proactive in doing technical design and documentation to avoid unseen problems arising during the development process. You can't predict everything, but it's better to have thought through a feature before starting the implementation.

I've seen that developers on teams can get siloed into their development areas. You might find that only one developer on a team understands a certain area of your application. It helps to pair people together from different areas to work collaboratively. People like to learn and teach, so make sure to give them those opportunities. You can pair a developer that knows an area well with a developer that doesn't know it. This can slow velocity for a bit, but most developers are excited to learn new things (and share with others). This definitely raised the enthusiasm of the team and eventually led to much better team velocity.

6.5.2   What are some ways that you've reduced technical debt?

I've seen that technical debt often builds up when long-running projects ignore it or if an organization doesn't have good communication. Communication is more difficult with large organizations, but small organizations can identify technical debt through retrospectives or something that allows the team to surface pain points.

To reduce technical debt, I'd suggest keeping a prioritized list of mitigation tasks with estimates. Then, move small chunks of those tasks into each sprint based on their priority. I like to order the task list by the effect each task will have and add a column with estimated effort. Then I can negotiate with the product team to add these tasks to lighter sprints where larger deliverables aren't being worked on, usually at the beginning or end of milestones.

Each product manager's understanding of technical debt is going to be different. With some, you may need to explain the WIFM (what's in it for me). I was in a situation where the product team was asking for features that we couldn't fulfill because the technical debt was so bad. Our client-side data management solution was homegrown, and it was increasing the development time and complexity by at least 2x. We needed to replace the entire component with a modern, open source implementation. In cases like this, where a significant part of your application is dragging everything down, it's important to communicate with the product team, create a list of things that need to be changed, and keep that list prioritized. Of course, proper estimation is also important, and you should set standards for story point estimates to ensure that any prioritized task is well-planned and sets your team up for success.

When working on long-term technical debt, it also helps to split the team to focus on either feature work or technical debt and then switch those developers every two sprints. This keeps developers from getting bogged down and frustrated because fixing most technical debt is hard.

6.5.3 *What advice do you have for lead developers to ensure that their development process is optimized?*

When working on a new project or application, I suggest you create tests before it's too late. Integration or end-to-end tests are fine. Unit tests tend to have a much lower ROI for the time they take to write. Also, I haven't found that unit tests help as much for new projects because your application's internals will likely change. Unless there is a lot of planning beforehand, this can create a lot of churn with unit tests.

We have a design doc process and documentation review at Reddit. Developers proactively brainstorm and plan how they'll develop an application, and the team can provide feedback. We have a meeting where we talk about the comments, and this helps us to find a lot of the "gotchas" before anyone starts the implementation. You should also take note of the areas of the project that cause bugs or break often, for example, things that break regression testing or something that takes much longer than it should. This will help you identify problem areas to smooth out the development process.

As a lead developer, don't always assume that your experience is everyone's experience. If something is easy for you, don't assume it's easy or working well for the rest of the team (especially with remote teams). Use sprint retrospectives to capture pain points and review developer velocity. Continually ask yourself and your team how things could be improved.

I like pair programming because it often prevents technical debt, surfaces opportunities to optimize the development process, and improves team camaraderie. Pair programming can reduce and prevent technical debt because you're coding with an objective reviewer. Both people aren't actually programming. One is typing, and one is watching and suggesting approaches. When I do this, my code is cleaner because I can focus on the best application structure, and the person I'm pairing with can help research and bounce ideas off each other. You can also learn from seeing the other person's workflow and working together to optimize the development process. Two minds are better than one, after all.

Summary

- Lead developers are crucial in ensuring the development process runs smoothly and efficiently, leading to better results, improved quality, job satisfaction, morale, teamwork, and cost-effectiveness.

- Pain points such as lack of clear direction or communication and lack of proper tools and resources can negatively affect the quality of the final product and lead to confusion, missed deadlines, and burnout.

- Process management is the systematic approach of designing, executing, controlling, and monitoring development processes.

- Lead developers must understand the perspectives and needs of all stakeholders involved in the development process, including both developers and nondevelopers, by gathering insights to create a comprehensive view and identify opportunities for improvement.

- When receiving constructive criticism, it's important to approach it with an open mind and not take it personally.

- Lead developers should be confident in their abilities, but they must also be humble enough to acknowledge that they don't know everything and be open to new ideas and perspectives from both developers and nondevelopers.

- It's important to identify opportunities to streamline the SDLC by automating repetitive and manual tasks, which can improve overall efficiency, reduce errors, and save time by using tools such as Jenkins for CI/CD and Selenium for automating web application testing.

- Lead developers can optimize the SDLC by taking a preventative approach to software development, which focuses on avoiding problems before they occur through design that is scalable, maintainable, and adheres to best practices, reducing the risk of technical debt and ensuring the codebase remains healthy over time.

- Documenting the QA process includes four key stages—planning, test design, execution, and reporting—to ensure the software's overall quality, as well as consistency and accountability across projects.

- Setting a maintenance schedule for documenting and continually improving the development process must involve all team members. Changes must be documented, and the process must be continuously improved to ensure efficiency, effectiveness, and relevance.

Working with project teams

This chapter covers

- Best practices for providing estimates
- Effects of incorrect estimates on projects
- Best practices for facilitating team communication
- Effect of effective versus poor communication
- Agile versus waterfall project management methods

Lead developers are key players in the software development process, as they oversee the technical aspects of projects. However, they can't achieve project success alone. Effective collaboration with project teams is essential to ensure that projects are delivered on time, within budget, and with high-quality output.

Working closely with project teams can help lead developers identify potential roadblocks, risks, and opportunities, as well as make informed decisions. Lead developers need to establish open lines of communication with project teams to ensure that everyone is aligned with project objectives, timelines, and deliverables. This can improve overall project morale and foster a sense of teamwork and collaboration.

In addition to collaboration, lead developers play a critical role in the project management process. They are responsible for establishing and adhering to project plans, monitoring progress against milestones, and communicating project status to stakeholders. By working closely with project teams, lead developers can ensure that resources are allocated efficiently, project risks are mitigated, and problems are addressed promptly.

7.1   *Cross-training project management skills*

Lead developers must have a deep understanding of the technical aspects of a project. However, it's equally important to develop project management skills. Managing projects effectively requires a broad skill set that extends beyond technical proficiency. Cross-training and learning project management skills by working with a mentor or studying independently can enhance lead developers' ability to navigate complex projects and lead teams effectively. One of the best ways to cross-train is to shadow their co-workers and learn how they approach project management and leadership.

By cross-training, lead developers can broaden their knowledge base, leading to more well-rounded decision-making. Project management skills such as agile and waterfall can help a lead developer anticipate and mitigate potential problems that may arise during the project's lifecycle. Furthermore, cross-training enables lead developers to communicate more effectively with project stakeholders, including other team members, clients, and executives.

Cross-training can improve project outcomes and can also have personal benefits. Developing project management skills can enhance a lead developer's career prospects, as they will be better equipped to manage larger and more complex projects. Furthermore, cross-training can improve job satisfaction by allowing lead developers to take on new challenges and expand their skill set beyond technical abilities.

Developing project management skills is essential for lead developers to succeed. While technical expertise is vital, it's only part of the equation. Regarding project management expectations, the roles of a lead developer and a project manager are distinct yet complementary. The primary focus for a lead developer is leading the development team, ensuring seamless collaboration, and delivering high-quality code. Project managers are responsible for orchestrating the entire project, juggling timelines, and allocating resources. While the lead developer brings technical brilliance to the table, the project manager provides the strategic vision and coordinates the team's efforts. These roles form a harmonious partnership, driving the project forward with their unique strengths and responsibilities. By broadening their skill set, lead developers can navigate complex projects, communicate more effectively, and improve their job satisfaction and career prospects.

7.1.1   *Reviewing the waterfall method*

The waterfall project methodology is a popular traditional approach to software development that has been used for many years. This approach is a linear and sequential process that consists of several distinct stages. It involves completing each stage of the project in a linear sequence. The stages of the waterfall methodology include requirements gathering, design, implementation, testing, and maintenance. Each project stage must be completed before moving on to the next. This approach is often used when the project requirements are well-defined and the project scope is clear. Figure 7.1 shows the typical phases of the waterfall methodology.

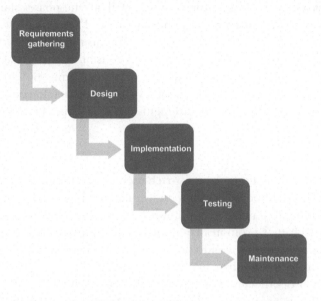

Figure 7.1 Waterfall method phases

One of the benefits of the waterfall approach is that it allows for a detailed plan to be created early in the project, which often helps to prevent scope creep. By having tight requirements and sticking to them, the unexpected, not estimated, or unfunded changes during the project are often eliminated or reduced. Stakeholders sign off on each stage of the plan before proceeding to the next stage. This helps to ensure that the project stays on track and that everyone involved knows what is expected of them. The waterfall approach can help prevent problems from arising later in the project. Completing each project stage in a linear sequence allows for problems to be identified and resolved early on. This can ultimately lead to a successful outcome for the project.

One example of a software development project that used the waterfall methodology is the development of the Microsoft's Windows operating system. The project was divided into separate stages, with the completion of each stage being a requirement for the next. The first stage involved gathering requirements, which was followed by the design stage. Once the design was finalized, the implementation phase began, where the actual coding of the operating system took place. The testing phase was next, where the software was thoroughly tested to ensure that it met the necessary requirements. Finally, the maintenance phase began, fixing any bugs or problems discovered during testing.

I've worked for companies that used waterfall, and I believe their projects took longer and had more problems than they would have had they used agile. For software development projects, the requirements are rarely fully known up front. Priorities shift, and waterfall doesn't have a mechanism to deal with shifting priorities, which can cause blockers. When there is a change to the project in waterfall, all the phases start over, beginning with the discovery or requirements gathering phase. Then, the project plan is revised and updated for the remainder of the project. You don't want to do this too often because it causes a loss of productivity. If priorities constantly change, agile is a better process because it's flexible and iterative instead of rigid and time-bound. While waterfall may not be suitable for every project, it's a valuable approach to consider for software development projects when the requirements are well-defined and the project's scope is clear.

7.1.2   *Defining agile*

The agile project methodology is a popular approach used in developing software and other related projects. This methodology values individuals and interactions over processes and tools, responding to change over following a plan. It's a flexible, iterative, and collaborative approach that promotes continuous improvement, customer satisfaction, and adaptability to change. The most popular frameworks used in agile project methodology include Scrum and Kanban.

Scrum is an agile framework that emphasizes collaboration, flexibility, and feedback. It's a simple yet powerful framework that encourages teams to work together and deliver high-quality products in short iterations called sprints. Scrum is based on three roles: the product owner, the scrum master, and the development team. The product owner is responsible for defining and prioritizing the product backlog, the scrum master ensures that the team follows the Scrum process, and the development team delivers a potentially releasable product increment at the end of each sprint. Scrum also has four activities: sprint planning, daily scrum, sprint review, and sprint retrospective. These activities enable the team to inspect and adapt their process, discuss progress and challenges, and plan for the next sprint. Table 7.1 lists Scrum terms and their definitions.

Table 7.1   Scrum terminology

Scrum term	Definition
Sprint	A fixed time-boxed iteration during which the team works on a subset of the product backlog, with the goal of delivering a potentially releasable product increment
Backlog	A prioritized list of product features, enhancements, or fixes that the team works on during a sprint
Product owner	The person responsible for managing the product backlog, prioritizing the work, and ensuring the team delivers value to the stakeholders
Scrum master	The person responsible for ensuring that the team follows the Scrum process, removing any obstacles, and facilitating collaboration and communication
Sprint planning	A meeting held at the beginning of each sprint during which the team reviews the product backlog, selects the items for the sprint backlog, and defines a sprint goal
Daily scrum	A 15-minute time-boxed meeting during which the team members discuss their progress, identify any obstacles, and plan the work for the day

Table 7.1   Scrum terminology *(continued)*

Scrum term	Definition
Sprint review	A meeting held at the end of each sprint during which the team demonstrates the completed work to stakeholders and receives feedback
Sprint retrospective	A meeting held at the end of each sprint during which the team reflects on their performance, identifies areas for improvement, and creates a plan for the next sprint
User story	A short, simple description of a product feature from the perspective of a user or customer
Velocity	A measure of the amount of work completed by the team during a sprint or over multiple sprints

Most companies I've worked for used Scrum, but many of them skipped the sprint review and sprint retrospectives. This results from a poor agile implementation or transformation from a more traditional project management methodology such as waterfall. Remember that having a daily scrum doesn't make an organization agile. Without a sprint review or retrospective, the core mission of agile to continuously improve the process won't happen. Conversely, I've worked for many companies that used Scrum to the full extent. These companies achieved standardized processes, which led to higher productivity and less technical debt.

Kanban is an agile framework emphasizing visualization, flow, and continuous improvement. It's a pull-based system that limits work in progress (WIP) to improve throughput and reduce cycle time. Kanban is based on three principles: visualize the workflow, limit WIP, and manage the flow. Kanban boards are used to visualize the workflow, with columns representing the different stages of work. Each column has a WIP limit, which prevents the team from starting new work until the existing work is completed. Kanban also has several metrics, such as lead time and cycle time, that help the team to measure and improve their performance. Figure 7.2 shows an example of a Kanban board.

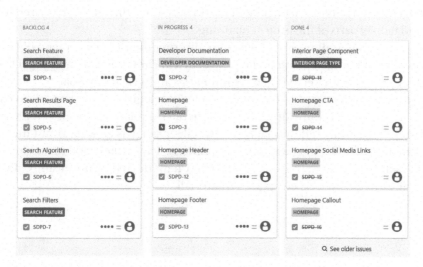

Figure 7.2 Example Kanban board

We use Kanban at my company, HoffsTech, which works well for us. I like to use the WIP limits to ensure that the team isn't overworked and the tasks are performed in a specific order. With Scrum, sometimes tasks are moved into a future sprint if they aren't completed in the current sprint, which can go on and on. Tasks in Scrum are often reprioritized on the fly, which isn't a fit for my team. I understand that priorities shift at times, but when that happens constantly, you spend time reacclimating to the task when you get back to it later. This results in a loss of productivity, so I prefer sticking to task completion using WIP limits in Kanban.

Scrum and Kanban have unique strengths and weaknesses, and the choice of framework depends on the nature of the project and the team's preferences. While Scrum provides a structured approach that promotes collaboration and communication, Kanban provides a flexible approach that promotes visualization and flow. However, both frameworks share common agile principles, such as customer satisfaction, working software, and responding to change. Whatever the choice of framework, the agile approach promotes continuous improvement and adaptability to change, resulting in successful and satisfying project outcomes.

7.1.3   *Comparing agile to waterfall*

Agile and waterfall are two distinct project management methodologies, each with its own unique advantages and disadvantages. While waterfall is a more traditional and sequential approach, agile is a more iterative and flexible approach. The main difference between the two methodologies is their approach to managing the development process. Agile focuses on flexibility, adaptability, and delivering value to the customer through continuous improvement. In contrast, waterfall focuses on detailed planning, execution, and delivering the project on time and within budget.

In an agile project, the focus is on delivering small, incremental improvements to the product or service to meet the evolving needs of the customer. This approach allows for greater flexibility and adaptability and ensures the development process always aligns with the customer's requirements. Agile works best when changes are factored into the time and money parts of the project planning.

In contrast, waterfall projects focus on delivering the project sequentially by planning and executing each phase of the project in a linear fashion. This approach is well-suited for projects with well-defined requirements and a clear end goal.

Another key difference between the two methodologies is the approach to change. In waterfall, change is difficult to incorporate once a phase has been completed and can result in delays and additional costs. In agile, change is expected, and the project team can adapt quickly to changing requirements. This makes agile more suitable for projects subject to frequent changes or with a high degree of uncertainty. Table 7.2 shows the differences between agile and waterfall.

Table 7.2 Agile vs. waterfall

Criteria	Agile	Waterfall
Definition	An iterative and flexible approach to project management that emphasizes collaboration, adaptability, and customer satisfaction	A linear and sequential approach to project management that emphasizes planning, documentation, and strict control
Focus	Customer satisfaction and delivering value	Meeting project requirements and staying within budget
Planning	Continuous planning throughout the project	Comprehensive planning at the beginning of the project
Requirements	Requirements not fixed and can change as the project progresses	Requirements fixed and defined at the beginning of the project
Testing	Continuous testing throughout the project	Testing at the end of each phase
Feedback	Regular feedback from customers and stakeholders	Limited feedback from customers and stakeholders
Risk management	Constantly monitoring and mitigating risks	Risk management done at the beginning of the project
Time frame	Shorter development cycles (two to four weeks)	Longer development cycles (three to six months or longer)

While waterfall is a more traditional approach suited for well-defined projects, agile is a more flexible approach suited for complex and dynamic projects. In my experience, agile works better for software development projects, but many organizations achieve success with waterfall. Ultimately, the choice of methodology will depend on the specific requirements of the project and the organizational culture.

7.2 *Providing accurate estimates*

Lead developers play a crucial role in ensuring the success of a project, as they are expected to provide accurate project estimates. Accurate estimates provide a clear understanding of the project's scope, timeline, and budget, which results in better project planning and management. On the other hand, inaccurate estimates can lead to problems such as missed deadlines, budget overruns, and project delays. This can result in losing trust and confidence among stakeholders, leading to project failures.

For example, if a lead developer underestimates the time required to complete a task, the team may work overtime to meet the deadline, causing burnout and decreased productivity. Working overtime only temporarily boosts productivity. If you do it week after week, your productivity will decrease because people need rest to produce high-quality work. On the other hand, if the estimate is too high, it could lead to unnecessary delays, and the project team may spend more time and resources than necessary. Therefore, it's important for lead developers to provide accurate project estimates for the smooth functioning of the project and to ensure its success.

Lead developers may use either hourly estimates or story points to provide project estimates. *Hourly estimates* involve estimating the number of hours required to complete a task or a project, while *story points* refers to a unit of measurement used to estimate the relative effort required to complete a task or project. The choice of which method to use depends on the nature of the project and the team's preference.

7.2.1 *Measuring hourly estimates*

For projects requiring high precision, such as software development projects with a fixed budget and tight deadlines, hourly estimates may be appropriate. This is because hourly estimates provide a clear understanding of the time required to complete a task and help with better project planning and management. If you're working on consultancy and services projects, hourly estimates can be used to estimate the time required to complete the project and to bill clients accurately. The following list includes the steps that lead developers should take to estimate projects accurately using an hourly scale:

- *Understand the requirements.* Before providing an estimate, it's important to clearly understand the project's requirements and scope. This will help you identify the tasks that need to be completed and the resources required to complete them.
- *Break down tasks.* Break down the project into smaller, manageable tasks. This makes it easier to estimate the time required to complete each task and identify potential challenges or roadblocks.
- *Use historical data.* If you've worked on similar projects in the past, you can use that data to estimate the time required for a task. This will help you provide more accurate estimates, as you already understand the challenges and resources required for a similar project.
- *Consider all factors.* When estimating the time required for a task, consider all factors that may affect the completion time. For example, if a task requires the collaboration of multiple team members, the estimate should consider their availability.
- *Review and revise.* Once you've provided the estimate, review and revise it if necessary. It's important to be realistic and to allow for unexpected challenges or roadblocks that may arise during the project.

I've worked on several web development projects with enterprise clients, and those types of projects are often complex. I've found that breaking down tasks with the development team and project manager is an effective way to organize projects. I always assign specific features to one developer and then assign any bug fixes to others on the team. That way, everyone will have experience with each feature in case someone isn't available.

When working with requirements, you must ensure they are understood. If I have any doubts or questions about requirements, I speak to the project manager and the client. Asking clarifying questions such as "What did you mean by this?" and using active listening help to mitigate misunderstanding. Repeating what the client says back to them will avoid miscommunication. I've also found this approach useful to uncover inaccuracies in the clients' requests.

Once you've broken down the tasks and finalized the requirements, you can assign estimates. Reviewing similar projects and using historical data to estimate tasks is helpful. For example, if I'm working on a web development project, most projects include creating page types such as the homepage and search results. Projects aren't all the same, but I like to look at the original estimate versus the actual time it took to finish each task. I may also review any problems that came up along the way that can be avoided to decrease the estimate. Measuring hourly estimates must be precise, so you should also include the team in the estimation process. We'll discuss this topic in detail later in this section.

Providing accurate hourly estimates is crucial for a project's success. By following these steps, you can ensure that your estimates are accurate and help prevent delays or budget overruns. As a lead developer, it's important to take the time to provide accurate estimates and communicate effectively with the team to ensure the project's success.

7.2.2 *Estimating in story points*

The story points unit of measurement used in agile project management estimates the relative effort required to complete a task or project. They have a flexible and adaptable approach to project estimation, considering the complexity of the task, the skill level of the team, and the availability of resources. Story points are valuable tools for lead developers, as they provide a clear understanding of the effort required to complete a project, helping to ensure that the project stays on track and that everyone is working toward the same goal. Using story points also allows for continuous improvement and adaptability, as they can be reviewed and revised during the project. Overall, story points provide a useful and effective method of estimating the effort required to complete a project in agile project management.

Several methods of estimating story points exist, including Planning Poker, T-Shirt Sizing, and the Fibonacci Sequence. Each method has advantages and disadvantages, so it's important for lead developers to choose the method that works best for their team:

- *Planning Poker*—This popular method of estimating story points involves team members using special cards with numbers on them to indicate their estimate for a task or project. This method is based on the idea that everyone has a different understanding of the effort required, so by discussing and sharing their opinions, the team can arrive at a consensus estimate.
- *T-Shirt Sizing*—In this method of estimating story points, tasks are given a size based on their relative effort. Sizes are typically assigned based on a scale from extra-small to extra-large, with extra-small being the lowest effort and extra-large being the highest effort. This simple and straightforward method makes it a popular choice among teams.

- *Fibonacci Sequence*—The Fibonacci Sequence is a mathematical series used to estimate story points. In this method, each number in the sequence represents the relative effort required to complete a task. For example, a task estimated as a 1 would require the lowest effort, while a task estimated as a 13 would require the highest effort. This method is based on the idea that tasks are interdependent and that the effort required to complete them increases as the complexity of the task increases.

A common approach is to use the T-Shirt Sizing or Fibonacci Sequence methods combined with Planning Poker to estimate story points accurately. Estimating story points on a scale from 1 to 5 is a simple and effective method of estimating the relative effort required to complete a task or project in agile project management. To do this, you must assign effort levels to each point on the scale, such as 1 being the lowest effort and 5 being the highest effort. Based on the effort levels, you should assign story points to each task based on the relative effort required to complete it. In my experience, it's important to document guidelines for measuring the complexity of each task as compared to other tasks in the project. I usually keep the scale small, from 1 to 5. An example of using this scale includes developing a search results page. Table 7.3 includes an example of measuring story points for a search feature.

Table 7.3   **Measuring story points for a search feature**

Story Points	Description	Tasks
1	Lowest effort	Creating an empty search page framework
2	Low to medium effort	Displaying search filters
3	Medium effort	Displaying search results
4	Medium to high effort	Implementing standard search functionality
5	Highest effort	Implementing search filters

In my experience, one of the biggest mistakes that companies make is assigning 1 h to 1 story point. Story points are a measure of complexity and shouldn't be mingled with hourly estimates. Table 7.4 shows the differences between hourly estimates and story points. If you want to make story points equal to hours worked, then you should use hourly estimates. This results from a poor agile transformation when companies attempt to move from a traditional project management method (e.g., waterfall) to agile. These methods are completely different, and many companies try to use their existing reporting tools for waterfall when they move to agile. They try to match story points to hours worked so that they don't have to update their reporting tools. This often results in poor estimates because story points were created to handle complex projects unsuitable for hourly estimates. We'll discuss agile and waterfall in detail later in this chapter.

Table 7.4 Hourly estimates vs. story points

Hourly estimates	Story points
Estimates the number of hours required to complete a task based on factors such as historical data, complexity, and risk	Relative estimation technique that estimates the effort required to complete a task based on its complexity, uncertainty, and risks
Provides a concrete metric that can be easily translated into cost or schedule	Focuses on the effort required to complete a task rather than the time required
Influenced by factors such as team productivity, individual skills, and work environment	Less affected by external factors and focuses on the work required to complete a task
Estimates specific, well-understood tasks, such as bug fixes or small enhancements	Estimates tasks that are uncertain or unclear, such as research or development of new functionality
Provides a precise estimate of time and cost to stakeholders or clients	Prioritizes tasks based on their level of effort and complexity, regardless of their time requirements
Predictable productivity levels with a well-established team	Breaks down tasks into smaller pieces for a new team or project

Most companies that I've worked for used a combination of Planning Poker with T-Shirt Sizing. Every organization should stick with one method of estimating story points to manage all projects according to the standard. T-Shirt Sizing is a more suitable method for estimating small or simple user stories that don't require high precision. The sizes in T-Shirt Sizing (e.g., XS, S, M, L, XL) are more subjective and can be quickly assigned to a user story based on its perceived size or complexity. Whichever method you use, keep in mind that you're expected to ensure that story points are estimated accurately to support the project's success.

7.2.3 Including the team

As a lead developer, involving your development team in task estimates is essential. Whether you're estimating in hours or story points, your team's input can make a big difference in the accuracy of your estimations. Including your team in this process is not only important for building trust and collaboration within your team but also for ensuring that projects are completed on time and within budget.

To gather accurate estimates, it's important to ask the right questions. You should start by defining the scope of a task, which is critical for estimating the effort required to complete the task. *Project scope* refers to the detailed definition of the work that needs to be completed in a project, including its objectives, deliverables, and the tasks involved in achieving those objectives. It outlines the boundaries and limitations of the project and defines what is and isn't included within the project. Be sure to ask your team members, including developers and project managers, for their input on the scope of each task, plus any dependencies or prerequisites that may be required. Before the work begins, communicate the scope as you understand it to the project manager to avoid working on tasks that are out of scope. Discussing the project scope with the project manager is imperative. I once made the mistake of adding features and functionality to the project to improve the quality without communicating the changes to the project manager. This resulted in many assigned tasks being out of scope, costing the company valuable time and increasing the budget.

Another approach that is sometimes used in agile projects is to ask, "What are the best possible solutions to the client's requirements?" Ask your team what you could deliver as a team within the sprint (usually two weeks). This is possible if your approach to managing requirements is goal-oriented rather than a list of "features" you hope will solve the customer's problem. This approach works well if your problem isn't buried under other requirements that are still open for discussion. For example, I've worked with organizations that set goals based on the users' needs, such as automating a manual process. Then, we wrote out the business and technical requirements to achieve that goal by integrating with an application programming interface (API) to automate reporting.

While planning and executing a software development project, you may encounter roadblocks or unexpected challenges. These can significantly affect the project's timeline and lead to a reduction in productivity or quality. Therefore, it's crucial to anticipate any potential problems that may arise during the project and take proactive measures to address them before they become bigger problems. You should encourage your team members to share any concerns they may have and to be as specific as possible. This could include identifying technical difficulties, such as the integration of different technologies or compatibility problems, as well as miscommunication that may arise between team members. Once you've identified potential problems, you can deal with them immediately. This may involve planning additional resources or time to address the problems, revising the project plan, or even changing the project scope. Additionally, you can work with your team to develop contingency plans if the problems arise to minimize the effect on the project timeline or deliverables.

When it comes to software development project estimation, making assumptions can often lead to inaccurate estimations. Assumptions are essentially taking something as true without necessarily having proof or confirmation of its validity. They can be made unconsciously or consciously and may stem from various sources, such as a lack of information or experience with the project. Identifying any assumptions being made during the estimation process is therefore essential to ensure that the estimates are as accurate as possible. Assumptions can lead to underestimating or overestimating the time required to complete a task, affecting the overall project timeline and budget. Therefore, it's crucial to evaluate the validity of any assumptions being made and adjust the estimates accordingly.

To identify assumptions, you should encourage your team members to share their thought processes when providing estimates. This can help to uncover any underlying assumptions that may be driving their estimations. It's also important to ask your team members specific questions to tease out any assumptions they may make. For example, you could ask questions like the following:

- Are you assuming that we'll have access to all the necessary resources?
- Are you assuming that the requirements won't change during the project?
- Are you assuming that there won't be any technical difficulties or challenges?
- Are you assuming that the client understands what they want versus what they need?

Once the assumptions have been identified, you can evaluate their validity and adjust the estimates accordingly. This may involve gathering additional information or seeking clarification on certain aspects of the project to eliminate any assumptions. In some cases, assumptions may be valid, but they may need to be factored into the estimates to ensure that the project is completed on time and within budget.

And finally, you must gather task estimates from your team. When asking your team members about task estimates, it's important to do so in a way that encourages accurate and detailed responses. Here are some examples of questions you could ask to gather more information about the estimated time required for a task:

- What steps will be required to complete this task?
- Are there any dependencies or prerequisites that must be completed before this task begins?
- Are there any technical challenges or obstacles that may affect the time required to complete this task?
- Are there any external factors (e.g., client requests, resource availability) that may affect the time required to complete this task?
- When might we see some progress toward our goal(s)?
- What do you need from the team to deliver what the customer needs?

By asking these types of questions, you can better understand the complexity of each task and what factors may affect the time required to complete it. Once you have a good sense of how long each task will take, you can work with the project manager to prioritize the backlog tasks based on their importance and the amount of time required. Then, you can work with the project manager to decide what will go into each sprint. This helps to ensure that the project stays on track and that the most critical tasks are completed first. It also allows you to allocate your team members effectively, ensuring that they are working on the most important tasks that match their skills and experience.

Including your development team in estimating tasks is essential for ensuring that your projects are completed on time and within budget. By gathering input from your team members and asking the right questions, you can refine your estimations and identify potential problems before they become larger problems. This collaborative approach also helps to build trust and collaboration within your team, creating a more positive and productive work environment.

7.3   *Facilitating communication*

As a lead developer, facilitating effective communication is essential to any successful project. Facilitating communication, or the act of creating an environment that promotes clear and open dialogue, is a crucial skill that can significantly affect the success of your team's work. In this context, *facilitating* means creating a space where team members can communicate freely and comfortably without fear of judgment or misunderstanding.

Having proper communication ensures everyone is on the same page and understands their role in the project. When there is proper team communication, tasks are completed more efficiently, and errors are minimized. In contrast, poor communication can lead to misunderstandings, frustration, and a lack of trust between team members. Miscommunication can also lead to wasted time, duplicated efforts, missed deadlines, and poor-quality work.

I've worked for organizations with excellent communication and others without. When I was a lead developer for the first time, I noticed that there were information silos in the organization, which is common in large corporations. I took the initiative to reach out to other teams to coordinate our efforts in both development and training. This helped increase the productivity in all the teams we worked with, as we avoided performing tasks already covered by another team. It also helped us uncover problems in our process pipeline that caused errors in our documentation and training materials, which improved the quality of our output. Table 7.5 shows examples of what happens when communication is properly facilitated and not facilitated.

Table 7.5   Properly facilitated communication vs. not facilitated communication

	Properly facilitated communication	**Not facilitated communication**
Teamwork	Team members collaborate effectively, share ideas and feedback, and work together to achieve project goals.	Team members working in silos with little collaboration, and a lack of clarity in roles and responsibilities can lead to duplicated efforts or important tasks being missed.
Productivity	Team members are able to work efficiently and productively because they understand their goals, roles, and tasks. They can easily ask for help or clarification when needed, reducing delays and mistakes.	Team members waste time and effort on tasks that are already completed or have been changed, and missed or misunderstood tasks can result in delays or even project failure.
Innovation	Team members communicate effectively, which allows for creative thinking and innovation, as they can share their ideas and perspectives to come up with new solutions and approaches.	Team members may be hesitant to share their ideas, leading to missed opportunities for innovation and growth.
Morale	Team members work in a positive environment where they feel valued and supported, and their ideas are heard and considered.	Team members feel isolated, frustrated, and undervalued, leading to low morale and burnout.
Quality	Team members can catch and address problems and mistakes early, leading to high-quality output.	Team members produce low-quality output that can lead to costly rework and project failure because of missed errors, unclear requirements, and misunderstandings.

Lead developers have a critical role in facilitating communication between teams. You must create an environment that promotes open communication and encourages your team members to share their thoughts and ideas. You must also listen actively and ensure that everyone feels heard and valued. By doing so, you can help your team to work more cohesively and produce better results. When you take the time to develop your communication skills, you'll create a positive and supportive environment that allows your team to thrive.

7.3.1 Connecting team members

As a lead developer, you're uniquely positioned to connect your development team with other people within the organization. When your team needs information or support to do their job effectively, you can help by building bridges between your team and other departments. This can help your team stay productive and engaged, and ultimately lead to more successful projects.

One of the most important things you can do as a lead developer is to create an open and communicative environment within your team. Encourage your team members to ask questions and seek help when needed. Make it clear that you're there to support them and that there are no stupid questions. I like to tell everyone on my team that the only stupid question is the one that you don't ask. By fostering a culture of open communication, you can help your team members feel more comfortable reaching out to others in the organization for help.

When your team members need help, it's important for them to know whom to contact. Take the time to build relationships with people in other departments, such as DevOps, QA, and project management. These people can be valuable resources for your team and can help provide the information and support your team needs to stay productive. By building relationships with these people, you can create a network of support for your team.

Another way to connect your team with other people in the organization is to create opportunities for collaboration. Encourage your team to work with people from other departments on projects and initiatives. This can help your team members build relationships and better understand how other parts of the organization operate. By working together, your team can also gain valuable insights that can help improve the quality of their work. Gaining insight into how other departments operate and their goals will also help your team cross-train different skills and achieve professional development.

I like to pair developers with user experience/user interface designers (UX/UI) so that they understand the purpose of what they are working on and how the users will interact with the application. In my experience, this helps to improve the quality of the developers' work. Working with UX/UI can also help with your system design to map fields within the interface to fields in a database. I've done a lot of work with the Sitecore Content Management System (CMS), and something that helped me a lot was working with UX/UI to create screenshots of every interface and the mapping for each field in the database. With this approach, I provided training and documentation for clients and stakeholders using visual representations that were easily understandable.

Finally, it's important to recognize the contributions of people outside your team who help your team be successful. Take the time to thank people who provide support and information to your team. This can be as simple as sending an email or sending a message to express your appreciation. By showing gratitude and recognizing the efforts of others, you can build stronger relationships and create a more collaborative and productive environment.

When you foster a culture of open communication, you can help your team stay productive and engaged. Lead developers should lead by example, and building relationships with people in other departments is crucial for the team's success. When you create opportunities for collaboration and recognize the contributions of others, you'll show your team how to find the people they need and watch as your projects become more successful and your team members grow and develop.

7.3.2   *Asking for help*

As a lead developer, you're expected to be the go-to person for all technical and leadership skills. With this responsibility comes a lot of pressure, and it's easy to feel like you must always have all the answers. However, remember that you're only human, and it's okay to ask for help when you're struggling. It's essential to lead by example and foster a collaborative environment where questions are encouraged. When you show vulnerability and ask for help, you create a safe space for your team members to do the same. This fosters a culture of teamwork and collaboration, where everyone can learn from each other's strengths and weaknesses.

The ability to learn from anyone is an essential skill that can lead to personal and professional growth. It means being open-minded, curious, and willing to listen to diverse perspectives and experiences. No matter whom we interact with, we can always learn something from them. Everyone has unique knowledge and insights to offer, whether a colleague, a friend, or even a stranger. By embracing a learning mindset and seeking out opportunities to learn from others, we can expand our horizons, challenge our assumptions, and become better versions of ourselves. Additionally, learning from anyone helps us build stronger relationships, increase empathy and understanding, and create a more inclusive and collaborative community.

When you're struggling with a technical problem, don't hesitate to ask your team members for their input. They might have experience with similar problems or have a fresh perspective that could help you find a solution. Furthermore, by involving your team members in the problem-solving process, you're helping them develop their own technical skills and fostering a sense of ownership in the project. I was once tasked with comparing hosting providers for a client, and I was unfamiliar with the newer options available, so I asked my team. A junior developer fresh out of college had taken a course on Azure when it was brand new, and they helped me get up to speed quickly. This enabled me to create a comprehensive report for clients to provide them with choices and recommendations.

Regarding leadership skills, it's important to recognize that no one is a perfect leader. Everyone has areas for improvement, and seeking feedback from your team members is a great way to identify these areas and work on them. Don't hesitate to ask your team for honest feedback on your communication and decision-making skills. This can help you identify blind spots and develop strategies for improvement. The first time I led a team, I was afraid to get negative feedback because I thought it would show the team that I didn't know what I was doing. I thought this because of imposter syndrome, and I assumed I got the job because my manager thought I knew everything already. Through trial and error, I found that asking for feedback from the team helped me to surface their pain points so that I could take a proactive approach to alleviate problems with our processes.

Asking for help doesn't make you weak, and it makes you a better leader. By showing your team that it's okay to ask for help and admitting when you don't know something, you're modeling the behavior you want to see in your team. This creates a positive work environment where everyone can learn, grow, and collaborate.

7.3.3   Avoiding miscommunication

Effective communication is essential for the success of any team or project. Miscommunication, on the other hand, can lead to misunderstandings, delays, and even failure. As a lead developer, it's important to understand what causes miscommunication and take steps to avoid it. One of the most common causes of miscommunication is unclear expectations. When team members are unclear on what is expected of them, they may misunderstand their roles and responsibilities, leading to confusion and delays. As a lead developer, you must set clear expectations for your team members and ensure that everyone understands their roles and responsibilities. Expectations should be set at the beginning of a project and reviewed throughout the project. As priorities change, expectations and responsibilities may also need to be adjusted.

Another cause of miscommunication is the use of technical jargon or acronyms that may not be familiar to everyone on the team. While it's important to use the correct terminology when discussing technical problems, ensuring that everyone on the team understands what is being discussed is equally important. This can be achieved by explaining or defining technical terms as needed. I like to create a glossary of terms for every project that I'm working on. Nondevelopers appreciate this because they can learn from it and understand what I'm talking about. Remember, people who aren't developers but work on development projects have technical skills, and you can rely on them to understand technical concepts. They may not be able to write code or set up servers, but they can conceptualize application development.

Lack of active listening is another factor that can lead to miscommunication. *Active listening* is a communication technique that involves paying close attention to what the speaker is saying, both verbally and nonverbally, and providing feedback to confirm understanding. It requires the listener to fully focus on the speaker and refrain from interrupting or making assumptions. Active listening involves techniques such as clarifying, paraphrasing, summarizing, and reflecting to ensure that the listener clearly understands the message being conveyed. This type of listening helps foster better communication and understanding between individuals and is an essential skill for effective communication in personal and professional relationships. It's essential that team members actively listen to each other and ask questions to clarify any misunderstandings. As a lead developer, you can encourage active listening by modeling it yourself and setting a positive example for your team. For example, if a project manager is telling you about a new feature that is coming up for an app your team is developing, you should listen, paraphrase what you understood, and repeat it back to them. This often helps to surface misunderstandings and fix them before they affect the project.

Other factors that can contribute to miscommunication are cultural or language barriers. When working with project teams or team members from different cultural backgrounds, it's important to be sensitive to cultural differences and to try to communicate clearly and respectfully. This may involve using simpler language, avoiding idioms and cultural references, and being patient and understanding when communicating with team members who may not speak English as their first language. When I work with people who aren't native English speakers, I like to avoid using contractions and too many acronyms. I talked about creating a glossary earlier to help nondevelopers, but this also serves to aid communication for developers who don't speak English as a first language.

Miscommunication can be caused by a lack of transparency or feedback. As a lead developer, it's important to ensure team members have access to the information they need to do their jobs effectively and provide regular feedback and support. This can help ensure everyone is on the same page and working toward the same goals. When there is no feedback loop, this leads to something even worse than miscommunication: no communication. I experienced an environment of no communication when working for an organization that had over-engineered the development processes to the point that they thought no communication was needed. I once sat in a development team meeting where they talked about automating Slack messages to provide deployment process updates. They expected the team to read the messages and then move on to the next step on their own. The problem was that these automated messages had no context for each specific project, and there was a lot of confusion. I suggested that the lead developer keep an eye on the deployment and update the team as to when the next step was starting, what to expect, and what tasks everyone needed to perform. This idea was initially dismissed until I took it upon myself to implement a communicative process and avoid the over-engineered process. Our deployments took less time and had fewer errors because the team was communicative throughout the entire deployment process.

Miscommunication can be a significant challenge for any development team. However, by understanding the causes of miscommunication and avoiding it, lead developers can help create a more effective and cohesive team. With the proper strategies in place, teams can work more effectively together and achieve their goals with fewer misunderstandings and delays.

7.4 *Improving project management processes*

Lead developers play a crucial role in overseeing the development process of software products as well as the project management process. As a lead developer, you largely manage projects and continually improve project management processes. When you take the time to learn project management skills, you'll have insight into the structured methods and procedures that guide the project manager in executing project activities from initiation to closure. A well-designed and executed project management process can ensure that the project is completed on time, within budget, and with high-quality output.

A comprehensive project management process involves a clear definition of project objectives, timelines, milestones, and budget. By establishing and adhering to a project management plan, lead developers can ensure that all stakeholders are aligned, resources are allocated efficiently, and the project is executed systematically. This approach can help to minimize the risk of delays, cost overruns, and scope creep.

Another key benefit of improving the project management process is that it helps to increase transparency and accountability. By regularly tracking and reporting progress against the project plan, lead developers can keep all stakeholders informed and provide them with a clear understanding of the project's status. This can help to build trust and confidence among stakeholders and also provide opportunities to identify and address any potential problems before they escalate.

Lead developers should recognize the critical role of project management in ensuring successful software development projects. By improving the project management process, they can help to ensure that projects are completed on time, within budget, and with high-quality output. This can increase stakeholder satisfaction, improve team morale, and create a more efficient and effective software development process.

7.4.1 *Supporting project managers*

Lead developers can support project managers by providing accurate and timely technical information and suggesting process improvements. Project managers often need to make decisions that have technical implications, and having a lead developer on the team who can provide the necessary information can help the project manager make better-informed decisions. By providing technical insights, lead developers can help the project manager plan and prioritize work more effectively.

Another way that lead developers can support project managers is by facilitating communication between the development team and other stakeholders. Lead developers are often able to communicate technical information to nontechnical stakeholders, such as clients or business managers. By doing so, they can help to ensure that everyone involved in the project is on the same page and working toward the same goals. Fostering a positive team culture is critical for a successful development project, and lead developers can play a key role in building and maintaining such a culture. They can help ensure team members are motivated, engaged, and working effectively toward the project goals. This can include things like recognizing team members for their contributions, providing coaching and mentoring to team members, and fostering an environment of continuous learning and improvement.

As a lead developer, you can offer valuable insights and suggestions for improving project management processes. One of the most effective ways to suggest improvements to project management processes is to approach the conversation with a positive and constructive attitude. Rather than simply pointing out what's wrong with the current processes, focus on suggesting specific solutions to help the team work more efficiently and effectively. It's also important to be clear and specific in your suggestions. Ensure you can articulate exactly what you think needs to change and why. This will help your project manager understand your perspective and the benefits your suggestions can bring.

I've worked for several companies that were shifting from waterfall to agile and having difficulty with their agile transformation. This is a common occurrence, resulting in a mismatched project management methodology known as "Wagile" or "Scrumfall". When I encountered this, I suggested that the project management team implement sprint retrospectives that included the project stakeholders. I explained that agile centers around open and frequent communication, mitigates blockers, and ensures everyone is up to date. I also sent them links to agile resources from Scrum.org (www.scrum .org) to help them understand the process. Through consistent discussion, we adjusted our processes until we were fully agile.

You must be open to feedback and discussion. The project manager may have a different perspective or constraints you're unaware of, so it's important to be open to their feedback and work together to find a solution that works for everyone. Remember, suggesting improvements to project management processes aims to make the project more successful and help the team work more effectively. By approaching the conversation with a positive and collaborative attitude, you can help your team achieve these goals and make a real difference in the project's outcome. By supporting project managers, you can help to ensure that projects are successful, efficient, and delivered on time and within budget.

7.4.2   *Integrating deployments with project management systems*

As a lead developer, you know that tracking deployments can be challenging. Monitoring deployments can be time-consuming, and it can be challenging to keep everyone informed about their status. However, integrating deployments with project management systems can make your life easier by automating the process and ensuring that everyone understands the task at hand.

Integrating deployments with project management systems means you can track deployments from one central location. You can see when a deployment starts, when it finishes, and whether it was successful or not. This information can be invaluable for tracking down problems and ensuring that deployments are completed on time. One example of integrating deployments with project management systems is using a tool such as Jira. Jira is a project management tool that tracks tasks, bugs, and problems. By integrating your deployment tool with Jira, you can create a deployment ticket that includes all the necessary information, such as the target environment, the deployment package, and any notes or instructions. When the deployment is completed, the ticket is updated automatically so everyone can see the deployment status.

I've used Jira at almost every lead developer job I've had over the past 10 years. One company I worked for used Jira for project management but didn't have it integrated with their deployments in Azure DevOps. I showed them the release feature in Jira and how to include Jira tickets in each deployment, which was a manual process for them before. We worked together to automate this process, which reduced human error and greatly improved productivity and reporting.

You can also connect your GitHub repository to Jira and create automation rules based on DevOps triggers. I like how you can connect code branches to releases and tickets in Jira by including the Jira ticket number in the name of the branch. When you do this, tickets are automatically updated whenever you commit code or do a pull request. This is an excellent way to improve communication while maintaining each release's history. GitHub and Jira also connect to communication tools, including Slack and Microsoft Teams, so that you can send updates to project teams on status updates, which is useful for deployments.

Another example of integrating deployments with project management systems is using a tool such as Trello. Trello is a project management tool that uses boards, lists, and cards to organize tasks. You can create a card for each deployment by integrating your deployment tool with Trello. The card can include all the necessary information, such as the deployment date, the target environment, and any notes or instructions. When the deployment is completed, the card is moved to a "Completed" list so everyone can see that the deployment is finished.

Remember that implementing automation for deployments and connecting them to your project management system helps to communicate the status of tasks and deployments, but you shouldn't over-engineer the process. You still must prioritize communication within the team. While automation is great, providing context to status updates isn't always possible. I like to be proactive and send a message to the team when updates need more context. Communicating with the team is important when you're assigning new tasks or when one task is finished and the next one is ready to begin, such as the testing phase during deployments. You should never expect an automated process to communicate for you.

7.4.3   *Assessing your defect rate*

In project management, it's crucial to measure the performance of your development team to ensure that you deliver high-quality software products. One of the essential metrics to track is the defect rate, which reflects the number of errors or defects in your code. The defect rate is an essential indicator of the team's efficiency and software product quality. By measuring this metric, you can identify the areas of your development process that need improvement and address them promptly.

In agile methodology, the focus is on delivering incremental changes to the software product in short iterations. The development team works in sprints, each delivering a working software product. The defect rate (aka defect count) is calculated by dividing the number of defects by the total number of stories completed in a sprint. The formula for calculating the error rate is

Error rate = (Number of defects ÷ Total number of stories completed) × 100

For example, if your team completed 10 stories in a sprint and found two defects, the defect rate would be

Error rate = (2 ÷ 10) × 100 = 20%

In the waterfall methodology, the focus is on completing the entire project in one go, starting from requirements gathering to delivery. The development team works linearly, and each phase must be completed before moving to the next. The defect rate is calculated by dividing the number of defects by the total number of lines of code in the software product. The formula for calculating the error rate is

Error rate = (Number of defects ÷ Total number of lines of code) × 100

For example, if your team wrote 1,000 lines of code and found 150 defects, the error rate would be

Error rate = (150 ÷ 1,000) × 100 = 15%

Reducing the error rate is a continuous process that requires consistent effort from the development team. You must identify the root cause of the defects and address them promptly. Talk to the team to get their feedback on what needs to be improved, and include them in maintaining the development process. It's also important to conduct code reviews to identify potential errors. Code reviews should never be rushed, no matter how small the task.

Performing thorough testing is critical to ensure the software product is working as expected. I'm a proponent of both automated unit testing and manual testing. Unit testing is great, but you can't automate testing the design of your product or user experience. Remember, too much automation isn't a good thing, and it can lead to a lack of communication when status updates need to be explained in greater detail.

The defect rate is an essential metric to track in project management. It helps you identify areas for improvement and ensure that you're delivering high-quality software products. By implementing checks and balances in your process, you can reduce the number of defects and improve your development team's efficiency.

7.5   *Case study*

Chloe Condon is a Bay Area–based developer advocate for Google Cloud and AI. Previously, she worked at Microsoft, as well as Sentry.io, where she created the award-winning Sentry Scouts program (a camp-themed meet-up featuring patches, s'mores, giant squirrel costumes, and hot chocolate) and was featured in the Grace Hopper Conference 2018 gallery featuring 15 influential women in STEM by AnitaB.org. Her projects and work in teaching cloud have ranged from fake boyfriend alerts to Mario Kart "astrology," and have been featured in *VICE*, the *New York Times*, and SmashMouth's Twitter account. Chloe holds a BA in Drama from San Francisco State University and is a graduate of Hackbright Academy. She prides herself on being a nontraditional background engineer and is likely one of the only engineers who has played an ogre, crayon, and the back end of a cow on a professional stage. She hopes to bring more artists into tech and more engineers into the arts. In this case study, Chloe offers her advice for avoiding miscommunication and her experiences supporting the success of project teams.

7.5.1   *How do you avoid miscommunication with your team members, and what are some important strategies you use?*

A lot of what I do involves helping product teams script out technical content for developers for videos. When I'm in planning meetings specifically for technical content, I make sure that everybody in the room knows what the product does and how it works, and I don't assume that they already know. I think sometimes we get into a room, and we assume that everyone knows what the product does, how it works, why it works, why developers would use it, and how developers would use it, but a really big part of my job is helping tell the developer story. Any time I enter a meeting, I don't assume that anyone is technical, and I don't assume that anyone isn't technical. I've been in situations where people have addressed that in a not-so-nice way, where they just assume everyone is nontechnical, or they assume everyone is technical. So finding that middle ground and making sure you're on the same page with everyone is really important to avoid miscommunication.

7.5.2   *Why is it important to ask for help?*

I've worked for a lot of larger companies like Microsoft and Google, and acronyms are always different for every company. When I first started at these companies, people were throwing around terms, saying that we need to make sure we get the XYZ on the ABC and the TTYL. I'm the one in the meeting always raising my hand to ask, "Can someone tell me what this acronym means?" When I'm in a meeting, I'll be the squeaky wheel asking questions because I just assume other people don't know either.

In terms of asking for help, my role is kind of unique because I work with a lot of different product teams to help create video content for their tools. A lot of times, these products either aren't generally available, so I can't even go to the documentation yet, or it's something that we're going to be announcing, like a feature that hasn't been released yet. So I had to get over the fear of asking for help very quickly in my current role. I used to fear asking for help because in previous jobs earlier in my career, I thought this made me look like I didn't know what I was doing or that I was weak. In my previous life as an actress, asking for help wasn't a part of that culture. Being an actress required a lot of figuring it out on my own. So in my previous life, asking for help felt incredibly intimidating, whereas if I don't ask for help in the tech industry, I would have no idea what I'm doing. I rely on so many other smarter people to be able to be successful at my job.

There are a couple of things that I do when I'm asking for help that have helped me. I ask for help the way that I would want to be asked for help. For example, "Hey, I'm trying to do an X, here are the three things that I've already tried. Can you help?" Because people often reach out to me for things, and I wonder if they've googled it, and I need to know what steps they have already taken to resolve the problem. I'm always very specific with my questions because I know that everybody's time is very valuable, especially when working with engineers, because steering an engineer away from a technical task isn't only distracting to them, but it's very costly for the company.

7.5.3 *How do you support project managers?*

I try to give project managers accurate time estimates. I know that I'm terrible at scoping (as many developers are). So I always try to set proper expectations in terms of timing. I have a buffer where I always add a couple of days or a week to whatever I think it's going to take me to get something done. It also helps to set up a weekly cadence of meetings, so they don't have to follow up and play tag with me as much. I give them updates when I have them, making sure that I communicate everything to them even before they ask.

I'm also very transparent with project managers, and I tell them that if they need to reach me, chat is best. I'm probably not going to see the message if it's in my email, so I like to communicate my communication preferences. If I'm working on a certain project, I'll have a group Google Chat. We touch base at least weekly because we're all working on so many things at once. Having that check-in every week is always helpful. Sometimes we touch base, and we've made no progress, and sometimes we have made a ton of progress. These check-ins allow the project manager to plan their schedule accordingly, and they don't have to chase me down. Making sure that I'm communicating with project managers gives me accountability, and also I think it shows that it's a priority to me/the team.

7.5.4 *How do you connect team members with the people and resources they need to finish a task if they're struggling?*

I connect with them immediately because otherwise, I'll forget. I also connect them with someone who can help if I can't help. I think there's sort of this etiquette when you introduce someone to someone else. It's a little different when you work at the same company. If someone on Twitter asks me to connect them with someone, I'll usually ask the person first. But if it's within a company, I provide context when I introduce them. For example, I'll say, "Jill needs help with [insert description here]. Jill, this is Jack. Jack needs help with [insert description here]. I think you could help each other." I try to send these messages as soon as I see them instead of writing myself a note because I know my brain, and if I don't do it right now, I won't do it.

Sending documentation is great, but it's better if I'm able to send a video that can walk people through what I'm talking about. That has been very useful, and I always assume, except in cases where it's a brand-new product that hasn't been released yet, that someone has already written or talked about it, or they have done a much deeper, better dive that already exists out there.

A lot of our job as developers is just knowing how to google, which I promise isn't an ad for Google because I work there. So much about being a developer is knowing how to search and what to search for, which has become very interesting and relevant with AI now that we're all discussing prompt tuning! Being able to create the right prompt is a huge part of getting the most accurate results. Oftentimes, I find that if I'm working with less technical people (or maybe folks who just don't know how to look for what they're searching for), it can even just be a matter of changing one word in the search query. So sometimes, part of onboarding and teaching teammates is showing them how to find internal documentation, resources, and so on. We're so lucky at Google, and my ADHD brain is very thankful for how easy it is to search for internal resources. It hasn't been as easy at other companies—easy and searchable access to information is so helpful in getting work done!

I think as developers, sometimes we underestimate how differently our brains work when using search tools. There's a great meme about developers searching for "how to kill a child" referring to a GitHub repository, and it tips off the FBI, but then they complete the search, and it says "repository." It's literally just a matter of changing one word or adding additional industry terms to find what you're searching for. A lot of being a more senior developer is knowing what to search for and how to search for it. If your documentation is difficult to understand or navigate, people are going to have a very difficult time getting their work done.

Summary

- Lead developers play a crucial role in ensuring a project's success, and they can use either hourly estimates or story points to provide accurate project estimates for better project planning and management.
- Inaccurate estimates can cause missed deadlines, budget overruns, project delays, burnout, decreased productivity, and a loss of trust and confidence among stakeholders, leading to project failures in software development projects.
- Regularly scheduled meetings, using collaboration tools, and establishing clear communication protocols are some of the best practices to facilitate communication and connect team members and stakeholders.

- Properly facilitated communication can lead to improved collaboration, timely problem resolution, and successful project outcomes, while lack of communication can result in misunderstandings, delays, conflicts, and project failures.
- Agile project management is an iterative and flexible approach that emphasizes collaboration and adaptive planning, while waterfall project management follows a linear and sequential process with predefined stages and specific deliverables.
- Integrating code management tools such as GitHub with project management systems such as Jira or Trello can provide real-time updates and better visibility into the status of software deployments.

Speaking with clients

8

This chapter covers

- Best practices for understanding client needs
- Using active listening for client communication
- Differentiating between client wants and needs
- Establishing client trust
- Staying calm and diplomatic with clients
- Handling difficult clients

As a lead developer, you've likely spent countless hours perfecting your technical skills and deepening your understanding of programming languages. However, as you advance in your career and take on more responsibilities, you may face a new challenge: learning how to speak to clients.

Speaking to clients can be daunting, even for the most experienced developers. It requires a different set of skills than programming, and you'll need time and practice to become comfortable with it. But the benefits of being able to communicate effectively with clients are numerous: you can build stronger relationships, improve your understanding of clients' needs, and ultimately deliver better solutions.

Throughout this chapter, you'll learn about the most common challenges you'll face as a lead developer dealing with clients. When I took on the role of lead developer for the first time, I struggled a lot when dealing with clients. I made many mistakes, but I learned from those mistakes to become comfortable with clients. I hope that reading about my experiences will give you the skills and confidence to effectively work with clients and manage your relationships. These skills can take time to develop, but they are essential for building strong relationships with clients and understanding their needs.

8.1   *Understanding your clients' needs*

When lead developers understand their client's needs, they can deliver solutions that truly meet their client's expectations. By listening to their clients, asking questions, and involving them in the development process, lead developers can gain a deeper understanding of what their clients need and how they plan to use the software. This can result in solutions that are tailored to their unique requirements, increasing the chances of success.

Understanding clients' needs can also help build stronger relationships with them. Lead developers can build trust and long-term relationships with clients by demonstrating a commitment to their success and involving them in the development process. This can lead to repeat business and positive referrals, essential for a successful business.

In contrast, when lead developers don't understand their client's needs, it can lead to a project that falls short of expectations. Without a clear understanding of what the client needs, lead developers may develop software that doesn't meet their client's needs or isn't functional. This can lead to frustration on both sides, with the client feeling like they wasted time and money on a solution that doesn't work for them and the lead developer feeling like they wasted their time and resources developing something that doesn't meet the client's needs. A poor result can damage the relationship between the client and the organization. Clients may feel like their needs weren't heard or understood, leading to a breakdown in communication and a loss of trust. This can damage the company's reputation and make it more difficult to win future business.

Throughout my career, I've taken the lead on many projects that weren't going well. I always assess the disconnect between the written requirements and what the client is asking for. I speak to the client directly and collaborate with them to come up with the best solution for their project, and most importantly, I listen to them. Clients don't always know what they want or need, but it's not the lead developer's job to make decisions for them. It's a collaborative process, and lead developers must understand how to assess their clients' needs.

8.1.1   *Using active listening*

Active listening is the process of fully engaging with the speaker and seeking to understand their message. As one of the most effective ways to understand your client's needs, active listening involves not just hearing what the speaker is saying but also paying attention to their tone, body language, and context. By listening actively and engaging with clients, you can get a clearer picture of what the client wants and needs from the software. This, in turn, can help you develop solutions that truly meet those needs, leading to successful projects and satisfied clients. Here are some examples of active listening for lead developers:

- *Ask open-ended questions.* Instead of asking yes or no questions, ask questions encouraging clients to share more information about their needs; for example, "Can you tell me more about how you plan to use the software?" or "What are your biggest challenges that this software will solve?"
- *Repeat back what you heard.* After the client shares their needs, repeat back what you heard to ensure you understand correctly. This demonstrates to the client that you're actively listening and seeking to understand their message.
- *Pay attention to body language.* Sometimes, what a client says verbally may not align with their body language. For example, if a client says they are excited about the project, but their body language is closed off and tense, it may indicate that they have reservations. Make sure to address their concerns and show empathy for their situation. Reassure them that they are being heard, and promote open conversation. Addressing negative body language in a positive manner will show the client that you care and will address their concerns.

Active listening can also help build trust and strong relationships with clients. Lead developers can build rapport and trust with clients by demonstrating a commitment to understanding their needs and actively engaging with them. This, in turn, can lead to repeat business and positive referrals.

When working with clients, at the end of every meeting, I repeat what we talked about and reiterate the action items we agreed on. I also work with the project manager to write meeting notes and send them to everyone afterward. Active listening can be applied to written communication as well as verbal. This is especially important if you're working with someone with a disability, such as being blind or deaf. You must use all communication methods to ensure everyone is on the same page and there is no miscommunication.

8.1.2   Asking insightful questions

Insightful questions are those that go beyond the surface level and seek to uncover the underlying needs and motivations of the client. They are designed to encourage the client to think more deeply about their needs and provide detailed answers that can inform the development process. By asking insightful questions, lead developers can better understand the client's needs and develop solutions that truly meet those needs. Table 8.1 provides some examples of insightful questions that lead developers can ask their clients.

Table 8.1   Questions for clients

Question	Purpose
What are your goals for this project?	Understanding the client's goals can help you prioritize features and functionality that will be most useful to the client. Many lead developers are accustomed to thinking about individual tasks, but you must also take a step back and understand the purpose of the entire project so that you can design the system components accordingly.
What challenges are you currently facing that this project will solve?	Identifying the client's pain points can help you develop solutions that address those challenges directly. Asking this question often leads to opportunities for automation to increase productivity and reduce human error.
How do you envision using the software in your day-to-day operations?	Understanding use cases for the software can help you design a user-friendly interface and prioritize functionality that will be most useful to the client. For example, when you're building websites, they are generally based on a Content Management System (CMS) so that users can manage their web pages without developer intervention. It's important to understand how the users will interact with such a system so that you can customize the interface to suit their needs.
What are your long-term goals for your business, and how can this software help you achieve those goals?	Understanding the client's long-term goals can help you develop a software solution to grow with the client's business. It's important for you as a lead developer to take a step back and understand how the project you're working on affects the overall business goals.
What are your expectations for the development process, and how can we ensure that those expectations are met?	Understanding the client's expectations can help you manage them and ensure a smooth development process. Just be careful to set reasonable expectations and deliver on your promises.

Asking these questions isn't a one-time event, and you must follow up with them. If a project isn't going well, check back frequently to address the problems and get everything back on track. I've been in situations where I met with the client daily for a short 15- to 30-minute conversation. With other clients, we had 1-hour meetings once per week. It depends on the severity of the problems and your relationship with the client. I like to use a checklist for their concerns, and once a fix is implemented, I ask them for feedback. It's important to remember that these questions are just a starting point, and you should be prepared to follow up with additional questions as needed to fully understand the client's needs.

8.1.3   *Interviewing the end user*

As a lead developer, you may be tasked with working on software projects designed to meet end users' needs. End users are the people who will use the software that you implement, and they may not be a part of the project team. To deliver a successful project, it's essential to have a deep understanding of those users' needs and preferences. I've worked on projects that were business-to-business (B2B), and I was customizing systems for internal use. In this case, I was able to connect with the end users personally. I've also worked on business-to-consumer (B2C) software as a service (SaaS) platforms for customers where I couldn't have contact with millions of users. I can tell you from experience that one of the most effective ways to understand the needs of the end users is by interviewing them using various methods.

Interviewing end users is a critical step in the development process because it allows you to understand the needs and preferences of the people who will be using the software. This understanding can inform key design decisions, feature prioritization, and the overall development process. Without this information, you risk delivering software that doesn't meet the needs of the end users, which can lead to poor adoption rates and a lack of engagement. Lead developers can use several different interview formats to gather insights from end users. Here are a few examples:

- *Structured interviews*—Structured interviews are highly organized and use predetermined questions. This format is useful when gathering specific information from end users or comparing answers across multiple interviews.
- *Semi-structured interviews*—Semi-structured interviews allow for more open-ended responses but still follow a general structure. This format is useful when you want to explore a topic in-depth but also want to allow for unexpected insights.
- *Unstructured interviews*—Unstructured interviews are the most open-ended format and allow for a free-flowing conversation between the interviewer and end user. This format is useful when exploring a topic in-depth and allowing for unexpected insights.
- *Focus groups*—Focus groups bring together a small group of end users to discuss their experiences and perspectives on a specific topic. This format is useful when gathering insights from multiple end users at once and facilitating group discussion.
- *User testing*—User testing involves observing end users as they interact with a prototype or early version of the software. This format is useful when you want to gather feedback on the usability and functionality of the software.
- *Surveys*—Surveys are the fastest way to gather information, and they can be a starting point before you engage in conversation with end users. You can compile the data to surface pain points and allow your users to provide anonymous critiques of the software. People are often more truthful if their feedback is anonymous.
- *Heatmaps*—A software heatmap is a tool that is commonly used to analyze user interactions with a website or application. You can assess which screens are never used and which paths are taken through the software. This can then lead you to ask more targeted questions of the user base.

In my experience, the combination of surveys and focus groups has worked well. I've worked with end users who were part of the client's internal team and external customers. In either case, I often found a disconnect between what the client requested and what the user needed. An example of this was when I worked with a client who had exceptional technical skills but also the tendency to over-engineer their software so that it was difficult for nontechnical users to understand. This was a B2B project, and I could schedule a focus group with every end user, as it was a small group. I asked them about their roles and how they expected to use the system. I listened to all of them and noted any discrepancies in our existing use cases. You may be unable to include every user if it's a large group, so a survey is more appropriate. If I hadn't interviewed the users, the software project would have failed due to mismatched requirements.

No matter which interview format you choose, it's important to prepare ahead of time and tailor your questions to the specific needs of the project and end users. Make sure to listen actively and take notes during the interview to capture important insights and observations. Clients often don't know all the pain points of the end users, and involving them in the development process will help to ensure the project's success. Interviewing both the client and end users will help you determine the best approach for your project to meet everyone's needs. When I find that there are discrepancies in the use cases or requirements, I discuss these in a meeting with the client and project team. I've had great success meeting with the project team to prepare our approach beforehand to ensure we all understand the plan. I've worked with some excellent project managers who presented the information we gathered from the interviews and only relied on me to explain how our technical approach needed to change to address the feedback from the end users. It's important to work together with the project team and the client to listen to the end users and implement solutions that meet their needs.

8.2   *Suggesting technical approaches*

When a lead developer successfully presents their technical approach to clients, the client clearly understands the problem and how the proposed solution addresses it. They see the expertise and passion exuding from the lead developer, instilling confidence in their abilities. A successful presentation fosters a sense of trust and collaboration between the client and the development team, setting the stage for a fruitful partnership. In such instances, the client is more likely to embrace the proposed technical approach wholeheartedly. They recognize its benefits to their business, whether it's improved efficiency, enhanced user experience, or increased profitability.

An unsuccessful presentation can harm the client's perception of the technical approach. A lack of clarity and effective communication may confuse the client, leaving them unsure of how the proposed solution solves their problem. They may doubt the lead developer's competence or question the approach's feasibility altogether.

An unsuccessful presentation can also lead to a breakdown in trust and hinder the client's willingness to embrace the proposed solution. Without a clear understanding of the benefits or tangible evidence to support the approach, the client may hesitate to invest their resources in the project. This can lead to missed opportunities, strained client-developer relationships, and even the loss of potential projects. Mastering the art of presenting technical approaches is therefore crucial for lead developers, as it showcases their expertise and paves the way for successful project outcomes.

8.2.1 Understanding wants vs. needs

As a lead developer, you must implement features based on current industry standards and practices. Therefore, you must understand the difference between what the client wants and what the client needs. Communicating what they need takes great care, as you don't want to hurt their feelings or make them feel like their ideas are poorly thought out. You should listen to them, ensure that you understand what they want, and then translate that into what they need. You may also find that some clients will propose their own solutions. This must be handled carefully to avoid implementing software that doesn't address their needs. At one company I worked for, the managers didn't know how to handle this properly, so they would always implement the client's proposed solutions. This was a tough client, and they were very headstrong, but by not pushing back on their ideas, the system became over-engineered and not user-friendly. This is how management at that company handled all their clients, so none of their projects were successful, and they were shut down. This is an extreme case, and I hope you never encounter a misunderstanding of the client's wants versus needs on this scale. Part of your job as a lead developer is to ensure that the systems you build are high quality and meet the users' needs. It's up to you to assess any proposed solution to ensure it will support the project's success.

Listening is the first and most crucial step in understanding what your clients want. Engage in active listening during meetings, discussions, and even casual conversations. Pay close attention to their ideas and preferences. With good communication and understanding of their expectations, you can build trust and demonstrate your commitment to their vision. While client wants are important, it's equally essential to identify their underlying needs. Needs address the project's core purpose, functionality, and long-term goals. This requires a deeper understanding of their business, target audience, and industry trends.

When I start on a new project, especially with a new client, during the first project meeting, I encourage open dialogue and active listening. I also create an environment where clients feel comfortable sharing their aspirations and concerns. By fostering a collaborative atmosphere, you lay the foundation for productive discussions. During initial meetings, I encourage clients to describe their dream application or website and actively listen to their ideas. They might desire eye-catching design, vibrant colors, or unconventional design elements. While these are wants, it's important to recognize them as valuable starting points for deeper conversations. Table 8.2 includes examples of client wants versus client needs.

Table 8.2   Examples of client wants vs. needs

Wants	Needs
"Simple" e-commerce website	Advanced inventory management, order tracking, and customer support systems
Implement every cutting-edge technology into a mobile app	Upgrade to cutting-edge technologies only as needed
Robust customer loyalty program with a login and dashboard	Creating a simple login and dashboard, and rolling out new features gradually
Flashy web design	Designing a user-friendly interface
Custom solutions tailored for a specific project	Scalable and sustainable technologies that provide long-term support and compatibility

As a lead developer, your role is to dig deeper and uncover the underlying needs behind clients' wants. Ask relevant questions to understand their business goals, target audience, and project expectations. By delving into the core purpose of their project, you can gain valuable insights. Ask probing questions to determine each feature's purpose and intended user experience. This exploration might reveal what they truly need.

If a client insists on incorporating their proposed solution into their project, even though it might not be necessary, you can gently explain the potential drawbacks. You can also talk to the project manager about your concerns, and they can help mitigate the problem with the client. When this happens, I usually meet with the client and project team to discuss the problems with their proposed solution. By offering alternative approaches and explaining the pros and cons, you empower your clients to make informed decisions.

8.2.2   *Considering the budget*

As a lead developer, it's important for you to keep your clients' budgets in mind when suggesting technical approaches. While striving for a high-quality product is essential, balancing budget constraints and delivering exceptional results is an art worth mastering. When you're starting a project, it's imperative to have a clear understanding of the client's budgetary limitations. Clients often have specific financial constraints to consider during the project's planning phase. By being mindful of the budget, you demonstrate empathy, trustworthiness, and a commitment to delivering value for your clients.

You should begin by identifying the core features that are essential for the project's success and allocate a significant portion of the budget to implement them effectively. Focus on the features that directly align with the client's objectives and bring the most value to their business. By understanding the priorities, you can allocate resources and efforts more efficiently. When I start a new project, I work closely with the project manager to prioritize features to determine what will bring the most value. When I'm building an e-commerce website, implementing secure payment gateways is one of my highest priorities. Without a secure payment gateway, an e-commerce project would never be successful.

Sometimes, the features that will bring the most value to the client aren't as obvious, and you'll have to explain your reasoning for prioritizing that specific feature. Clients won't balk at the idea of prioritizing security; however, they may not understand the importance of robust inventory management to support a user-friendly checkout process. They may want to prioritize search or a recommended products widget, and while these are important features for any e-commerce website, you must support the checkout process first. When I'm explaining this to clients, I like to use the metaphor of building a house. You need the foundation built first, including anything that supports the rest of the house. After that's built, then you can move on to the next set of features.

While it's tempting to build complex and sophisticated solutions, it's important to strike a balance between functionality and complexity. Over-engineering a project can significantly affect the budget, both in terms of development time and ongoing maintenance costs. Suggesting lean and scalable technical approaches can help optimize costs. Consider using existing libraries, frameworks, or open source solutions to avoid reinventing the wheel. By using proven technologies, you can save time, reduce development effort, and ultimately minimize expenses for your client.

I once worked with a quirky client who wanted everything custom-built, and he hated Angular. I knew that Angular was a good solution for his project and that what he asked us to do would cost more. So I talked with him about his previous experience with Angular to figure out why he was so averse to it. Apparently, a previous developer had built something for him using Angular that he didn't like. This led him to form an unconscious bias against Angular, and I had to mitigate his feelings. It took several discussions, but I researched other options and presented him with each option. After we weighed the pros and cons together, we determined that Angular would be a better approach than building a custom library.

If a project has gone over budget, you should analyze the reasons why the project has exceeded the budget. Identify the factors contributing to the overruns, such as scope changes, unexpected problems, inaccurate estimates, or resource constraints. Work with the project team to brainstorm and identify potential solutions to address the budget overage. This may involve exploring different approaches, reevaluating project priorities, reallocating resources, or seeking additional funding if feasible. It also helps to evaluate the team member allocation within the project and ensure that the available people are used efficiently. Consider reassigning tasks or optimizing workflows to improve productivity and reduce unnecessary expenses.

Using the agile project management methodology can be instrumental in balancing the budget and product quality. In agile, you have an iterative development cycle where you break down the project into smaller milestones, allowing regular feedback loops with the client and providing continuous delivery. With continuous delivery, each release goes through automated testing and integration, which helps identify and fix bugs early in the development process. This leads to higher-quality software with fewer defects. This iterative process ensures that the client's vision aligns with the development progress and helps identify potential budgetary challenges early on. By incorporating continuous feedback, you can adjust along the way, ensuring that the development stays within budget and meets the client's expectations. It also provides an opportunity to address any scope creep and make informed decisions about feature enhancements or tradeoffs without compromising the overall budget.

8.2.3   *Presenting your case*

When it comes to presenting your technical approach to clients, it's important to remember that effective communication is key. You must be able to convey your ideas in a clear, concise, and compelling manner. It's important to understand your audience so that you can tailor your presentation to speak to their interests and concerns. You should listen to your clients and use active listening to reiterate back to them your understanding of the problem so that it's clearly defined and nothing is missed. Before you present your case, you must ensure that you and your client are in agreement and that you understand the requirements completely. You won't be set up for success if you go into a presentation with the wrong approach. I've been there, and it's very embarrassing. In my early days as a lead developer, I was tasked with presenting to a new client. I went in there equipped with my own ideas, not realizing that they had a technical expert on their end who had outlined their own ideas, which I had missed. My presentation didn't address their ideas, so it went awry. The client pushed back on nearly everything I presented, and we didn't accomplish our meeting goals. It took some time and teamwork to get back on track by addressing the miscommunication and discussing their requirements.

It helps to outline your technical approach using visuals such as diagrams or flow-charts. This enables a nontechnical audience to understand the concept that you're presenting. It's important to avoid using too much jargon in your presentations and not assume that everyone knows these terms or acronyms. Using real-world examples to illustrate your key points helps your client connect your concept to something tangible and measurable. I always present key metrics from past projects that were used to measure success to show that my team has a proven track record of successfully implementing similar projects.

Of course, part of presenting your case is addressing your client's concerns. Preparing your presentation by anticipating questions about feasibility, scalability, or potential risks is a good idea. When you preemptively answer these questions, it shows that you're experienced and you know what their concerns are because you've worked on similar projects. If you haven't worked on similar projects, you can still research similar projects and provide case studies. Encourage your clients to communicate their concerns and handle them in a professional manner. Answer every question they propose in a thoughtful manner and ensure that they are satisfied with your answer. When you're presenting your case for a technical approach, you're facilitating a conversation with your client to make decisions. You must take care to ensure that your client feels listened to and that their concerns are addressed. Table 8.3 includes a summary of the steps involved in presenting your case for a technical approach to a client, including descriptions and examples.

Table 8.3 How to present your case

Step	Description	Example
Understand your audience.	What are their goals, concerns, and priorities? Tailor your presentation accordingly to ensure that your message resonates with them.	If your client is primarily focused on cost efficiency, emphasize how your approach can optimize resources and reduce expenses.
Clearly define the problem.	Explain the challenges and pain points your client is facing. Use relatable examples and analogies to help your client grasp the concept.	Compare an e-commerce website to a physical store where customers abandon their shopping carts due to long queues at the checkout counter.
Outline your technical approach.	Break down complex concepts into jargon-free explanations. Use visuals such as diagrams or flowcharts to illustrate the various stages of your approach.	Visualize the process of optimizing page load times with a flowchart showing the before and after effects of each optimization step.
Highlight the benefits.	Emphasize the positive effect the project will have on their operations, user experience, and overall bottom line. Quantify these benefits wherever possible, using metrics such as increased conversion rates, reduced bounce rates, or improved customer satisfaction scores.	Explain how your proposed improvements in website load times can lead to a 25% decrease in bounce rates and a 15% increase in conversions. Explain how these improvements directly translate into higher revenue and a competitive advantage in the online market.
Address potential concerns.	Anticipate questions about feasibility, scalability, or potential risks. Provide well-thought-out answers and solutions that instill confidence in your approach.	Address concerns about code optimization by explaining your thorough testing and QA processes. Highlight successful implementations of similar approaches with other clients.
Use real-world examples.	Support your presentation with real-world examples that showcase the effectiveness of your proposed technical approach. Share success stories from past projects or relevant industry case studies.	Highlight the metrics and results achieved in a previous project where you improved website performance, such as reduced page load times, increased customer engagement, and improved search engine rankings.

I struggled to present my technical approach when I first became a lead developer. I had a hard time facilitating conversations about my client's concerns, but this became second nature over time and with practice. I also tend to work on very similar projects, so I've gathered a playbook that includes questions to ask, frequent concerns, and case studies. Now when I go into these presentations, I can connect with the client and communicate my team's approach in a way that they can understand. For example, I worked with a client needing a CMS for their website and app. They weren't technical and had difficulty understanding the underlying technology, but they were also curious. So I took the time to answer their questions and create flowcharts for them to visualize the architecture. They also had budgetary concerns, so we approached the project with the minimal viable product in mind. They appreciated my patience and attention to detail and thanked me constantly. I provided them with the information they wanted but never had before. I helped them learn new skills, which increased their confidence in themselves and the project. Remember, part of presenting your technical approach is facilitating a conversation with your clients and addressing any concerns that they have. Doing so will build trust and set you up for success.

8.3   *Forming relationships with clients*

Software development is often perceived as a technical endeavor, but it's crucial to remember that there is also a human element. Clients are real people with their own aspirations, concerns, and ideas. By investing time and effort in building client relationships, lead developers can establish trust, foster open communication, and gain a deeper understanding of their clients' needs. This human connection lays a strong foundation for collaboration and paves the way for a successful partnership.

The collaborative spirit essential for successful project outcomes diminishes without a strong working relationship. Ideas may be confined within information silos, which will hinder innovation. The absence of open communication channels means missed opportunities for valuable insights and improvements. As a result, the final product may fall short of the client's vision, leading to dissatisfaction and strained professional relationships. Without a positive experience, clients are unlikely to recommend the organization to others or seek their services in the future.

With a solid working relationship in place, collaboration between lead developers and clients becomes seamless. They function as a unified team, working toward a shared goal. The exchange of ideas becomes vibrant and dynamic, enabling lead developers to provide valuable insights and recommendations based on their technical expertise. Clients can offer unique perspectives and domain knowledge that enrich the development process. This collaboration results in a final product that meets the client's expectations and aligns perfectly with their long-term vision.

8.3.1   *Establishing trust with clients*

Trust is the cornerstone of any successful project, and establishing it from the very beginning is vital. Trust fosters open communication, enables effective collaboration, and instills confidence in the lead developers' expertise. It leads to streamlined processes, greater flexibility, and timely delivery of high-quality work, resulting in client satisfaction and the potential for long-term partnerships. On the other hand, a lack of trust can impede progress, hinder effective communication, and diminish client satisfaction, jeopardizing project success and fruitful relationships.

When I start a new project, the first thing I do is establish trust with my clients. One of the best ways to do this is to listen to them and consider their ideas. They are the experts in the business needs that their projects will support, so it's important for lead developers to understand the client's point of view. When clients feel understood, this leads to more effective collaboration and helps to build long-lasting relationships.

I've worked on many projects where I've taken over for another lead developer. When you go into a project that is already in progress, you should talk with the client and ask them what they would like to improve. Make sure to approach this conversation without blaming the previous lead developer, especially if they are still working for the same organization. You don't want to make the organization look bad by throwing anyone under the bus. This approach also works if it's a new client. You can ask them what pain points they've had with previous projects.

An effective method of establishing trust is to deliver high-quality work on time and within budget. Delivering high-quality work should be your goal, and doing so within budget can be difficult. Budgeting is generally up to the project manager, but you can help them by adhering to deadlines and minimizing technical debt. It's far easier to do this when you communicate and collaborate with the entire team frequently, which is the backbone of the iterative approach used in the agile project management methodology. Part of delivering high-quality work is to build stable systems using best practices.

Your team should also run maintenance tasks at regular intervals to ensure that you avoid downtime and errors. I've worked on many projects where maintenance was skipped, and systems would go down frequently. Some lead developers don't see this as a bad thing if the systems can be brought back up quickly. It can take more time to run maintenance tasks than it does to bring a system back online; however, this is a gamble. If you skip maintenance, you never know when a major error will occur, so it's best to schedule it regularly. Many clients I worked with were under the impression that downtime was normal in any software development project and accepted it, but didn't like it. When I showed them how regular maintenance works to avoid these problems, they were happy to add time for maintenance to the schedule. Furthermore, they trusted me because I was going above and beyond what they were used to.

Taking ownership of your work and being accountable for your actions is integral to earning trust. When mistakes happen, acknowledge them promptly, accept responsibility, and work toward finding solutions. Avoid shifting blame or making excuses, as this can undermine trust. My biggest pet peeve is working with developers who never apologize or hold themselves accountable. Some people fear telling the truth when they've made a mistake, but if you're caught in a lie, that is the worst thing that can happen. Your clients will doubt you at every turn, and even when you're telling the truth, they may not accept it. Demonstrating accountability shows clients that you're committed to rectifying any problems and maintaining their confidence in your abilities.

8.3.2 *Getting to know your clients*

As a lead developer, forming personal connections with your clients will help to establish a rapport that goes beyond project requirements and lays the foundation for a lasting working relationship. To truly get to know your clients, embracing the human element of your interactions is essential. While discussing project details, take a genuine interest in their lives, passions, and experiences. Doing so creates a comfortable environment that encourages open communication and strengthens the client–developer bond.

Project meetings should begin with a short, casual conversation as you wait for everyone to join. During these conversations, I discovered that many of my clients enjoyed running, which is something that I'm also interested in. I would explore their interests by discussing our favorite races and exchanging recommendations. This established a personal connection and showcased my willingness to go beyond the project scope and engage with my clients on a human level. Seeking common ground with your clients can be a powerful way to establish a connection that goes beyond the professional realm. I've had success getting to know my clients during a team lunch at a conference we all attended. These techniques will help you discover shared interests, hobbies, or even similar career backgrounds. These shared experiences can form the basis for conversations that transcend project-related discussions. It's these connections that make clients feel understood and valued, fostering a sense of loyalty and trust.

Lead developers can create a strong bond with their clients by displaying empathy and understanding. Put yourself in their shoes to understand their challenges, aspirations, and concerns. By demonstrating that you genuinely care about their needs, you build a foundation of trust and establish yourself as a reliable partner. I've worked with many clients who were concerned about tight deadlines or budget constraints. In these cases, I always acknowledge their worries and work together to find feasible solutions. By actively listening and providing support, you show that you're invested in their success and are committed to helping them overcome obstacles. You can also show empathy for what they are going through in their personal lives. You never know what people are going through, and if you recognize that they are having a bad day or aren't themselves, you can gently ask them if they are okay. One question I started asking at the start of meetings during the pandemic is "How are you really?" This goes beyond asking "How are you?," to which the usual response is "I'm fine," even if the person is clearly not fine. Adding "really" to the question shows the other person that you want to hear the truth. You would be surprised at some of the conversations I had with clients about mental health by asking this question. People want to feel supported, and it helps immensely when they feel that they aren't alone.

Acknowledging and celebrating project milestones and achievements is another way to deepen your client relationships. Whether it's the successful launch of a new feature or reaching a significant project milestone, you should take the time to recognize and commemorate these achievements together. If you're a fully remote or hybrid team, you can plan a virtual celebration such as a happy hour or game night. I prefer to travel to the client site for an in-person celebration, usually lunch or dinner. I find that being in person makes for a more effective celebration. It's possible to have a celebration online, but keeping the party going takes more effort because people can multitask. When you're in person, there is a more human connection, and people are less likely to be distracted. By sharing these moments of success, you create a positive association between your collaboration and positive outcomes, fostering a lasting bond and ensuring future collaboration.

8.3.3   *Remaining diplomatic*

Diplomacy plays a major role in effective collaboration, building trust, and delivering successful projects. It involves setting realistic expectations and managing them effectively. It's important to be transparent about project timelines, potential challenges, and any constraints that may affect the delivery. When facing unrealistic demands, you should explain the limitations and propose alternative solutions. I also like to offer insights into industry best practices and use my experience to guide clients toward more feasible options.

One thing that clients often request is that we deliver additional features within the same timeline. I always ask clarifying questions to understand why these features are a priority and if there is other work that we can postpone instead. Priorities are always changing. That is why we have project managers. But lead developers must communicate any problems that may occur by altering the priorities. When I'm working with clients, I tell them that adding additional work to the current timeline might affect the overall quality and stability of the project. Then, I offer alternative solutions that address their requirements while maintaining the project's quality. It's important to prioritize quality over everything else to ensure the highest level of customer satisfaction.

Your language has a major effect on how your message is received. You can use the power of positive language to inspire confidence, promote collaboration, and create a pleasant client experience. Using words that convey optimism and possibility can instill trust and enthusiasm in your clients. Using negative words will have a detrimental effect, as you come off as a negative person. Clients may respond to negativity by feeling negative about the project and your capabilities as a lead developer. You should be aware that misery loves company, and it's human nature for people to seek out others who will complain about the same thing.

With very negative clients, something that helped me was to learn how to reframe negative thoughts as positive thoughts. I learned about this in therapy, and it's called Cognitive Behavioral Therapy (CBT). CBT is a goal-oriented form of psychotherapy that focuses on changing negative thought patterns and behaviors by challenging and replacing them with more balanced and helpful alternatives, aiming to improve mental health and well-being. This is a great skill to master, and it has helped me in my personal life and career. An example of this is changing "We can't do that" to "That is an interesting idea; let's talk about how we can accommodate your request." I've worked with clients who didn't understand how the technology we were using worked, so they constantly asserted their opinion as to how it should work. Instead of telling them they were wrong, I would reframe the thought into this: "I understand where you're coming from, and you're not alone. Many people are confused by this; let me clarify some details for you." Things aren't often black and white; there are gray areas that must be clarified so that your clients understand your technical approach.

When you're being diplomatic, it's important to also be authentic. Don't get angry or impatient with your clients. Your overall goal is to ensure customer satisfaction. You should care about them, their interests, and their opinions. If you're saying positive words with a negative tone, people will be able to observe your behavior and see that you're not being entirely truthful. In addition, be mindful of your body language. If you're frowning or have your arms crossed in front of you, this is a sign that you're not pleased. Instead, you should maintain a neutral expression and sit up straight with your shoulders back and chest forward. This more inviting stance will encourage your clients to collaborate and share their thoughts. This goes a long way to forming lasting relationships with your clients.

8.4   *Dealing with difficult clients*

Appropriately dealing with difficult clients is of utmost importance for lead developers, as it can significantly affect project outcomes and client relationships. Several positive outcomes can be observed when difficult clients are dealt with appropriately. Appropriate handling of difficult clients enables lead developers to steer the conversation toward a more constructive path. By maintaining professionalism, lead developers can create an atmosphere conducive to open dialogue and problem-solving. This fosters a healthier working relationship and increases the likelihood of finding mutually satisfactory resolutions.

In contrast, several negative consequences may arise when difficult clients aren't dealt with appropriately. Reacting impulsively or losing your cool can worsen the situation, leading to strained relationships, poor communication, and project delays. The client's frustrations may escalate further, increasing tension and potential project disruptions. In extreme cases, inappropriate handling of difficult clients can even lead to contract terminations or reputational damage for the lead developer or their organization.

When difficult clients aren't handled appropriately, it can negatively affect the overall team morale and motivation. Team members may feel demotivated or frustrated when witnessing tense interactions or experiencing the consequences of mismanaged client relationships. This can lead to decreased productivity, lower quality output, and increased turnover within the team. Inadequate communication and ineffective conflict resolution can also hinder the team's ability to collaborate effectively, impeding the project's success.

I've dealt with my fair share of difficult clients in my career, which I struggled with a lot. The worst is when clients are rude or demeaning to you. I remember working with a client's systems administrator who was so rude to me and didn't provide any help. I escalated the problem to the project manager, and they initially brushed it off. But I pushed the problem, and they assigned a different systems administrator to work with me. We worked well together, and all our problems were addressed. Knowing how to act in these situations and how to diffuse tensions is so hard. It's especially hard when the client's requests are unreasonable and they are unwavering. As a first-time lead developer, you want to impress your clients and co-workers. When your clients are unhappy, it can make you feel like you're inadequate as a lead developer. Just know that you're not alone; this is one of the hardest parts of the job. Keeping your manager in the loop when clients are difficult is important. They may be able to escalate the problems to bring in someone who can help you mitigate them. When I learned how to stay calm and rely on my team, I started to have more success in diffusing tensions and turning a negative situation into a positive one.

8.4.1 Staying calm

When faced with a difficult client, it's natural for emotions to run high. However, reacting impulsively or losing your cool can have detrimental consequences. Maintaining a calm and collected demeanor can lead to more positive outcomes for both you and the client. Staying calm allows you to think clearly and make rational decisions. When emotions are running high, it becomes challenging to assess situations objectively. By remaining composed, you can better analyze the client's concerns, identify the root causes of their frustrations, and develop appropriate solutions. This measured approach fosters a sense of trust and confidence in your abilities as a lead developer.

Staying calm also helps diffuse tense situations. Difficult clients often express their frustrations with increased intensity and may resort to abrasive language or unreasonable demands. By responding calmly, you can avoid escalating the situation further. Your composed demeanor counterbalances their emotions, enabling you to steer the conversation toward a more constructive path.

A good way to stay calm when dealing with difficult clients is to put yourself in their shoes and try empathizing with their situation. Understand that their concerns may stem from external pressures or expectations. Demonstrating empathy creates a safe space for open dialogue and collaboration.

> **NOTE** Don't take things personally. There is often more than one reason for a client to be difficult.

Developing self-awareness will help you remain calm as you recognize your own emotional triggers and understand how they might affect your reactions. By being mindful of your emotions, you can choose how to respond rather than react impulsively. Take a moment to pause, breathe, and assess the situation before formulating a thoughtful and composed response. If you can't respond on the spot, you can tell your client that you'll do some research and get back to them. Knowing this will help you avoid getting upset or anxious because you know that you'll have time to respond. If the client requests an immediate response, you can tell them that you don't want to provide inaccurate information and that you must research the problem before you get back to them. Let them know that this is needed for you to support the project's success.

It's essential to have a support system in place when you're dealing with difficult clients. Reach out to your team members, mentors, or trusted colleagues to discuss your challenges. They can provide valuable insights, advice, and perspective to help you maintain your composure and develop effective strategies for handling difficult clients. When you're working on project teams, it's important for you to forge good working relationships so that you can seek their help when you need support. I'm lucky to have worked with many supportive project teams over the years, and we banded together when we worked with difficult clients. We often met with the internal project team directly after a client meeting to discuss how it went. We talked about how to handle the clients' comments, and it helped each of us to know that we weren't alone in our feelings. Knowing my team members well and having those meetings helped me to stay calm because I knew they felt the same way. When you don't feel alone, it helps you mitigate your triggers and feelings so that you can respond appropriately.

It's hard not to take things personally when a client is unhappy with your work. Remember that you're a part of a team, and failure is never a single person's fault. The ability to remain calm comes from within, and it helps if you remain confident in yourself and your skills as a lead developer. Having confidence enables you to approach challenging situations with a positive mindset and a belief in your abilities. You should reflect on past successes and remind yourself of the value you bring to the table. You can also gather feedback from team members or mentors who can provide valuable reassurance and help you identify areas for improvement. Having confidence allows lead developers to navigate difficult client interactions by remaining calm, staying positive, and diffusing the situation.

8.4.2 *Letting them talk*

When a client expresses their concerns or frustrations, you must listen to them regardless of whether or not you agree with what they are saying. Show that you genuinely understand their perspective by paraphrasing their statements and reflecting them back. This active listening approach helps defuse their emotions and allows you to effectively gather essential information to address their concerns. We discussed active listening earlier in this chapter, and it's an essential skill to practice when dealing with difficult clients.

Difficult clients often have specific concerns or challenges they want to address. By allowing clients to talk, you can gain valuable insights into the root causes of the client's dissatisfaction. Through active listening, lead developers can identify the underlying problems, understand the client's perspective, and develop tailored solutions. This demonstrates empathy and enables the lead developer to provide effective guidance and support to the client, leading to a more satisfactory resolution.

Clients may have unrealistic expectations or lack a clear understanding of the development process. By listening attentively, you can identify any misconceptions or gaps in knowledge and work toward bridging them. Through patient explanation and clarification, you can manage expectations and align them with what is feasible within the project's scope and constraints. By proactively addressing potential misunderstandings, you can mitigate conflicts and establish a realistic framework for collaboration.

The most difficult client I worked with would often have unrealistic expectations and a strict timeline. When they expressed dissatisfaction with the project's progress, I would respond empathetically by saying, "I understand how important this project is to you. Let's work together to identify the areas where we can improve and find a solution that meets your expectations." I listened to their feedback, asked clarifying questions, and worked with them to develop a viable solution. I empathized with them and asked them what expectations they were facing on their end. I let them know that my goal was to support their success as well as the success of the project. It took some time, but the client came to trust me and the project team even when things didn't go as planned because we had established lines of communication, and they felt that we were listening and taking their feedback into consideration.

Some clients don't know how to articulate their dissatisfaction, and you should take cues from their body language and tone. Sometimes, you need to ask them questions to get the conversation started and find out what they would like to see improved. I usually ask them point-blank what can be improved. This shows them that I'm open to having this conversation and that it will be handled in a professional manner. The following list includes questions that help get the conversation started:

- Can you please describe the specific challenges or problems you currently face with the project?
- What were your initial expectations for the project, and how do you feel they have been met or not met?
- Could you provide examples of specific project features, functionalities, or aspects that don't meet your requirements or expectations?
- Is there any aspect of the project that you find confusing or unclear? If so, could you please elaborate?
- Are there any communication gaps or breakdowns you noticed during the project?
- Can you explain any instances where the project may have deviated from your original vision or requirements?
- Have there been any challenges or obstacles on your end that have affected the project's progress or outcomes?
- What specific outcomes or results were you hoping to achieve through this project, and do you feel they have been adequately addressed?
- Are there any specific concerns regarding the timeline, budget, or resource allocation that you would like to discuss?
- What would you consider the ideal resolution or improvement for the problems you've raised?

Once the conversation is started, clients are better able to articulate their concerns. When they are prompted to provide specific information, it helps to frame their thoughts and guide them to give relevant information. These questions aim to encourage open dialogue and help lead developers gain a deeper understanding of the client's perspective. Without an open conversation, dissatisfaction builds and can lead to miscommunication and conflict. By actively listening to the client's responses, you can work toward finding effective solutions and addressing the client's concerns to enhance the overall project experience.

8.4.3   *Remaining engaged*

One of the key aspects of engaging with difficult clients is establishing and maintaining clear communication lines. By doing so, lead developers can effectively address any concerns, manage expectations, and keep clients informed about the project's progress. Regularly scheduled meetings, email updates, and collaboration platforms can be effective communication channels. When I'm working on a project with a difficult client, I always schedule a weekly meeting to discuss progress, address concerns, and set realistic goals. By providing regular updates and a platform for open communication, I find that this successfully engages the client and builds trust.

It also helps to be proactive and regularly update the client on the project's status, challenges faced, and the steps being taken to address them. Transparency builds trust and reassures clients that their concerns are being addressed promptly. When a difficult client raises a pressing problem, respond calmly with transparency, saying something like, "I appreciate you bringing this to my attention. Let's discuss it openly to find the best course of action together." I usually build a dashboard for clients, including progress reports so they can stay informed about the project's development. These reports can highlight completed milestones, upcoming tasks, and any potential roadblocks or risks. Providing transparency through progress reports demonstrates accountability and reassures clients about the project's trajectory.

Some clients may have unrealistic expectations or demands. Instead of dismissing their requests outright, calmly explain the project's limitations, and propose alternative solutions that align with their goals. This approach demonstrates your commitment to finding a compromise while managing expectations effectively. For example, if a client requests additional features with a tight deadline, you can calmly respond by saying, "While I understand the importance of these features, implementing them within the given time frame may compromise the project's stability. How about we prioritize the most critical ones and plan for the others in subsequent phases?"

One of the most important approaches to remaining engaged with your clients is to go into every conversation with an open mind. When clients are difficult, you may want to avoid them. However, avoiding them will only lead to more conflict and problems with the project. You have to dig in and have difficult conversations with them to surface problems so that they can be addressed.

Dealing with demanding, unresponsive, or overly involved clients can sometimes lead to frustration within the project team and hinder a project's progress. However, by adopting a proactive and engaged approach, lead developers can build better relationships with difficult clients, ensure project success, and maintain client satisfaction. Every difficult client presents an opportunity for growth and improvement. By implementing these strategies and adapting them to specific project dynamics, you can transform difficult clients into satisfied partners in achieving project success.

8.5 *Case study*

Jamie Maguire is an independent software architect, Microsoft MVP in Artificial Intelligence, technical author, and SaaS founder. He is a lifelong tech enthusiast with more than 20 years of professional experience using Microsoft technologies.

Jamie is also a Pluralsight author, LinkedIn Learning Instructor, and Cloud Academy Trainer. He creates introductory courses and deep dives into topics that include but aren't limited to Twitter API, conversational AI, Microsoft Azure, text analytics, and computer vision. He has collaborated on and delivered many projects, including working with Twitter, national healthcare organizations, departments of corrections, National Geographic, and other academic institutions and businesses.

Jamie is a keen contributor to the technology community and has gained global recognition for his written articles and the software he has built. He is a STEM Ambassador and Code Club volunteer, inspiring interest at a grassroots level. He shares his story and expertise at speaking events, on social media, and through podcast interviews. He has authored and co-authored books, including working with 16 fellow MVPs demonstrating how Microsoft AI can be used in the real world. He regularly publishes material to encourage and promote the use of AI and .NET technologies on his personal blog, Twitter, LinkedIn, and YouTube.

He designed, built, and released the social media SaaS Social Opinion (https://socialopinion.co.uk). He also built and launched the AI-powered online journaling and mood-tracking tool called Daily Tracker (https://dailytracker.co). You can find Jamie at www.jamiemaguire.net. In this case study, Jamie offers his experience and advice for working with clients.

8.5.1 *How do you establish trust with your clients?*

I'm active online in the IT and technical community. I find that sharing ideas, thoughts, and tips on my personal blog, LinkedIn, and Twitter builds social proof and trust. By the time someone has contacted me about a potential contract, they have often seen my online activity and have a feel for who they are dealing with, what I can offer, and how I conduct myself.

Professional, academic accreditations, publicly available GitHub repos, my social media scheduling SaaS, and YouTube demos provide further evidence of my skills and the value I can add. This collection of digital footprints makes people feel comfortable and helps potential clients feel confident that they can trust me.

During initial consultations and exploratory calls, to build further trust, I take time to fully understand the client's "ask" or pain point. I'll tap into prior experience or explain how I've been able to implement a similar solution in the past (at a high level). If a project is remote (and a lot are these days), I make sure to turn my camera on.

If there are gaps in my knowledge, understanding, or experience, I let the client know there and then. I personally find that saying, "I don't know, but we can find out" is perfectly acceptable, and clients appreciate that. If I have an existing prototype that performs a similar function to the client's requirements, I'll provide code or a video demo. When a project is underway, delivering what you say you will and when is very important. Doing this consistently over time naturally builds trust and often leads to additional projects.

8.5.2 How do you handle clients who request features that are out of scope?

I politely remind them this wasn't agreed upon within the initial statement of work, and if we want to include the additional feature request, we can add it to the backlog and price the effort at a suitable time. As an independent consultant, I feel it's important to be disciplined about this. Of course, throughout the duration of a project, smaller requests may be requested due to unforeseen circumstances. Those can be accommodated. I treat each situation according to its own unique circumstances.

8.5.3 What makes a successful presentation to outline your technical approach?

My personal blog has proven to be useful in helping communicate how I build software, my thought process, and how I might deliver a project. I find this can mean I don't need to pitch many presentations. That said, if I need to present a technical approach, I find being concise, to the point, and using simple language is the best approach. In terms of actual content in a presentation, opening with an introduction of myself, my skills, and playing back my understanding of the client's problem or challenges helps frame the discussion.

I'll then list the main pain points or client requirements before moving on to a potential solution, any benefits, and the value the new solution will bring. Any risks, third-party costs, cross-team, or data dependencies are also identified along with any "unknown unknowns." Identifying these gives the client further confidence. Diagrams or short demos that show how components interact in the proposed solution are also useful tools to ensure a successful presentation.

8.5.4 How have you dealt with difficult clients?

Fortunately, I haven't had to deal with many difficult clients. The level of technical understanding or expertise can sometimes mean you need to be patient. If a client doesn't understand your explanation, I personally feel it's my responsibility to find another way to communicate my reasoning or solution. For contractual difficulties, I'll refer to the contract and original statement of work that was agreed upon to realign expectations and get us back on track.

Summary

- Understanding and meeting clients' needs through effective communication and collaboration is critical for lead developers to deliver successful projects and build strong, long-term relationships.
- Using active listening is a crucial skill for lead developers to understand their client's needs, and it involves engaging fully with the speaker, asking open-ended questions, repeating back what was heard, and paying attention to body language.

- Balancing client budgets with exceptional results requires a clear understanding of budgetary limitations, prioritizing core features aligned with client objectives, and suggesting lean and scalable approaches.

- Establishing trust with clients is done by actively listening to their needs, having transparent communication, and delivering high-quality solutions within agreed-upon timelines.

- Being diplomatic helps to establish trust and deliver successful projects by setting realistic expectations, proposing alternative solutions to unrealistic demands, and using positive language to inspire confidence.

- Maintaining a calm and composed demeanor when dealing with difficult clients can be achieved by empathizing with clients, remaining self-aware of emotional triggers, and seeking support from team members.

Being a mentor

9

This chapter covers

- Best practices for mentoring
- Mentor expectations
- Building trust with mentees
- Guiding mentees in career planning
- Importance of being a positive role model
- Growing as a mentor

When a lead developer becomes a mentor, they take on the responsibility of guiding and nurturing the skills and potential of aspiring developers. This role goes beyond simply imparting technical knowledge; it involves fostering personal growth, instilling confidence, and cultivating a strong sense of teamwork. By sharing their expertise, experience, and industry insights, lead developers can help their mentees navigate through challenges, avoid common pitfalls, and improve their skills. Their guidance can significantly shorten the learning curve for the mentees, enabling them to level up their skills and knowledge much faster than they would on their own. Mentors shape their mentees' careers and professional trajectories, foster a positive work culture, and inspire a new generation of developers to excel. By investing their time and energy into mentoring, lead developers play a vital role in cultivating the next wave of talented and capable professionals, leaving a legacy within the global tech community.

Being a mentor has been one of the joys of my professional career. Being able to impart my wisdom and experiences to the next generation of developers is something that I don't take lightly. Mentors are responsible for encouraging their mentees to grow both professionally and personally by guiding them through their careers and any challenges they may encounter. I've mentored more than 100 people whom I met at work and in the global development community. I'm happy to have the opportunity to work with people from all over the world and learn about their struggles. This also helps me grow personally and professionally because I'm open to learning from my mentees. Watching my mentees succeed in their careers makes me feel like I'm positively affecting the tech industry.

9.1 What is a mentor?

A *mentor* is an experienced and knowledgeable individual who provides guidance, support, and advice to a less experienced person. They have achieved a certain level of expertise, and they voluntarily share their knowledge, insights, and personal experiences to assist their mentees in their personal and professional growth. Mentors play a vital role in shaping the mentee's skills, knowledge, and mindset. This helps mentees navigate challenges, set goals, and reach their full potential. A mentor is a trusted advisor, role model, and source of inspiration for their mentee.

As a lead developer, you can guide and shape your team members' careers. A good mentor possesses genuine empathy and actively listens to their mentees. They understand that everyone has unique strengths, weaknesses, and aspirations. A good lead developer should be abreast of their team members' technical/functional strengths and weaknesses and work with them to fill those gaps. They can provide tailored guidance and support by putting themselves in their mentees' shoes. If a mentor lacks empathy, they may dismiss their mentees' concerns, offer bad advice, or push their own agenda. This harms communication and discourages mentees from seeking guidance. A lack of empathy often creates a negative and unsupportive mentorship experience, hindering the mentee's growth and development. No advice is better than bad advice. Receiving bad advice can derail a mentee's path to their goals, causing frustration and a bad experience.

A good mentor provides constructive feedback, including specific and actionable advice. They highlight areas for improvement while also acknowledging accomplishments. They challenge and support their mentees, fostering an environment of continual growth. They encourage their mentees to step out of their comfort zones and embrace new opportunities, providing guidance along the way. Mentors may belittle their mentees' efforts if they give demeaning criticism or fail to provide meaningful support. This negative approach can result in lowered confidence for the mentee. A bad mentor may also neglect their mentees' needs, leaving them feeling unsupported and undervalued.

Mentors must inspire their mentees through their own actions and achievements. They lead by example, demonstrating a positive approach to challenging situations. Their enthusiasm motivates mentees to embrace challenges and pursue excellence. They generously share their experiences and knowledge, empowering mentees to navigate their paths to success. If a mentor fails to provide clear direction, mentees feel lost and uncertain about their professional journey. A bad mentor may also hoard knowledge, refusing to share valuable insights or collaborate with their mentees, stifling their development. This tends to happen when a mentee surpasses the mentor in a certain skill set. Sometimes the mentee will outgrow the mentor, which is a good sign that the mentor did their job. Table 9.1 lists some approaches to being a mentor and the result of a good versus a bad mentor.

Table 9.1   Good mentor vs. bad mentor

Approach	Good mentor	Bad mentor
Practicing empathy	Uses empathy to build trust and provide a supportive environment for their mentees	Ignores mentees' concerns and offers generic advice that doesn't address their specific needs
Providing constructive feedback	Guides mentees to improve their skills	Demeans mentees, making them feel unsupported
Leading by example	Cultivates a positive working environment where mentees thrive	Cultivates a negative working environment by allowing toxic behavior
Facilitating networking opportunities	Introduces mentees to relevant contacts, industry events, and communities	Fails to introduce mentees to relevant contacts, limiting their opportunities for professional growth

Becoming a good mentor requires a genuine commitment to the growth and success of your mentees. It takes time to cultivate your mentoring style, and you may make missteps along the way, and that is okay! Mentoring takes practice and self-awareness to pinpoint the skills you're lacking. When you embrace the role of a mentor with dedication and compassion, you'll witness the profound effect you can have on the lives and careers of those you guide.

9.1.1   *Comparing mentors and trainers*

The roles of mentors and trainers are crucial pillars of professional growth. While the terms *mentor* and *trainer* might appear interchangeable, lead developers need to comprehend the differences between the two. Mentors impart their experience and wisdom to mentees, offering guidance, support, and motivation as they navigate their careers. This role extends beyond the mere transfer of technical skills; they become a source of inspiration and encouragement.

Mentors lead by example and help mentees reach their true potential. They cultivate nurturing relationships, taking the time to understand their mentees' aspirations, strengths, and weaknesses. The guidance of a mentor is built upon mutual respect and trust, focusing on comprehensive personal and professional development. Mentoring is one of my favorite ways to give back, and I've gained a lot from it. You should learn from your mentees and get as much as you give. I've mentored people on social media and others whom I've worked with directly. When I mentor anyone, we focus on building our mentor/mentee relationship and developing their career plan, which we'll discuss in detail later in this chapter.

Trainers, on the other hand, share knowledge, expertise, and practical skills. They possess specialized proficiencies and employ structured instructional methodologies to teach specific competencies. Unlike mentors, trainers typically have a narrower scope, concentrating on specific skill sets or domains. They design comprehensive training programs, curate hands-on experiences, and provide constructive feedback. Trainers empower individuals by equipping them with the tools and skills necessary to excel in their respective roles. I've also been a trainer, and I think the major difference is that when someone takes my course, I generally don't have any further interaction with them. As a mentor, I meet consistently with my mentees, and we work through their problems in real time. I'm invested in the futures of both my mentees and students, but I'm not on a strict timetable with mentees.

I was once part of a mentoring program that was highly structured and centered around training. I suggested that they change the program to make it more flexible and prioritize career advice over training. Some mentees expected a focus on training and learning new skills, but when we started to focus on their careers and guiding them through their challenges, they began to thrive. The program had approximately 30 mentors but enrollment for mentees had been low. When we made these changes, we started to get more mentees interested in our program through word of mouth.

The roles of mentor and trainer often intersect. It's common for mentors to incorporate elements of training in their guidance, offering practical insights and resources to mentees. Similarly, in pursuit of excellence, trainers often cultivate mentoring relationships with their students, extending their influence beyond technical expertise. Both mentors and trainers serve as catalysts for personal and professional advancement. They share a common purpose: a genuine desire to witness people flourish and succeed. Whether learning from a mentor or a trainer, both can contribute immensely to our growth by offering unique perspectives, challenging us, and nurturing our talents.

9.1.2 *Mentoring expectations*

One of the primary roles of a mentor is to share wisdom and experience they have acquired over their career. Mentors draw from their successes, failures, and lessons learned, offering valuable perspectives to help you navigate challenges and make informed decisions. Mentors are expected to provide a safe space for you to discuss your aspirations, concerns, and goals. A mentor listens attentively, asks thought-provoking questions, and offers constructive feedback. Their guidance can range from technical advice to career development strategies, helping you chart a path that aligns with your ambitions.

My mentees often encounter the same problems I encountered in the past in my career. I like to explain to them what happened to me and how I handled it with the caveat that things change over time, so the outcome for them may not be the same. One of the main problems I've discussed with my mentees is how they can overcome failure. Failure is a learning experience that is necessary to achieve success. In my early career, when I failed, I felt guilty, ruining my motivation. Sometimes, what I perceived as my own failure was entirely out of my control, as I hadn't been set up for success. In one situation, I was hired as part of a team to migrate a desktop application to a web application. As the project progressed, every developer except me left the company, but they weren't replaced. Everything fell on my shoulders. I asked for help repeatedly and was denied. The project was also way over budget and ultimately failed. I was let go, and it devastated me. I thought it was my fault until I told the story to one of my mentors, and they told me that it wasn't my fault. They told me that the biggest sign of mismanagement in a company is when there is a lot of turnover, and if I encounter this, I should start looking for another job. This experience made me more resilient and able to deal with failure based on my previous experiences. My mentees relate to this story, as layoffs are quite common in the tech industry, which is something many of them deal with.

I also tell my mentees that everyone has different experiences, so I tell them what worked for me, but they must forge their own path. This is an important distinction to make so that your mentees don't try to copy you 100%. We're all on our own journey, and your mentees must develop career strategies that work for them. Sharing your experience and knowledge will provide insights to help your mentees navigate challenges and make informed decisions.

A mentor can suggest learning resources, give access to new opportunities, and introduce mentees to valuable connections within the industry. They serve as advocates for career advancement, offering guidance on navigating promotions, leadership roles, and professional challenges. Mentees should be encouraged to expand their skills, explore new technologies, and embrace continuous learning. Mentors must recognize the importance of soft skills, such as effective communication, leadership, and collaboration, and offer guidance on practicing these skills. The feedback that my mentees provided about my focus on developer soft skills inspired me to write this book.

A mentor should provide an open space for their mentees to discuss their aspirations, challenges, and insecurities. They maintain confidentiality and demonstrate empathy, understanding their mentees' pressures. Trust allows for candid conversations, constructive feedback, and the freedom to explore new ideas without judgment. I've often found that my mentees were a bit shy at first and uncomfortable telling me what was happening. However, over time, as we built a rapport, they began to open up, and I was better able to help them when I had a clear picture of what was troubling them. It's important to understand that trust doesn't happen immediately, and the relationship must be cultivated. We'll discuss this topic in detail in the next section.

A good mentor will challenge their mentees to push boundaries, explore new opportunities, and embrace new perspectives. They foster a growth mindset, helping mentees embrace failure as a stepping stone to success. Most people fear failure, and I always tell them that failure is a learning experience. If you learn from it, it's not truly a failure. I've failed many times, and I tell my mentees how I failed and what I learned from it. This helps them not to feel alone, and it's a good way to build trust by being authentic. When mentors are open to discussing their own struggles, mentees appreciate their candid communication, resulting in a stronger bond.

9.1.3 *Achieving success as a mentor*

The most effective mentors lead by example. They demonstrate a strong work ethic and are dedicated to self-improvement. They understand that learning is a lifelong journey of actively seeking new knowledge and skills. They encourage their mentees to set personal and professional goals that inspire them to strive for excellence. I take my position as a mentor and role model very seriously, and I try to keep things positive. However, we all have our bad days, and mentors should be honest about their feelings. If you're having a bad day, it's important not to take it out on anyone, as this can influence your mentees to do the same. Bad behavior trickles downward when people are shown that such behavior is acceptable.

Every mentee is unique, with their own learning style and aspirations. A good mentor will take the time to understand everyone's strengths, weaknesses, and goals. Your mentoring style should be tailored to suit the needs of each individual mentee. Some may thrive with hands-on coaching, while others may benefit from more independent problem-solving. Flexibility is key to helping them unlock their full potential. I have some mentees who prefer a structured approach with more hands-on coaching and others who need me to point them to the proper learning resources to learn independently. Assessing someone's learning style is something that you learn as a trainer, which is a useful skill as a mentor. Some people thrive in the traditional learning environment that we're given in school, but others prefer to learn on the job. Both approaches can and should yield the same results.

The best way to assess your mentees' learning style is by simply asking them what they prefer. What has worked for them in the past? What are their strengths and weaknesses in various learning environments? Observe their preferences and behaviors during the learning process. Pay attention to how your mentees engage with different types of information, such as visual, auditory, or kinesthetic. Then, you can tailor your mentoring approach to best suit the mentees' individual learning styles and optimize the learning experience.

A successful mentor empowers their mentees to take ownership of their work and make independent decisions. They gradually delegate responsibilities, allowing their mentees to grow their skills and gain confidence in their abilities. Mentors should provide guidance when needed and trust their mentees to find solutions. This autonomy not only enhances your mentees' skills but also fosters a sense of ownership and pride in their work. If you only tell your mentees what to do, this will stunt their growth. You should guide their thought process so that they come to their own conclusions. This type of coaching will help your mentees retain information better than if you just fed them answers. Because I have a background in training, this was a hard skill for me to learn. My job was to provide answers, but as a mentor, I found this to be the wrong approach. My first mentee felt very overwhelmed when I would feed them answers, and when we talked about it, I realized that it was because I was giving them too much information all at once. They needed to work some of it out on their own, and once we adjusted the mentoring strategy, they started to make better progress.

Mentors should help their mentees identify opportunities for professional growth and development. I encourage my mentees to attend conferences, participate in workshops, or contribute to open source projects. If they are working on my team and I have the budget, I like to give them time to work on these things on the job so they don't have to use their personal time. However, this isn't always possible, so be aware that people need rest and relaxation, which means they may take more time to progress if done in their personal time. Provide guidance on choosing the right learning resources and recommending books, online courses, or tutorials based on the tech stack they are learning. Advocate for their advancement within the organization, whether it's through challenging projects or promotions. The best mentors will also assess if a person has no upward mobility at their current job, and they will help them figure out their next move, even if it's outside of the organization. This is hard to do, especially if the company you work for frowns upon that mentoring strategy. I've been with organizations that require a certain amount of personnel retention to measure the success of a leader. This isn't a good practice, as sometimes there is frequent turnover because a leader is a good mentor who helps their employees grow, even if they grow out of their current job.

Mentoring is also about personal growth and overall well-being. Successful mentors take a genuine interest in their mentee's life outside of work. They offer guidance on work-life balance, stress management, and self-care. I find that it's helpful when you celebrate their achievements both at work and in their personal life. I had a mentee who was afraid to be a public speaker due to bad experiences giving presentations at school. We talked about what happened and why it still affected them in the present. I related to them because I also had unpleasant experiences when I gave presentations in high school and college. I offered them support, and we celebrated together when they had their first successful presentation at a conference. They had a hard time viewing their presentation as a success because it wasn't perfect, but I assured them that this achievement needed to be celebrated. I encouraged them to apply for more speaking engagements, and, over time, they got much better. One of the best things about being a mentor is watching as your mentees flourish, becoming the next generation of successful developers.

9.2   *Forming relationships with mentees*

Mentors can form strong and meaningful relationships with their mentees through various approaches. Building trust and rapport is crucial. Mentors should foster a safe and supportive environment where mentees feel comfortable sharing their goals, challenges, and aspirations. Practicing empathy and approaching mentees with a nonjudgmental attitude helps mentors establish a strong foundation for mentoring relationships. By being accessible and reliable, mentors can form a relationship based on mutual respect, understanding, and shared goals.

I've always been a very empathetic person, and people tend to trust me quickly and tell me their problems. I'm a good listener, and my mentees respond to that. I tell them that anything we discuss is confidential and that I won't judge them. I try to be reliable, but that isn't always possible, so if I have to reschedule a meeting, I give them as much notice as possible. If I can't meet, I find another way to communicate with them, such as email or chat. This works well for me, and my mentees still feel that I'm invested in the mentoring relationship.

Several negative consequences can arise when lead developers fail to form relationships with their mentees. Mentees may hesitate to approach their lead developer without a strong connection for guidance or clarification. This can lead to misunderstandings, delays, and suboptimal work. Additionally, mentees may feel disconnected, unsupported, and undervalued, resulting in decreased motivation and disengagement. The lack of a supportive relationship also hinders effective knowledge transfer and limits the mentees' growth potential.

Without strong mentoring relationships, a development team may experience a lack of cohesion and collaboration. Communication breakdowns and siloed knowledge become more common, leading to duplicated efforts, inefficient problem-solving, and decreased overall productivity. The absence of a supportive environment can also affect team morale and cohesion, potentially leading to higher turnover rates and a loss of talent. That's why it's crucial for a lead developer to become a successful mentor by forming relationships with their mentees and becoming their trusted advisor.

9.2.1 *Establishing trust with mentees*

Establishing trust with your mentees is vital for fostering a positive and productive mentoring relationship. Trust is the foundation for effective learning, growth, and open communication. You must communicate your expectations of your mentees from the beginning. Your mentees should help you set the goals and objectives of the mentoring relationship, the desired outcomes, and the level of commitment required from both parties. Clearly communicating mentoring initiatives helps mentees understand what is expected of them and enables them to work toward meeting those expectations.

Being authentic and transparent is key to building trust. You should share your experiences, successes, and failures with your mentees. Being open about your own journey fosters a sense of authenticity and showcases your own vulnerability. When I discuss my challenges and how I overcame them, I can often see something click with my mentees. Transparency helps mentees see that everyone faces obstacles and that learning is a continuous process. No one starts out being perfect or knowing everything. It takes time to gain experience, and having a trusted mentor will help your mentees achieve their goals faster.

Being transparent also includes giving unpleasant news and avoiding white lies. If you're caught in a lie, that will break any trust you've established with your mentees.

Some people tell white lies to avoid conflict, but it's imperative that you always tell the truth. I had a mentor early in my career who would review and approve my code but then make changes later. When I asked him about it, he told me that my work was excellent and not to worry about it. When he continued to do it, I felt uneasy about it, but I was unsure why. When I became a mentor, I realized that he was preventing my growth by not being able to give me constructive criticism. It would have been better if he used comments on my code in pull/merge requests as a way to work through this problem and help me learn best practices. You'll always learn something new when you work on code reviews together.

As a lead developer, you're expected to have a high level of technical expertise. Demonstrating your competence and knowledge instills confidence in mentees. You can share your insights, follow best practices, and offer explanations when introducing new concepts. However, it's important to strike a balance between showcasing your expertise and allowing mentees to explore and learn on their own. Encouraging mentees to find solutions will nurture their growth and critical thinking skills. I've asked team members to shadow me while I'm coding to help them learn new skills. As they watched me work, they learned a lot and respected my skill level, which led to trusting relationships.

As a mentor, you must understand that your mentees are human. Be patient and understanding, as they may make mistakes as they learn and grow. Patience and understanding are vital in establishing trust during these times. You should avoid being overly critical or impatient when mentees encounter difficulties. Instead, offer guidance and support. Help your mentees analyze their problems, identify potential solutions, and guide them in the right direction.

One of the most crucial aspects of a trusting mentoring relationship is respecting confidentiality. Open communication should be encouraged, but make it clear that any personal or sensitive information shared will be treated with the utmost confidentiality. Respecting privacy builds a safe space for mentees to share their concerns, insecurities, and professional aspirations without fear of judgment or repercussions. This is especially important when you're mentoring people within your team. I've dealt with mentees who were having personal problems, such as divorce or illness, that they didn't want the team to know about. I encouraged them to be open with their team members, but if they were uncomfortable with that, I didn't push it further. One of my worst mentors would reiterate my personal information to friends we had in common. This was a complete violation of trust, and I was very hurt when I found out. I felt that nothing I disclosed was kept confidential, and I didn't trust them. I had to end that relationship.

As a mentor, you're expected to be a trusted advisor. When your mentees trust you, they will be more open to telling you what is really going on and what challenges they are facing so that you can better guide them. Remember, trust takes time to develop, so you must invest in building and nurturing relationships to help your mentees thrive and grow into confident developers.

9.2.2 *Getting to know your mentees*

Getting to know your mentees personally helps you understand their strengths, weaknesses, goals, and aspirations, enabling you to provide tailored guidance and support. As a lead developer, you should schedule regular one-on-one meetings with your mentees to encourage discussion. These meetings allow you to discuss their professional and personal interests, experiences, and career goals. Mentees can share their challenges, aspirations, and any roadblocks they may be facing. This is a good opportunity for you to ask open-ended questions and provide guidance based on their unique circumstances. I always ask my mentees about their career aspirations and what they hope to achieve in the short and long term. Understanding their motivations and identifying areas where you can provide guidance will help them reach their goals. The following list includes open-ended questions you can ask your mentees to get the ball rolling:

- How do you manage work-life balance, and what strategies do you find effective in maintaining your well-being?
- What are your hobbies outside of software development?
- What role does your support network (family, friends, etc.) play in your personal and professional development?
- How do you recharge and care for your mental and physical well-being outside of work? What are some practices you find helpful?
- Are there any specific life skills or areas of personal development that you're interested in exploring or improving upon?
- How do you prioritize and make time for activities or relationships that are important to you outside of work?

Participating in team-building activities with your mentees allows you to interact with them in a more relaxed and informal setting. Group activities or social events provide an opportunity to bond, share experiences, and build rapport outside the usual work environment. These activities can be company-sponsored, or you can organize them yourself. I've used company retreats, picnics, and conferences to spend time with my mentees away from work. I use these occasions to have more casual conversations and get to know my mentees' hobbies, learn about their interests, and allow them to tell personal stories. This informal setting can foster stronger connections and a deeper understanding of their personalities. By showing genuine interest in their well-being beyond their professional lives, you create a sense of camaraderie and establish a deeper connection.

I once worked with a fully remote team, and we would schedule one week to meet in person occasionally. I would take them out to lunch every day and make sure not to talk about work. It's natural for people to gravitate toward work as a topic of conversation with people they work with. However, it's important for you to initiate conversations to discuss nonwork-related topics such as books, movies, hobbies, or current events. These conversations can reveal common interests and provide a more holistic understanding of your mentees' personalities. Investing time and effort in getting to know your mentees will lay the foundation for a successful and rewarding mentor-mentee relationship.

9.2.3   *Finding common ground*

Finding common ground fosters trust between you and your mentees. Shared experiences and interests create a sense of familiarity and understanding, promoting a more relaxed and open environment for communication. When mentors and mentees have shared interests or backgrounds, they can use that commonality as a starting point for discussions, making it easier to relate to and understand each other's perspectives.

When you don't spend the time to get to know your mentees personally, this can harm your relationship and limit the mentees' growth and development. Without a personal connection, mentees may feel a lack of trust and engagement. They might perceive mentorship as merely a formal obligation rather than a genuine effort to support their professional and personal development. This can lead to a misalignment of goals and expectations. You may struggle to provide personalized guidance that addresses the unique needs of your mentees.

I've worked under some lead developers who were highly technical early in my career. They didn't spend any time getting to know me or schedule regular meetings for us to talk. When I encountered problems and I went to them for guidance, they didn't understand why I was encountering problems because they didn't understand my educational background. I felt unsupported, and my confidence was low. When I worked for lead developers who took the time to get to know me on a personal level, they understood my thought process and why I encountered problems. They were able to assess the situation and provide the guidance I needed to overcome the problems I was facing.

Building a personal connection facilitates effective communication between you and your mentees. Without this connection, mentorship conversations may lack depth and authenticity, hindering the mentees' willingness to openly discuss challenges, seek guidance, and share their perspectives. Establishing a rapport and connection with mentees is essential for creating a supportive and collaborative environment. When mentees don't feel a personal connection with their mentors, their motivation and engagement in the mentorship process may decrease. They may become disinterested or disengaged, limiting the overall effectiveness of the mentoring relationship. To ensure a successful mentorship experience, you should prioritize investing time and effort in getting to know your mentees personally. By establishing a personal connection, you can foster trust, open communication, and tailor support that empowers your mentees to grow and succeed both professionally and personally.

You can learn much about your mentees by following them on social media. I like to follow my mentees on GitHub to see what they are working on and ask if they need any assistance. When I see they are making progress, I bring it up at work and congratulate them on their achievement. If they post about it on a platform such as LinkedIn, I add a supportive comment. Showing public support helps to grow your mentoring relationship and show your mentees that you care. This is something that mentors often miss, but it's very important in today's landscape of social media. Connecting on social media is a great way to forge your relationship so your mentees trust that you care about their well-being.

9.3 *Inspiring personal and career growth*

As a lead developer, inspiring your mentees to achieve both personal and career growth is essential for their success. When your mentees pursue personal growth, they feel encouraged to enhance their skills, knowledge, and abilities beyond their current capabilities. This fosters a continuous learning mindset and helps them become well-rounded professionals. Personal growth can include developing strong communication skills and maintaining a work-life balance. These qualities benefit their careers and contribute to their overall personal development.

When you set a positive example, your mentees will feel inspired and motivated to grow. They will be more likely to be engaged and committed to their work. Your guidance and encouragement can ignite their passion for their craft and instill a sense of purpose. By setting high standards and demonstrating your own enthusiasm, you can inspire them to push their boundaries, take on challenges, and achieve their full potential. By setting clear goals for yourself, you can help your mentees set goals for themselves. By sharing your own experiences and insights, you can help them make informed decisions and navigate potential obstacles along the way.

When you prioritize your mentees' personal and career growth, you foster a positive work culture that values continuous improvement and development. This sends a powerful message to the entire team that growth is a shared priority and encourages a collaborative and supportive environment. The ripple effects of this culture can lead to increased morale, productivity, and overall team satisfaction. By investing in their growth, you contribute to their professional journey while strengthening the overall capabilities of your team.

9.3.1 *Making a career plan*

To help your mentees reach their full potential and grow into successful professionals, it's essential to establish a career plan. A career plan helps your mentees gain clarity and direction based on their professional aspirations. Setting specific goals and milestones is important to provide mentees with a clear road map to follow. This ensures that their efforts are focused and serve a purpose. Having a career plan empowers mentees to visualize their desired career trajectory and understand the necessary steps to achieve it.

A well-defined career plan motivates mentees to strive for growth and progress. Having a clear understanding of the skills they need to acquire helps them become more engaged in their work. This fosters a sense of ownership, commitment, and enthusiasm, leading to increased productivity and overall satisfaction. I have several mentors who have helped me form a career plan, and it has changed over time. It's important to remember that interests may change if a mentee becomes burned out in their current industry. Some people want to specialize in specific programming languages or tech stacks, but others want to try a bit of everything. To keep your mentees engaged, you should encourage them to learn every skill they are interested in and prioritize them based on their goals. Setting targeted goals and learning objectives ensures that your mentees receive the appropriate guidance and resources to develop their skills. This approach enables them to continually enhance their skill set and remain relevant in a rapidly evolving industry.

Having a solid career plan helps identify professional growth opportunities for your mentees. By aligning their aspirations with organizational needs, you can help them navigate promotions, projects, or even job rotations that will enable their professional advancement. This alignment benefits the mentees and contributes to the team's overall success and growth. By equipping them with the necessary skills, experiences, and opportunities, you create a talent pipeline within your organization. When your mentees are prepared to take on more significant responsibilities, it ensures continuity and reduces any disruptions that may arise due to attrition or promotions.

One of my mentors noticed that I was interested in leadership early on in my career, and he helped me set goals and learn new skills. Some of my early goals included running meetings, writing project plans, and meeting with other teams within the organization. He encouraged me to apply for a promotion when a new position opened for a development team lead. We discussed what that role would entail, and to my surprise, I had already been doing similar work because of the goals we had set. I was prepared to move forward in my career, and I did get that job! Creating a career plan for your mentees can change their careers. Figure 9.1 illustrates how a career plan can be structured for a mentee aiming to become a lead developer.

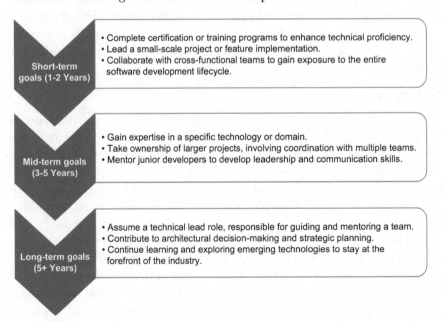

Short-term goals (1-2 Years)
- Complete certification or training programs to enhance technical proficiency.
- Lead a small-scale project or feature implementation.
- Collaborate with cross-functional teams to gain exposure to the entire software development lifecycle.

Mid-term goals (3-5 Years)
- Gain expertise in a specific technology or domain.
- Take ownership of larger projects, involving coordination with multiple teams.
- Mentor junior developers to develop leadership and communication skills.

Long-term goals (5+ Years)
- Assume a technical lead role, responsible for guiding and mentoring a team.
- Contribute to architectural decision-making and strategic planning.
- Continue learning and exploring emerging technologies to stay at the forefront of the industry.

Figure 9.1   Example career plan

A career plan isn't something that you create once and always follow the same plan. You should conduct regular check-ins with your mentees to discuss progress and adjust the career plan as necessary. Provide constructive feedback and guidance to address areas of improvement, and celebrate their successes. A career plan isn't set in stone and should evolve with your mentee's changing interests and goals. Regularly reassess and refine the plan to ensure alignment with their aspirations and the organization's needs. I've often changed my career plan when I lost opportunities and had to pivot my career. I once lost a promotion to a senior web developer, and I wanted to do something different. My mentor at the time suggested that I investigate technical writing or training. I had never considered either of those options because I didn't know much about them. We updated my career plan to include instructional design and technical writing. I completed several courses within one year, and the results were excellent. When you help your mentees maintain a career plan, you empower them to navigate their professional journey successfully to cultivate the next generation of lead developers.

9.3.2 Identifying skills to improve

Identifying the skills that your mentees should improve is important for their professional growth. By recognizing areas of improvement, you can provide targeted guidance, resources, and opportunities that will enable them to enhance their skill set. Assessing the technical competencies of your mentees is essential for determining skill gaps. Examples of evaluation methods include the following:

- *Code reviews*—Regularly review your mentees' code to identify areas for improvement in coding standards, efficiency, and maintainability.
- *Technical assessments*—Conduct assessments or quizzes to gauge their understanding of key concepts, algorithms, data structures, or specific programming languages.
- *Pair programming*—Engage in pair programming sessions to observe their problem-solving approach, code organization, and debugging skills.

You should seek feedback from colleagues, team members, and stakeholders who interact with your mentees. Their perspectives can surface areas where your mentees may need improvement. Speak with their teammates to gain insights into their collaboration skills and ability to work in a team setting. Project managers can help you understand how well your mentees align with project objectives, meet deadlines, and handle project complexities. Collecting feedback from clients and project stakeholders is important to measure the quality of deliverables and their overall satisfaction with your mentees' work.

In addition to technical competencies, soft skills play a vital role in career growth. Observe and assess your mentees' soft skills to determine areas of improvement. Assess their ability to convey ideas, actively listen, and collaborate effectively with team members and stakeholders. To measure their leadership potential, focus on their decision-making abilities and their aptitude for guiding and mentoring other team members. Ensure that your mentees are organized and able to meet project deadlines.

When identifying areas of improvement, you must consider your mentees' career goals and aspirations. Discuss their professional interests and aspirations to identify the skills they need to improve in their desired areas. If a mentee expresses interest in moving into a different role, identify the required skills and help them focus on developing those skills. If a mentee wants to specialize in a particular technology or domain, identify the necessary skills and provide opportunities for them to work on relevant projects or receive training.

Identifying the skills your mentees should improve is critical to mentoring and nurturing their growth. Providing targeted guidance, resources, and opportunities will empower your mentees to enhance their skill set, paving the way for their continued professional success. Remember, a supportive mentorship relationship coupled with consistent skill development efforts can unlock the full potential of your mentees.

9.3.3   *Being a role model*

As a lead developer, you significantly affect the growth and development of your mentees. Your actions, values, and behaviors serve as a guide to achieving success. You should set high standards of excellence and professionalism, inspiring mentees to strive for greatness. I instruct my mentees to pay attention to details, which is significant to show thoroughness and precision in their work. This is especially important for developers, as we're dealing with many moving parts, and it can be difficult to keep track of everything. I show my mentees the effect of paying attention to details by preemptively assessing possible errors and offering solutions. For example, if I see a test case is missing, I'll suggest the addition and work with the QA team to ensure the change is appropriate. You should show your mentees how to think about every aspect of what they are working on and support the success of the rest of the team.

You can provide an example of continuous learning by staying updated with the latest technologies and industry trends. Share your knowledge with your team, and point them to the resources you use to stay current. You should also share your journey to personal development and what you learn along the way. I mainly focus on self-awareness for personal development, as that can surface opportunities for personal and professional improvement.

Lead developers should show effective communication skills within the team and with clients and stakeholders. We've discussed active listening throughout this book, and it's important for you to provide an example of this to your mentees. This will demonstrate respect and attentiveness to others' perspectives and promote a positive working environment. You should also show your mentees how to communicate ideas and technical concepts in a clear and concise manner. Treat nontechnical team members respectfully, and answer all their questions using language they understand.

You must foster a collaborative and supportive team environment and inspire your mentees to value teamwork. You can promote a culture of sharing knowledge and expertise within the team by participating in code reviews and knowledge-sharing sessions. Cultivating a supportive team can be achieved by acknowledging the team's success. This shows the importance of teamwork and collaboration in reaching milestones. I've worked for organizations that didn't do this, and the results were mixed. Some people took it upon themselves to congratulate the team, which helped, but others felt unappreciated by leadership. Showing your team that you appreciate them as a leader will also help them appreciate each other.

One of the most important things you can do as a role model is to demonstrate a strong work ethic and accountability. This will instill these values in your mentees. You should set an example by consistently meeting deadlines and emphasizing the importance of punctuality. Be on time for meetings, and communicate if you have a calendar conflict. This will show that you respect the time of your co-workers, as everyone's time is valuable. If you make mistakes, hold yourself accountable. Taking responsibility for your actions and actively seeking solutions will demonstrate that mistakes are growth opportunities.

Having a strong work ethic is great, but you should strive to achieve a healthy work-life balance. Encourage your mentees to prioritize their well-being as a part of a strong work ethic. No one performs well if they are burned out, and everyone needs rest. You should take regular breaks and engage in self-care. This will show your mentees that you support their personal well-being. I used to be quite a workaholic because the leaders I worked for were workaholics, and they didn't prioritize self-care. Many of them checked in on work during their vacations when they were supposed to be spending time with their family. Taking this approach will influence your mentees to follow suit because they want to impress leadership to ensure job stability. When I became burnt out, I felt like I wasn't good enough to be a senior developer because I kept making silly little mistakes. It wasn't until I took time off that I realized I just needed a break. That is why it's important for you to share your own experiences and practices for achieving work-life balance, such as setting boundaries, delegating tasks, and making time for personal interests. Your actions speak louder than words, and being a positive role model will have a lasting effect on the development and success of your mentees.

9.4 *Paying it forward*

Mentoring allows lead developers to give back to the global development community that has supported their own journey, providing personal fulfillment and a sense of purpose. You should embrace the opportunity to positively affect the community to empower the next generation of tech professionals. You should give as much as you take. If you have an amazing mentor, then you should mentor others. This will ensure that the development community has a continuous supply of mentors who offer their time and expertise to support community members. As you share your expertise and guidance, you positively affect the lives and careers of aspiring developers. By investing your time and knowledge in others, you contribute to advancing the tech industry. The satisfaction of witnessing your mentees succeed and grow is immeasurable, and it reinforces the value of paying it forward.

9.4.1   *Empowering mentees to become mentors*

While mentoring is an effective way to guide and support individuals, there is an even greater opportunity to empower mentees to become mentors themselves. A mentee who demonstrates a strong understanding and mastery of the knowledge and skills within their field of expertise may be ready to take on a mentoring role. They should be able to effectively communicate and explain concepts, demonstrating their passion for teaching and guiding others. Encouraging the transition from mentee to mentor benefits your mentees and leads to the development team's overall growth and success. When mentees become mentors, they have a unique opportunity to reinforce their knowledge and skills. Mentoring others requires a deeper understanding of technical and soft skills, as mentors often need to guide their mentees in these areas. Being a mentor helps solidify their knowledge, uncover gaps in their understanding, and seek new perspectives to answer questions. This will enhance their expertise to help them become more well-rounded and confident in their abilities.

The transition from mentee to mentor is a natural progression in the learning journey. Encouraging mentees to become mentors creates a continuous cycle of learning within the team. When mentees become mentors, they are exposed to fresh challenges and questions from their mentees, which motivates them to seek new knowledge and explore innovative solutions. This continuous learning process benefits the mentors and enriches the team as new ideas and perspectives are brought to the table. It's important for senior developers to transition into mentorship even if they aren't interested in being lead developers. They are still expected to mentor junior developers to help them overcome learning blockers and learn new skills. Junior developers can also benefit from being mentors, although they often feel that they aren't experienced enough. I suggest that junior developers learn mentoring skills because there is always someone who is less skilled than you in a particular area. I've worked with many junior developers who didn't realize that they were already mentors because they shared their expertise via personal projects or blogs and helped guide others to do the same.

Empowering mentees to become mentors promotes a culture of collaboration and support within the development team. They will gain insights into different learning styles and adapt their mentoring approach accordingly. This shift in mindset encourages a culture where team members support one another, share knowledge, and grow together. The bond formed through mentorship promotes a sense of unity and cohesion, resulting in increased productivity, creativity, and overall job satisfaction. Mentors should get as much as they give, and your team should be open to learning from anyone. Everyone on your team could be a mentor and share their expertise to guide their team members to improve their skills.

The transition to mentorship plays a significant role in developing leadership and communication skills among mentees. Mentors are responsible for guiding and motivating their mentees, which requires effective communication and providing constructive feedback. By taking on this role, mentees have an opportunity to hone their leadership abilities and strengthen their emotional intelligence. These skills benefit their mentoring relationships and prepare them for future leadership positions within the team or the organization. When mentees are allowed to mentor others, they feel valued and recognized for their growth and expertise. This provides them with a sense of purpose and responsibility, which can boost their job satisfaction and loyalty to the team. By nurturing a pipeline of mentors from within the team, the organization can ensure a smooth transition of knowledge and leadership as more experienced members retire or move on to other roles.

The most important reason to empower your mentees to become mentors is to provide the development community with a continuous stream of new mentors. Without suggesting mentorship, how will we ensure that there will be mentors in the development community? You have a responsibility to your organization and the global community to cultivate the next generation of mentors. This is how your mentees can pay it forward: by connecting with others and guiding them through their careers as you did for them.

9.4.2 *Mentoring people outside of your organization*

Lead developers possess a wealth of knowledge and experience that can benefit your immediate team and the global development community. While mentoring everyone within your development team is crucial, expanding your reach to mentor individuals outside of your immediate circle can profoundly affect the development community. By extending your mentoring efforts beyond the confines of your organization, you can disseminate your expertise and contribute to the growth and development of aspiring developers, junior professionals, and even experienced practitioners. The act of sharing our expertise creates a ripple effect, fostering an environment of continuous learning and improvement across the global development community.

Mentoring developers outside of your organization allows you to contribute to diversity, equity, and inclusion efforts in the development community. By reaching out to mentees from different backgrounds, cultures, and regions, you can expand opportunities for underrepresented groups. Mentoring individuals with limited access to resources or networks can help level the playing field and empower them to thrive in their careers. Your guidance and support will contribute to building a more inclusive and diverse development community that grows the strengths of every individual. By engaging with mentees from around the world, you can broaden your perspectives and gain insights into diverse cultures and practices. These interactions facilitate the exchange of ideas, collaboration, and mutual learning. Furthermore, the relationships you forge through mentoring can extend beyond professional boundaries, creating a network of supportive individuals with shared goals and aspirations. These connections can lead to collaborations, partnerships, and lasting friendships that enrich your own personal and professional journey.

Whether you're a senior developer or a lead developer, you have technical expertise that you can share with the development community. You also don't have to go out of your way to find mentees outside of your organization. I only mentor people who ask for it. Otherwise, I would never have the time to mentor everyone I encounter.

Mentoring beyond your organization plays a major role in nurturing the next generation of leaders in the development community. By taking aspiring developers under your wing, you provide them with valuable guidance that will shape their career trajectories. You can inspire and motivate others to reach their full potential. By sharing your experiences, offering advice, and serving as a role model, you can develop confident and capable leaders who will, in turn, make positive changes in their respective organizations and communities. I mentioned at the beginning of the chapter that I've mentored more than 100 developers over the years, and those have been some of the best experiences I've had as a developer. Many of my mentees are now mentors themselves, and I love to see their mentees achieve success.

9.4.3 *Participating in mentoring communities and events*

Participating in mentoring communities and events enables lead developers to share their expertise and contribute to the growth of other developers. You'll refine your communication and teaching abilities by offering your time as an organizer or speaker at these events. This will allow you to give back to the community that has nurtured your growth. By sharing your knowledge, experiences, and insights, you contribute to developing the next generation of developers, helping them navigate their career paths and overcome challenges.

Mentoring communities and events offer an invaluable opportunity to build a strong professional network. Connecting with other developers allows you to establish meaningful relationships, share experiences, and collaborate on projects. Building a network of like-minded professionals can lead to potential partnerships, career advancement opportunities, and a sense of belonging within the developer community. Engaging in these communities exposes you to diverse ideas and approaches that can inspire you to think creatively and adopt new techniques. Collaborating with developers from different backgrounds and skill sets can lead to creating groundbreaking projects and cultivating fresh perspectives.

Participating in mentoring communities and events offers personal and professional fulfillment. Witnessing the growth and success of developers whom you've mentored can be immensely rewarding. Contributing to the collective knowledge of the developer community gives a sense of purpose and accomplishment. Moreover, mentoring provides an opportunity for self-reflection, reinforcing your own skills and boosting your confidence as a lead developer. Table 9.2 lists some of the industry's best mentoring communities and events.

Table 9.2 Mentoring communities and events

Community or event	Description
Meetup.com	A platform that hosts various developer meetup groups in different cities around the world. These groups bring developers together to network, share knowledge, and learn from each other.
Dev.to	An online community for developers that offers mentorship programs. It provides a platform for developers to connect, share ideas, and find mentorship opportunities.
GitHub	A space for developers to connect and collaborate on open source projects. It also offers mentorship programs such as the GitHub Campus Experts and the GitHub Mentorship program.
Codementor	This online platform connects developers with mentors who can help them with specific programming challenges or provide guidance on their career paths.
Women Who Code	A global nonprofit organization that offers mentorship and networking opportunities for women in technology. They organize events, workshops, and mentorship programs to support and empower women developers.
CodeNewbie	An inclusive community for people learning to code or transitioning into tech careers. They host regular Twitter spaces, podcasts, and virtual meetups, offering mentorship opportunities and support for beginners.
Developer conferences	Developer conferences, such as Google I/O, WWDC (Apple's Worldwide Developers Conference), and Microsoft Build, often feature mentorship programs, workshops, and networking events. Attending these conferences can provide valuable learning and mentorship opportunities.

I've been a speaker at many of these events, but my favorite so far has been Women Who Code. I attend a lot of their online events, and they reached out to me to be a speaker for an online panel on personal branding for developers. After the event, I received many messages from female developers asking for career guidance. I always try to answer every message I receive from someone asking for help. It may take me some time to get to every message, but I understand that I have influence in this industry, and I have a responsibility to mentor anyone who asks for it. This is why I'll continue to speak at these events. I love meeting new developers and getting to know them. I encourage people to reach out to me when I speak at events and let them know that I try to answer every message. This gives them the sense that I'm open to mentoring anyone who asks for it, and it goes a long way toward making them comfortable contacting me. It's important to tell people that you're available. Otherwise, they may assume that you don't have time for them. By embracing the opportunity to speak at mentoring events and participate in mentoring communities, you can positively affect the lives of aspiring developers and contribute to their career success.

9.5 *Case study*

Steve Buchanan is a principal program manager with a leading global tech giant focused on improving the cloud. He is a Pluralsight author, the author of eight technical books, Onalytica's Who's Who in Cloud? Top 50, and a former 10-time Microsoft MVP. He has presented at tech events, including DevOps Days, Open Source

North, Midwest Management Summit (MMS), Microsoft Ignite, BITCon, Experts Live Europe, OSCON, Inside Azure management, and user groups. He has been a guest on over a dozen podcasts and has been featured in several publications including the *Star Tribune* (the fifth largest US newspaper). He stays active in the technical community and enjoys blogging about his adventures in the world of IT at www.buchatech.com. In this case study, Steve gives his expert advice on achieving success as a mentor.

9.5.1 *Tell a story about one of your many achievements as a mentor. How did you help your mentees, and what success did they achieve?*

I've done mostly short-term mentoring, but now I'm doing more long-term mentoring. I'm more focused on the career planning aspect with my long-term mentees; you don't have the chance to see short-term mentees through their careers. Some of my mentees became Microsoft MVPs, authors/co-authors, and conference speakers. Some make moves in their career direction, and they are always looking for recommendations for their next move. I've also walked my mentees through how to handle situations they may encounter in the workplace.

9.5.2 *How do you help a mentee make their career plan?*

Because the tech industry is changing quickly, mentees must have a solid career plan. I also mentor people on how to get through layoffs. They need direction, so I have a conversation to take a step back and figure out where they want to go, and then we work backward from there. I suggest that everyone identify people who are doing what they want to do and study their journey. Everyone is on a different journey, but you can be influenced by others. I also use tools like Microsoft Visio to plot their career path. I start at the end goal and work back from there. For example, you want to be an expert on identity or security—what is it going to take to do that?

9.5.3 *Do you have any examples of mentoring communities or events? What is your experience with these events?*

I spoke at a conference called Blacks in Tech in Minnesota. My session was about building a personal brand and aiming to be a tech influencer. I was also a speaker at Oscon by O'Reilly on how to lead technical teams. The session was made to influence aspiring and current technical leaders. These speaking engagements often surface opportunities to create content around those topics. I'm planning to do my own courses based on these topics: managing your career, building a brand, and leading technical teams.

9.5.4 *What advice do you have for lead developers who have never mentored anyone before?*

Remember that your mentees are humans. They are prone to error, and you should be there for them when it happens. Spend some time researching the topic "What does it take to be a good mentor?" There are plenty of videos and resources to help you learn. Keep in mind that 90%+ of the ownership is on the mentee for driving things and getting things done. I like to ask them to set a duration and schedule for meeting up. They should determine what they want to get out of mentorship. You need to make sure the mentee has bought into the relationship and that it's worthwhile. As a mentor, you're getting mentorship from your mentees as well, and you should keep yourself open to learning from anyone. Mentorship goes both ways, and it's important for you to get as much as you give. In addition, make sure you have a group of mentors yourself. You should have more than one mentor because not every mentor will suit all your needs.

Summary

- A mentor shares wisdom and experiences, provides guidance tailored to individual journeys, helps set meaningful goals, and fosters trust and growth by being transparent and authentic.

- A successful mentor leads by example, tailors their approach to each mentee's needs, empowers independent decision-making, fosters professional growth, and supports personal well-being, celebrating achievements and guiding mentees through challenges.

- Establishing trust with mentees is achieved through authentic and transparent communication, technical competence, patience, and respect for confidentiality.

- Creating a career plan with specific goals and milestones helps mentees gain clarity, aligns their aspirations with organizational needs, and creates a talent pipeline for professional growth and advancement.

- Mentors should encourage their mentees' growth and development by setting high standards of excellence, emphasizing attention to detail, demonstrating a strong work ethic and accountability, and prioritizing work-life balance as a positive role model.

- Empowering mentees to become mentors fosters continuous learning, collaboration, leadership development, and a sense of purpose within the development team while also ensuring a sustainable pipeline of mentors for the development community.

Taking the lead

10

Lead developers are responsible for guiding and coordinating a team, making critical decisions, and ensuring the successful execution of projects. When developers take the lead, they establish a clear vision and direction for the team. They set goals, define project milestones, and outline a road map for success. This proactive approach instills confidence and aligns everyone toward a common objective. Figure 10.1 shows some of the benefits of taking the lead.

When lead developers fail to take the lead, their colleagues will go off independently to find the information they need to perform their daily tasks. I've worked under these conditions, and it's chaotic. When there is no leadership on the development team, communication breaks down, and the wrong decisions are made due to a lack of information.

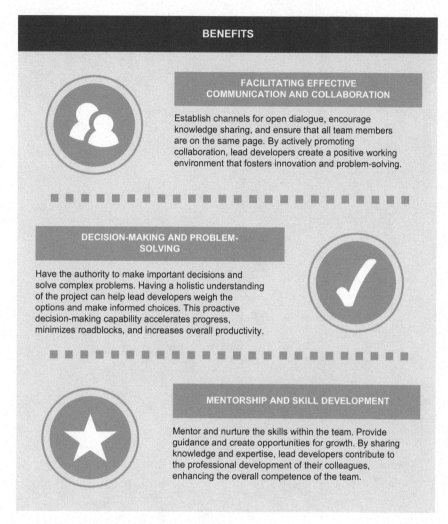

Figure 10.1   Benefits of taking the lead

I remember one instance where the lead developer would start a deployment to production and then expect the rest of the team to handle any problems that came up. This would be fine if the team had been trained in the process and there was a playbook on what to do if there were errors. He was also not responsive when we needed help. This resulted in deploys lasting much longer than they should have and outages that caused our clients to be upset. This could have been avoided with relevant leadership guiding us and training us in the proper process. Figure 10.2 outlines how a lack of leadership affects development teams.

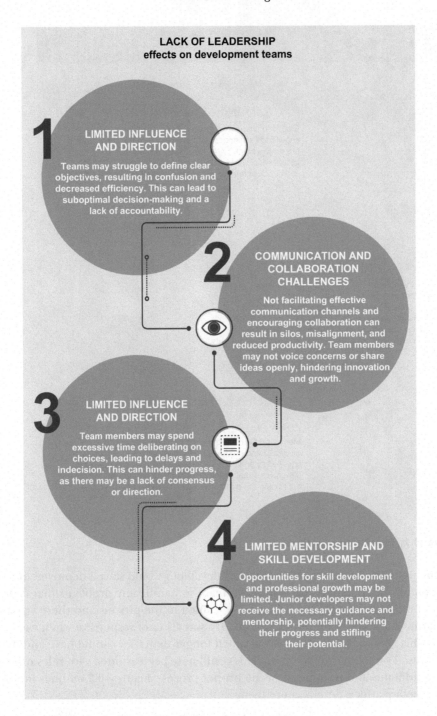

Figure 10.2   Lack of leadership effects on development teams

While taking the lead entails greater responsibilities, it also offers opportunities for personal and professional growth. However, it's essential to acknowledge that not everyone aspires to be a leader, and some may excel in individual contributor roles.

10.1 Providing instructions

Lead developers must provide clear instructions to their team members. Effective communication of instructions ensures that everyone is aligned, understands expectations, and can work efficiently toward a common goal. Table 10.1 illustrates the outcomes when lead developers do give clear instructions versus when they do not.

Table 10.1   Clear instructions vs. unclear instructions

Desired outcome	Clear instructions	Unclear instructions
Alignment and clarity	Clear understanding of objectives and tasks	Ambiguity and confusion
Efficiency and time management	Efficient prioritization and task completion	Delays and wasted effort
Quality and consistency	High-quality work adhering to standards	Inconsistencies and rework
Confidence and empowerment	Increased confidence and empowerment	Uncertainty and hesitancy
Communication and collaboration	Smooth collaboration and reduced miscommunication	Misunderstandings and conflicts
Productivity	Increased productivity and progress	Decreased productivity and lack of progress
Accountability	Clearly defined roles and responsibilities	Lack of accountability and ownership

Example scenario

You're working with your development team on a new web development project with tight deadlines. The project is challenging with many frequent changes, including scope creep, and it's hard to keep up. This project requires multiple application programming interface (API) integrations that lack documentation, and it's difficult to stay on track and not cause technical debt. You don't feel like you have the time to keep up with documentation. However, you continue to be inundated with questions, and your team isn't delivering their work on time. They don't take ownership of their work and lack accountability.

Without proper leadership, the team begins implementing API integrations that go against best practices. Because they lack documentation, they can't know the proper approach. They start asking the same questions regarding the lack of documentation, and you tell them that they need to figure it out on their own. This leads to confusion and lower productivity.

Then, you communicate more with the team to ensure they understand the requirements and timeline. You encourage them to collaborate with each other and document

(continued)

everything. The team works together to make decisions and prioritize tasks. This results in an improved quality of work and increased confidence among the team. The project improves, and your team is back on track.

10.1.1 Speaking with confidence

When lead developers speak confidently, their words carry weight and inspire trust among their teams. Confidence conveys a sense of authority, expertise, and competence, leading team members to rely on their guidance and decisions. When lead developers lack confidence, it undermines the trust and credibility they need to lead their teams effectively. If a lead developer doubts their abilities, team members may question their decisions and hesitate to follow their guidance.

When you're confident, you're more likely to make decisive and assertive decisions. Conviction in your own knowledge and skills allows you to trust your judgment and act promptly. When faced with complex technical challenges or critical project decisions, confidence helps you remain composed and make well-informed choices.

> **TIP**   Instead of saying, "I might be wrong, but shouldn't we use the latest version of the framework?" be more confident by saying, "I think we should use the latest version of the framework."

I had a hard time being confident in my early days as a lead developer, which made me indecisive and slowed down the decision-making process. I kept second-guessing my choices and hesitated to make tough calls. This led to delays and missed opportunities. I was in a situation where a project was late, and the project manager asked questions, trying to find a path forward. I presented several options but couldn't decide which one was best. I ended up taking weeks to study every option, only to end up using the first option. I should have trusted my instincts because I knew that option was the industry standard while the others were experimental. I wasted so much time, which could have been avoided. I should have been more confident, as I had learned from past mistakes.

How to trust your instincts

Lead developers can develop a strong sense of trust in their instincts through a combination of experience, continuous learning, and self-awareness. Consider a scenario where you're faced with a critical project deadline. Despite thorough analysis suggesting a particular technical approach, your instinct tells you that there might be a more efficient alternative.

You decide to explore the alternative approach, which turns out to be a game-changer, resulting in both meeting the deadline and producing a higher-quality result. This experience reinforces your trust in your intuition. You're reminded that your expertise and intuition often complement data-driven decision-making, leading to more innovative and successful outcomes.

A lack of confidence in your communication can have a detrimental effect on team morale. When team members sense hesitation or uncertainty in your words, it can foster a culture of doubt and insecurity. Insecure communication may discourage team members from openly sharing their ideas or concerns, fearing potential repercussions or dismissal. This can limit the diversity of perspectives and ideas, resulting in suboptimal outcomes. Expressing your ideas and requirements with conviction clarifies expectations and ensures everyone is on the same page. Confident communication encourages open dialogue, as team members feel comfortable discussing their perspectives, concerns, and suggestions. It fosters an atmosphere of trust and collaboration, where diverse viewpoints are valued and integrated for better outcomes.

10.1.2 Being clear and concise

Clear and concise instructions eliminate ambiguity, ensuring that developers fully understand their objectives. By providing explicit guidelines via email or a project management system, lead developers empower their team members to work with clarity, purpose, and confidence.

When you provide clear instructions, you set clear expectations. That way, developers can align their efforts toward a common objective, resulting in efficient collaboration and improved overall performance. I've experienced what happens when instructions are unclear and inconsistent, leading to chaos. I always dig deep and think about what will be involved in an assigned task from start to finish—and sometimes even after it's finished.

There are a few key things to remember when writing clear and concise instructions. First, be sure to use plain language that everyone on the team can understand, especially when you're working with nonnative English speakers. Avoid using jargon or technical terms that may not be familiar to everyone. It's also a good idea to avoid idioms and colloquialisms, which can be confusing. Be specific, and provide all the necessary information. Don't leave anything to chance that could lead to confusion and errors. Get to the point quickly, and avoid rambling.

Example of clear and concise instructions

The following is an example of providing clear and concise instructions for a user authentication feature:

"Develop a RESTful API endpoint that retrieves user data from the user authentication SQL database via a secure connection. The endpoint should accept a GET request at

(continued)

'/user/{id}' and return the user's name and previous orders in JSON format. Make sure to handle error cases, including invalid IDs or database connection failures."

These instructions are excellent because they follow each task to its logical conclusion. You should include as much information as possible, including the names of the database tables, views, methods, and so on, that the task will use. Provide all the necessary information without being too wordy.

When providing written instructions, it's important to make the information easy to read. Developers are busy, and they don't want to read a novel for every task. It's better for information retention to streamline your written instructions, calling out the highlights. If a developer goes back to read the instructions again, they should be able to skim them to find the details they need. Figure 10.3 includes some additional tips for writing clear and concise instructions.

Writing clear and concise instructions

1. Use active voice.

2. Write short sentences and paragraphs.

3. Use numbered lists or bullet points.

4. Use visual aids, such as screenshots or diagrams.

5. Proofread your instructions carefully before

distributing them.

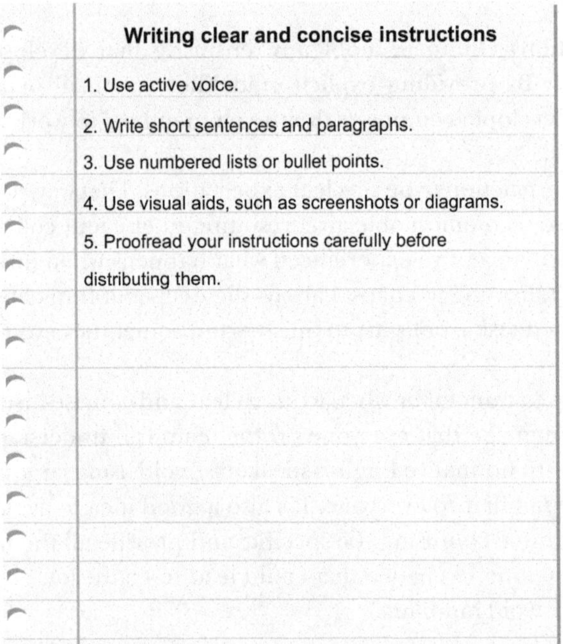

Figure 10.3   Writing clear and concise instructions

I've helped companies improve their instructions throughout my career by implementing these guidelines. In most cases, the instructions were too short and lacked much detail. Developers often had many questions about the intended functionality, so I started thinking about the instructions I was giving from the developers' point of view. I thought about their level of knowledge, what knowledge they needed from me, and how I could enable them to figure out the rest for themselves. For example, I changed an instruction for "Add a new user" to "To add a new user, open the user management page, and click the Add User button. Enter the user's name, email address, and password. Click the Save button." Providing detailed information like this helped organizations I've worked with increase productivity and developer satisfaction.

10.1.3 Documenting frequently asked questions

FAQs are a valuable resource for both developers and nondevelopers. They can help to answer common questions about a project and reduce miscommunication. To assess the most common questions that need to be addressed, you can observe questions asked during meetings, review support tickets, or gather feedback through surveys. You can create a solid foundation for your FAQ document by identifying these common queries.

When I was working on a large project for an enterprise client, we used JIRA as our project management system, and the client commented on our tasks. I noticed that they kept asking about data security, which was part of our technical approach, but they weren't clear on the level of security we were implementing. I brought it up at a project meeting to get everyone up to speed, and then I added it to the FAQ document we created in Confluence. That way, everyone had access to it and knew where to go for answers. The client appreciated this, as we spent less time going back and forth on things that had already been decided.

You can use several systems to manage FAQs, depending on your audience. For internal project FAQs, I like to use an information tool such as Confluence, which integrates with JIRA (a project management system). I've also used Zendesk and Basecamp. For external user FAQs, I've built these out using a standard Content Management System (CMS), but there are better methods to automate some of the heavy lifting. You could also use tools such as Document360 or ProProfs. As a lead developer, you may not have full autonomy to decide what system to use, but you should review the options available to provide your suggestions. Figure 10.4 shows an example of FAQ documentation in Confluence.

Organizing questions into categories helps readers quickly find the information they need. You can organize the FAQs by topic, question type, or product feature. For example, you could organize your FAQs by product features, such as "How to create a new account," "How to log in," and "How to reset my password." Grouping questions thematically makes the FAQ document more user-friendly and enhances its usability. This was a useful approach for me when I was working with public-facing platforms that needed FAQs for users. Allowing the users to navigate to the information they needed in an easy way reduced the number of support tickets. We got comments from users thanking us for the quality of our FAQs, which helped to raise team morale.

Figure 10.4   Example FAQ documentation in Confluence

As your product or service evolves, you must update the FAQs to reflect the changes. This will ensure that the information in your FAQs is always accurate and up to date. If the information is inaccurate, your project teams or users may be misled. A well-maintained FAQ document can help to improve the user experience of your product or service. Users will be able to find the information they need quickly and easily, making them more satisfied with your product or service.

10.2 Giving feedback

Feedback can be a powerful tool for improving individual and team performance. It can help developers identify areas where they need to improve, learn from their mistakes, and develop new skills. However, feedback can also be difficult to give and receive. It's important for lead developers to provide feedback in a constructive and actionable way. Figure 10.5 includes tips on providing effective feedback.

Providing effective feedback

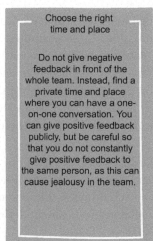

Choose the right time and place

Do not give negative feedback in front of the whole team. Instead, find a private time and place where you can have a one-on-one conversation. You can give positive feedback publicly, but be careful so that you do not constantly give positive feedback to the same person, as this can cause jealousy in the team.

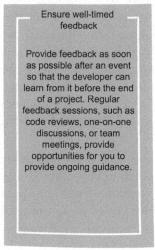

Ensure well-timed feedback

Provide feedback as soon as possible after an event so that the developer can learn from it before the end of a project. Regular feedback sessions, such as code reviews, one-on-one discussions, or team meetings, provide opportunities for you to provide ongoing guidance.

Be open to feedback

Your team should feel comfortable giving you feedback on your performance. This will help you to understand how your feedback is being received and to make sure that you're providing feedback in a way that is helpful and constructive.

Figure 10.5 Providing effective feedback

I've worked with several global teams, and one thing I've learned about giving feedback is that you have to keep cultural differences in mind. Some cultures aren't accustomed to blunt feedback, and being blunt is seen as unprofessional. I struggled with this because I can be very blunt. Sometimes, it was due to a busy schedule, and I didn't feel I had much time for feedback discussions. This was a terrible mistake because it caused dissidence within my team. It also helps to inject some humor into the conversation to diffuse tension. Nothing makes feedback discussions work better than a healthy dose of humor. Don't speed through feedback sessions; they are important for the growth of your team, and you must ensure that you have enough time to discuss every problem in detail.

10.2.1 Providing positive feedback

As a lead developer, one of your key responsibilities is to provide feedback to the development team. While constructive criticism is essential for growth, positive feedback is equally important in motivating your team. Positive feedback isn't just about recognizing achievements; it's about empowering your team to reach new heights and encouraging them on their journey toward success. The following list includes best practices for providing positive feedback:

- *Be specific and genuine.* You need to be specific about what the team member did well. General praise may not have the same effect as highlighting specific accomplishments or skills demonstrated. For example, instead of saying, "Great job," you could say, "I'm impressed at how you solved that complex problem. Your attention to detail and problem-solving skills are exceptional." Being genuine in your praise and acknowledging the effort and talent of your team members will make your feedback more meaningful and effective.

- *Foster a growth mindset.* Focusing on the individual's growth and progress is important. Emphasize the effort and determination that contributed to their success. By highlighting their growth, you motivate individuals to continuously learn, improve, and take on new challenges. When recognizing a team member's strengths, consider how you can further support their professional growth. Offer learning resources or new responsibilities that align with their skills and interests. By investing in their professional development, you'll support their continued success.

- *Encourage peer recognition.* While your positive feedback as a lead developer is valuable, fostering a culture of peer recognition can be equally powerful. Encourage team members to acknowledge and appreciate each other's achievements. This reinforces positive behaviors and promotes collaboration, camaraderie, and a sense of shared success within the team.

> **TIP**   Maintain a feedback journal or document for each team member. Whenever you notice something worth mentioning, positive or constructive, jot it down immediately. This will help you recall specific instances during performance reviews.

What I love most about giving positive feedback is the reaction of the person receiving feedback. Many people have told me how much they appreciate it because they hadn't received specific feedback before. They felt a bit lost, never knowing if what they were doing was the right approach. I've often assessed leadership potential in developers I've worked with, and I let them know that they excel in skills such as communication and leading team meetings, which transfer to leadership. I had one developer who liked to lead team meetings, so I let them. We worked on the agenda together, and at first, they shadowed me to get a sense of how I run meetings. After a while, they had the skills they needed to lead the meetings without my assistance. Other team members noticed this and gave them feedback on how the meetings were going and if anything needed to be adjusted. I enjoyed seeing the team work together in this way to support each other's success, and it made a big difference to the team. We became a close-knit team, and it was a pleasure watching everyone grow into different roles and move forward in their careers.

10.2.2 *Giving negative feedback*

Giving negative feedback can be difficult to master, but it's an important part of being a leader. Without it, developers may not know what they could improve upon. Negative feedback can also have an adverse effect if it's not given correctly. You could damage the developer's confidence or motivation if you're not careful. The following list provides tips on how to provide negative feedback:

- *Be constructive.* The goal is to help the developer improve, not to chastise them. Focus on what the developer can do to improve rather than just pointing out their mistakes. Offer to help them, and provide resources to learn the skills they need to be successful.
- *Be respectful.* Remember that negative feedback is a two-way street. A developer may not agree with your feedback, and that's fine. The important thing is to respect their opinion and have a constructive conversation.
- *Listen to the developer's perspective.* After you've given your feedback, you should listen to the developer's perspective. They may have different opinions on the problem, and you need to hear them out. This will help them feel that this isn't an attack but rather a conversation, which will go a long way to reducing tension.
- *End on a positive note.* Even if you're giving negative feedback, try to end the conversation on a positive note. This will help the developer feel motivated to improve.

Providing negative feedback isn't a one-time event. It requires ongoing support and follow-up. After delivering negative feedback, schedule follow-up meetings to check on the individual's progress and offer guidance. Show your commitment to their growth by offering mentorship, training opportunities, or project assignments that allow them to develop the required skills. Consistent support will reinforce their confidence and demonstrate your investment in their success.

> ### Example of negative feedback
>
> When you're giving negative feedback, be specific, and use "I" statements: "I'm concerned," "I noticed," "I think." Don't point the finger at them by saying, "You didn't do this right." By focusing on yourself and your perception, you'll make the conversation less of an attack, reducing tension and making the individual feel more comfortable.
>
> "I'm concerned about the quality of your code. I've noticed a few errors. I recommend taking more time to test your code locally before submitting it so that you can catch any errors. I'm happy to provide guidance when you need it; just ask."

One of my worst managers gave me negative feedback in the hallway in earshot of the entire development team. I felt so embarrassed, and I could hear people snickering. This was early in my career, and it hurt my confidence. When you're giving negative feedback, you must do this in private one on one.

> **TIP**   When you're a lead developer for the first time, you may feel the urge to invite someone to the meeting to give negative feedback so that you don't have to do it. Please resist this urge—it will hurt your relationship with the individual receiving the feedback, as they can feel like you're ganging up on them.

It's difficult to shadow someone to learn how to give negative feedback, but you can take inspiration from negative feedback you've received throughout your career. Ask yourself how it made you feel and what you wanted to happen. This will help you gain perspective and empathize with the developers on your team. You may have a few missteps along the way, but you'll become comfortable giving negative feedback with practice.

10.2.3 *Planning feedback sessions*

Constructive feedback plays an important role in fostering growth in your team. Planning and participating in feedback sessions can be a delicate task that requires careful consideration and tact. Before conducting a feedback session, you should define clear objectives and potential outcomes. What specific problems do you want to address? Are there any specific goals or performance expectations that need to be discussed? Clearly outlining the feedback session's purpose helps you and your team focus on relevant topics and facilitates a more productive conversation. For example, if a developer on your team has been struggling with meeting project deadlines, your objective for the feedback session could be to identify the problem's root causes and collaboratively develop a plan to improve time management.

You must select an appropriate time and setting for the feedback session to ensure an atmosphere of privacy, comfort, and minimal distractions. Ideally, you should find a neutral space where both you and your team members can engage in an open and honest conversation without interruptions. Consider the individual's preferred communication style, and try to adapt accordingly. If a team member prefers a casual setting, you could schedule a feedback session over a coffee break in a quiet office corner or outside. You don't have much choice in a fully remote team, and it should be a videoconference. However, you can move yourself to a more relaxed environment and urge your team members to do the same. I live in Florida, so I like to have casual video calls from my porch with palm trees in the background. I find that this puts people at ease and sets a positive tone for the call.

> **DEFINITION**   The Sandwich technique, also known as the Feedback Sandwich or Praise-Critique-Praise method, is a popular approach for delivering constructive

feedback in a balanced and effective manner. It involves structuring the feedback session by sandwiching the criticism or areas for improvement between two layers of positive feedback or praise.

You should plan to begin the feedback session by providing positive reinforcement to acknowledge the team member's strengths, achievements, or areas where they have excelled. This sets a positive tone for the conversation, boosts morale, and highlights the individual's valuable contributions. For example:

> *I wanted to commend you on your recent work. Your attention to detail and problem-solving skills were outstanding. The code you wrote was clean, efficient, and well-documented.*

Once you've established a positive tone, discuss the specific areas where the team member can improve or grow. Provide constructive criticism by identifying gaps in their performance or highlighting what they could improve upon. It's essential to be objective and offer actionable suggestions or examples for improvement. The following is a good example of constructive criticism:

> *While your technical skills are excellent, there were a few instances where your communication with the team could have been better. For example, during the last sprint, there was some confusion about the project timeline and requirements. To enhance collaboration, I suggest actively engaging in team discussions and being proactive by providing regular updates to ensure everyone is on the same page.*

Finally, conclude the feedback session by reiterating positive aspects and expressing confidence in the individual's abilities. Emphasize that the critique or suggestions will help them grow and succeed, rather than undermining their overall value. For example:

> *Despite the communication challenges, I have no doubt that you have the skills and potential to excel in teamwork. Your technical expertise and dedication are valuable assets to the team, and I believe that with improved communication, you'll further enhance your collaborative skills.*

When I plan feedback sessions, I like to outline the flow of the conversation. If the conversation drifts away from my intended plan, I gently bring it back. I've had team members who dwell on constructive criticism and apologize profusely for not recognizing that they needed to improve. I always tell them that is part of my job, and without feedback, how would they know what they need to improve? It's a team effort, and no one can improve without feedback.

10.3 Handling emergencies

As a lead developer, you play a major role in guiding your team through unexpected challenges. Emergencies can strike anytime, threatening project timelines, system stability, and morale. Having the ability to effectively navigate emergencies is an essential skill for any lead developer. We'll explore the contrasting scenarios of having a leader versus not having one during an emergency and provide a comprehensive guide on how lead developers should handle such situations efficiently.

When an emergency arises, such as a systems failure or a data breach, having a leader in place ensures clear and concise communication channels. The leader becomes the central point of contact, disseminating vital information to team members and stakeholders. This helps prevent confusion, reduces panic, and enables quick decision-making. I was once in a situation where the lead developer I was working with bailed during an emergency early on in my career. A website we were working on went down, and there was panic within the team. The lead developer remained quiet and offered no guidance. Everyone on the team was scrambling, and we made even more errors. We weren't communicating effectively, which led to duplication of work. It took us a very long time to figure out how to fix the errors. This process could have been much more streamlined and less stressful if the lead developer had a plan. Now let's learn what should have happened and how to handle emergencies properly. Figure 10.6 shows the five phases you should keep in mind when handling emergencies.

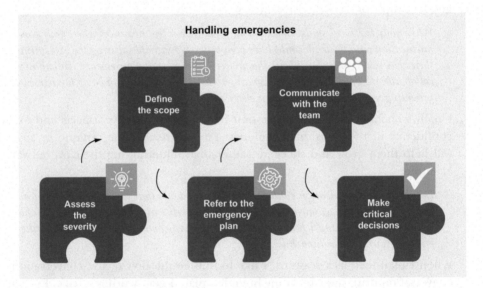

Figure 10.6   Handling emergencies

When you're facing an emergency, your first step is to assess the severity and scope. Gather all available information, including the effect on systems, users, and stakeholders. This initial assessment will help you understand the urgency and formulate an appropriate response plan. You should have a well-defined emergency response plan in place ahead of time. That way, you can activate the plan immediately, ensuring all team members know their roles and responsibilities. This plan should include predefined communication channels, escalation procedures, and a decision-making hierarchy. We'll discuss this topic in detail later in this section, including going over an example emergency response plan.

Proper communication is vital during an emergency. You should establish communication channels with your project team, such as a team chat or an open conference line. Continually provide updates on the situation, progress, and any changes in the response plan. Encourage open dialogue, address concerns, and ensure everyone is informed and aligned. You'll need input from the team to make critical decisions quickly while under pressure. Analyze available options, evaluate risks, and consider the long-term effect of each decision. The way you handle emergencies reflects not only your technical competence but also your leadership skills. When you can handle emergencies well, you'll inspire confidence in your team and stakeholders.

10.3.1 *Remaining positive*

Maintaining a positive mindset during an emergency is crucial for effective leadership and achieving successful outcomes. When emergencies happen, it's natural for stress and negativity to overshadow the work environment. However, a positive attitude can significantly affect how you and your team respond to these challenges. By maintaining an optimistic outlook, you inspire others to persevere and give their best in the face of an emergency. A positive leader sets an example for their team, fostering resilience and encouraging a can-do attitude. Figure 10.7 includes strategies to cultivate and sustain positivity within yourself and your team during an emergency.

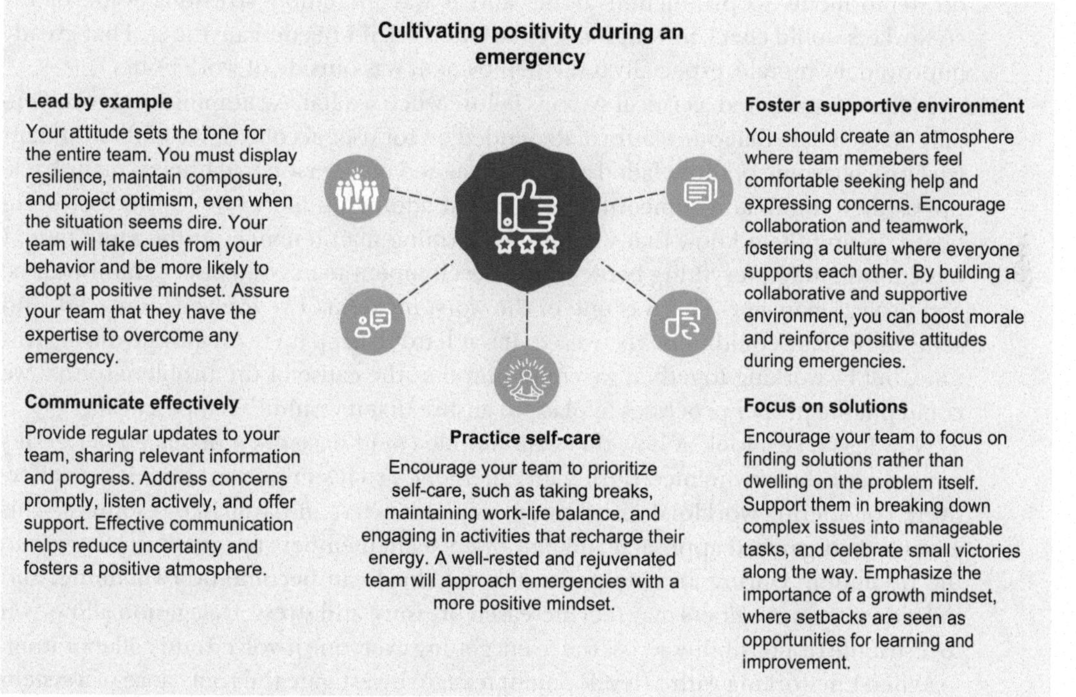

Cultivating positivity during an emergency

Lead by example
Your attitude sets the tone for the entire team. You must display resilience, maintain composure, and project optimism, even when the situation seems dire. Your team will take cues from your behavior and be more likely to adopt a positive mindset. Assure your team that they have the expertise to overcome any emergency.

Communicate effectively
Provide regular updates to your team, sharing relevant information and progress. Address concerns promptly, listen actively, and offer support. Effective communication helps reduce uncertainty and fosters a positive atmosphere.

Foster a supportive environment
You should create an atmosphere where team memebers feel comfortable seeking help and expressing concerns. Encourage collaboration and teamwork, fostering a culture where everyone supports each other. By building a collaborative and supportive environment, you can boost morale and reinforce positive attitudes during emergencies.

Practice self-care
Encourage your team to prioritize self-care, such as taking breaks, maintaining work-life balance, and engaging in activities that recharge their energy. A well-rested and rejuvenated team will approach emergencies with a more positive mindset.

Focus on solutions
Encourage your team to focus on finding solutions rather than dwelling on the problem itself. Support them in breaking down complex issues into manageable tasks, and celebrate small victories along the way. Emphasize the importance of a growth mindset, where setbacks are seen as opportunities for learning and improvement.

Figure 10.7   Cultivating positivity during an emergency

When I'm supporting a team during an emergency, the first thing I like to do is to assure them that we're a highly capable team and that we'll get through it. Emergencies happen, and they are always a learning experience. I think sometimes people become more nervous to speak up during an emergency because they feel overwhelmed. I make it clear that I need their input, and without it, I may overlook something that they have expertise in.

The first time I recognized the need to practice better self-care during an emergency was when I was handling a deployment to production that went very wrong. Ten hours into it, I was feeling very irritable, so that when people asked me questions, my answers became very short. I felt impatient that the problems weren't fixed yet, and I just wanted it to be over with. One of my team members recognized that I wasn't acting like myself, and she suggested that I take a break because the QA team was testing, so I was waiting for any questions that may arise. I thanked her and took a 15-minute break to eat and stretch. While I promoted self-care for my team, I didn't follow my own advice. You must take care of yourself before you can support the success of others. When you're relaxed, you can better focus on being positive and resilient during an emergency.

10.3.2 *Bringing the team together*

When facing an emergency, it's imperative to promote a culture of team spirit. Everyone has a part to play, and no one is alone. I've worked for companies that had me do deployments to production alone, and it was incredibly stressful. Some of my co-workers would check in with me regularly and ask if I needed anything. That greatly improved my morale, especially if the deployment was outside of work hours.

I once encountered a critical systems failure when a database administrator accidentally deleted data that our platform depended on for user accounts. We had redundant backups, but some of those failed as well. I assigned one person to gather as many backups as they could, and someone else handled adding an alert box to the user dashboard, letting them know that we were performing maintenance. At the same time, I was coordinating everything between the development team, database administrators, and project manager. This was one of the worst incidents I've ever encountered, and some of the data couldn't be recovered. It was hard to keep up team morale during this time, but by working together, we could pinpoint the cause of the problem so that we could put the proper processes in place to ensure that it wouldn't happen again.

Now let's take a look at how the team morale could have been managed better. It's natural to feel overwhelmed during an emergency, so it's important to delegate effectively, considering workload distribution, dependencies, and available resources. This ensures an organized approach and empowers team members to contribute actively to the resolution. During an emergency, the workload can become overwhelming, and individual team members may feel increased pressure and stress. Delegation allows you to distribute responsibility across the team, getting everyone involved and collaborating.

When I'm working with a development team to investigate the root cause of a system failure, I always delegate communication with stakeholders to someone else, usually the project manager. Some errors take a while to work out, and I must be heads down while I'm working with a development team to troubleshoot and work out a plan. I consider each team member's expertise and delegate tasks accordingly. This approach ensures that all essential tasks are addressed concurrently and shared among the team. Every team member possesses their own skills and strengths that can be helpful during an emergency. Delegation allows you to use the diverse expertise within your team and assign tasks based on individual skill sets.

When teams are under extreme pressure, confidence can easily waver due to increased uncertainty. By delegating tasks, you empower your team members and demonstrate your trust in their abilities.

10.3.3 Outlining a plan

An emergency plan helps minimize downtime by providing a clear action plan for handling critical problems. It ensures that all team members know their roles and responsibilities, expediting efforts to mitigate the effect of emergencies. Having a solid plan can reduce recovery time and minimize disruptions to project schedules. You should be proactive and identify potential emergency scenarios affecting the system or project. Consider factors such as system failures, security breaches, data loss, and natural disasters. Understanding the potential risks allows you to tailor the plan to address specific challenges facing each individual project.

Effective communication is imperative during emergencies. An emergency plan establishes communication protocols, channels, and escalation procedures, ensuring that information is shared among team members and stakeholders. Clear communication enables prompt decision-making. The following list includes items to address regarding communication in an emergency plan:

- Identify team members' roles and responsibilities, such as developers, system administrators, and project managers.
- Establish primary and backup communication channels for team members and stakeholders. This may include email groups, chat platforms, or dedicated emergency contact numbers.
- Ensure all team members and stakeholders have up-to-date contact information. There should be a central document with this information, and each team member should include their contact information in their email signature.
- Create a clear and concise communication protocol outlining how and when to report incidents, provide updates, and escalate problems. You can timebox updates so that they are done every half hour or hour based on the severity of the problem. Problem reporting and escalation protocols should be clearly stated with a backup plan if necessary. Critical errors should be escalated to a team, not an individual, to avoid problems if an individual isn't available.

An emergency plan provides a framework for strategic decision-making, enabling you to make informed choices based on predefined criteria and contingencies. By considering potential risks and available resources, you can prioritize actions, allocate necessary resources, and minimize the effect of emergencies on the project and system. Evaluating available options and risks associated with each potential solution is important. All decisions should be documented and include the rationale behind them. As new information becomes available, your team must work together to reassess and adjust the response strategy accordingly.

One of the most important parts of an emergency plan is the incident response guidelines. As the lead developer, you should be notified immediately when a critical system problem occurs. Key stakeholders should also be added to the notification list as necessary, for example, project managers to communicate with stakeholders. If there is a natural disaster or a mass layoff is announced, everyone should be notified and come together as a team to process the information. Keep in mind that emergencies aren't always technical in nature. There are nontechnical emergencies to consider as well. I was working at a company that had to shut down, and when they announced it, many people left, creating a mess. I worked with the project manager to gather the resources needed to finish the project we were working on before the company closed. She helped me find another job and acted as a counselor through the process to help me remain positive and level-headed. The team got through it together, and we all went on to achieve success in our next roles.

As a lead developer, it's your job to gather all available information and assess the severity and scope of the incident. Outline step-by-step procedures for responding to different types of emergencies. Include guidelines for assessing the situation, identifying critical systems or components, and coordinating with the team. Delegate tasks and responsibilities to team members based on their expertise and availability. You are the point of contact, and it's important to constantly update the team regarding progress, challenges, and any changes to the response plan. Provide stakeholders with the expected resolution time, and inform them of any necessary actions on their part. Fully document the incident, and clearly define decision-making processes and escalation paths to ensure an efficient response. Figure 10.8 shows an example of an emergency plan in Confluence.

Once the emergency has been addressed, it's important to conduct a thorough analysis to identify root causes and evaluate the effectiveness of the response. Gather feedback from team members and stakeholders to document lessons learned. That way, you can update the emergency response plan to enhance preparedness for future emergencies. I always keep the team informed of changes to the emergency plan when they occur so that everyone is aware and up-to-date. Additionally, when I'm onboarding new developers, part of their training is to review the plan so that they know the procedures when an emergency occurs. It's better to be proactive than reactive regarding emergency preparedness to foster a culture of proactive response and readiness.

🖉 Defining an incident

Working to define what your business considers an incident will save you critical time and headspace when you're in the midst of a service outage.

1. e.g., more than 10% of customers must be impacted
2.
3.

🦃 Incident roles & responsibilities

List the current incident response roles at your company. If you don't have defined incident roles, check out this resource to learn more about common setups.

Role	Owner	Responsibilities
Major Incident Manager (MIM)	@ mention the Owner here	e.g., • Assess the severity (service and customer impact) • Escalate to the appropriate people on-call • Track changes, decisions, and fixes (and confirm final fix) • Hold a post-incident review meeting • Decide if a public post-mortem is needed
Communication Officer	@ mention the Owner here	• Quickly identify the incident status • Pull in appropriate departments needed for communications • Provide public and internal updates • Decide the appropriate communication channels

🎤 Incident communication channels

Establish how and where you'll communicate updates to relevant audiences during an incident.

Communication channel or tool	When do we use it?	Who or which departments should use it?	How do we use/access it?
Where are you communicating with your customers? (e.g., Service desk, Statuspage, Twitter, email, chat tool)	What type of incidents do we use this for? (e.g., only incidents with x amount of customer impact, only incidents that last x hours long, Sev 1, 2)	Who is authorized/trained on communicating from this channel? (e.g., Product Marketing, Communication Lead)	Instructions on how to use it, how to get access/login info for it, etc. (e.g., Password, Ask for user account)

✦ Incident Response Procedures

Even the most comprehensive incident response plan lacks guidance for more subjective, nuanced situations that can and will arise.

Stage	Explanation
Identify	Document the type of incident and severity.
Assess	Conduct impact analysis and risk evaluation.
Respond	Notify the project team and relevant stakeholders. Regularly update stakeholders on the incident status, expected resolution time, and any necessary actions on their part.
Mitigate	Prioritize actions based on urgency and potential impact. Document decisions made throughout the process and adjust the response strategy as new information becomes available.
Review	Document the root cause analysis and identification of areas for improvement. Share the findings and recommendations with the team to enhance preparedness for future emergencies.
Maintain	Document lessons learned and update the emergency plan accordingly. Update the plan based on changes in project requirements and team composition.

Figure 10.8   Example emergency plan in Confluence

10.4   *Improving your confidence*

Improving confidence in your abilities can have a significant effect on both your personal life and career. As a lead developer, you must set achievable goals and break them down into smaller milestones. You'll gain confidence in your skills and abilities when you consistently meet these milestones. This confidence spills over into your personal life, as you feel more in control of your aspirations and personal goals. Many people fear failure to the point that they never go out of their comfort zone. Instead of shying away from challenges, lead developers should embrace them as opportunities for growth. Even if you fail, learning from the situation and applying those lessons enhances your confidence in handling future obstacles, both professionally and personally. I used to get very upset when I perceived my own failures. Sometimes, my colleagues assured me that I didn't fail, as I wasn't set up for success in the first place. Assessing the cause of failure is a good step toward improving your confidence. With experience, you can ensure that you're set up for success so that you don't fail.

Empowering your team members through mentoring and skill development is a good way to boost your confidence. Recognize the positive effect of your guidance. When I think about all the people I've mentored throughout my career, I feel proud when they achieve a new accomplishment. I keep in touch with my mentees through social media, and I love to see when they post an update about a new job or certification exam they passed. This especially helps when I'm feeling down on myself, which happens to everyone occasionally. You must mitigate your feelings of self-doubt to be an effective leader. Doubting yourself isn't always a bad thing, as it keeps you humble. If you always thought highly of yourself, you wouldn't learn from your mistakes.

10.4.1   *Assessing your strengths and weaknesses*

Self-assessment is a vital step in personal and professional growth. By acknowledging the areas where you excel and the areas where you need improvement, you can make informed decisions on how to improve. Confidence doesn't mean achieving perfection. It comes from understanding yourself and making continuous efforts to grow and learn.

Start by evaluating your technical skills and expertise. Reflect on the skills you're most comfortable with and have mastered. I always consider the projects I've successfully led or the complex challenges I've overcome. Recognizing your technical strengths will instill confidence and help you make informed decisions during project planning and execution. It's important to assess your leadership and communication skills objectively. Ask yourself if you're skilled at providing clear instructions and constructive feedback. Do you actively listen to your team members and value their input?

Assessing weaknesses can be challenging, but it's crucial for personal and professional development. You should identify areas where you may lack expertise or experience. It could be a specific programming language, unfamiliarity with a particular technology, or difficulty leading your team. The key is to tackle these weaknesses head-on. My biggest weakness as a leader used to be conflict management and resolution. I would shy away from dealing with conflict, which only results in more conflict. I understood that this was a problem, so I created a professional development plan to seek out training opportunities and learn the leadership skills I needed to manage conflict effectively. As I learned new skills and gained experience, I made progress, which lifted my confidence as a leader.

One of the best ways to assess your strengths and weaknesses is to gather feedback from your team members. Encourage them to be open and honest. Ask for their input on your leadership style, communication effectiveness, and overall performance. Constructive feedback can be a powerful tool for making positive changes and enhancing your confidence as a lead developer. I gather feedback from developers on my team when we meet one on one. I've found that this is a good time for two-way feedback, and it's important for your team members to feel that they can and should also give you feedback.

When you receive negative feedback from your team members, it's important not to take it personally. When I got my first leadership role, I was promoted above my team members, which was initially difficult. If they gave me negative feedback, I would take it personally and think that they were just jealous because of my promotion. Over time, I realized that I was internalizing my own self-doubt and allowing it to damage my progress. I became a better leader once I started listening to them and making the proper adjustments. You can't improve your leadership skills without feedback, and you must take it as it comes. By taking proactive steps to address areas that need improvement and fostering a continuous learning environment, you'll enhance your confidence and become a more effective and influential lead developer.

10.4.2 Avoiding comparing yourself to others

Comparing yourself to others is a natural human instinct, but it can be detrimental, especially in a professional setting. As a lead developer, you should be mindful of the negative effect of comparisons on your confidence and self-esteem. Everyone has a diverse skill set and perspective to bring to the table. Instead of comparing yourself to others, celebrate your individuality and the unique strengths you offer. Emphasize the areas where you excel and your valuable contributions to the team. Recognize that your strengths are what make you an essential asset to the organization.

You should limit your time on social media. Social media platforms can become breeding grounds for comparison and self-doubt. As a lead developer, you must be cautious about comparing yourself to others on these platforms. Social media often portrays a curated and idealized version of reality. People don't often post their struggles; they focus on their achievements. You can't know what is really going on in someone's life or how they accomplished their goals. That is why I make it a point to discuss my struggles publicly so people know that my life isn't perfect. I've had a hard time writing this book because a lot has been going on in my life during this time, and I feel that it's important to talk about it. I wish others would do the same. Whenever I get a response, and someone is comparing themselves to my seemingly perfect life and career, I set them straight and tell them not to compare themselves to me. Instead, focus on your unique journey and progress in your career.

It helps to surround yourself with supportive communities and seek mentorship from experienced professionals. Engage in networking opportunities, and participate in developer communities where individuals can share experiences, insights, and lessons learned. When you engage with developer communities, keep in mind that everyone is on their own journey. Just because someone else is further ahead in their career doesn't mean that you're not good enough. It's important to celebrate your own progress along the way.

Practicing self-compassion means being kind to yourself. You should acknowledge that everyone has strengths and weaknesses. Don't be too hard on yourself when you fail and someone else succeeds. Treat yourself with the same understanding and compassion you would offer a friend. This is difficult for me, and I'm very hard on myself. While that quality pushes me to achieve great things, it also causes a lot of stress in my life. I understand that about myself and know that it's a trigger for me. I try to think about the present and not worry too much about the past or the future. One of Walt Disney's most famous quotes is, "Keep moving forward." This is one of my mantras that helps me when my confidence is shaken.

10.4.3 *Challenging negative thoughts*

Negative thoughts can often creep into the minds of even the most skilled lead developers, leading to self-doubt and diminished confidence. The first step in challenging negative thoughts is to recognize when they arise. Be mindful of your emotional responses to different situations, and identify any recurring negative thought patterns. Once you identify negative thoughts, take a moment to assess their validity objectively. Ask yourself if the thought is based on evidence or if it's merely a product of self-doubt or unfounded fear. Often, negative thoughts stem from irrational beliefs or past experiences, and they might not accurately reflect your current abilities or potential.

Something that used to happen to me often was that I would think it was my fault when a system failed or there was turnover on my team. This stemmed from past experiences when I was treated as a scapegoat by poor leaders. I didn't realize it at the time, but I've since learned that no one should place blame on one single person for a failure when they are working on a team. Everything is a team effort, and we should endure failure together. When you have bad experiences with leaders you look up to, this can make you question yourself and your abilities. I find that talking about these situations with team members or mentors helps me gain clarity on these situations so that I can overcome my negative feelings toward myself.

Intrusive thoughts are unwanted, distressing, and often disturbing mental images that unexpectedly and involuntarily enter a person's mind. These thoughts can be unsettling, causing anxiety or fear. While intrusive thoughts are a common human experience, they can become problematic when they interfere with daily functioning and mental well-being. To mitigate intrusive thoughts, you can practice several strategies. Figure 10.9 includes some strategies you can follow.

You can challenge negative thoughts by reframing them into more realistic and balanced statements. For example, if you think, "I'm not skilled enough for this task," reframe it as, "I may face challenges, but I have the knowledge and experience to overcome them." By shifting your perspective, you'll replace self-doubt with a more positive and constructive outlook.

The company you keep can significantly affect your confidence levels. Surround yourself with supportive colleagues who encourage your growth and celebrate your achievements. Engaging in positive and constructive discussions with like-minded individuals can help combat negative thoughts and reinforce your confidence. Try to stay away from toxicity in the workplace, and be a positive influence on others. I create a support system of people I can count on to be there for me when the going gets tough. Everyone has bad days and needs support sometimes. You should be kind to yourself and seek help when needed so that your own negative thoughts don't prevent you from achieving success.

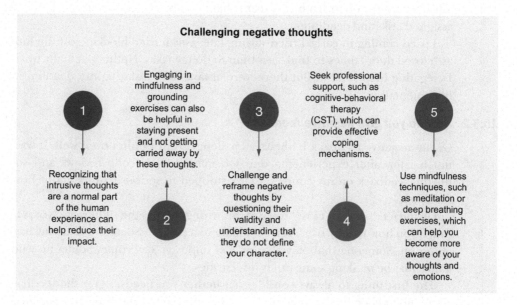

Figure 10.9   Challenging negative thoughts

10.5   *Case study*

Deborah Kurata started as a software developer and quickly became a project team lead and then a software development manager. Later, she started her own software consulting company that grew to 30 consultants at the peak of the company.

Deborah loves teaching and creating content for developers. For her work supporting software developers, she's been recognized with the Microsoft Most Valuable Professional (MVP) award in Developer Technologies and is a Google Developer Expert (GDE) in Angular.

You can contact her on Twitter at https://twitter.com/DeborahKurata, find her Pluralsight courses at https://mng.bz/6YYZ, access her freeCodeCamp articles at https://mng.bz/o002, and view her YouTube content at https://mng.bz/n00e. In this case study, Deborah shares her advice for taking the lead.

10.5.1 How did you know you were ready to be a leader?

For me, it wasn't a laid-out path or a matter of choice. I fell into it. And with no real experience or mentor, I learned by failing . . . a lot.

I tried many different techniques for organizing projects and providing team motivation. In the days before "standups" were all the rage, I used to "manage by walking around." I'd often spend the day walking around the office checking in with each of the team members. We'd talk about design ideas or code together or debug something. Then, it was on to the next person. That seemed to work well.

One big challenge was getting my own work done. Especially when starting out as a leader, you're often leading a team that you also are a part of. And you also have assigned tasks and deadlines.

I tried coming in early. I tried staying late. I even tried blocking off the lunch hour as "closed door" times to find *some* time to do my tasks. Nothing actually worked well. Delegating helped a bit. But there were always more tasks, tighter deadlines, missing documentation.

10.5.2 How do you give negative feedback?

Giving negative feedback is always a challenge. And I didn't do it well. It wasn't until much later, after experiencing one too many useless code reviews and some very hurtful feedback on my courses, that I stopped to seriously think about how to give feedback.

Giving feedback isn't just "You did this wrong, here is the right way." Nor is it "I need to tell you how to improve." You're talking to a person. Someone that may have things going on. Someone that may already feel imposter syndrome. Someone whose arrogance may be masking some inner insecurities.

The first thing to always consider is whether you need to give the feedback at all. Chris didn't code that routine the same way that you would. Do you really need to tell them "You could have done x, y, or z instead?" Or is it good enough? Sometimes we all get a little focused on perfection when most often "good" is "good enough."

If you determine that you really need to provide feedback, set up a time to talk. And don't just send a slack message "We need to talk tomorrow" and let them sweat all night. Instead, request a time to "check in" on the project or "review the prior day's meeting."

When you meet, always start with something positive. "The client was very happy with your presentation." And be specific: "They appreciated the organization and detail. They really liked how you handled the questions." Then, get to what needs to be improved: "The client was a bit surprised to see you spent the rest of the meeting playing a game on your laptop. They thought it was disrespectful to the other speakers."

Don't go on and on. Make the point, and then let them respond. Help them get to how *they* think they can improve.

And if at all possible, don't clean up their messes. Don't redo their code. Don't rewrite their documentation. Rather, provide guidance on how they can make the needed changes to rectify the problem.

10.5.3 What is your experience with leading a team through an emergency?

The biggest emergency I've led a team through was 9/11. This was in 2001 before we had good internet everywhere, so we were all grouped around one computer trying to get the latest news. Back then, everyone couldn't be hitting the network all at the same time because there wasn't enough bandwidth. At lunchtime, we told everyone to go home because no one was working anyway. It was a difficult time, and I didn't feel like I was doing much leading because I was in shock. Everyone was in shock, and it took a long time for us to get through it.

Another emergency I encountered was a mass layoff. A company I worked for got bought out by a company out of Los Angeles, and I live in the San Francisco Bay Area. All of our team were working in Silicon Valley at the time, and there was an announcement that they were moving all of their operations to Los Angeles. And the people in Silicon Valley didn't want to move. So I worked with all the team members there to talk through their frustrations, and it was very difficult because at that point, everyone was angry and going through the stages of grief. A layoff isn't unlike losing a loved one. Losing a parent is significantly worse, but during a layoff, you still go through the same stages of grief: denial, anger, frustration, and so on.

And through that, the company still needed us to transition the team. Because no one was going to move, it was difficult to work with the team members to share in their frustrations and their anger. But we still had to try to accomplish something in terms of the turnover process. So that was quite a challenging experience. And I was five months pregnant at the time. Luckily for me, because no one wanted to move, they actually hired me back as a consultant to help finish the transition before everyone had left. It's a difficult time to lead when you're also feeling disappointed and let down. You have to push that down a little bit so that you can help the team members get through it.

10.5.4 What advice do you have for lead developers who aren't sure if they are ready to take the lead?

Since I fell into leadership, I didn't really have time to think about it, which was probably a good thing because I didn't have a chance to stress about it. And then the questions became "How are you going to do it?" "How are you going to make it happen?" "How are you going to succeed in this role that you don't really know how to do?" It was really important for me to try different things and be creative—and to focus as much as possible on what the team needs.

One of the things that happens is that people internalize things and think they aren't good enough or they don't know how to do this. I know as a leader, it's important not to internalize things but look outward. Ask yourself, "What can I do for the team?" "How can I lead them and make them comfortable when they are overwhelmed or stressed out?" Figure out how to help without doing someone else's job. You need to provide assistance without overdoing it.

I remember doing a consulting project where I wrote technical documentation. I would spend hours understanding a programming language to get the information I needed. When I submitted it to the project lead, he would completely rewrite it and then send it to the client. It made me feel like, "Why am I even here?" When I would ask him about it, he said I was doing fine, and he was just touching it up a little bit. When you're in leadership, you have to support your team members by providing feedback so that they know what needs to improve. That is one of the hardest things, especially if you're a lead developer who was promoted from within. You can't inject yourself too much into other people's work; they need you to sit down with them and tell them what they can improve upon so that they can get better. It's often easier for you to just redo their work yourself than to spend the time with them to explain what's wrong with it. But over time, if you keep doing all the work yourself, that's not helping anybody.

Leading a team isn't like getting an award. It's more like getting a puppy. Sure, it's cute and can be fun . . . but it's also a huge responsibility. And if you don't pay attention and provide proper guidance, it can become an unruly pet. My advice is to give it a try. It will be difficult, and you'll make mistakes. Learn from those mistakes, and don't give up.

Summary

- Providing clear and concise instructions is essential for developers to understand their objectives fully, prevent confusion and wasted time, and encourage efficient collaboration and improved performance.
- Using "I" statements while giving negative feedback can create a more comfortable and supportive environment to avoid conflict.
- Using the Sandwich technique for giving feedback involves sandwiching constructive criticism between two layers of positive feedback to create a balanced and supportive approach.
- Maintaining a positive mindset during emergencies is crucial for effective leadership, as it fosters resilience, creativity, and problem-solving skills, and supports the team in overcoming challenges and achieving successful outcomes.
- Having a well-defined emergency plan is crucial for minimizing downtime and disruptions, enabling effective communication, strategic decision-making, and swift resolution.
- Building confidence yields benefits in your personal life and career, allowing for setting achievable goals, embracing challenges, empowering team members, and mitigating self-doubt, leading to a more fulfilling and successful life overall.

11

Leading with emotional intelligence

Emotional intelligence is a crucial skill set that encompasses understanding, managing, and effectively expressing emotions. In the dynamic world of software development, emotional intelligence plays a pivotal role in determining the success of lead developers and their teams. Emotionally intelligent lead developers foster a positive and supportive team culture. They actively listen to their team members' concerns, show appreciation for their efforts, and provide constructive feedback.

DEFINITION   Emotional intelligence is the ability to recognize, understand, and manage one's emotions effectively while also perceiving and empathizing with the emotions of others.

Conflicts are a natural part of any workplace, but it's essential to resolve them quickly. Emotionally intelligent lead developers ensure that conflicts don't escalate and negatively affect team dynamics.

Lead developers often deal with tight deadlines and high-pressure situations. Emotionally intelligent lead developers can handle stress effectively, keeping calm in an emergency and guiding their team members through challenging times with composure and resilience.

Employees will remain loyal to the organization when the lead developer is supportive and provides a safe space for them to learn and grow. Employees respond well to an emotionally intelligent leader who takes the time to understand what makes every individual team member happy. Leaders must also sense when a team member is having a bad day and provide the support that they need to get through it.

Lead developers must recognize the importance of emotional intelligence and invest in fostering this skill to ensure the long-term success of their projects and overall team satisfaction. In this chapter, we'll explore the meaning of emotional intelligence and walk through some scenarios to show you how to apply it to benefit your team.

11.1   *What is emotional intelligence?*

Emotional intelligence comprises five key components: self-awareness, self-regulation, motivation, empathy, and social skills (see figure 11.1). A lead developer with high emotional intelligence is attuned to their emotions and those of their team members. Through self-awareness and empathy, they can adapt their behavior according to the emotional needs of their colleagues and project circumstances. Self-regulation helps in conflict resolution when a lead developer can keep their emotions in check. Oftentimes, conflict can be avoided by showing empathy toward your team members and motivating them to work together to achieve success. Effective communication, collaboration, and conflict resolution are important social skills that every lead developer should have for them to be emotionally intelligent leaders.

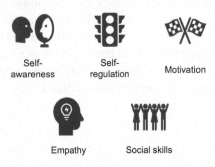

Self-awareness   Self-regulation   Motivation

Empathy   Social skills

Figure 11.1   Five key components of emotional intelligence

I've found that team members work better together and achieve professional growth when they work with an emotionally intelligent leader. The team has less conflict, as everyone respects each other and learns from their different experiences. By mastering the principles of emotional intelligence, you'll enhance your leadership abilities and cultivate an environment where team members feel valued, motivated, and empowered.

Table 11.1 breaks down different aspects of emotional intelligence to compare the result when lead developers are emotionally intelligent versus when they lack emotional intelligence.

Table 11.1 Emotional intelligence vs. lack of emotional intelligence

Aspect	Emotional intelligence	Lack of emotional intelligence
Self-awareness	Recognizes personal emotions and triggers, managing them to maintain a composed leadership style	Often ruled by their emotions, which can lead to conflict and poor decision-making
Conflict resolution	Handles conflicts diplomatically, finding win-win solutions and maintaining team harmony	More likely to escalate conflicts, which can damage team morale and productivity
Stress management	Handles stress effectively, maintaining focus on tasks and ensuring team members' well-being	Succumbs to stress, becoming overwhelmed and negatively affecting team productivity
Empathy	Demonstrates genuine care for team members' well-being, supporting them through challenges	May be insensitive to the needs and feelings of others, which can lead to frustration and resentment
Building relationships	Builds strong relationships with their team members and promotes a positive working environment	Difficulty building trust and rapport with their team members, which can lead to a lack of cooperation and productivity
Communication	Actively listens and understands team members' perspectives, encouraging open dialogue and collaboration	Disregards team members' opinions, leading to poor communication and reduced team morale
Employee retention	Creates a supportive and respectful work environment, reducing turnover and retaining talent	Fosters a toxic atmosphere, leading to a high turnover rate and difficulty in attracting and retaining talent

11.1.1 Understanding the four-branch model

Emotional intelligence encompasses a range of skills and competencies that enable individuals to navigate the complexities of emotions and human interactions. The term *emotional intelligence* was first introduced by psychologists Peter Salovey and John D. Mayer, but the term gained widespread recognition through the pioneering work of psychologist Daniel Goleman.

While the concept of emotional intelligence has been explored by various researchers, the four-branch model of emotional intelligence proposed by Salovey and Mayer in 1990 stands out as one of the most influential and comprehensive frameworks.

Unlike earlier models that treated emotional intelligence as a single construct, their model breaks it down into four distinct branches, each representing a different facet of emotional intelligence. The four-branch model provides lead developers with a well-rounded framework to understand, develop, and apply emotional intelligence skills. By mastering these components, lead developers can create a healthier and more productive work environment, build stronger relationships with their team, and effectively lead projects to success. The following list defines each of the four branches:

- *Perceiving emotions*—The ability to perceive emotions accurately in oneself and others. This includes recognizing emotions expressed through facial expressions, body language, and vocal cues. Individuals with strong perceptions can decipher the emotional states of others, forming the foundation for empathetic responses and effective communication.

- *Using emotions*—Using emotions to facilitate thinking and problem-solving. Individuals harness their emotions to aid decision-making, prioritize tasks effectively, and creatively approach challenges. They understand that emotions carry valuable information and can influence cognitive processes to achieve better outcomes.

- *Understanding emotions*—The capacity to comprehend complex emotions and the relationships between different emotional states. This branch of the model goes beyond basic emotional recognition and extends to understanding the causes and consequences of emotions. This helps individuals navigate their emotional experiences with greater clarity and insight.

- *Managing emotions*—The ability to manage emotions in oneself and others. Individuals can regulate their emotions in response to various situations, avoiding impulsive or destructive reactions. They can also assist others in managing their emotions, providing support and empathy when needed.

Being able to perceive emotions is a necessary skill for any leader. Lead developers must recognize both positive and negative emotions to understand and empathize with their team members. When people feel positive, they will appear upbeat and optimistic in the face of challenges. They may smile more often and show appreciation and gratitude toward their co-workers. Negative emotions may be harder to recognize because they are often tied to behaviors and not words. When someone is experiencing negative feelings toward their job, they may disengage and avoid participation in group activities. They may appear irritated, stressed, or fatigued. Figure 11.2 illustrates some of the most common positive and negative emotions and how to recognize them.

Understanding emotions, perceiving them accurately, and effectively managing them is vital for personal growth and overall well-being. Lead developers often have to guide their teams through challenges such as tight deadlines or organizational restructuring. Understanding their own emotions and how their use of emotions affects the team is crucial to ensuring their team's success. If a lead developer feels frustrated, they must manage their emotions when communicating their problems with the team.

If a team member exhibits negative emotions, the lead developer must deal with the situation by listening and empathizing with them. A lead developer can manage the emotions of their team members through guidance and coaching to mitigate negative feelings.

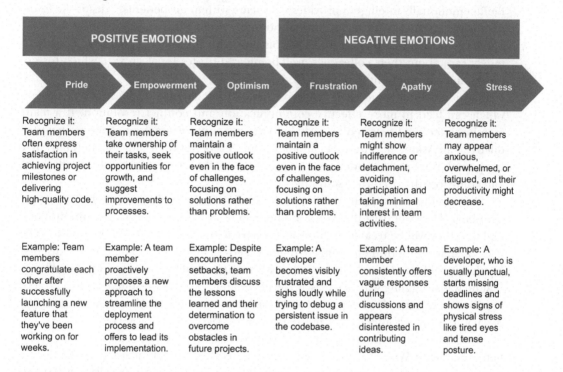

POSITIVE EMOTIONS			NEGATIVE EMOTIONS		
Pride	**Empowerment**	**Optimism**	**Frustration**	**Apathy**	**Stress**
Recognize it: Team members often express satisfaction in achieving project milestones or delivering high-quality code.	Recognize it: Team members take ownership of their tasks, seek opportunities for growth, and suggest improvements to processes.	Recognize it: Team members maintain a positive outlook even in the face of challenges, focusing on solutions rather than problems.	Recognize it: Team members maintain a positive outlook even in the face of challenges, focusing on solutions rather than problems.	Recognize it: Team members might show indifference or detachment, avoiding participation and taking minimal interest in team activities.	Recognize it: Team members may appear anxious, overwhelmed, or fatigued, and their productivity might decrease.
Example: Team members congratulate each other after successfully launching a new feature that they've been working on for weeks.	Example: A team member proactively proposes a new approach to streamline the deployment process and offers to lead its implementation.	Example: Despite encountering setbacks, team members discuss the lessons learned and their determination to overcome obstacles in future projects.	Example: A developer becomes visibly frustrated and sighs loudly while trying to debug a persistent issue in the codebase.	Example: A team member consistently offers vague responses during discussions and appears disinterested in contributing ideas.	Example: A developer, who is usually punctual, starts missing deadlines and shows signs of physical stress like tired eyes and tense posture.

Figure 11.2 **Recognizing positive and negative emotions**

I once led a team through organizational restructuring, and emotions were high. Many team members experienced anxiety, as they felt unsure about their futures. I also felt unsure about my own future, but I tried to stay positive. I noticed that some team members stopped offering their ideas and couldn't stick to deadlines. No one told me how they were feeling, so I had to read between the lines and perceive their emotions through their actions. We ended up losing a few people during the restructuring, and managing the emotions of the remaining team members was a challenge for me. I made it a point to meet one on one weekly during the restructuring, and I listened to each team member and reiterated my empathy for their situation. I offered support during the difficult times, and I managed my emotions to show an example of perseverance in the face of adversity. It took some time, but the team members eventually felt comfortable with their job stability, and we got our projects back on track.

Effective lead developers combine their technical skills with emotional intelligence. Leaders who possess emotional intelligence can adapt to changing circumstances and handle conflicts with diplomacy. Emotionally intelligent individuals can use their emotions to enhance decision-making processes. By recognizing the effect of emotions on cognition, they can make more well-rounded and thoughtful choices.

11.1.2 *Teaching yourself to be emotionally intelligent*

Being emotionally intelligent provides your team with many benefits. Trust is the foundation of any successful team, and emotionally intelligent lead developers excel at building and maintaining trustful relationships with their team members. They genuinely care about their colleagues' well-being and professional growth, which fosters loyalty and commitment to the team's goals.

Emotional intelligence can help you better understand the emotions of others, which can lead to more effective communication and conflict resolution. If a team member is feeling frustrated, you can help them communicate their concerns in a productive way. Asking how they feel about a conflict is better than only asking them what happened. You need to understand how they feel so that you may empathize with them and come together to form a solution.

When you're emotionally intelligent, you'll be trusted and respected by your team members. They will trust that you can understand and empathize with their emotions and that they will be treated with respect. I have a mentor who taught me how to gain trust by sharing his own emotional struggles. People will be more comfortable discussing their problems if you share yours first. My mentor used to ask me for input on things that he was struggling with, such as anxiety over an important presentation and project deadlines. He trusted my expertise and respected my opinion. That behavior trickled down and positively affected the entire team, which led us to great success.

Considering the emotional effect of your decisions on others can help you make better decisions. When I'm presented with several different technical approaches by my team members, from which I can only select one, I consider how the decision will make the team feel. In several scenarios, I had to decide whether to prioritize new features or improve the existing codebase and fix bugs. The team expressed their frustration with the existing codebase and wanted to fix everything before implementing new features. However, we had a project schedule to think about, so we compromised and fixed bugs that directly affected the features we were working on. I listened to their concerns about each approach, and we agreed on a plan that would eventually fix everything. I could see beyond the immediate business goals and recognize the importance of maintaining a positive work environment. This led to a more holistic decision-making process that considered not only technical factors but also the well-being and motivation of the development team. In the long run, this approach resulted in higher-quality work and improved team dynamics, contributing to the project's success.

I've worked with some lead developers who weren't emotionally intelligent. I worked for lead developers early in my career who never tried to get to know us as people, and our communication was always formal. This led to discomfort on the team, especially when they quickly shut down small talk during meetings. They didn't listen to anyone on the team, and we never felt appreciated. If someone was having a bad day, they weren't met with understanding. Instead, they were chastised. There was a lot of turnover on the team, and those lead developers didn't last long.

I've also worked with lead developers who were very emotionally intelligent. I learned a lot from them, and they inspired me to become a better leader. One lead developer I worked for noticed my leadership potential and supported me, which led to my professional growth and promotions. What impressed me most was that it felt like sometimes he could read my mind. He was perceptive and recognized when I struggled, even if I was putting on a brave face. People may not always tell you the truth until they trust you, so you have to take cues from their body language and tone of voice. Learn to focus on people's actions over what they are saying. If a team member tells you that everything is fine, but they continue to struggle with deadlines, this may be due to something they are going through that they don't feel comfortable discussing. While it's not your place to pry, you should provide the support they need to get back on track. This can be accomplished by listening to their struggles and lifting them up by appreciating their successes. When someone is having a bad day, reminding them of the value they bring to your team is helpful. Doing this will inspire loyalty so that you can retain top talent.

11.1.3 Teaching your team to be emotionally intelligent

Now that you're mastering emotional intelligence yourself, how do you teach your team? Teams often encounter challenges, including missing project deadlines and learning blockers. Emotionally intelligent teams are better equipped to handle these challenges because they can manage stress and regulate their emotions effectively. When faced with adversity, they maintain composure, analyze problems objectively, and seek constructive solutions rather than falling into destructive patterns of blame or negativity. The following list includes examples of how you can teach your team to be emotionally intelligent:

- Model emotional intelligence by being aware of your own emotions, managing your emotions effectively, and being empathetic to the emotions of others.
- Provide feedback to team members on their emotional intelligence skills. This feedback can be specific and constructive, and it should be given in a respectful and supportive way.
- Create opportunities for team members to practice their emotional intelligence skills. This could include role-playing exercises, simulations, or real-world experiences.
- Offer training in emotional intelligence. Many training programs on emotional intelligence are available. Some reputable sources include the Harvard Division of Continuing Education and LinkedIn Learning. Lead developers can allow their team members to participate in one of these programs.

You don't have to be the perfect model of emotional intelligence to teach others what you have learned. It takes time to master this skill, and you'll continue to learn new things along the way. When I'm teaching my team to be emotionally intelligent, I convey the benefits of emotional intelligence and how it can help them in their careers. They will learn more from their fellow team members when they are open to understanding and supporting different perspectives. This will go a long way in helping them achieve professional and personal development to support their career objectives.

When you're leading a development team, they must work well with each other as well as clients and customers. Teaching your team to be emotionally intelligent with each other will support their success in working with people outside of your organization. I like to use role-playing exercises based on real-world experiences to provide feedback on team members' skills in emotional intelligence (see figure 11.3). One exercise I often use is a coding challenge that requires collaboration and integrating different components. Developers often have to work together when one person develops a feature that is related to another feature being worked on by someone else. Participants in this exercise should focus on task delegation, sharing progress updates, and addressing any problems that arise. During the exercise, I introduce unexpected changes to the requirements to gauge how the team handles pressure and adapts to change.

One situation I often observe is that people tend to think their idea is best, and they don't fully listen to their co-workers. In this case, I meet with them individually to address the problem. During team meetings, if I encounter this behavior, I call it out immediately by saying, "Let's listen to everyone's ideas." I encourage people to speak up and collaborate. Often, I find that each idea can be combined to promote innovation. This is a great way to get the team to work together and avoid the idea of "being right." Multiple people can be right at the same time.

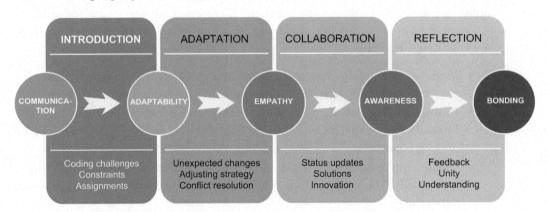

Figure 11.3   Example role-playing exercise

Developers must adapt quickly, communicate changes to their teammates, and collaborate to find solutions. The following list includes resources that I've shared with my teams to learn emotional intelligence:

- *Emotional Intelligence 2.0* (TalentSmart, 2009) by Dr. Travis Bradberry and Dr. Jean Greaves

- *Emotional Intelligence: Why It Can Matter More Than IQ* (Bantam, 2006) by Daniel Goleman
- *HBR Emotional Intelligence* Boxed Set (Harvard Business Review, 2018) by Daniel Goleman, Annie McKee, Bill George, and Herminia Ibarra

These resources helped me learn how to apply emotional intelligence in my personal and professional life. It has been an interesting journey, and I've watched teams flourish under emotionally intelligent leadership. In the next section, we'll explore everything I've learned and my experiences with emotional intelligence.

11.2 Using emotional intelligence

Emotional intelligence is a crucial factor in the success of a lead developer's leadership. Developing and prioritizing emotional intelligence allows for effective management of working relationships, leading to a more cohesive and high-performing team. Figure 11.4 describes the steps to becoming emotionally intelligent.

When you're facing a critical problem or tight deadline, you may encounter various challenges and obstacles to overcome. This may make you feel stress and pressure, which can result in negative body language, such as crossing your arms or using a tense tone of voice. When you recognize your emotions, you can better control them. Stay focused and remain calm under pressure to show a positive example of leadership. Show appreciation for your team, and keep your tone positive and upbeat.

A common emotional trigger for me is feeling responsible for my team and pressure to support their success. This can lead to burnout if I spend too many hours balancing my technical and leadership tasks. It's important to be open with your manager and let them know when you're feeling overwhelmed so that you can get the time you need to rest. The best leaders will notice when their team members are getting burnt out even before the members notice it. Common symptoms include appearing fatigued, having trouble concentrating, and exhibiting loss of control. I worked for a great manager who taught me a lot about preventing burnout, and they detected the signs early to help me through it. Now I can avoid burnout by limiting my work time and focusing on a good work-life balance.

Sometimes, you may not have much time to self-regulate your emotions, especially when you're under tight deadlines. When you feel stressed or overwhelmed, I suggest you take a moment to do a quick breathing exercise or meditation. I've found that closing my eyes and counting to 10 while breathing deeply helps to mitigate negative emotions. You can also do a full body scan meditation. Several apps are available to walk you through meditation exercises in 10 minutes or less. My favorite is the Calm app.

Expressing your emotions concisely, especially in writing, can be difficult. People are busy, so it's crucial to get to the point and tell them only what they need to hear to support your needs. Be clear about your emotional state or the emotional effect of a situation, either verbally or in writing, but avoid unnecessary emotional language that might cloud the message.

BECOMING EMOTIONALLY INTELLIGENT

1 Be aware of your own emotions

Pay attention to how you feel in different situations and why you feel that way. Be aware of your body language and tone of voice, as these can give away your emotions even if you do not realize it.

2 Understand your triggers

What are the things that make you feel angry, sad, or stressed? Once you know your triggers, you can start to develop strategies for managing your emotions in these situations.

3 Learn to self-regulate

Be able to calm yourself down when you are feeling angry or upset. There are several techniques that can help you with self-regulation, such as deep breathing, meditation, and exercise.

4 Empathize with others

Try to understand how other people are feeling and why they feel that way. Everyone experiences emotions differently, so it is important to be open-minded and understanding.

5 Communicate effectively

Be able to express your emotions concisely. Listen to others, and understand their point of view.

6 Build strong relationships

Be able to connect with others on a personal level. Build trust and rapport with others, as this will help you resolve conflicts effectively and create a positive work environment.

Figure 11.4   How to become emotionally intelligent

Avoiding unnecessary emotional language

Scenario: A project is facing a critical delay due to a team member missing a deadline.

Unnecessary emotional language: "I can't believe this is happening! This is a disaster, and it's all your fault!"

Clear and professional expression: "I want to discuss the situation with the missed deadline. It's causing a significant delay in the project, and we need to address it urgently."

In the second example, the lead developer expresses their frustration and urgency without using emotional language that might escalate the situation. This approach focuses on the problem at hand and invites a more constructive conversation about finding a solution to the problem.

Becoming emotionally intelligent is a gradual process that requires patience and consistent effort. On the journey to increased emotional intelligence, be kind to yourself and others, and celebrate the progress you make along the way. Embrace emotional intelligence as a core element of your leadership journey. Being emotionally intelligent can elevate your team and bring you to new heights of success and fulfillment.

11.2.1 Becoming self-aware

Self-awareness is the ability to recognize and understand your own emotions, thoughts, beliefs, and behaviors. It involves having a clear perception of your strengths, weaknesses, values, and motivations. When you're self-aware, you're conscious of how your emotions and actions affect you and others, allowing you to make more informed decisions and navigate social interactions effectively.

Two components of self-awareness

Internal self-awareness: Understanding your emotions, values, beliefs, and personality traits entails recognizing the various facets of your identity and gaining insights into how these aspects influence behavior and decision-making.

External self-awareness: The ability to perceive how others perceive you involves being attuned to the effect of your actions and communication on others, which helps you adjust your behavior and responses in different social situations.

As a lead developer, being self-aware will help you identify your leadership style and understand how it may be perceived by others. You must make the necessary adjustments to ensure effective interactions with team members and stakeholders. Your leadership style should evolve over time to support the different skills and personalities of yourself and your team members. Self-awareness allows you to be more adaptable in different situations. You can identify when to be more directive or participative, depending on the team's needs and project requirements. For example, if a team is experienced and self-motivated, you might adopt a more hands-off, servant-leadership approach. In contrast, a less experienced team may benefit from more guidance and direction.

I've worked with teams with various personalities that required different leadership styles. Some people prefer more of an "all business" feel, while others are comfortable opening up to their co-workers and being more personal. This was hard for me because I wanted to get to know my team as individuals. When someone isn't comfortable opening up, I ask myself if they are uncomfortable being personal or if they are uncomfortable being personal with me. Sometimes, I recognized that I overstepped too quickly, asking them questions about their life. When this happened, I apologized if I made them uncomfortable and told them they didn't have to answer the question. I perceived that they didn't want to open up to me because they were shifting in their seat and not making eye contact with me. You must take great care in understanding how your actions affect others and try to make things as smooth as possible so that you build trust.

A good way to become self-aware is to engage in self-reflection. You should take time for introspection. Analyze your emotional responses and behavior in various situations, especially when you're under pressure or providing feedback. Consider how your emotions in these situations affect your decision-making and interactions. You can often feel the tension in the room when you have said or done something that people didn't like. Ask yourself why you reacted the way you did and how you could have handled the situation differently to achieve a more positive outcome.

Empathy is closely tied to self-awareness. Putting yourself in others' shoes and trying to understand their emotions can help you become more self-aware as you reflect on your own reactions. If you have a team member who is struggling with a task, try to empathize with their challenges and consider how you would feel if you were in their position. This goes a long way toward understanding the perspectives of your team members so that you don't chastise them for the wrong reasons. We'll discuss empathy in depth later in this chapter.

Self-awareness is a hard skill to master, as it often uncovers toxic behaviors that you exhibit. No one is perfect, and everyone makes mistakes. I've been hard on team members who weren't performing well because I didn't know that my decision-making process was compromised due to my own emotions. To be fully self-aware, you must recognize your own faults and improve yourself. This will enable you to increase your level of emotional intelligence, empathize with others, make better judgments, and foster healthier relationships.

11.2.2 *Managing working relationships*

Lead developers must be able to build strong relationships with their team members to be successful. Lead developers with strong empathetic skills can put themselves in their team member's shoes. This helps them understand their team members' concerns, frustrations, and aspirations. By actively listening and acknowledging their team members' emotions, lead developers can build trust and rapport, creating a safe space for open communication. The following list includes tips on how to manage working relationships:

- *Be respectful.* Listen to your team members' ideas and opinions, even if you don't agree with them. Be mindful of your words and actions, and avoid making disrespectful comments or jokes.

- *Be honest.* Be up front with your team members about your work, your expectations, and your needs. If you have a problem with someone, be direct and honest about it.

- *Be there for your team members when they need help.* This could mean offering to help them with a project or simply being a listening ear. It's important to be supportive of their ideas and goals.

- *Be clear about your expectations and open to feedback.* Communicate regularly with your team members about work-related and personal matters.

- *Be willing to compromise.* No two people are exactly alike, so there will be times when you need to compromise with your team. This doesn't mean giving up on your own needs or wants but rather being willing to meet them halfway.

- *Be forgiving.* Everyone makes mistakes. If a team member makes a mistake, be willing to forgive them. This doesn't mean forgetting about the mistake but moving on and not holding it against them.

Communication is the key to building working relationships, and using emotional intelligence will help facilitate communication and collaboration within your team. Being compassionate and sensitive to the emotions of yourself and others will put others at ease and build rapport. I've been in situations where I learned that the person was having a conflict with someone else on the team, but they didn't feel comfortable addressing it with the person directly. I've worked for many managers who urged me to handle conflict on my own before I was in leadership, and this isn't the way to build relationships. It made me feel unimportant when I asked for help to deal with the conflict and was denied. Furthermore, the conflict was never resolved, so I didn't stay with those companies for very long.

When I notice someone struggling, I schedule a one-on-one meeting to figure out what is going on immediately. If they are having a conflict with someone else on the team, I bring the people involved in the conflict together and listen to both sides without judgment. In one case, I had a team member who fell ill and missed a lot of work. Another team member didn't know what was happening and felt upset when deadlines kept getting pushed because of this person being out a lot. I apologized for my shortcomings, but I should have made a better contingency plan to keep things on track. The ill team member was uncomfortable divulging what was going on in their personal life, and I didn't push the issue. I handled it by putting the focus on myself instead, and we worked out a plan together. It took some time, but the team members eventually overcame their differences and began collaborating effectively. The person who was ill ended up taking time off, and when they were better, they returned to a welcoming and supportive team.

11.2.3 *Achieving personal growth*

Learning how to become emotionally intelligent will help you not only in your career but also in your personal life. People respond very well to emotionally intelligent individuals, and you'll be able to form deeper relationships. The more attuned you are to the needs of others, the closer you become to them emotionally. Compassion and sensitivity to others are vital for building strong relationships. As well as helping to put others at ease, it builds rapport and helps you act tactfully in delicate situations.

My superpower has always been getting people to open up. I've had friends and family who never opened up to anyone but me, and I think the key is that I listen. I don't offer advice unless they ask because sometimes people just need to vent. If you give advice, they may feel like you're telling them what to do, which may derail the conversation. In our desire to help and show concern for our loved ones, it's common to find ourselves tempted to offer unsolicited advice. Whether it's about their relationships, career choices, parenting decisions, or personal habits, we often believe that our well-intentioned suggestions can improve their lives. However, giving unsolicited advice can be more harmful than helpful, and it can strain relationships and lead to unintended consequences.

Your support and encouragement will be appreciated by everyone around you. If you have faced similar situations, share your experiences without insisting they follow the same path. Let them draw insights from your story if they find it relevant. I always tell people that this was my experience and theirs may be different. I don't want people to copy what I'm doing 100% because what worked for me may not work for them. And I don't want to cause conflict if it doesn't work out for that person.

Learning emotional intelligence can help you make better decisions in your personal life. When you understand your own values and priorities, you're better able to make decisions that are in line with your goals. This can help you achieve your goals and live a more fulfilling life. When I was young, I engaged in a lot of toxic relationships and wasn't happy with my life. I was taking care of others before myself, and through experience and self-awareness, I began to understand my role in these relationships. I'm not perfect, and I was feeding into the toxicity with immature behavior. I was able to repair some relationships, but I had to cut ties with some people. You must have people in your life who support you and your goals, which will help with both your personal and professional growth.

11.3 *Learning radical empathy*

Radical empathy requires us to be willing to listen to and learn from others, even if their experiences are different from our own. It's about understanding their perspective and why they feel the way they do. This helps you see the world through their eyes and attempt to experience their emotions as they do. Radical empathy is an extension of traditional empathy, as shown in figure 11.5, where you seek to understand those you don't agree with or dislike. It can be difficult, but learning radical empathy is a powerful skill for building relationships and creating a more compassionate working environment.

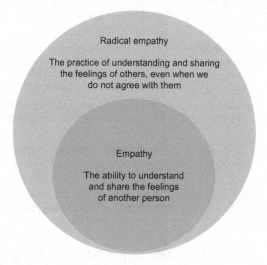

Figure 11.5 **Defining empathy and radical empathy**

One of the primary drivers of workplace conflicts is miscommunication. Practicing radical empathy will create a positive working environment that values open and honest communication. When team members feel genuinely heard and understood, they are more likely to express their concerns and seek constructive resolutions, thereby preventing misunderstandings from festering into full-blown conflicts. When conflicts occur, using radical empathy can lead to de-escalation. Instead of responding with defensiveness or aggression, team members are encouraged to listen and empathize with each other's differing viewpoints. This approach helps find common ground and collaborative solutions, diffusing tensions and animosity. Throughout this chapter, you'll be provided with examples of radical empathy from my career to help you understand how to use this skill to support your team's success.

11.3.1 Comparing empathy to radical empathy

Empathy is the ability to see things from another person's point of view and understand their emotions and perspective. *Radical empathy* goes one step further, encouraging individuals to deeply connect with others and address the underlying problems contributing to conflict. It involves actively seeking to comprehend the concerns and experiences of team members in the context of larger societal, organizational, and personal factors. Radical empathy is a more active and engaged form of empathy than traditional empathy. It's focused on social issues, looking beyond the person as an individual to understand the historical and societal context of where they are. Table 11.2 illustrates the differences between the two.

Table 11.2 Empathy vs. radical empathy

Aspect	Empathy	Radical empathy
Focus	Individual experiences and emotions	Individual experiences and broader social, cultural, and systemic factors influencing those experiences
Response	Providing emotional support and validation to the person experiencing the emotions	Promotes taking action to address the underlying problems and challenges faced by the person, aiming to create positive change and alleviate suffering
Scope	Connecting with and understanding the emotions of one person or a small group of individuals	Recognizing patterns of marginalization and oppression affecting various groups of people
Goal	Providing comfort and showing understanding to the person in distress	Building a more compassionate and just society by challenging societal norms and advocating for social change
Effect	Positive effect on individuals by helping them feel heard and understood	Transformative effect on individuals and communities by promoting social justice and equity

Lead developers who go beyond traditional empathy to practice radical empathy are more likely to be perceived as approachable and understanding. They can inspire their teams to follow their example, creating a positive and supportive workplace culture. This can reduce the likelihood of conflicts and enhance overall employee satisfaction and engagement.

I've been treated poorly in the workplace due to my invisible disability. I have a moderate stutter, and although my speech is usually fluent, I've experienced periods when I stuttered a lot. Sometimes, when I was stuttering at work, my manager or client would sigh loudly and talk over me, or in extreme cases, I would lose my job. These discriminatory practices had a negative effect on me, causing me intense emotional distress. In these situations, I used radical empathy to put myself in their shoes even when I was being discriminated against. It helped me to overcome the hardship by attempting to understand where they were coming from, as most people are ignorant of the plight of the disabled. Luckily, I've had two managers who didn't avoid the situation and assured me that they would never discriminate against me for having a disability. They comforted me in times of need, which supported not only my success but the team's success as well. They made sure that I was comfortable talking about stuttering and asked me questions so that they could learn more to support me better. They also addressed problems of systemic discrimination by creating focus groups. I've taken the same approach when I worked with people with medical needs, and they became very successful.

11.3.2 *Understanding others*

Cognitive bias is one of the primary obstacles to understanding others with differing opinions. *Cognitive bias* refers to the systematic patterns of deviation from rationality or objectivity in the way people process information, make judgments, and form decisions. These types of biases can lead individuals to interpret information in a way that may not be based on reality. Biases often influence our perceptions and actions unconsciously. Our minds tend to favor information confirming our beliefs and dismiss or ignore ideas that challenge them. Radical empathy empowers individuals to recognize these cognitive biases and consciously engage in open dialogue. As people learn about biases, they often have questions about what constitutes bias so that they can avoid being biased themselves. By discussing these issues, we create an opportunity for personal growth and learning, as well as foster a culture of respect and inclusivity.

As a lead developer, you must be open to being challenged. Leaders should never surround themselves with people who always agree with them. You want a team that you can rely on to give you advice based on their expertise. When individuals from diverse backgrounds come together, their differing perspectives lead to innovation and creativity. Radical empathy allows teams to harness diversity effectively. By understanding and valuing different viewpoints, team members are more likely to collaborate, combining their strengths to solve problems creatively. This dynamic enhances the quality of work and cultivates a workplace culture that celebrates individuality and inclusivity.

It's natural to want your team members to support your ideas and points of view. I struggled with this because I used to feel that my ideas were being attacked if someone suggested something different. It made me feel as though my leadership skills were in question. I was once in a situation where I had a team member who constantly pushed back on my ideas. It got so bad that it was disruptive, especially during meetings. This made me dislike the person because I constantly anticipated their disagreement. The way they expressed their ideas wasn't from a helpful perspective. They always asserted that they were right no matter what. This caused the team to avoid that person, leading to miscommunication and decreased productivity. It took me too long to speak to them one on one about it, but when I did, I uncovered cultural differences that I hadn't considered. I learned that some cultures communicate using blunt statements, while others are so diplomatic that you often can't understand when they are providing criticism, and you may take it as a compliment. We discussed cultural sensitivity, and I helped them understand how to get their point across more professionally. It took some time, but they did improve and even went on to a role in leadership.

Individuals tend to view each other as adversaries when there is conflict, making it challenging to find common ground. Radical empathy encourages a shift in mindset, recognizing that everyone's experiences and perspectives are valid. Radical empathy teaches us to see one another as humans, which goes a long way to breaking down barriers and fostering relationships.

Radical empathy also involves embracing and celebrating diversity. Lead developers should encourage an inclusive environment where co-workers from different backgrounds feel valued and respected. I enjoy learning about other cultures, and I've been fortunate in that I've had the opportunity to travel to several countries. Working with people from different cultures can be challenging when your experiences and perspectives are vastly different. Even if you don't agree with someone's point of view, it's important to consider their experiences to understand their perspectives. I once worked for an organization that held a cultural festival yearly to celebrate the richness of diverse teams. They included exhibits for each culture, including traditional cuisines. These festivals helped me open a dialogue with my team members to discuss their experiences not only with their own culture but with other cultures as well. This went a long way in harnessing our team's diversity effectively. By understanding and valuing different viewpoints, the team members were more open to collaboration, combining their strengths to solve problems creatively. This dynamic improved the quality of work and cultivated a workplace culture that celebrated individuality and inclusivity.

11.3.3 Connecting on a deeper level

Listening with empathy is a powerful skill that enables lead developers to truly understand and relate to their co-workers' experiences and emotions from a personal and professional perspective. You should take the time to listen to your team members' challenges and aspirations without judgment and offer support or encouragement. This empathetic approach fosters trust and creates a safe space for open communication.

When you communicate openly with your team members, you should encourage them to share some information about their personal lives. Recognizing their personal milestones demonstrates care and appreciation for your team members beyond their professional successes. I've celebrated team members' achievements, including parenthood, marriage, and reaching fitness goals. I worked with many people who participated in long-distance running, from 5Ks to marathons. I didn't think that I could be a runner, but they encouraged me to try it, and I kept an open mind. Eventually, I was inspired to start my own journey, and I've completed 27 races to date, including 5Ks, 10Ks, and half-marathons. I remember my first 5K. I was nervous, and my team members advised me on training and pushing through the mental challenge of running. We formed a bond and even organized a virtual 5K for the entire company so that fully remote teams could participate. After the event, we shared photos of our achievements on a Slack channel. What I loved about this was that it allowed my team to connect with others and form relationships. We discussed our challenges with running, and everyone was supportive and nonjudgmental. I'm still in contact with many of the people I worked with, and we celebrate each other's achievements on social media.

11.4 Having difficult conversations

Having difficult conversations and resolving conflicts are key skills that lead developers need to have to be successful. I once faced a situation where one of the developers on my team was acting out and missing deadlines. They were very irritable, and anything could set them off. It was a difficult situation, and many team members came to me to complain. They told me that the developer who was acting out wasn't communicative, and the team needed their expertise to be productive. Let's discuss how you might handle this situation with emotional intelligence.

When you're discussing performance problems, it's important to understand that you never know what someone is going through. There could be mitigating factors contributing to their performance. In this case, I gathered information from the team regarding their co-worker's behavior. I told the team that their team member needed our support to be successful and we shouldn't judge them. When I spoke to the team member about their performance, I first asked them how they were versus jumping right into addressing the performance problems. I found that they were dealing with several problems in their personal life that had an effect on their mental health. I worked with human resources to provide the team member with a list of available mental health resources. We also discussed options for taking leave to care for family problems. They ended up taking time off, and when they returned to work, I ensured them that they had the team's full support.

By effectively using emotional intelligence in difficult conversations, lead developers can create a more empathetic and productive work environment. This will foster stronger relationships within the team and promote successful conflict resolution. For example, you may need to discuss behavioral or performance problems with a team member. I've had many conversations like this, and you must be prepared. Gather all relevant information and facts related to the problem at hand. Being well-prepared helps in presenting arguments clearly and reduces the chances of emotional reactions. Figure 11.6 shows the steps in the process of having a difficult conversation as a lead developer.

Figure 11.6   Difficult conversation process

During a difficult conversation, you must manage your emotions effectively. Deep breathing and taking short breaks when needed can help you stay composed and focused. Be prepared for potential negative reactions, and respond with patience and understanding. Never react defensively, as this will escalate the conflict. You should always be aware of signs of escalation and implement de-escalation techniques if necessary. Some of the signs to look for include increased tension, heightened emotional responses, and avoidance behavior. If you encounter any of these behaviors, you must redirect the focus to the main problem and keep your emotions in check. You should listen, and even if you don't agree with their perspective, you must validate their feelings. Putting yourself in the shoes of others to understand their perspectives and feelings will go a long way to de-escalate tension.

Emotional intelligence will help you empathize with your team members and support their career growth when you have a difficult conversation. If you look at things from their point of view, you can better understand their perspective and handle the conversation with care. Ultimately, you want to come to a resolution that is agreed upon by all parties. Using emotional intelligence will help you understand what compromises will help support your team's success. With practice, you can apply your skills in emotional intelligence to turn difficult conversations into productive ones.

11.4.1 *Preparing before the conversation*

One of the most challenging aspects of the lead developer role is managing a team of developers. While you may not be responsible for hiring and firing your team members, there will inevitably be moments when difficult conversations are necessary. You must handle these situations with empathy, clear communication, and a constructive approach. It's critical to prepare for difficult conversations to maintain a healthy team dynamic and foster growth among team members.

Approaching a difficult conversation with the right tone can set you up for a productive discussion. You should plan to begin the conversation with a positive intent by emphasizing that your goal is to find a solution and improve the situation rather than point fingers or lay blame. When you send a message to schedule a meeting, it's important to use the right tone:

> *Hey [Name], I would like to discuss the recent problems with the project. I value your contributions, and we'll work together to provide you the support you need to succeed.*

Notice how this message begins with "Hey" and not "Hello" or "Dear [Name]," as these are more formal. "Hey" is more informal and will put the person at ease. If you use a formal greeting, it sounds serious, especially if you don't usually send messages using that greeting. You should use "I" statements following the greeting, as they go a long way to ensure that you're not putting the person on the defensive, which we discussed in a previous chapter. Your message should end on a positive note, ensuring that the person knows that this is a collaborative meeting and not a formal reprimand.

As you prepare for the conversation, collect relevant data and specific examples of the problem you want to discuss. Having evidence to support your concerns will make your conversation more objective. Avoid assumptions or hearsay, and stick to observable behaviors and results. I've often had conversations with developers about the number of bugs encountered when their code is tested by QA. I prepare for these discussions by gathering metrics that are available to me. This usually includes estimated time versus actual time and the number of times a ticket or task is sent back to the developer from QA.

There can be several reasons for a task to fail testing, and you should consider all options before meeting with the developer. For this particular example of bugs, I consider the reasons their testing failed. Sometimes, the developer didn't test their code in the QA environment. This often happens when deployments take time to finish, and the developer has moved on to another task, or their local development environment had a different configuration than QA, causing the test cases to fail. Testing failures can also happen if the business requirements or technical requirements are inaccurate. I've also experienced bottlenecks that caused my own code to sit in the deployment queue for too long, and my code conflicted with new features or bug fixes.

There may be other reasons for failed testing or overall performance problems. It's best to come prepared with some ideas, but be open to listening to your developers to uncover the cause of these problems so you can work together to devise a plan of action. Remember that difficult conversations can also lead to positive change and improved team dynamics when handled thoughtfully.

11.4.2 Listening more than you talk

Effective communication is the key to having a successful outcome from a difficult conversation. While it might be tempting to rely on your technical expertise to drive these conversations, the art of listening is an invaluable skill in difficult conversations. If you dominate the conversation and dismiss the team member's concerns without truly listening, this can result in frustration and resentment among your team members.

Listening goes beyond simply hearing the words being spoken; it involves paying attention to the person's tone, body language, and emotions. Listening demonstrates that you value the opinions and perspectives of your team members or project stakeholders. By showing genuine interest, you create an environment where individuals feel respected and valued, fostering trust and rapport. By practicing active listening, you'll gain insights into the problem at hand. After the speaker has shared their thoughts, paraphrase what you heard to confirm your understanding. This shows that you're actively processing the information. This leads to a deeper understanding of the problems, which allows you to make informed decisions and address concerns effectively.

When you don't listen to your team members, you can cause conflict in your team. Take, for example, a situation where a lead developer didn't listen to my suggestion for a technical approach that followed best practices. They told me that there was no time to implement my approach and that theirs was better overall. I tested their approach, and it caused errors in our existing system. They continued to assure me that their approach would work in production, and we implemented their solution. This caused errors in QA, and we took on technical debt. My solution was implemented, but we lost valuable time because the lead developer didn't take the time to listen to me and didn't fully understand my solution.

Being a good listener includes asking probing questions that delve into the root causes of a problem. This helps in uncovering underlying problems that might not be immediately apparent. Encourage the speaker to elaborate by asking open-ended questions.

Asking open-ended questions

Scenario: A developer on your team has become less productive than they used to be, and you must have a difficult conversation about their performance.

Open-ended questions to ask:

(continued)

How do you feel about your current performance and progress on the project?

Can you share your perspective on the feedback you've received so far?

What challenges or obstacles do you think are affecting your performance?

How do you believe we can work together to address any areas of improvement?

What support or resources do you think would be helpful to enhance your performance?

Can you tell me about your approach to problem-solving and decision-making in recent tasks?

What aspects of your role or responsibilities do you find most satisfying?

In what areas do you think you have excelled in your performance?

What specific feedback or assistance do you need to enhance your coding/design skills?

What work-life balance adjustments, if any, do you believe would contribute to your overall performance?

When I ask open-ended questions, I don't interrupt the person speaking. You should allow the speaker to finish their thoughts before responding. Interrupting can break the flow of the conversation and hinder understanding. I always give my undivided attention to the conversation. I ensure that I have no distractions, and I maintain eye contact to show my engagement. It's harder to keep distractions at bay when you're accustomed to multitasking, so you should turn off all notifications to stay engaged with the conversation.

11.4.3 *Following up on difficult conversations*

Having a difficult conversation to resolve a conflict or address a performance problem is just the starting point. The follow-up process is where you can solidify the outcomes of those conversations and demonstrate your commitment to the team's growth and well-being. Following up shows that you take the conversation seriously and are genuinely invested in resolving the problem or helping the person improve their skills. Follow-up conversations provide an opportunity to clarify any uncertainties that might have arisen during the initial discussion. I've found that people often form new opinions after they have had time to think about the conversation. I usually schedule a follow-up meeting at least two weeks after the initial conversation to gauge how well the person is progressing toward the desired outcome and provide additional support if needed. I ask them if they felt that the conflict was resolved. If they say yes, then we discuss how it was handled and any feedback they have. If they say no, then the conflict is still ongoing, and I ask them what they need from me to resolve it. We work together to devise a solution, which often entails another mediation with the team members involved in the conflict. I follow up again and again until everyone tells me that the conflict is resolved. If I do my job well, only two to three follow-ups may be needed.

If the person has made positive changes, it's important to acknowledge their efforts. This recognition can motivate them to continue improving and reaffirm your support. Depending on the situation, you can offer resources such as training materials, mentorship, or coaching that can aid in overcoming challenges. I've worked with many developers who were slow to start, and this was often due to a steep learning curve based on the cutting-edge technologies we were using and the corporate language that they weren't accustomed to. In many cases, the initial discussion included setting goals and providing guidance on achieving those goals. But when I followed up, I found that they were still struggling. In these cases, it's important to be patient and show empathy. Call out their positive changes so far, and inspire them to continue. Take the time to address any concerns or questions they may have. I've achieved great success using this approach, and I've witnessed developers improve greatly after several follow-up meetings.

Depending on the situation, you may need to follow up multiple times after the initial difficult conversation. The first follow-up should be two weeks later, and I would suggest that all subsequent follow-up meetings be scheduled in two-week intervals. This gives the person some time to work on the goals that you set and show some progress. Every follow-up meeting is an opportunity to set new goals with the person to work toward continuous improvement. Emphasize that your door is always open for further discussions. Encouraging open communication builds a culture of trust and transparency.

After the initial conversation and follow-up meetings, you should engage in self-reflection. Consider how you can improve your emotional intelligence and communication skills for future interactions. Consider whether your initial approach was effective or if any adjustments are needed for future conversations. This will reinforce your leadership skills and ensure that the outcomes of challenging discussions yield positive results.

11.5 *Avoiding imposter syndrome*

Imposter syndrome affects everyone, regardless of their experience level. Many people are surprised that I often suffer from it. If it's not managed properly, imposter syndrome can keep you back and hinder your success. Being able to avoid imposter syndrome will help you be a successful lead developer, which helps when you're deciding if you're ready to be a lead developer. Throughout this section, we'll discuss ways that you can avoid imposter syndrome.

> **DEFINITION** Imposter syndrome is that lingering feeling of self-doubt where, despite all your successes and achievements, you can't shake the worry that you're not truly deserving. It's like fearing that others might suddenly discover you're not as capable as they think, even though you've proven your abilities time and again.

Imposter syndrome has had negative effects on my career over the years. When I feel inadequate, I fall into the trap of comparing myself to others, which is an unhealthy mindset, as any therapist will tell you. When you compare yourself to others, you're likely unaware of the full picture. People often attempt to conceal their problems, so you never know what someone is dealing with. When I suffer from imposter syndrome, I tend to avoid opportunities where I feel I won't succeed. However, I'm often successful when I challenge myself and overcome imposter syndrome. I try to focus on my success and, more importantly, how my success contributes to the success of my team.

Mitigating imposter syndrome involves adopting strategies and practices that promote self-awareness, build confidence, and foster a positive mindset. Table 11.3 includes several effective strategies for addressing and mitigating imposter syndrome.

Table 11.3   Effective strategies to address and mitigate imposter syndrome

Strategy	Description
Acknowledge and accept	Recognize that imposter syndrome is a common phenomenon experienced by many high-achieving individuals. Accept that it's a normal part of the human experience and doesn't define your true capabilities.
Celebrate achievements	Take time to acknowledge and celebrate your accomplishments, no matter how small. Keep a record of your successes and revisit them when feelings of self-doubt arise. This can serve as a tangible reminder of your competence.
Set realistic goals	Break down larger tasks into manageable goals. Set realistic and achievable objectives, and celebrate your progress along the way. This helps in avoiding the overwhelming feeling of having to be perfect.
Embrace feedback	View constructive feedback as an opportunity for growth rather than a sign of failure. Understand that everyone, regardless of their level of expertise, can improve. Use feedback as a tool for refining your skills.
Share your feelings	Be open about your experiences and feelings with trusted colleagues, mentors, or friends. Discussing your insecurities and challenges can help you gain perspective, receive support, and realize that you're not alone in your feelings.
Keep a brag document	Maintain a document where you write down positive feedback, successful outcomes, and instances where you overcame challenges. Reflecting on these entries can reinforce your achievements and provide a more balanced perspective.
Reframe negative thoughts	Challenge negative self-talk by consciously reframing your thoughts. Replace self-deprecating statements with positive affirmations. Focus on your strengths and the progress you've made instead of dwelling on perceived shortcomings.
Seek mentorship	Connect with mentors who have experienced imposter syndrome themselves. Their guidance and shared experiences can provide valuable insights, encouragement, and practical advice on how to navigate challenges.
Mindfulness and self-compassion	Practice mindfulness techniques and self-compassion to stay present and kind to yourself. Meditation, deep breathing exercises, and other mindfulness practices can help manage stress and foster a more balanced perspective.
Join supportive communities	Participate in professional communities where individuals share their experiences and challenges. Knowing that others face similar struggles can provide a sense of camaraderie and support.

Imposter syndrome is a common experience among lead developers, with characteristics such as persistent self-doubt and a fear of being inadequate. It often arises from the unrealistic expectation of knowing everything and the reluctance to show vulnerability. Remember that overcoming imposter syndrome is an ongoing process, and different strategies work for different people. Try experimenting with these approaches, and tailor them to fit your personal preferences and circumstances. Mitigating imposter syndrome will not only set you up for success but also enable you to fully contribute to your team's success.

11.5.1 *Practicing self-compassion*

Self-compassion involves treating oneself with empathy and understanding, especially in the face of setbacks. By incorporating self-compassion into their daily routines, lead developers can create a supportive environment for their development team. Throughout this section, we'll discuss some practical strategies to cultivate self-compassion and counteract imposter syndrome.

Instead of viewing mistakes as failures, you should see them as opportunities for growth and learning. Making mistakes is a natural part of the personal and professional development process, and it doesn't diminish your skills or accomplishments. Consider normalizing the experience of making mistakes and using them as guidelines for improvement. My first failure as a lead developer was when I made a poor technical decision that caused a big delay in the project. I felt like it was all my fault, and I was very hard on myself. I was afraid that I would lose my job, which affected my concentration, resulting in a reduction in my performance. There is a famous quote from Walt Disney that helped me greatly when dealing with my first failure as a lead developer:

> *I think it's important to have a good hard failure when you're young. I learned a lot out of that. Because it makes you kind of aware of what can happen to you. Because of it, I've never had any fear in my whole life when we've been near collapse and all of that. I've never been afraid. I've never had the feeling I couldn't walk out and get a job doing something.*

When you begin to embrace failure, you become unstoppable. It will still hurt when you fail, but if you know from experience that there are lessons to be learned, then it's much easier to have a positive outlook. Remaining positive helps you to avoid imposter syndrome by quieting negative thoughts. Instead of taking failure at work personally, you begin to see it as a stepping stone to success. After I acknowledged my error in the technical approach, I brought the team together to discuss a better approach, which I didn't do the first time around. I learned that I needed to make use of the expertise of my team and never make an important decision like that alone. This resulted in better performance by the development team overall.

It's important to take the time to acknowledge and celebrate your successes, both big and small. It's easy to overlook smaller achievements in the pursuit of constant improvement. For example, if you find a way to reduce a little technical debt, you should celebrate that accomplishment! Reflect on your accomplishments and recognize your value to the projects you lead. This will help you combat self-doubt and negative thoughts. When you have these thoughts, try reflecting on one of your accomplishments. This will help take your mind off whatever caused the negative thoughts to get you back on track.

Don't hesitate to reach out for support from your mentors. Remember that everyone faces moments of self-doubt, and discussing them openly can help you foster a culture of empathy within your team. By embracing self-compassion, you can overcome imposter syndrome and create a positive and empowering work environment. Cultivating a mindset that acknowledges both strengths and areas for improvement fosters continuous growth and resilience, ultimately leading to more confident and effective leadership.

11.5.2 *Sharing your feelings*

Being open and sharing feelings with team members can be a powerful antidote against imposter syndrome and a significant step in determining readiness for the lead developer role. By fostering a culture of openness and vulnerability within the team, developers can create a supportive environment to discuss their insecurities and challenges without fear of judgment. Sharing feelings helps build trust and camaraderie among team members and provides reassurance and perspective. It allows developers to realize that they aren't alone in their struggles and that their experiences are valid and shared by others. This sense of connection and understanding can boost confidence, mitigate feelings of inadequacy, and provide a clearer path toward assessing readiness for leadership. Ultimately, by fostering an environment where feelings can be shared freely, developers can gain the emotional resilience and self-awareness needed to step into the role of a lead developer with confidence and clarity.

When you're open about your struggles, it humanizes you to your team. Sharing your feelings fosters trust and rapport, making team members more comfortable expressing their concerns. This transparency creates a culture of openness and understanding. I've worked for a company where executive leadership spoke about their struggles with mental health openly, and as a result, their working environment was incredibly positive and supportive. Their employees thrived, and the company was able to hire top talent due to great employee reviews.

You don't have to reveal your deepest insecurities right away. Start with small, relatable anecdotes about challenges you've faced in your career or specific moments of self-doubt. This gradual approach can help team members connect with your experiences.

Confidence in vulnerability is a powerful leadership trait. When sharing your feelings, be confident in handling challenges and uncertainties. This attitude sets a positive example for your team, demonstrating that vulnerability isn't a weakness but a strength.

When discussing difficulties or mistakes, frame them as opportunities for growth and learning. Emphasize the lessons you've gained from these experiences and how they have contributed to your development as a lead developer. This reframing helps normalize setbacks as part of the journey to success.

Actively promote an environment where team members feel comfortable sharing their feelings. Consider implementing regular sessions where individuals can discuss both professional and personal challenges. This can be done during sprint retrospectives, team meetings, or one-on-one sessions. I've experienced firsthand how an environment promoting collective vulnerability fosters a sense of unity and support. I've worked for organizations that were in the process of redefining their organizational culture, and there were growing pains. The development team wasn't used to sharing feelings, and they were reluctant to do so. It took me time to coax them to be more open, and that came with many challenges. I remember one instance when a developer on my team was very combative. In this case, I worked with them during several one-on-ones to get to the root of the problem. By sharing my experiences and challenges, they could relate to me on a deeper level, which helped them feel comfortable sharing their feelings. We ended up coming to an agreement to help them present their feelings in an assertive manner versus being aggressive. They were also interested in leadership, and I stressed how important it was for them to take my lead and cultivate a positive team environment. This helped them work more cohesively with the team, and it helped them in their decision-making process for their career trajectory. They eventually took on leadership positions within the organization and were successful.

Sharing your feelings as a lead developer isn't a sign of weakness but a demonstration of authenticity and strength. By opening up about your experiences, you create a culture of empathy and understanding within your team, actively combating imposter syndrome. As a result, you enhance your well-being and contribute to a more resilient and cohesive team. Remember, shared experiences can be a powerful catalyst for growth and success in the collaborative realm of software development.

11.5.3 Discouraging perfectionism

If you've ever found yourself tirelessly striving for perfection, only to feel like a fraud when you fall short, you're not alone. Imposter syndrome can creep in when you're a perfectionist, making you doubt your skills and contributions. Throughout this section, we'll explore how embracing imperfection can be a game-changer in mitigating imposter syndrome.

As leaders in the dynamic world of software development, it's easy to fall into the trap of perfectionism. We set high standards for ourselves, aiming for flawless code, seamless processes, and impeccable leadership. But here is the truth: perfection is an illusion, and pursuing it can be a breeding ground for imposter syndrome.

Instead of seeing success as synonymous with perfection, redefine it as progress and growth. Acknowledge that each step forward contributes to your success as a lead developer, no matter how small. Celebrate milestones and achievements, even if they aren't flawless. For example, if I'm working on a small bug fix or a feature, I give myself a pat on the back when I complete it successfully. Sometimes, I buy myself a gift or celebrate at my favorite restaurant. Then, I remember those occasions when I feel like an imposter. This helps me to push forward and remove doubt from my mind.

It's no secret that perfectionists hate making mistakes. However, you should view mistakes as opportunities to learn and improve. Mistakes aren't indicators of incompetence but rather stepping stones toward mastery. Adopting a culture that values learning from failures and iterating on solutions will help you be a good lead developer, as you can apply this culture to your team. Learning from failure is one of the hardest skills to master if you're a perfectionist. We often want control over situations, and when we fail, we feel out of control. This can lead to self-doubt and avoidance of situations in the future. I once made a bad decision and went against best practices to complete an application programming interface (API) integration quickly. This led to many bugs and technical debt. I was unwilling to address my mistake and learn from it, so I avoided API integration tasks in the future. I missed an opportunity to learn from my mistake, which stunted my professional growth.

When you make mistakes, try to cultivate a habit of honest self-reflection. Acknowledge and explore your own challenges and uncertainties. Being open with yourself breaks down the facade of personal perfection. It helps me to write down my challenges in a journal. The process of putting thought into what you're writing is a great way to engage in self-reflection and learn from your mistakes. It also helps to put things into perspective. I often realize that the big mistake I thought I made wasn't so big after all. I often reflect on mistakes only to find a solution to move forward with a fix.

Try to enjoy the process of growth and professional development rather than fixating solely on the end result. Recognize that the journey is filled with learning opportunities and that personal perfection is an unrealistic destination. Instead of attempting to write perfect code, focus on learning best practices. Your learning journey should begin with the specific skills you need to learn to get your job done, and it should end with knowledge retention. When your goal is knowledge retention versus output, the pressure isn't on you or your code but rather on the quality of the learning materials and your ability to remember what you've learned so that you can complete similar tasks in less time. This will help you achieve innovation by shifting your mindset away from your current task to considerations for future projects.

Embracing imperfection creates opportunities for authenticity, growth, and innovation. Remember, it's okay not to have all the answers, and it's okay for your code to be a work in progress. When you learn from your imperfections, imposter syndrome will take a back seat to your journey of continuous improvement.

11.6   *Case study*

Gabriela Martinez is a senior software engineer and mentor currently working at Microsoft Research, where she develops, designs, and collaborates on projects to solve today's computational problems. Previously, she worked for different companies in the software industry, developing systems that help customers solve their business challenges. She also worked in open source software implementing tools for web developers. In addition, she has written and talked about her learnings in blogs and talks for communities for cloud and software development. Finally, she has volunteered in organizations such as Technovation and Women Who Code to mentor women and students seeking or starting a software development career in the software industry. She looks forward to contributing and advocating for inclusiveness and collaboration in any work environment. In this case study, Gabriela offers her thoughts on practicing emotional intelligence.

11.6.1 How has practicing empathy affected your relationships at work?

Empathy is an important aspect of communication, whether you're working with customers or with different roles in the organization. To build relationships at work, you need to try to see the other person's point of view. I think you're always learning, and there are varying personalities that you get to work with at different levels. You can work with junior developers or you can work with senior developers, and their perspectives are very different. When you're developing software, that involves working relationships with customers and team members, and there are many different aspects.

You can also apply empathy to the end user of your software. Ask yourself, "How can I make this easier for the user?" When I first started, I was focused on developing web pages, and I thought about just the requirements. Now I think beyond requirements to reflect on the user experience. Go through test cases, and put yourself in their shoes. However, sometimes the "end user" isn't a person but a system, such as an API for a service. Even if the end user isn't a person, you can still create a persona for this. Perhaps it could be a support engineer who uses your software to connect to another API. You should always think about what the value is and how you can put yourself in that role so you can develop better software with a better user experience.

11.6.2 What lessons have you learned through self-awareness?

A lot of people aren't self-aware, are they? I think self-awareness starts with yourself. It's that piece of your personality that will help you get through challenges that you have when you're learning or when you're growing in your professional career. I think you need to be able to ask yourself, "What are the things that I need to improve or work on myself in order to deliver value to my work and working relationships?"

I've had experiences where I didn't get the results I was looking for, and I learned to get perspectives from others about what I could improve. It's important to have a mentor or manager who will give you a very honest point of view about what kind of things you can improve about yourself. You also have to be honest with yourself. Nobody else knows you as well as you know yourself. Being aware of your own shortcomings and working to improve yourself is a skill that I admire. It will enable you to overcome challenges and grow professionally.

11.6.3 How can emotional intelligence help balance a difficult conversation?

When I worked with smaller teams of two to three people, it was hard to communicate something I wasn't happy about. You don't want to make comments that are too critical or harsh, so I always try to be polite and thoughtful. After I gained more experience, I had some conversations that weren't so easy for me, and I recognized that it's good to have difficult conversations. People think difficult conversations are negative, but it's good to have disagreements. No matter how much you try, there is always something that you may not agree with. You're going to have a disagreement with someone because no one thinks the same as you. When you disagree with someone, if you communicate with respect and honesty, that's valuable, even if it's something the other person doesn't want to hear. Being able to express what you think freely is valuable. You can learn about your own feelings, insecurities, or things that you find difficult to express. It's valid to say that you don't agree, and it's important to call out to ensure that the team is delivering projects with value and the team's values are aligned with the values of the organization.

11.6.4   *What advice do you have for practicing emotional intelligence in the workplace?*

I think that it starts with you: the more honest you are with yourself and learn self-awareness, the more that will reflect on all of your interactions with people who are working with you. It could be your manager, your team members, or the CEO of the company you're working for. I suggest that you look for learning opportunities and be curious about how you can improve those interactions. You can rely on a mentor or someone you can trust to give you honest guidance.

We have so many tools and so much information to help us create abilities about communication, self-awareness, and resilience. Emotional intelligence is a wide subject, and you can look for many resources. Many companies are offering workshops and creating content for employees to teach emotional intelligence and give recommendations. You can also talk to a manager or someone who can relate to you and who shares the same values. Ask them for learning resources such as books, courses, or talks to help you improve your skills in emotional intelligence. The following list includes my favorite resources for learning about emotional intelligence in the workplace:

- Books:
  - *Start with Why: How Great Leaders Inspire Everyone to Take Action* (Portfolio, 2009) by Simon Sinek
  - *Switch: How to Change Things When Things Are Hard* (Crown Currency, 2010) by Chip Heath and Dan Heath
  - *Think Again: The Power of Knowing What You Don't Know* (Penguin, 2023) by Adam Grant
  - *Emotional Intelligence: Why It Can Matter More Than IQ* (Bantam, 2006) by Daniel Goleman
  - *Dare to Lead: Daring Greatly and Rising Strong at Work* (Random House, 2018) by Brené Brown
  - *Lean In: Women, Work, and the Will to Lead* (Knopf, 2013) by Sheryl Sandberg
- Talk I've found inspiring:
  - Esther Perel: "The Power of Relational Intelligence"

Summary

- Emotional intelligence is the ability to recognize, understand, and manage one's emotions effectively while also perceiving and empathizing with the emotions of others.

- Self-awareness is recognizing and understanding your emotions, thoughts, beliefs, and behaviors.

- Being self-aware is important for lead developers to understand how their actions affect others and make better decisions.

- Radical empathy is the practice of understanding and sharing the feelings of others, even when we don't agree with them.

- Effective communication in difficult conversations using open-ended questions can uncover underlying problems and promote deeper insights, ultimately leading to informed decisions and effective problem resolution.

- Following up after a difficult conversation is vital to ensure progress while emphasizing open communication and personal growth through self-reflection.

- Imposter syndrome affects individuals regardless of experience level, but can be managed through celebrating achievements, setting realistic goals, and embracing feedback, ultimately contributing to personal growth and team success.

12
Being a successful lead developer

Deciding when you're ready for anything is difficult, let alone moving from a technical position to leadership. Determining your readiness to become a lead developer extends beyond technical prowess. Are you the team member who naturally coordinates and assists others? Do you find satisfaction in the success of your projects and team development? These inclinations are foundational to leadership potential.

Leadership isn't just about managing—it's about inspiring, strategizing, and unlocking the potential in others. If you align more with these elements, it's a strong indication that you might be ready to don the mantle of leadership. Yet, cultivating the necessary soft skills—communication, empathy, and conflict resolution— is an ongoing process that doesn't end with a title change. You might be ready for leadership if you're actively working on refining these skills and eager to expand them further.

Impostor syndrome can serve as a hurdle on your path to leadership. It's a common thread woven into the fabric of the tech industry's rapid-paced environment, where the next innovation is always on the horizon. But impostor syndrome, while a challenge, can also be a catalyst for growth. The very fact that you question your readiness is a sign of conscientiousness, a valuable trait for any leader.

No leader is an island, and gathering a diverse group of mentors is a strategic step in preparing for a leadership role. Mentors provide invaluable perspectives from their own journeys and can offer both the encouragement to overcome self-doubt and the critical advice needed to sharpen your leadership skills. They serve as a compass that helps navigate the complex team leadership territory.

I never thought I was ready for leadership, and I just dove right in. I wish that I had taken some time to set myself up for success versus learning on the job. You'll have to learn on the job somewhat, but there are also things you should do to help the transition go smoothly. Throughout this chapter, we'll discuss the common hardships facing potential lead developers and how you can mitigate them to set yourself up for success.

12.1 Assessing your skill level

Embarking on the journey from a senior developer to a lead developer is a natural progression in your career, but it's crucial to recognize when you're truly ready to take on the responsibilities of leading a team. Assessing your own skill level is a key step in determining when the time is right to step into the role of a lead developer. As a developer, you're constantly learning and evolving. Your technical expertise grows with each project, and your skill set expands as you tackle new challenges. Assessing your skills helps you understand your strengths and areas for improvement, providing a road map for personal and professional growth.

Becoming a lead developer isn't just about writing code or solving intricate technical puzzles. It involves a shift in perspective and a broadening of responsibilities. You'll find yourself tackling complex technical problems, guiding and supporting your team members, making high-level decisions, and collaborating with other departments. So how do you know when you're ready to take on these additional responsibilities? Self-assessment is the key.

First, you must evaluate your technical proficiency. As a lead developer, you'll be the go-to person for technical guidance. Assess your understanding of coding languages, architecture, and development methodologies. This can include taking online courses with an assessment or even passing a certification exam. Ask yourself if you've mastered the skills required for the types of projects you'll be overseeing. Confidence in your technical abilities indicates that you're ready for a leadership role.

Of course, leadership isn't just about coding but also about effective communication. Assess your ability to convey complex technical concepts to both technical and nontechnical stakeholders. Before I became a lead developer, I put effort into learning how to speak about technical concepts to my co-workers who weren't developers. I learned how to speak to them at a high technical level without getting too much into the weeds. I encouraged them to ask questions and assured them they could understand these concepts. Anyone who works in tech possesses technical skills, and even if they aren't a developer, they are exposed to a lot of terms and information. My co-workers noticed the effort I put into educating them, and they appreciated it. Once leadership observed my success, I was promoted to lead developer. Remember, a lead developer serves as a bridge between different teams, translating technical jargon into understandable language. You're on the right track if you find joy in mentoring others and can articulate your ideas clearly.

Becoming a lead developer is a significant step in your career journey, and taking the time to assess your readiness is okay. Self-reflection and honest evaluation of your skills will empower you to make informed decisions about when to step into a leadership role. Remember, it's not just about the destination; it's about the journey of personal and professional growth. When you can combine technical mastery and effective communication, you'll be ready to inspire and lead your team to new heights. Throughout this section, I'll show you how to prevent the struggles I had to deal with so that you can succeed.

12.1.1 *Shadowing other lead developers*

Shadowing is an immersive learning experience where you follow a seasoned lead developer, observing their day-to-day activities, decision-making processes, and the environment they cultivate in their team. You can view it as a peek into your future leadership role. It's a chance to assess your skills, identify gaps, and understand the nuances of leading a dynamic development team. Shadowing provides a front-row seat to the technical expertise of lead developers. You get to witness how they navigate complex coding challenges, make architectural decisions, and balance the art of coding with the science of project management. It's a crash course in technical mastery tailored just for you. If there are no lead developers within your organization, you should connect with lead developers on social media or developer communities. Connecting with lead developers outside of your organization and growing your mentor network are important steps to take to become a successful lead developer. We'll discuss growing your mentor network later in this chapter.

Shadowing becomes a self-reflective journey, allowing individuals to compare and assess their own skills against those demonstrated by established leads. This process sheds light on areas of strength, areas needing improvement, and the overall readiness to step up to the responsibilities of a lead developer role. Every situation allows you the opportunity to compare how you might have handled that situation versus how the lead developer you're shadowing handled it. Every situation is a learning experience, especially those with negative results. Through shadowing, developers can refine their technical prowess, enhance their problem-solving abilities, and develop the interpersonal skills necessary for effective leadership in the dynamic world of software development.

When there is an emergency situation, lead developers shine as problem-solving heroes. Shadowing exposes you to the roller coaster of real-time problem-solving.

You'll see how they troubleshoot, make decisions under pressure, and guide the team through challenges. I once worked with a team of three people—a junior developer, a senior developer, and myself. We had a particularly difficult deployment to production that lasted for 14 hours. Everything went wrong, from failed tests to a disk space problem on one of our servers. I walked the team through the troubleshooting steps and delegated responsibilities while answering everyone's questions. It was a difficult day, but we worked together, and they expressed how much they learned afterward. The senior developer even documented the experience in case we had similar problems in the future.

Shadowing other lead developers allows you to witness their adaptability in action. How do they stay ahead of technological trends? How do they integrate new methodologies seamlessly? These insights help you cultivate a continuous learning mindset, a hallmark of successful leaders. When I shadowed a lead developer for the first time, we worked together on a new search filter logic feature for an enterprise web development project. I found it interesting that they suggested we use a relatively new technology at the time because I'm not an early adopter. However, the technology had been around for a few years, and they wanted to avoid a situation where we implemented something that quickly became outdated. The project had its challenges, and the lead developer successfully adapted to the constant changes we needed to make so that the filter logic worked properly. I learned a lot from that experience, and it's something that I carry with me today.

How do you get started shadowing a lead developer? You should let your desire to shadow a lead developer be known. Most leaders appreciate eagerness to learn and grow. It's a win–win—you get to learn, and they get a motivated, aspiring leader in the making. I shadowed many lead developers for years before I became one myself. I asked the first lead developer I worked with if I could shadow him, and he gladly accepted. Another lead developer later in my career wasn't as enthusiastic about it because it made them nervous. They were new to the role, so I didn't push the issue with them, but in hindsight, they were probably feeling imposter syndrome. I think that any lead developer should be happy to pass on their knowledge, and I wish I had the opportunity to learn more from them.

When you're in the shadows, be like a sponge—absorb everything. Observe keenly, ask questions, and seek guidance. This is your chance to learn, so make the most of it.

Before starting the shadowing experience, define your goals and expectations. What specific skills or knowledge do you want to acquire? Discuss these goals with the lead developer you'll shadow to ensure alignment. Figure 12.1 illustrates my goals when I shadowed other lead developers.

Pay close attention to the lead developer's decision-making process, problem-solving techniques, and communication style. Observe how they prioritize tasks, manage their time, and interact with team members. While shadowing, try to actively participate in meetings, discussions, and collaborative activities. Offer your insights and opinions when appropriate. This will demonstrate your engagement and provide you with opportunities to learn and contribute. Use this opportunity to build relationships with other team members and stakeholders. Networking is crucial in any leadership role, and engaging with various individuals can broaden your professional connections.

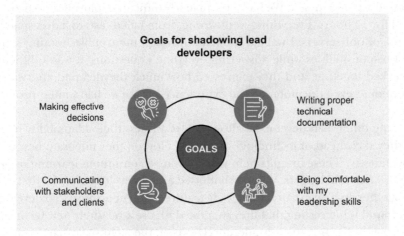

Figure 12.1   Goals for shadowing lead developers

You should constantly ask questions to get the most out of your shadowing experience. Don't be afraid to ask stupid questions. The only stupid question is the one you don't ask. I wish someone had told me that earlier in my career because I kept my mouth shut too often when I should have felt comfortable asking questions. If someone makes you feel stupid for asking a question, they have no place in leadership. You should have a feedback loop between you and the lead developer to ensure proper communication and goals. Be curious and seek clarification on any aspects that you find unclear. This is an excellent way to deepen your understanding of the role and the industry.

> **TIP**   After your shadowing experience, seek feedback from the lead developer. What did you do well? In what areas can you improve? Constructive feedback is the compass that guides your journey toward leadership.

After each shadowing experience, take time to reflect on what you've learned. Consider how you can apply these insights to your own work and development. Reflecting on the experience will help solidify your understanding. Remember, the goal of shadowing is to assess your skill level to decide if the role of lead developer is for you. By being proactive, setting goals, and gathering feedback, you can make the most out of your shadowing experience as an aspiring lead developer.

12.1.2 *Building technical architecture from scratch*

When you're assessing your technical skill level, it's important to understand how to build technical architecture from scratch. However, you should aim to create a reusable prototype so that you don't have to build any project from scratch. This will save your team and organization valuable time and improve productivity. Building an application from the ground up isn't just about writing code; it encompasses a range of processes and considerations fundamental to any software project's success. Possessing this technical skill set will help you decide when you're ready to be a lead developer.

Building an application from scratch provides lead developers with invaluable insight into the entire development lifecycle. From project planning and requirements gathering to design, implementation, testing, and deployment, lead developers who have hands-on experience with every stage of the process are better equipped to make informed decisions and anticipate challenges.

While navigating being a lead developer for the first time, I didn't have a prototype to work with, so I had to lead the team while we built the application from scratch. This involved many challenges, including figuring out the proper architecture, configuring continuous integration/continuous delivery (CI/CD), and supporting the project manager. I struggled because I was leading the team for the first time and trying to learn the skills I needed to succeed.

A simple "Hello, World" application begins the process of learning how to build technical architecture. Implementing the simplest approach possible will teach you the basics, and you can build your skills from there. Often, before you're a lead developer, you work on building features, but you may not have experience implementing the architecture for building features. Before I became a lead developer, I focused my skills on integrating third-party application programming interface (API) connectivity. The architecture for building out features and search was already done for me, so I was unfamiliar with that process, and I had to learn on the job the first time I was a lead developer.

Learning how to build technical architecture while also trying to learn the necessary soft skills to succeed in a technical leadership role presents many challenges. If you're unfamiliar with this process, it's good practice to make use of the knowledge on your team. I've often worked with team members who have knowledge of building technical architecture for a specific type of feature. Even if they haven't built everything from the ground up, you can work with them to reverse engineer the build. You need to be cognizant of best practices and ensure that you follow them to create clean code for your applications.

Understanding how to build technical architecture from scratch is a cornerstone for developers aiming to assess their readiness for the lead developer role. This skill empowers developers to design comprehensive, scalable, and efficient systems from the ground up. It involves considering various factors such as system requirements, scalability, security, and maintainability. When developers can architect solutions independently, they develop a deep understanding of the intricacies of creating robust software systems. This knowledge becomes pivotal in assessing one's readiness for a leadership position, as it showcases a developer's ability to think strategically, plan for the long term, and foresee potential challenges. Essentially, proficiency in building technical architecture demonstrates technical expertise and signifies the capability to lead a team in developing innovative and reliable solutions to complex problems.

12.1.3 *Cultivating a positive working environment*

Leadership often involves solving problems beyond the scope of coding. You must evaluate your problem-solving and critical-thinking skills in a broader context to help you assess your leadership skills. Can you analyze situations, make decisions under pressure, and lead your team through challenges? These qualities are vital for a lead developer navigating the dynamic landscape of software development. When you possess the soft skills to lead, you'll cultivate a positive working environment that will go a long way to aid your decision to become a lead developer. Figure 12.2 shows how to cultivate a positive working environment.

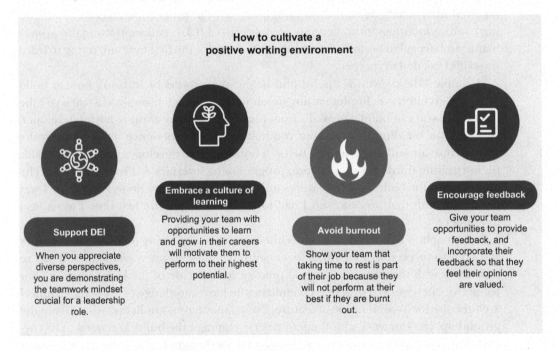

Figure 12.2   How to cultivate a positive working environment

You must stay ahead of the curve and stay current with your leadership skills. I thought I was done with them once I learned soft skills. However, like technical skills, soft skills are also ever-changing. In recent years, leadership practices have evolved to be more inclusive. Diversity, equity, and inclusion have been at the forefront of these changes, and it's important for you to learn to support these initiatives within your organization. I stay up to date by subscribing to publications such as the *Harvard Business Review*, which has excellent leadership articles, and read books that are relevant to anyone in a leadership position.

A lead developer isn't a lone wolf. You must foster a collaborative and inclusive environment. If you enjoy helping others succeed, appreciate diverse perspectives, and can motivate your team, you're demonstrating the teamwork mindset crucial for a leadership role. Being open to diverse perspectives will help drive innovation on your team. I often remember when smartphones were fairly new, and facial recognition consistently didn't recognize dark-skinned individuals. This happened because companies didn't test this feature properly, and they used light-skinned individuals for test subjects. This problem caused discourse within tech companies, and while flaws like this have improved, we still have a long way to go. Think about the language we use in tech: master/slave has become main/secondary, and blacklist/whitelist has become disallowed/allowed. I'm sure there are things that we still need to improve, and things will continue to change, so we have to adapt our leadership skills accordingly.

I often fell into the trap of disregarding a good work-life balance, and I expected others to put in overtime. This was a product of years of poor leadership making me feel like I needed to work overtime consistently. However, this isn't tenable in the long run. You'll burn out, and so will your team members. You must lead by example and work smarter, not harder. Taking time to rest is part of your job because you won't perform at your best if you're burnt out. I remember once, before I was a lead developer, a woman on my team lost a family member, and the lead developer asked her to work over the weekend, knowing that she had a funeral to go to. She ended up logging into work on her laptop from the funeral. That was the moment when I spoke up about a lack of work-life balance for the first time. I told the lead developer that it was ridiculous to expect someone to work when they had experienced loss. The lead developer said they didn't mean for my co-worker to work from the funeral, and she should have found another weekend to work. I realized that they acted like that because upper management also treated them like that.

If you don't have proper mentors in upper management, it's likely that you won't be successful as a lead developer due to a toxic company culture. As a lead developer, you should avoid being a "yes" person. It's important for you to protect your team and ensure that they have the tools they need to be successful. If you consistently agree with everything that upper management asks you, you won't provide your team with a proper example of good leadership. Speaking up when you or a team member needs help is a crucial skill that you must master. Learning these soft skills will help you lead by example and show your team how to navigate challenges and achieve success.

12.2 Taking the leap

You may ask yourself, "How do I know when I'm ready to become a lead developer?" Honestly, you'll never know for certain. A lot of parents have told me they didn't feel ready to raise a child, but you just get thrown into it and must do the best that you can. Even if you're not ready, you can set yourself up for success. You should also embrace the idea that you'll likely fail from time to time, and that's okay! When you do fail, you need a group of mentors to help you through it. Everyone needs support and guidance to overcome failure and learn valuable lessons.

I certainly didn't feel ready when I accepted my first lead developer position. However, I did set myself up for success. I took it upon myself to study leadership, and I often volunteered to lead meetings with the development team. I became a mentor to many developers on my team, and my manager noticed. He pushed me to hone my leadership skills and was confident in my ability to lead even when I didn't feel ready. Throughout this section, we'll discuss how you can ensure you're prepared to take the leap to become a lead developer.

12.2.1 *Gathering a group of mentors*

The best advice I was ever given was to gather a group of mentors before I became a lead developer. Developers can greatly benefit from assembling a group of mentors even before stepping into the lead developer role, as this proactive approach aids in evaluating their readiness for such a pivotal position. These mentors, ideally a diverse set of experienced professionals, provide invaluable guidance, feedback, and insights based on their own journeys in leadership. Engaging with mentors allows developers to tap into a wealth of knowledge, learning from the successes and challenges of those who have walked similar paths before. Through mentorship, developers can gain clarity on the skills, experiences, and mindset required to thrive as a lead developer. Mentors offer a sounding board for ideas, help navigate complex situations, and provide honest assessments of one's strengths and areas for growth. By fostering these mentor relationships early on, developers can make informed decisions about their readiness for leadership, charting a course that aligns with their aspirations and ambitions while benefiting from the wisdom and support of seasoned mentors.

You shouldn't have just one mentor. Cultivating a diverse group of mentors is important to help hone your skills from their different backgrounds. If you have only one mentor, you may fall into the trap of trying to be just like them. However, we all have different experiences, and what drove success for one person may not work for another person. Before reaching out to potential mentors, take the time to clarify your needs, goals, and areas where you could benefit from guidance. Consider your current role, your career aspirations, and your specific challenges. This self-reflection will help you identify the types of mentors who can best support your growth and development. Figure 12.3 lists some ways to gather a group of mentors.

Building a mentor network requires intentionality and effort. It involves identifying individuals whose expertise aligns with your needs and reaching out to cultivate those relationships. This might mean attending industry events, using social media, and seeking training programs to connect thought leaders in the field. I met most of my mentors via social media and online events. Technology has made it easier to connect with mentors virtually, transcending geographical boundaries. Online communities offer avenues to find and engage with mentors who can add value to your professional journey.

I've worked in technical training for more than 15 years, and I've had many students reach out to me after I gave a workshop or they watched my online courses. I know many instructors who mentor their students when asked. If you encounter someone who is a thought leader in the industry, you can always ask them for help. The best thought leaders will give you some of their precious time because they want to help. I often tell people that I teach because I don't want people to struggle as I have. That is why I've mentored more than 100 people throughout my career. All they have to do is ask.

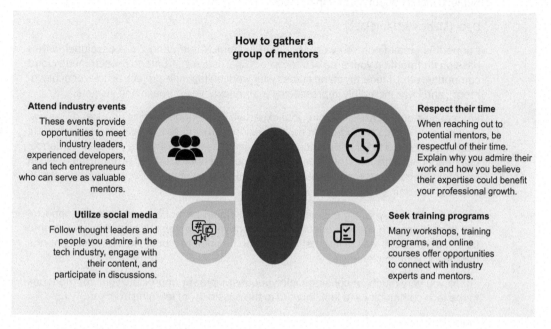

How to gather a group of mentors

Attend industry events
These events provide opportunities to meet industry leaders, experienced developers, and tech entrepreneurs who can serve as valuable mentors.

Respect their time
When reaching out to potential mentors, be respectful of their time. Explain why you admire their work and how you believe their expertise could benefit your professional growth.

Utilize social media
Follow thought leaders and people you admire in the tech industry, engage with their content, and participate in discussions.

Seek training programs
Many workshops, training programs, and online courses offer opportunities to connect with industry experts and mentors.

Figure 12.3 How to gather a group of mentors

The first step in establishing a mentorship relationship is often the most daunting—reaching out for that initial contact. Before you even begin drafting your email, take the time to research your potential mentor. Learn about their background, expertise, and contributions to the tech industry. This will help you tailor your message and demonstrate your genuine interest and admiration for their work.

Mentors, especially those in high-demand roles, are often busy individuals. With this in mind, keep your email concise, clear, and respectful of their time. Aim to convey your message in a few paragraphs, focusing on the key points without overwhelming them with unnecessary details. Start your email with a personalized introduction to grab their attention. Mention specific reasons why you admire their work or expertise. This could be a project they led, an article they wrote, or a talk they gave at a conference. Showing that you've done your homework goes a long way in making a meaningful connection.

Be up front about why you're reaching out and what you hope to gain from the mentorship. Whether you're seeking advice on career growth, technical challenges, or leadership development, clearly articulate your goals. This helps the potential mentor understand how they can best assist you.

Close your email by expressing your gratitude for their time and consideration. Acknowledge that you understand they are busy and that you would greatly appreciate the opportunity to connect. A genuine expression of appreciation shows respect for their expertise and time.

Example email to a potential mentor

Subject: Inquiry about Mentorship Opportunity

Dear [Mentor's Name],

I hope this email finds you well. My name is [Your Name], and I'm a developer with a passion for [mention your area of interest or expertise, e.g., frontend development, cloud computing, etc.]. I recently came across your work on [specific project, article, or achievement], and I was incredibly impressed by your innovative approach and insights.

I'm reaching out because I admire your expertise in [mention specific area], and I believe your insights could greatly benefit my professional growth. As a developer, I'm navigating challenges related to [briefly mention your challenges or areas where you seek guidance, e.g., team collaboration strategies, adopting new technologies, etc.]. Your experience in [mention mentor's expertise] would be invaluable in helping me overcome these obstacles and becoming a lead developer.

I understand that your time is valuable, and I would be honored to have the opportunity to connect with you. I'm eager to learn from your experiences and gain insights into [specific topics or areas of interest]. Would you be open to a brief virtual coffee chat or a meeting at your convenience?

Thank you very much for considering my request. I greatly appreciate your contributions to the tech community and look forward to the possibility of learning from you.

Warm regards,

[Your Name]

[Your Contact Information]

After sending your initial email, give your potential mentor some time to respond. If you haven't heard back within a week or two, sending a polite follow-up email as a gentle reminder is acceptable. However, avoid being persistent or overly insistent, as this may be perceived as pushy.

While you may have a specific mentor in mind, don't hesitate to explore other potential mentors if your first choice is unavailable or unable to commit. The tech industry is full of talented individuals with valuable insights to offer, and each mentorship relationship can bring unique benefits.

By following these steps and crafting a thoughtful, respectful email, you'll increase the likelihood of making a positive impression on your potential mentor. Remember, mentorship is a two-way street, and approaching the relationship with sincerity and a willingness to learn will set the foundation for a rewarding journey of growth and development.

12.2.2 *Starting your first project*

Leading a project for the first time can be exhilarating and daunting in equal measure. It marks a significant transition from being a team contributor to a leader, responsible for not just your own work but also guiding the efforts of an entire development team. As you embark on this journey, there are several key strategies and pieces of advice to keep in mind to set yourself up for success as you start your first project.

Before diving headfirst into the development process, take the time to thoroughly understand the project. This means understanding the technical requirements and the broader context: the business goals, target audience, timelines, and any constraints. Clear communication with stakeholders, product managers, and designers is crucial here. A shared understanding will prevent misunderstandings down the line and ensure everyone is aligned on the project's objectives. The first project I led was an enterprise web development project, and I took the time to meet with the project manager to get the lay of the land before I started. This enabled me to see things from their perspective and understand the business objectives. I used this information to help tailor the technical requirements to those objectives. This went a long way to support the successful implementation of the project.

You may have risen to the position of lead developer due to your technical prowess, but it's essential to recognize that you can't do everything yourself. Delegate tasks based on team members' strengths and expertise. Empower your team by giving them ownership of their work while providing guidance and support when needed. Effective delegation lightens your workload and cultivates a sense of ownership and accountability among team members. Delegation is something that I struggled with, and I would often overextend myself by doing tasks that I could have delegated. You must let go of control and understand that your team members possess technical expertise and can learn on the job. If you don't understand how to perform a task, you must rely on your team to get the job done. Otherwise, you'll burn yourself out while not supporting your team members' professional growth. I've seen this type of environment lead to a high turnover rate, as employees didn't feel valued or like they had a career trajectory within the company. Losing talent is costly to any organization, so you want to strive to retain the talent on your team.

No matter how meticulously you plan, unexpected challenges can and will arise during a project. Anticipate potential roadblocks such as technical hurdles, resource constraints, or changes in requirements. Develop contingency plans to mitigate these risks, whether it's allocating additional resources, adjusting timelines, or having alternative solutions in place. Being prepared will help you navigate uncertainties with confidence. I've often dealt with resource constraints as a lead developer without always handling them properly. I fell into the trap of wanting to impress the leadership in my organization by meeting strict deadlines no matter what.

While meeting deadlines is important, never compromise on the quality of your deliverables. As a lead developer, you are responsible for upholding coding standards, conducting code reviews, and ensuring thorough testing. Encourage a culture of quality within your team, where each member takes pride in delivering clean, maintainable code. Quality should be the primary goal, and to achieve the highest quality possible, you must work with project managers to assure that your team isn't overworked. I used to be a workaholic because I worked for companies that required their employees to meet deadlines no matter the cost. This mentality is detrimental to producing high-quality products and services because people aren't at their best when they are burnt out. You should be open to working with the team to estimate tasks and ensure the proper resources are in place.

Effective communication is the glue that holds a project together. It's a best practice to keep all stakeholders informed of progress, challenges, and decisions. Establish regular check-ins with the team to discuss updates, blockers, and priorities. Use project management tools and communication channels to ensure everyone is on the same page, whether it's through Slack, Jira, email updates, or face-to-face meetings.

No matter how experienced you are, there's always room to grow and improve. Solicit feedback from team members, stakeholders, and peers throughout the project. Reflect on what worked well and what could have been done better. Actively seek learning opportunities, whether attending conferences, taking online courses, or reading industry publications. A growth mindset benefits you personally and enriches the entire team.

Becoming a lead developer and leading your first project is a significant milestone in your career that comes with challenges and rewards. By focusing on understanding the project, building a strong team, embracing agile practices, and prioritizing communication and quality, you can confidently navigate your first project and set the stage for continued success in your leadership role.

12.2.3 *Setting yourself up for success*

Transitioning from a developer to a lead developer comes with its unique challenges. While you may not know when you're ready to be a lead developer, you can set yourself up for success. When I first became a lead developer, I jumped in with few goals or guidance. I learned very quickly that I was in over my head because I wasn't confident in my leadership skills. This led to dissonance in my team, as they didn't trust me to make key decisions. I was in a bad place, both personally and professionally, but I dug in my heels and learned on the job. Before you take the leap, figure 12.4 gives you some key strategies to set yourself up for success in your first lead developer role.

Successful leadership is built on trust and collaboration. You must take the time to build strong relationships with your team members, peers, and stakeholders. Understand their strengths, weaknesses, and motivations. Foster a positive team culture where ideas are freely exchanged and everyone feels valued. Clarity is key to success. Clearly define project goals, expectations, and timelines for your team. Make sure everyone understands their roles and responsibilities. Regularly communicate progress, changes, and updates to keep everyone aligned.

When I was in a position where my team didn't trust me, I turned it around through communication, and I allowed radical candor. I didn't shy away from asking for feedback from my team and supervisors. Constructive feedback helps you understand what you're doing well and where to improve. Continuously seek growth opportunities, whether through training, certifications, or learning from experienced leaders. Incorporating my team members' feedback into my leadership style made them feel empowered and motivated them to seek feedback themselves. This resulted in the team's professional growth, and some even got promotions.

Setting yourself up for success
Becoming a lead developer

Build strong relationships $\rightarrow$ Learn to delegate tasks $\rightarrow$ Set clear goals and expectations $\rightarrow$ Manage time effectively $\rightarrow$ Seek feedback

Figure 12.4 Setting yourself up for success

Trying to do everything yourself can be tempting, especially if you're used to being a hands-on developer. However, as a lead developer, your role is to guide and support the team. Learn to delegate tasks effectively, trusting your team members to deliver. This not only lightens your workload but also helps in team development. With multiple responsibilities, staying organized is crucial. Use project management tools, calendars, and task lists to stay on top of deadlines and priorities. Time management skills will help you juggle various tasks efficiently and delegate tasks accordingly.

Taking on the lead developer role for the first time is a rewarding journey of growth and learning. By building relationships, delegating tasks, and staying organized, developers can set themselves up for success in this pivotal role. With the right mindset and approach, the transition can be a fulfilling step toward a successful career in software development leadership.

12.3 Working with management

When lead developers actively engage with management to craft and manage budgets, they ensure that projects are well-funded and aligned with business objectives. This alignment is essential for maintaining the momentum of development teams and avoiding the pitfalls of underspending or overspending.

Similarly, involvement in hiring and firing decisions allows lead developers to directly influence the composition and capability of their teams. By advocating for the skills and team dynamics needed, they can build a more cohesive and productive team environment.

Setting policies for AI tools is another area where lead developers must have a strong voice. As AI integration becomes more prevalent, establishing clear guidelines on the ethical use, capabilities, and limitations of these tools is critical. This protects the company legally and reputationally while also promoting innovation within safe and practical boundaries.

The consequences of failing to communicate effectively with management in these areas can be significant. Without input from lead developers, management may make decisions that aren't technically feasible or that are misaligned with team capabilities, leading to project delays, budget overruns, and low morale among developers. In this section, you'll gain insight into forming your policies and plans and then presenting your case to management.

12.3.1 Planning a budget

As a lead developer, one of your pivotal roles involves collaborating with the project management team to form a practical and efficient budget. Your technical expertise and experience are crucial in forecasting costs, assessing resource requirements, and managing expectations. This section will discuss how you can effectively contribute to budget formation.

Begin by thoroughly understanding the project's scope and technical requirements. This understanding is foundational for accurately estimating the resources and time needed for development tasks. Engage with stakeholders to clarify features, performance criteria, and deployment needs, ensuring that all technical aspects are considered in the budget. Use your technical knowledge to provide detailed cost estimates for different project components:

- Accounting for software tools, development environments, and necessary licenses
- Estimating costs related to servers, hosting, and any specialized hardware
- Detailing the number and level of developers needed, considering the complexities of the project
- Including the resources required for thorough testing, including third-party services if needed
- Anticipating costs for ongoing support, bug fixes, and potential upgrades post-launch

You must work with project managers to prioritize project features based on value, cost, and effect on the overall project. This helps make informed decisions about what to include in the initial development phase and what can be added later, optimizing available resources. Always include a contingency budget to manage unexpected expenses or changes in the project scope. Depending on the project's complexity and risk factors, a contingency of 10% to 20% of the overall budget is typically recommended.

Recommend and use effective project management tools with budget tracking and resource allocation features. These tools help keep the project on track and within budget, providing real-time insights into spending and resource usage. I've often used Microsoft Excel to budget complex projects, including project estimates and the cost of our tooling. Table 12.1 includes some of the most popular tools for budgeting.

Table 12.1 Popular tools for budgeting

Tool	Purpose
Microsoft Excel, Google Sheets	Create detailed breakdowns, apply formulas to estimate costs, and adjust variables. These tools are useful for maintaining granular control over the budget elements and can be easily shared and updated.
Jira, Microsoft Project, Asana, Monday.com	Integrated budgeting features that help you plan and track expenses against actual spend. These tools often include visual dashboards that provide real-time insights into budget health, helping you stay on track and make informed decisions quickly.
QuickBooks, Xero	Traditionally used for overall business accounting; can also be adapted for project budget management. These tools offer features for tracking expenses, managing invoices, and even handling payroll, which can benefit larger projects or ongoing maintenance phases.

Allocating resources wisely involves prioritizing expenses that maximize value and contribute directly to critical project outcomes. Historical data from past projects can help forecast costs more accurately and identify areas where you can optimize spending, such as choosing more cost-effective technology solutions or using open source tools. I've worked for several agencies implementing enterprise web development projects using a reusable prototype. Most of the projects included the same features. I used the historical data, including the original estimates versus the actual work performed, to aid me in estimating the resources needed to develop the initial budget. I considered the lessons learned from previous projects and their risk assessment. The resulting budget showed improvements in the burn-down rate, significantly affecting the success of the budget.

You must always include a contingency budget to account for unforeseen expenses or changes in project scope. A typical contingency budget might range from 10% to 20% of the total budget, depending on the project's complexity and risk. Tools such as risk management software can help identify potential risks and quantify their financial effect, allowing you to adjust the contingency budget accordingly. The situation that has affected me the most has been turnover. The cost of losing a developer with significant knowledge of a project and the cost of hiring and training a new developer is a contingency you must account for, especially in larger projects spanning several years.

Budget planning isn't a one-time task but an ongoing process. As the project progresses, regularly review the budget with the project management team, using the tools at your disposal to track expenditures and adjust as necessary. Always keep the lines of communication open, and update project managers when the cost of tools increases or a contingency occurs. This dynamic approach helps you manage changes efficiently and ensures the project remains financially viable throughout its lifecycle.

12.3.2 *Hiring developers*

As a first-time lead developer, one of your critical responsibilities will be building a capable and cohesive team. Lead developers are often expected to assist in the hiring process even though the engineering manager is the hiring manager. Start by reviewing résumés. Focus on identifying candidates with relevant experience in your team's programming languages, frameworks, and tools. Additionally, consider the complexity and scale of their past projects, which can indicate their readiness for your work.

Pay attention to résumés highlighting problem-solving abilities, showcasing specific problems the candidate faced and the solutions they implemented. This can reveal their analytical skills and creativity. Because software development is a collaborative effort, prioritize candidates with experience working in teams, mentioning collaboration tools, team projects, and contributions to group efforts.

Given technology's rapid evolution, hiring developers committed to continuous learning is crucial. Look for evidence of ongoing education, such as courses, certifications, or participation in tech communities. Finally, a well-structured, error-free résumé often indicates a candidate's attention to detail. In contrast, poorly formatted résumés or those with spelling and grammatical errors might suggest a lack of thoroughness. I like to see résumés that are formatted well and and with the relevant information easy to find. You may have hundreds of résumés to review, so you can't review them all. Good résumé writers understand this and will focus on relevant information for the job description, making it easier for reviewers to find the information they need by skimming the résumé.

The interview process allows you to delve deeper into a candidate's skills, experience, and fit for your team. Technical questions should include coding exercises to assess their coding skills, logical thinking, and problem-solving approach. System design questions can help you understand their ability to think at a higher level and handle complex projects, such as designing a scalable e-commerce platform. Debugging scenarios can evaluate their diagnostic skills and attention to detail by presenting them with a piece of code containing a bug and asking them to identify and fix it. I always assign a short coding test to assess the candidate's skill level before the interview. Coding tests should take one hour maximum so that you don't overwhelm the candidate but are respectful of their time. When they pass the coding test and move on to the interview, choosing the right questions is crucial to uncovering the candidate's true potential. Table 12.2 lists questions I like to ask and why they are relevant.

Table 12.2   Interview questions

Question	Relevance
Describe a challenging project you worked on. How did you handle it?	Assesses problem-solving skills, resilience, and the ability to handle stress
How do you keep up with the latest developments in technology?	Gauges the candidate's commitment to continuous learning and staying current in a fast-paced industry
Describe a time when you had to work closely with others. How did you ensure successful collaboration?	Evaluates interpersonal skills and the ability to work as part of a team

Table 12.2 Interview questions *(continued)*

Question	Relevance
What is your approach to debugging and testing code?	Ensures the candidate has a methodical approach to ensuring code quality and reliability
How do you prioritize tasks when you have multiple deadlines to meet?	Measures time management and prioritization, which are essential for productivity and meeting project timelines

By carefully reviewing résumés and strategically conducting interviews, you can build a strong development team that meets technical requirements and aligns with your company's culture and values. As a first-time lead developer, these hiring practices will help you identify the best candidates who can contribute to your team's success.

12.3.3 Firing developers

One of the more challenging and sensitive duties for a lead developer is determining whether a developer should be dismissed from the team. As a lead developer, you're instrumental in assessing team performance and dynamics. However, it's crucial to understand that while you may be involved in the decision-making process, you may not be present in the actual firing meeting. This separation is designed to maintain your working relationship with the team and focus on your primary leadership responsibilities. I suggest dismissal should only occur after you diligently work with the developer to resolve any problems.

Before suggesting dismissal, you must take several crucial steps to ensure the decision is justified and well-documented. Initially, it's important to set clear, measurable objectives and performance standards for each team member, including regular feedback sessions to discuss progress and areas for improvement. If a developer consistently fails to meet these standards, the lead developer should implement a formal Performance Improvement Plan (PIP), clearly outlining the expectations and the timeline for improvement. Throughout the PIP, you should provide ongoing support and coaching, documenting all interactions, progress, or lack thereof. Regular consultations with HR to review the developer's performance against the PIP are essential to ensure compliance with company policies and legal standards. Only after these steps, if there is no significant improvement, should dismissal be considered and discussed with upper management and HR, presenting a detailed case based on documented evidence and objective assessments.

The first step in the process is identifying the problems that might warrant dismissal. These can range from consistently missing deadlines, poor quality of work, and a negative effect on team morale to more severe problems such as breaches of company policy. It's important to document all incidents and patterns of behavior that contribute to this perspective, as this documentation will be critical in discussions with HR and upper management. Once you've documented the problems, the next step is to present this information to HR and your direct supervisors. Here are some tips for building a strong, objective case:

- Use specific instances where the developer failed to meet expectations. Provide dates, project names, and detailed descriptions of the incident(s).
- Discuss how the developer's actions or lack thereof have affected team performance and morale.
- If a performance improvement plan was implemented, provide a detailed account of the plan and the developer's response. Highlight any failures to adhere to the plan or lack of improvement.
- HR can guide the legal and procedural aspects of the dismissal process. Engaging them early ensures all actions comply with company policy and employment law.
- Be prepared to discuss potential backlash or morale problems within the team post-dismissal. Have a plan for addressing these problems and supporting your team through the transition.
- It's important to handle these situations with professionalism and empathy. The way you communicate your case can affect your credibility and the trust you hold with your team.

Lead developers may not be involved in the actual firing meeting, but they'll play a critical role in shaping the decision through their detailed assessments and evidence-based approach. This process requires a thorough understanding of the developer's performance and effect on the team and a tactful and empathetic approach to communicating with management and HR. By following these guidelines, lead developers can ensure that they fulfill their responsibilities effectively while maintaining the integrity and performance of their team.

12.3.4 Setting policies for AI tools

As a lead developer, one of your key responsibilities is to assess and integrate emerging technologies, including AI tools, into your development processes. When considering the adoption or rejection of AI tooling, it's crucial to maintain a balanced approach that prioritizes the team's needs, the specific benefits of the technology, and the potential risks involved. This section provides guidance on how to thoughtfully evaluate AI tooling and communicate your recommendations to management effectively.

Before suggesting the use of any AI tooling, begin by evaluating how it aligns with your team's current and future projects. Consider whether the AI tool can improve productivity and streamline workflows by automating mundane tasks, thus freeing up developers for more complex problems. It's also important to assess the quality of the output the AI tool produces, its error rates, and how well it integrates with your existing tools and workflows. AI tools should be able to seamlessly integrate without requiring significant changes to current processes.

Introducing AI tooling also comes with risks that need to be carefully managed. Teams may become too reliant on AI, potentially degrading problem-solving skills and limiting innovation. Security and privacy are also crucial, especially in how AI tools handle data and whether they comply with relevant data protection regulations. Beyond the initial investment, consider the long-term costs associated with training, integration, and maintenance. Table 12.3 lists some of the most popular AI tools and their uses.

Table 12.3 Popular AI tools

AI tool	Purpose
GitHub Copilot	An AI-powered code assistant helping developers write code faster by suggesting whole lines or blocks of code as they type. It's built on OpenAI's Codex model and is integrated directly into Visual Studio Code.
Kite	An AI-powered code completion tool that helps developers write code faster and with less effort. It integrates with multiple IDEs and supports languages such as Python, JavaScript, Java, and more, providing smart completions based on the project's context.
Tabnine	AI code assistant offering code completions for a variety of programming languages. Powered by machine learning, it integrates with popular IDEs to provide predictive text functionalities to improve coding efficiency.
Code Climate	Uses AI to analyze source code and identify problems that might affect maintainability, such as complexity, duplication, and potential bugs. It provides actionable insights to improve code quality and maintainability over time.
DeepCode	Uses AI to analyze codebases for bugs, security vulnerabilities, and performance problems in real time. It suggests improvements and best practices to enhance code quality.
TensorFlow and PyTorch	These machine-learning libraries allow developers to create AI models that can process data, make predictions, and learn from experiences. They are widely used for developing everything from simple algorithms to complex neural networks that perform tasks such as image recognition and natural language processing.
IBM Watson	Provides a suite of AI services and tools that enable developers to build, train, and deploy AI models. Watson services include natural language processing, speech to text, text to speech, and machine learning capabilities.
Google Cloud AI and machine learning products	Google offers a range of AI and machine learning products that help developers build and deploy AI models more efficiently. These tools include AutoML for training custom models with minimal effort and AI Platform for building and deploying machine learning models at scale.

When you're prepared to present your case for or against AI tooling, structure your communication to address the specific concerns and priorities of the management team. Demonstrate how the AI tooling aligns with the broader business goals. For example, if the company aims to accelerate product development, highlight how AI can speed up certain processes. Provide a detailed analysis of the expected return on investment (ROI) and a breakdown of the costs and benefits, not just in financial terms but also in terms of developer satisfaction and retention improvements. Clearly outline the potential risks and your strategies to mitigate them to build trust and show thoughtful consideration.

There may be situations where management is enthusiastic about implementing more AI tooling than is practical. In such cases, educating stakeholders on what AI can and can't do is crucial to setting realistic expectations to prevent future disappointments. Suggest implementing the AI tools in phases, each evaluated for effectiveness before proceeding. This reduces the risk and allows for adjustments based on practical experience. I recommend starting with a pilot program involving a small, manageable project that allows for evaluating the tool's effect without committing extensive resources.

As a lead developer, your role is to guide your team and management through the technological landscape with a balanced perspective on adopting AI tools. Your ability to critically evaluate these tools and communicate their benefits and risks effectively is crucial in shaping the technological direction of your team and organization.

Summary

- Shadowing experienced lead developers offers an immersive learning experience, providing insight into leadership roles.

- Understanding how to build technical architecture from scratch is crucial for lead developers, but it presents challenges that can be mitigated by using team knowledge and adhering to best practices.

- Cultivating a positive work environment will hone your leadership skills as you advocate against a toxic culture to drive innovation and success.

- Lead developers benefit significantly from a group of mentors, as they can provide diverse perspectives, a wealth of expertise, and a supportive network for holistic growth and informed decision-making.

- When transitioning to a lead developer role, building trust and collaboration is essential, as well as delegating effectively, communicating clearly, staying organized, and seeking feedback to guide the team and grow in the role successfully.

- Forming an efficient budget by using your technical expertise is important for accurately estimating costs, assessing resource requirements, managing expectations, and prioritizing features.

- Focus on building a cohesive team by reviewing résumés for relevant experience, problem-solving, teamwork skills, and continuous learning. Conduct technical interviews to assess candidates' skills and fit, ensuring alignment with your team's needs and company culture.

- Deciding on dismissal requires thorough performance assessment, setting clear objectives, providing feedback, and using a PIP. Consult with HR, document all interactions, and if no improvement occurs, present an evidence-based case to management. While you may not attend the firing meeting, your detailed evaluation is vital for a justified decision.

- Evaluating and integrating AI tools is a key responsibility. Assess whether AI tools align with your team's projects, improve productivity, and integrate seamlessly with existing workflows. Consider potential risks, such as overreliance on AI and security concerns, while weighing long-term costs.

- When presenting to management, align AI benefits with business goals, provide a detailed ROI analysis, and propose phased implementation. Your balanced evaluation and effective communication are critical in guiding your team and organization through AI adoption.

index

RELATED MANNING TITLES

Think Like a Software Engineering Manager
by Akanksha Gupta

ISBN 9781633438439
352 pages, $49.99
June 2024

Skills of a Successful Software Engineer
by Fernando Doglio

ISBN 9781617299704
192 pages, $49.99
June 2022

Think Like a CTO
By Alan Williamson
Foreword by Ankit Mathur

ISBN 9781617298851
320 pages, $49.99
February 2023

How to Lead in Data Science
by Jike Chong and Yue Cathy Chang
Foreword by Ben Lorica

ISBN 9781617298899
512 pages, $59.99
November 2021

For ordering information, go to www.manning.com

A new online reading experience

liveBook, our online reading platform, adds a new dimension to your Manning books, with features that make reading, learning, and sharing easier than ever. A liveBook version of your book is included FREE with every Manning book.

This next generation book platform is more than an online reader. It's packed with unique features to upgrade and enhance your learning experience.

- Add your own notes and bookmarks
- One-click code copy
- Learn from other readers in the discussion forum
- Audio recordings and interactive exercises
- Read all your purchased Manning content in any browser, anytime, anywhere

As an added bonus, you can search every Manning book and video in liveBook—even ones you don't yet own. Open any liveBook, and you'll be able to browse the content and read anything you like.*

Find out more at www.manning.com/livebook-program.

*Open reading is limited to 10 minutes per book daily

MANNING

The Manning Early Access Program

Don't wait to start learning! In MEAP, the Manning Early Access Program, you can read books as they're being created and long before they're available in stores.

Here's how MEAP works.

- **Start now.** Buy a MEAP and you'll get all available chapters in PDF, ePub, Kindle, and liveBook formats.

- **Regular updates.** New chapters are released as soon as they're written. We'll let you know when fresh content is available.

- **Finish faster.** MEAP customers are the first to get final versions of all books! Pre-order the print book, and it'll ship as soon as it's off the press.

- **Contribute to the process.** The feedback you share with authors makes the end product better.

- **No risk.** You get a full refund or exchange if we ever have to cancel a MEAP.

Explore dozens of titles in MEAP at www.manning.com.